ENCOUNTERING US EMPIRE IN SOCIALIST VENEZUELA

PITT LATIN AMERICAN SERIES
CATHERINE M. CONAGHAN, EDITOR

ENCOUNTERING US EMPIRE IN SOCIALIST VENEZUELA

THE LEGACY OF RACE, NEOCOLONIALISM, AND DEMOCRACY PROMOTION

TIMOTHY M. GILL

UNIVERSITY OF PITTSBURGH PRESS

Published by the University of Pittsburgh Press, Pittsburgh, Pa., 15260
Copyright © 2022, University of Pittsburgh Press
All rights reserved
Manufactured in the United States of America
Printed on acid-free paper
10 9 8 7 6 5 4 3 2 1

Cataloging-in-Publication data is available from the Library of Congress

ISBN 13: 978-0-8229-4744-8
ISBN 10: 0-8229-4744-7

Jacket design by Melissa Dias-Mandoly

This book is dedicated to my family: Aiola, Sebastian, and Fiona. I'm so grateful for you. You make every day worthwhile.

CONTENTS

Acknowledgments

ix

Introduction. US Empire in the Twenty-First Century

3

1. The Rise of Hugo Chávez and the Evolution of US-Venezuelan Relations

17

2. Theoretical Perspectives on US Democracy Assistance

38

3. Understanding Venezuelans, Understanding Chávez: The Endurance of Racist-Imperialist Mentalities

71

4. Coaching Opposition Political Parties I: The International Republican Institute

95

5. Coaching Opposition Political Parties II: The National Democratic Institute

116

6. Promoting Free Market Economics and Traditional Labor Unions in Chávez's Venezuela

130

7. Funding Anti-Chávez Voices in Civil Society:
The National Endowment for Democracy

153

8. Transforming Chavistas, Encouraging Protest:
The US Agency for International Development in Venezuela

175

9. Chávez Responds:
Terminating Foreign Funding for Political Parties and NGOs

190

Conclusion. Making Theoretical Sense of US Democracy Assistance
Efforts in Venezuela

207

Notes

221

Bibliography

225

Index

247

ACKNOWLEDGMENTS

This manuscript is the culmination of over a decade of graduate study, research, and writing.

It's strange, frightening, and quite satisfying to write that. When I think about it, the genesis of this project perhaps even lies closer to over two decades of thought.

As a young kid, I was introduced to punk rock, and it flipped my world upside down. In some ways, it was when my education truly began.

Growing up in Cleveland with my mother as a nurse, my father as a pipefitter, and an associate's degree between the two, many things seemed out of reach. Some folks made a lot of money, some made enough to get by, and some were living on the street. None of that seemed fair. Punk music talked about all of this in a way that helped me to start making sense of my life. It helped to start formulating my sociological imagination, if you will.

Elsewhere, at my Catholic grade school, we were taught to honor the United States and its history. Columbus was presented as a remarkable man, and US wars were presented as necessary and a source of freedom and liberation.

When I listened to those punk bands, and when I read their lyrics and their liner notes, I learned something much different. Those bands brought me to Noam Chomsky and Howard Zinn. All of their insights into the realities of US foreign policy and US history—both punks and scholars—shocked and unnerved me in a way that has never left.

In academia, we're often taught to intellectualize things in a way that's divorced from how we really feel. What I mean to say is that I could tell a story about how I came to this project because I was interested in theoretical contributions and the changing nature of the world in the twenty-first century, and so on. Yes, of course, as a scholar, I'm focused on theoretical contributions and pushing our understandings of US foreign policy and democracy promotion ahead. Should all of that literature already existed, perhaps I would have selected a different topic.

Yet, the reality of how I settled on this topic is rooted in those early days as a young kid, finding my way in and coming to understand the world around me. When I took a sociology course, my first thought was that it was "Wow . . . this is the punk rock subject!" I found folks like C. Wright Mills, for instance, conducting scientific research on corporate power—a common topic on punk albums.

Now, here I am. With a book of my own. I try to be as objective as possible, but there is no doubting that my experiences have shaped my topic of study.

Thank you so much to Josh Shanholtzer for all his work shepherding this manuscript to completion, as well to the anonymous reviewers who have undoubtedly made this a stronger analysis.

Herein I present many voices, particularly from the US foreign policy and Venezuelan NGO community. I'm grateful to all those who were willing to meet and speak with me. These are sensitive topics, and no one had any mandate to speak with me. Indeed, some folks did not. I appreciate those who did, as they seemingly understand the importance of research and scholarship.

I must also thank Private Chelsea Manning for her release of a trove of embassy cables, without which my research would be much less thorough. The cables that Manning released are a data gold mine. They detail backstage discussions and dynamics that would otherwise be inaccessible. Anyone who has submitted Freedom of Information Requests requests knows of the great many redactions that cover the pages. Over the past decade, it has been rollercoaster of responses to my use of these documents, which were published by Julian Assange. It has been fascinating to see the tide turn against him, particularly around the time of the 2016 US presidential election. We know more than ever about the workings of US foreign policy as result of his and Manning's efforts.

Without the formal and informal guidance from my dissertation chair and friend David Smilde, there would be no academic career for me, no book, no public writings, and much less of a joyous life thus far. I could never say enough about David's willingness to work with, trust, and encourage me. From the beginning of my time at the University of Georgia, David made me feel appreciated and acknowledged. He treated me like a scholar from the start and showed me so much warmth. Academia was a confusing place for me. David understood me and has continued to offer me guidance. Thank you so much for everything. I owe you many fine stouts until the end.

Patricia Richards and Pablo Lapegna served as dissertation committee members for me, and I also now call them friends. I appreciate their dedication to my project and all of the time they spent reading my comprehensive exams, prospectus, and final work.

I am also thankful for Jim Dowd, who has continually shown me warmth and kindness. Jim was a constant source of discussion and conversation. I am grateful for our friendship.

I also wish to thank Peter Meiksins, Jim Chriss, Bill Morgan, and Howard Ramos at Cleveland State University. I completed an MA at Cleveland State and was still only slowly developing research skills. Peter and Howard worked with me on my master's thesis and met me where I was at the time. They could have easily torched my work. They were kind, and I always remember that when I work with my own students.

In addition, I completed a BA at John Carroll University. Several folks also showed me kindness along the way as an undergraduate student: Gloria Vaquera, Paul Lipold, Janet Larsen, Richard Clark, Duane Dukes, Wendy Wiedenhoft, James Krukones, and Ken Eslinger.

I wish to thank my parents and my brothers. My parents provided me with a Jesuit education and have encouraged my studies since I was a young boy. My mother and stepfather helped my now-wife and I move to Georgia and on every other move thereafter. When one of my flights to Venezuela was cancelled at the last minute I was to leave for research, my mom stepped in and bought me a ticket. It was no small thing. When I told my mother about an annoyance I was having as a graduate student, she wanted to call the university. I didn't let that happen. But that's the mother I have.

My father passed away at age fifty-nine in 2014. I was two years away from finishing my degree. He didn't get to see me graduate or his two grandchildren, but he lives on within me. He dropped out of college after a semester and became a janitor, and later a pipefitter. He was not a trained sociologist, but he had a sociological eye. He was my wrestling coach for many years, too. I learned so very much from him, and I hope I see him again.

I thank all those friends who have stuck with me all along the way. Phil Lewin enriched and continues to enrich my life. We argued over sociological theory in the day, and punk song structures at night. They say dedicate your life to books in graduate school, but we found time to put together a new band and even go on a ten-day tour. What a great time. Thanks to Nico Gomez, Andrew Epstein, and Patrick Goral for also enriching my days in Athens as bandmates and friends.

Thanks also to Becca Hanson—my cohort mate also focused on Venezuelan politics. We worked on many projects together, including the workshop, the blog, and a recent piece in the *Nation*. My time as a graduate student and scholar was and is all the more exciting because of your presence and friendship.

There are too many other friends to thank, but you know who you are, and I appreciate all of the warmth you showed me over the years—from our times in seminars, at shows, in bars, at conferences, at our apartment watching professional wrestling. We were just above the poverty line, and it was frustrating ... but it was a good time.

Finally, and most importantly, I wish to thank my family: Aiola, Sebastian, and Fiona. You are everything to me.

Sebastian and Fiona, I hope you grow up in a country that's much less mean, much less hateful, and much less materialistic than the country I knew as a child. I hope you never feel the financial burden of education and healthcare. You bring me more joy than you could ever imagine. I love you so much.

To Aiola, thank you for first moving with me from Cleveland to Georgia. You hadn't yet lived in the country for a decade, before packing up and moving with me to a new area that neither of us had any experience with. We were twenty-four, and we only knew each other for a little over a year. It took me awhile to speak to you in our statistics class at Cleveland State. But, finally, I did, and you agreed to come and see my own punk band one April evening, in an abandoned Chinese restaurant that had been taken over by anarchists.

We've been together ever since.

The life of a graduate student is not romantic. There's little pay, long hours of reading, and annoying debates with other doctoral students. You knew I could finish. You stuck by me through it all. You understood when I left for research, and you've read my work and believed in me.

We've moved now four times in our time together. When I look back, it's just amazing. From New Orleans to Wilmington to Tennessee, we've made it all work out. We've traveled to places I never thought I'd go: Ireland, Albania, Peru, Ukraine. Thank you for everything. I love you. You're the best friend I've ever had.

ENCOUNTERING US EMPIRE IN SOCIALIST VENEZUELA

Introduction

THE VENEZUELAN GOVERNMENT AND US EMPIRE IN THE TWENTY-FIRST CENTURY

At the turn of the twenty-first century, the US government possesses and maintains a global empire. This might sound nefarious or hyperbolic. It might even sound conspiratorial. The existence of the US Empire, however, is widely accepted among many contemporary scholars, journalists, and politicians (Go 2011; Immerwahr 2019; Kaplan 2020; McCoy 2017). When we speak of the US Empire, what is meant, quite simply, is that the US government and its functionaries wield disproportionate influence over global affairs through the exercise of a number of modalities, such as, for example, economic coercion and military intervention. While it remains true that some regional powers exist, such as China and Russia, and while it remains true that these countries possess some influence over some of their neighbors, the US Empire remains hegemonic in the sense that US government decisions remain far more consequential and wide-ranging than the decisions of any other global actor. The US government, for example, wields far more leverage than any other country over a far wider array of government leaders and international organizations, such as the International Monetary Fund and the World Bank (Babb 2009; Mann 2013; McCoy 2017; Nye 2015).

Despite US preponderance of global power, though, challengers have continued to confront the US government well into the twenty-first century. US government leaders, for instance, charged the Russian government with interfering in its 2016 presidential elections by infiltrating Democratic and Republican Party electronic messages and databases, promoting the Trump candidacy, and transmitting partisan material over social media in order to sow discord during the electoral season. The Chinese government, for another, continues to court allies throughout many parts of the world with its One Belt, One Road initiative, and the US government has recurrently accused the Chinese government of intellectual property theft in order to unfairly bolster their domestic economy and outcompete US-based corporations. Over the course of the last decade, too, several Latin American countries have openly defied the US government by asserting their claims to national sovereignty, removing US government agencies from their territory (e.g., the Drug Enforcement Agency, and the US Agency for International Development), and calling for the creation of a multipolar world system free from US global domination, including countries such as Bolivia, Cuba, Nicaragua, and Venezuela.

No government has been more vociferous in this endeavor than the Venezuelan government, formerly under socialist President Hugo Chávez, and now led by Chávez's successor, President Nicolás Maduro.[1] Under the socialists, the Venezuelan government has condemned the global war on terror, established intensive relations with US government foes (e.g., Belarus, China, Iran, Russia), and expropriated US businesses. All the while, Venezuelan leaders have sought to cultivate a new socialist model to combat free-market economic policies championed by US government leaders.

Throughout recent history, the US government has forcefully, and often successfully, targeted and deposed Latin American leaders who have challenged its dominance. In the 1950s, President Dwight D. Eisenhower permitted the Central Intelligence Agency (CIA) to assist dissident and exiled military forces in Guatemala in overthrowing the democratically elected government of Jacobo Arbenz. In the 1960s, President Lyndon B. Johnson ordered a US military invasion in the Dominican Republic to ensure that leftist forces would not achieve presidential power, and President John F. Kennedy ordered an invasion of Cuba led by exiles living in Florida to defeat the Castro government. In the 1970s, President Richard Nixon failed to prevent socialist President Salvador Allende from attaining presidential power in Chile, but, thereafter, succeeded in deposing, and, ultimately, killing him by permitting the CIA to work with dissident military forces led by General Augusto Pinochet. Although Congress reined in on CIA activity following hearings lead by Senator Frank Church in the 1970s, CIA and US government leaders under the Reagan administration still found ways to work with counterrevolutionary forces in Nicaragua to violently destabilize the leftist Sandinista government in the 1980s, even after Congress prohibited these efforts.

Two dynamics, however, distinguish the arrival of the Venezuelan socialist government from earlier instantiations of leftist governance in Latin America during the twentieth century. First, the Soviet Union no longer exists, and, as a result, no other superpower seriously threatens to replace the US Empire as the world's most powerful entity. Regional powers surely exist, but their capacity for global influence is limited. Russia might maintain some degree of influence over Belarus and parts of Ukraine, and China might wield some degree of influence over North Korea, for instance, but they do not command the extensive sort of influence that the US Empire now commands across the globe. What is more, though, given the absence of the Soviet Union, the threat of socialism and/or communism as a justification for aggressive US foreign policy seems hardly defensible. US government leaders might denounce Venezuelan socialism, but the country hardly appears to pose the same existential threat that the Soviet model formerly posed to the US government.

Second, Venezuela has, until very recently, remained an upper-middle-income society that possesses more oil reserves than any other country in the world.[2] As a result, the Venezuelan government has not been as vulnerable as other Latin American countries that had previously experimented with socialist and leftist policies at earlier points in time. While the US government easily overthrew the Guatemalan and Grenadian governments, for instance, the United States would conceivably face more formidable obstacles in an attempt to forcefully depose the Venezuelan government. Indeed, if the US government could not, and has not been able to, depose the Cuban government—a country that has faced much international isolation and suffered much misery across the last few decades—there is only more doubt that it could easily overthrow the Venezuelan government and dismantle its accompanying Bolivarian Revolution.

Despite these impediments, US government leaders have in no way abandoned imperial efforts to control political-economic dynamics inside Venezuela. US government agencies have continually sought to steer the country in a direction that US government leaders would prefer. This book, in part, examines how the US government has sought to undermine socialist governance in Venezuela, promote liberal democracy, and bring the Venezuelan opposition to power. In doing so, I show how the US government has primarily used democracy assistance to pursue these objectives. Through agencies like the National Endowment for Democracy (NED) and the US Agency for International Development (USAID), the US government has, for example, provided funding and training for opposition political parties and opposition-oriented nongovernmental organizations (NGOs). Although the US government and its democracy-promoting agencies have claimed that such funding remains neutral and nonpartisan, this is anything but the case. In Venezuela, these agencies have continually sought to bolster the opposition. In response, the Venezuelan government has pushed back against these initiatives with several legal maneuvers. Yet, despite this, US government intervention has continued. I briefly turn to the origins of US imperialism, before outlining the path ahead for this this text, and the arguments that I will put forth in ensuing chapters.

The Origins of US Imperialism

Until the turn of the twentieth century, US government efforts toward territorial expansion had focused on the elimination of Indigenous populations across "the American Frontier." The US government continued to push its boundaries further west under a settler-colonial model until they reached the Pacific Ocean. Settlers pushed Native American tribes off their land, murdered many of those Native Americans who resisted their displacement, continually broke formerly existing treaties, and thereafter circumscribed the land upon which Native Americans could reside (Bulmer-Thomas 2018; hooks 1982; Horne 2020; Horsman 1981; Jung 2011). In addition, American revolutionaries pushed for emancipation from England, in part, so that they might continue to enslave Africans and African Americans, a practice that persisted until the mid-nineteenth century (Horne 2016). Thereafter, white US leaders developed a racial, patriarchal dictatorship wherein only white propertied men could vote, govern, and maintain political office (hooks 1982; Horne 2014, 2020; Horsman 1981; Jung 2011).

As White Anglo-Saxon Protestant (WASP) men cultivated what bell hooks (1982, 27) terms a "white imperialistic order," US government leaders such as Benjamin Franklin and Thomas Jefferson thoroughly believed that they were a chosen people destined to manage the entirety of the Americas (Horsman 1981; Immerman 2010; Fitz 2017; Krenn 2006). They supported some nineteenth-century Latin American revolutionaries, such as Simón Bolívar, in their efforts to overthrow Spanish rule, but US government leaders believed that the Americas remained a US government sphere of influence, and they eventually codified this belief in 1823 under the Monroe Doctrine (Fitz 2017; Krenn 2006; Schoultz 2018). To the south and to the west, US government forces annexed large portions of Mexico and warred with the country from 1846 to 1848. Much like their depiction of Native Americans, US government leaders depicted Mexicans as culturally backward, possessing impure blood, and thus unworthy of managing such vast territory (Fitz 2017; Horsman 1981). To these leaders, it was only natural that US Americans should remove it from them.

In 1898, though, US imperial efforts moved beyond the continental mainland. With the support of much of the US populace, President William McKinley deployed the US military to assist in the removal of Spanish forces from Cuba, Guam, the Philippines, and Puerto Rico. Following the Spanish defeat, President McKinley and other US politicians had much difficulty in deciding upon an exit plan. This would become a turning point in US history. US government leaders underwent little existential anguish extending their boundaries across the continental mainland, but what about an overseas empire?

This situation indeed provoked much soul-searching among US political elites. But, following lengthy congressional debates concerning US values and the future of the US role throughout the world, President McKinley decided that the United States would temporarily remain in the formerly Spanish-controlled colonies (Bulmer-Thomas 2018; Go 2011; McCoy 2017). These temporary dealings have long since spiraled into indefinite stays in some places (Guam, Puerto Rico) in comparison with others (Cuba, the Philippines). McKinley, more than anyone else, consecrated the contemporary origins of US global empire. With his initiation of overseas military engagement, the door opened for a global US government presence. At the turn of the twentieth century, the British government continued to operate as the world's hegemonic superpower, and other European powers, such as the French and Portuguese, continued to retain colonial possessions throughout the world. But, while the US government did not claim many additional lands beyond those garnered from Spain and did not pursue the acquisition of formal colonies, US government leaders commenced a pattern of gunboat diplomacy and military invasion, particularly throughout Central America and the Caribbean (Grandin 2006; McPherson 2016; Schoultz 2018). In fact, these areas would serve as the training grounds for future US imperial efforts—that is, in the years before the US government would eventually reach hegemonic maturity after World War II (Go 2011; Grandin 2006).

Indeed, it was not until the conclusion of World War II that the US Empire reached maturity as a hegemonic force and ushered in an era of widespread US global empire-building. Following the war, the US portion of global GDP reached roughly 35 percent, former European colonial powers turned many of their military bases over to the United States, and the US government began a cold war with the Soviet Union, continuing to engage in invasions and battles in places such as the Dominican Republic, the Korean Peninsula, and Vietnam (Mann 2013). On the cultural front, too, Hollywood films and US corporately produced music came to dominate much of the airwaves across the world, and US cultural products, from sports jerseys to toys and gadgets, found their way into global markets, solidifying US cultural imperialism.

Interestingly, though, as the United States became a globally hegemonic power, it did not pursue colonial arrangements, as previous European empires had. Some have interpreted this is in a benign light, claiming that the US Empire has ruled over the world system in a benevolent manner, commanding a new form of empire built upon freedom, liberty, and democracy (see, e.g., Kaplan 2020). Many more social scientists, however, argue that little evidence exists to support these claims (Bulmer-Thomas 2017; Go 2011; Immerwahr 2019; Mann 2013; McCoy 2017). Instead, they view the US Empire as continuing to engage imperial strategies in a similar effort to control and dictate both the domestic affairs of foreign countries and global affairs writ large, albeit in a more indirect and informal, rather than formal and colonial, manner.

Firstly, many scholars reject the idea that the US Empire is historically unique in comparison with previous empires. Historian Victor Bulmer-Thomas (2018) and sociologist Julian Go (2011), for instance, point out that the US government indeed engaged in colonial arrangements even during the first few decades of its existence, long before the Spanish-American War and the pursuit of overseas aggression. As the US government expanded its boundaries beyond the initial thirteen colonies, the federal government ruled over newly acquired territories, such as Louisiana, for substantial periods of time without territorial citizens possessing the same rights as citizens in official states (Bulmer-Thomas 2018; Go 2011). Some politicians even challenged the presidential candidacy of Republican senator Barry Goldwater, for example, given that he was born in Arizona before it achieved official statehood in 1912 (Bulmer-Thomas 2018).

In the wake of World War II, it remains true, though, that the US Empire has not pursued formal colonial efforts in the same manner as European colonial powers throughout earlier centuries. Go (2011) dispels the notion that this is due to American exceptionalism and a unique form of benevolence—that is, in contradistinction to former European colonial powers. Like Bulmer-Thomas (2018), Go (2011) points out that the US government pursued colonial efforts both on the US American mainland and beyond. More importantly, though, he points out that global dynamics prevented the US government from pursuing colonies. In the wake of World War II, the US Empire contended with the Soviet Union, and, while the United States could have pressured European powers to turn their colonies over to the United States, Soviet support for decolonization in many parts of the world precluded such efforts. Given that some revolutionary movements received support from the Soviets, US government leaders feared that should they succeed, and should the US Empire pursue colonies or support continued European colonialism, successful revolutionary movements might align with the Soviets and turn against the United States. As a result, these structural conditions stifled any consideration of such pursuits.

In addition, Go (2011) points out that US government leaders could not simply claim territories as European colonial powers had done so during, for example, the scramble for Africa. Rather, in the post–World War II period, territories were defined, nation-state lines were drawn, nationalist movements developed, and at least some local governance was established within many formerly colonialized territories, even if that local governance could easily and formally be undercut by governors and other colonial rulers. The global terrain had changed since Europeans colonized the world, and US government leaders had to adjust to these new circumstances.

Second, and more importantly, social scientists have documented how under these new arrangements, the US government deployed other sorts of imperial methods—beyond colonization efforts—in order to maintain a global empire. Michael Mann (2013) has identified four informal methods of imperial control that the US Empire has deployed in lieu of formal colonialization efforts, but no less intended to ensure global domination. These efforts include military force, support for proxy governments, economic coercion, and hegemony. While the US government has persistently been at war since World War II in places such as Iraq and Vietnam, it has also relied upon authoritarian rulers in many parts of the world, who have embraced US foreign policy interests. During the Cold War, the US government supplied not a few dictators with economic and military support, such as General Augusto Pinochet in Chile. Even in the present, the US government continues to intensively work and maintain friendly relations with authoritarian governments in places such as Azerbaijan, Honduras, and Saudi Arabia. In addition, the US government has exerted control over the policies of foreign governments through the threat of removing bilateral aid or vetoing multilateral aid. Finally, many world leaders have simply accepted the global leadership position of the United States and have fallen in line behind US global policies, such as when British and Australian leaders quickly supported US counterterrorism policies, including the invasion of Iraq.

Mann (2013), among other social scientists, remains much justified in spotlighting these particular imperial modalities. However, these methods include only the most visible strategies undertaken by the US Empire. Many of these methods are not frequently deployed in most areas of the world. More importantly, these methods are often not deployed against some of the US Empire's most formidable opponents, including those middle-income countries that pose a serious challenge to the future of US global power, such as China, Iran, Russia, and Venezuela. In such middle-income countries, the US government often relies upon far more subtle methods in its attempts to steer political-economic dynamics in a direction consonant with US imperial visions of how foreign governments should operate.

Given that the US government cannot invade all countries, and given that the United States often cannot economically coerce middle-income countries due in part to their independence from international financial institutions, how have US government leaders responded to such challenges?

US Empire Building in the Twenty-First Century

In some instances, the US Empire continues to use the aforementioned sorts of informal tools to exert control over global affairs. There is no question about that. Many social scientists focused on US imperialism, however, often entirely miss an understudied, yet consequential US foreign policy initiative that has become widely used at the turn of the twenty-first century: democracy assistance. In in the 1980s, US foreign policymakers began to establish programs and agencies specifically charged with providing governments, newly developing political parties, and NGOs in Africa, Asia, Eastern Europe,

Latin America, and the Middle East with financial and technical support, or democracy assistance, for transitioning to and constructing democratic political systems (Carothers 1999; Geogehan 2018; Robinson 1996). While the US government has distributed this aid within many low-income countries, it has also provided such assistance within several middle-income countries, such as Belarus, Colombia, Russia, and Venezuela.

By the 1980s, it had become clear that communism had begun to lose its international vitality, as communist governments faced recurrent domestic protest and began to formally transition away from authoritarian modes of political-economic governance. Mikhail Gorbachev, for instance, initiated policies of glasnost and perestroika, or a loosening of restrictions on civil liberties and private enterprise, alongside freedom for nearly all imprisoned critics. The Reagan administration, for its part, recognized that the days of communism were limited and wanted to shape what political-economic system replaced the Soviet model in many locations across the world. Administration members also believed that the inspiration that the Soviet Union formerly offered, had now dissipated. Some disagreement remains, though, as to the ultimate basis for the beginnings of democracy assistance. Thomas Carothers (1999), for one, argues that the global shift away from communism allowed the US government to adamantly, and, finally, pursue democracy promotion without the suspicion that foreign citizens might elect socialist or communist-inspired leaders who might align with the Soviet Union and threaten US national security interests. In contrast, William Robinson (1996, 2006) has argued that as popular social movements were beginning to unseat authoritarian dictators in places such as Iran and Nicaragua, US government leaders searched for a new policy that would prevent these developments and allow the United States to more carefully manage global affairs. What is more, Robinson has argued that dictators had become anachronistic vestiges who prevented the full spread of neoliberal economic policies, as these leaders often engaged in crony capitalist policies such as awarding domestic businesses to friends, family members, and political supporters. In his view, moderate and right-leaning governments that were democratically elected could thus provide the best stability for global capitalism and the spread of transnational corporations. Taken together, Robinson (1996, 2006) argues that these two dilemmas—increasing social unrest and crony capitalist policies within dictatorial countries—pushed the US government to advance a new form of imperialism that would allow for long-term control over other countries.

Since this time, the US government has developed several agencies that provide governments, political parties, and NGOs with democracy assistance. Specifically, this has included offices within the US Agency for International Development (USAID) and the Department of State. In addition, US policymakers created the National Endowment for Democracy (NED) and its four associated groups—the International Republican Institute (IRI), the National Democratic Institute for International Affairs (NDI), the Solidarity Center (SC), and the Center for International Private Enterprise (CIPE)—to provide political parties and NGOs with complementary assistance. The NED and its associated groups receive nearly all of their funding from Congress, but they possess independent boards of directors and must only provide Congress with annual reports on their programs and policies throughout the world. They exist as a sort of semi-government institution in contrast with US offices within USAID and the Department of State. All together, these groups encompass the heart of what Thomas Melia (2006) has termed "the democracy bureaucracy," which also includes a smattering of additional private organizations, foundations, and other groups that contract with these state organizations, all of which I discuss in later chapters.

Similar to mid-twentieth-century US foreign policy endeavors, contemporary US democracy assistance practices remain controversial. Neo-Marxist scholars, for instance, have argued that the US government only provides democracy assistance to a select array of political actors (Burron 2013; Petras 1999; Robinson 1996, 2006). These include political parties and NGOs that champion neoliberal economic policies, including trade liberalization, privatization of formerly nationalized industry, and economic deregulation. In a word, neo-Marxists claim that the US government supports actors that pave way for the spread of transnational capitalism and transnational corporations, many of which are headquartered in the United States. Although elections might appear free and fair, they argue that the US government seeks to cultivate political leaders that only it deems worthy of leading countries abroad. To do so, they argue that the US government lavishes such leaders and organizations with funding and assistance.

Government leaders throughout the world have also criticized democracy assistance and, in some places, they have curtailed and criminalized the practice (Carothers 2006; Christensen and Weinstein 2013; Gill 2016). For one, the Egyptian government has prohibited some NGOs from receiving US government assistance, and, in February 2012, Egyptian law enforcement arrested forty-three civil society workers, including several US citizens working in the country. In the same year, the Russian Duma under President Vladimir Putin passed legislation that labels NGOs that receive foreign aid as "foreign agents" and subjects them to financial regulations. Putin has also shut down USAID offices and expelled its workers from the country. Similar episodes have occurred in places such as Belarus, Bolivia, Nicaragua, and Hungary.

Government leaders throughout Latin America, including President Hugo Chávez in Venezuela, President Daniel Ortega in Nicaragua, President Evo Morales in Bolivia, and President Rafael Correa in Ecuador, also criticized, circumscribed, and, in the instance of Venezuela, entirely prohibited political parties and politically-oriented NGOs from receiving US democracy assistance and other forms of foreign aid. In 2010, after years of condemning USAID and other US government funding practices in the country, the Venezuelan legislature successfully passed the Law for the Defense of Political Sovereignty and National Self-Determination, which prohibits political parties and political NGOs from receiving foreign funding. While it does not apply to all NGOs, the language of the law remains ambiguous as it extends its jurisdiction to include any organization that has as its purpose "to promote, divulge, inform, and/or defend the full exercise of citizens' political rights." Since many NGOs support the expression and defense of what could be understood as political rights, such as electoral rights and freedom of the press issues, it is conceivable that the Venezuelan government could subject a range of NGOs and their leaders to fines and prosecution based on this new legislation. These measures, however, have not deterred US government agencies, as they have continued to openly fund civil society groups in the country.

US Democracy Assistance and the Venezuelan Government

In chapter 1, I provide a short history of Venezuelan politics, and US-Venezuelan relations. I show how political-economic discontent throughout Venezuela during the 1980s paved way for the success of outsider presidential candidate Hugo Chávez, who critiqued socioeconomic inequalities in the country and offered an opportunity to break with the Venezuelan two-party system. In addition, I lay out how under Chávez, US-Venezuelan relations increasingly deteriorated to the point where the two countries expelled their respective ambassadors. What is more, I detail some of the basic claims laid out by scholars concerning US intervention into Venezuela during these years, including how the United States used democracy-promotion efforts to undermine the Chávez government.

In chapter 2, I discuss the various US government agencies that carry out foreign policy abroad, including their origins, official mandate, and how they have used funding. I also lay out the two major perspectives that exist concerning the provision of democracy assistance, including a neo-Marxist perspective and a neo-Tocquevillian perspective. Although many scholars have neglected to examine this form of intervention, these two perspectives comprise what scholarly work exists on these practices. Throughout this book, I build upon the neo-Marxist perspective and provide a comprehensive understanding of US democracy assistance efforts abroad. As a result, I complement this analysis by drawing upon postcolonial work from scholars such as W. E. B. Du Bois, as well as the work of critical historians examining US foreign policy in Latin America.

What is more, I show that the neo-Tocquevillian perspective does not offer an accurate view of US democracy assistance efforts abroad. Taking influence from the work of Alexis de Tocqueville and his belief in the inherent beneficence of civil society groups, neo-Tocquevillian scholars have argued that governments such as the United States should furnish political parties and NGOs with financial and technical support in order to cultivate a healthy civil society and a pluralist political model (Carothers 1999; Diamond 2009; McFaul 2004 Wiarda 2003). Such scholars, many of whom have worked within the US democracy assistance community, believe that civil society and democracy are mutually reinforcing, and each would not properly function without the other. In addition, such scholars portray democracy assistance as unbiased, nonpartisan, and flowing to a diverse array of political actors, including a multiplicity of NGOs and political parties. They claim that these political actors strengthen the societies they inhabit, and, where democratic consolidations have not transpired, they believe that NGOs and political parties can play an essential role in solidifying democratic change.

My analysis shows that a liberal democratic framework has undergirded US democracy assistance efforts. In addition to private property rights, liberal democratic politics involve policies that promote individual rights, including voting rights, limited government, decentralization of services, law enforcement, and, indeed, private property rights. The US government has embraced the centrality of the individual citizen in contrast to a strong centralized state. What is more, my analysis links democracy assistance with a history of US foreign policymaking that has involved racism, neocolonialism, and paternalism within the region. US policymakers believe it is their duty to show Venezuelans their true interests and to turn them away from Chávez and his allies. They envision Chávez and his allies as uncivilized and undemocratic, and as manipulating Venezuelan citizens, who remain rather irrational and cannot understand their true interests. Indeed, this serves as the justification for US intervention and for the use of democracy assistance in the first place.

In chapter 3, I specifically examine the racist and neocolonial underpinnings involving US foreign policymaking toward contemporary Venezuela. One of the primary assertions that I render in this book is that US global empire persists into the present, and, what is more, it persists with much ideological continuity since the days of the Monroe Doctrine, the Mexican-American War, and President McKinley's decision to initiate an overseas empire. In particular, I argue that visions of US exceptionalism, US political-economic supremacy, and US racism, neocolonialism, and paternalism guide and justify US foreign policy efforts in Venezuela. US government elites believe it is their duty to promote their vision of democracy—that is, a liberal democratic vision—within Venezuela and to convince Venezuelan citizens what politicians they should support, which excluded Chávez, the politician that Venezuelan citizens, of course, did continually evidence support for. I show that US government actors have viewed Chávez's supporters as emotionally beholden to him and as a frenzied mass that cannot think for themselves. However, with US guidance, government functionaries believed they could enlighten Chávez supporters (Chavistas), teach them to reject him, and cultivate an allegiance for the Venezuelan opposition. In rendering this argument, I centralize the work of W. E. B. Du Bois, but also Edward Said and Aníbal Quijano, and their emphases on the global color line, Orientalist thought, and coloniality. While Du Bois's ideas help us to make sense of how the US government continues to exert control over countries abroad in a neocolonialist manner, Said's work on Orientalism and Quijano's work on coloniality assists us in making sense of the cultural dichotomies that US government functionaries draw upon to justify intervention into Venezuela. Together, such thinkers help us to make sense of the superiority evidenced by US government actors and their sense of paternalism over countries in Latin America and the choices their citizens make.

In chapters 4–8, I carefully detail the array of US democracy assistance efforts in Venezuela, including the work of the NED and its associated groups (chapters 4–7), and USAID (chapter 8). Throughout these chapters, I show that US government functionaries promote US global supremacy in the realm of political-economic life, and they understand their vision of democratic politics as superior to all other manifestations and understandings of democratic politics. This particular US understanding of democratic politics is closely aligned with the liberal democratic tradition of politics that champions civil liberties, individual rights, and limited government—or, in other words, civil and political rights. This deeply contrasts with the Venezuelan government's vision of democratic socialist politics that prioritizes social and economic rights and, at times, involved the transgression of individual rights, such as private property rights for corporations and landholders.

Chapters 4–7, respectively, lay of out the funding efforts of the NED, the IRI, the NDI, and, finally, CIPE and the SC. Although the NED provides funding for its associated groups, it also directly funds NGOs. In Venezuela, such funding has prioritized liberal democratic features of governance, such as, for example, civil liberties, decentralization of government, power, and human rights training for law enforcement officers. For its part, the IRI has run training seminars for political parties that include suggestions on how, for example, the opposition might recruit youth supporters, reach out to voters, hold press conferences, and construct a political platform. Within interviews, former IRI representatives quite plainly state that these efforts were designed to help the opposition defeat Chávez. The NDI, on the other hand, has maintained more of a mixed record in terms of its support for projects in Venezuela. On the ground, it largely worked with opposition mayors on infrastructural issues. However, it also engaged in electoral observation projects, including the creation of an electoral watchdog group composed of both opposition and government members that would eventually verify Chávez's electoral victories.

In chapter 6, I show how CIPE exclusively worked with members of the opposition and sought to promote neoliberal economic policies throughout the country, particularly through funding for a libertarian-oriented think tank, as well as through training programs for poor Venezuelans to learn about the alleged advances of free-market capitalism. Finally, I discuss how the SC primarily worked with labor groups opposed to the Chávez government and its labor policies. The group initially worked with one of the country's largest organized labor groups, the Confederación de Trabajadores de Venezuela (CTV), whose leaders had participated in a 2002 coup d'état and a subsequent lockout strike designed to unseat Chávez. In later years, the SC helped to establish a new labor organization designed to push back against Chávez's socialist policies, including his emphasis on cooperatives and worker councils.

In chapter 8, I detail the efforts of USAID and its Office of Transition Initiatives (OTI). While the NED and its associated groups worked with political parties, business groups, labor groups, and NGOs, USAID and OTI primarily worked within civil society to pull supporters away from Chávez and to assist the burgeoning, opposition student movement, all in the wake of the 2002 coup d'état that temporarily removed Chávez from power. In this chapter, I show that USAID and OTI unsuccessfully attempted to pull Chávez's supporters away from him by establishing seemingly neutral community groups in working-class neighborhoods of Caracas that incrementally criticized government practices and promoted a liberal democratic vision of politics. When these efforts failed, USAID and OTI shifted their focus primarily from poor barrios to student groups within the country. This chapter draws on interviews with former USAID and OTI workers, and their contractors, who operated programs in Venezuela, as well as unredacted US diplomatic cables describing these efforts in the country.

The final substantive issue that this text addresses involves the Venezuelan government's response to US government intervention. In chapter 9, I discuss how and why the Venezuelan government eventually prohibited foreign funding for political parties and NGOs at the time that it decided to do so, in December 2010. Much classical political sociological theory has centered on the domestic sphere and the composition of the domestic electorate to explain the passage of legislation. In Venezuela, though, Chávez and his supporters dominated all branches of government since 2000. Instead of directing attention toward the concerns of classical political sociology, which fail to help us understand these dynamics, I show how the shifting nature of Venezuelan international relations helps us to make sense of the timing of such legislation.

I show that when the Venezuelan government sought to pass anti-NGO legislation at earlier points in time, it still remained keyed into a nexus of relations with the United States, Western European countries, and several multilateral institutions. These embassies, institutions, and their representatives successfully persuaded the Venezuelan government to stall anti-NGO legislation, particularly in 2006, as the government remained highly concerned with its reputation throughout the world and did not wish to further damage relations with the these groups.

Following a presidential election in 2006, however, Chávez consolidated relations with an anti-US network of allies, including Belarus, China, Iran, and Russia—who were also pursuing and passing similar pieces of legislation, in addition to a regional, anti-imperial network of allies, including Bolivia, Ecuador, and Nicaragua, that recently came to power, establishing what has become known as the Latin American Pink Tide. Likewise, Venezuela diminished relations with the United States, Western Europe, and several multilateral institutions. When anti-NGO legislation came onto the agenda in 2010, the Venezuelan government did not consult with these latter countries and institutions or even seem concerned with their perspective on the legislation, as they had several years earlier. Rather, Venezuela had consolidated a newfound set of international relations, and, within this new nexus of relations, anti-NGO legislation was not transgressive, but, in fact, normative, as these same countries were also pursuing similar pieces of legislation and a process of diffusion had emerged among them.

Moving Forward

Over the past two decades, US foreign policy has been extraordinarily controversial in Venezuela—first under Chávez and now under Maduro. Venezuela is hardly the only location, though, where the US government has designed and operated interventionist programs carried out under the auspices of democracy assistance. The Venezuelan government is also hardly the only country that has pushed back against US government intervention and taken aim at foreign funding for NGOs and political parties—a new pattern that is developing among many countries throughout the world (Carothers 2006; Christensen and Weinstein 2013; Gill 2016). Other governments such as China and Russia are allegedly developing their own interventionist plans to target the United States, and we know that Russia, for one, has been involved in attempts to manage affairs in Eastern Europe, such as in Georgia, Serbia, and Ukraine. Given these global dynamics, a case study involving Venezuela provides an excellent opportunity to examine these newfound trends and, subsequently, to build upon and extend existing theory with regards to the US government and its contemporary imperial modalities.

Chapter 1

THE RISE OF HUGO CHÁVEZ AND THE EVOLUTION OF US-VENEZUELAN RELATIONS

Following presidential candidate Hugo Chávez's victory in the 1998 Venezuelan presidential election, US political leaders were unsure how he might govern the country. On the campaign trail, Chávez railed against socioeconomic inequalities, criticized the corrupt two-party system that had dominated Venezuelan politics since the 1950s, and promised to rewrite the Venezuelan constitution and create a participatory democracy that truly included all sectors of Venezuelan society (Buxton 2011; Ellner 2008; Lander and López Maya 1999; López Maya and Lander 2000). The specifics of his policies, though, were not entirely clear. Chávez spoke about respecting the rights of private business, and even received some support from some private business leaders during his 1998 campaign, yet he also maintained a strong friendship with Fidel Castro and the Cuban government (Gates 2010; Lander and López Maya 1999; Smilde 2011).

Shortly after his victory, President Chávez traveled to the United States to test out his relations with the US political and business community. He rang the bell at the New York Stock Exchange, met with private investors, and even threw out the first pitch at a New York Mets baseball game (Gill 2016; Kelly and Romero 2002. Indeed, the latter might have surely exhilarated Chávez, whose initial impetus to join the Venezuelan military was driven by his desire to move from rural Venezuela to the capital city of Caracas and pursue his childhood dream of eventually becoming a professional baseball player in the United States.

Despite these gestures, though, it increasingly became evident that Chávez would seek to forge his own international path and follow no other leadership than his own. Defying US government orders, Chávez traveled to the United States following a visit to Cuba with Castro, and, shortly following this trip, Chávez would become the first leader in years to visit Saddam Hussein in Iraq (Kelly and Romero 2002. While there initially existed a mix of tendencies within Chávez's discursive and behavioral repertoire, his inclinations became transparent in 2001 when he encouraged and signed legislation that allowed him more control over the military and the lifeblood of the Venezuelan economy: the oil industry. By 2001, Chávez began to explicitly criticize US foreign policy, including the US invasion of Afghanistan and subsequently, and more vociferously, its invasion of Iraq. From then onward, relations between the two countries plummeted, arriving at a point where there are no longer any ambassadors maintained between the two countries.

It is worth recounting several key events in the trajectory of the relationship between the United States and Venezuela in order to fully wrestle with additional questions concerning US government intervention into the country. Chávez was indeed elected by citizens on several occasions, in internationally and domestically monitored elections. So, why did the US government intervene in the country with its use of democracy assistance programs? In other words, if democracy already existed, why would any additional need exist for the US government to attempt to import democracy into the country? This chapter engages these questions and brings into relief the historical trajectory of the relationship between the United States and Venezuela under Chávez. I begin, though, by detailing Chávez's rise to power and some of the basic contours surrounding his historically exceptional presidency within the country.

Island of Liberal Democratic Stability Turned Socialist Democracy

Even among the most seemingly stable of Latin American countries, the relative failure of neoliberal economic policies catalyzed the development of social movements that eventually destroyed what had appeared as quite durable institutional foundations. Such is the story of Venezuelan politics at the end of the twentieth century. Throughout much of the latter half of the twentieth century, Venezuela served as the political-economic model that the US government held up for the rest of the region (Miller 2016; Kelly and Romero 2002). After decades of military dictatorship, the Catholic Church, the Venezuelan military, and then-dominant political parties agreed in 1958 to participate and share power within a liberal democratic political system that would promote specific political-economic goals irrespective of what party held power, under an agreement called the Pact of Punto Fijo (Buxton 2001; Ellner 2008; Lander and López Maya 1999). Until nearly the end of the twentieth century, Venezuela retained a relatively stable political-economic climate. Although tensions existed behind the scenes between the United States and Venezuela, and many Venezuelan leaders feared that the US government might encourage a military dictatorship should their government fail to eradicate domestic guerillas who were receiving support from Cuba, successive US administrations publicly praised Venezuela as an example of how Latin American countries could experience a democratic transition without embracing socialist or communist causes (Miller 2016).

During the mid-twentieth century, two parties dominated Venezuelan politics: Acción Democratica (AD), which was then led by President Romulo Betancourt, and Comité de Organización Política Electoral Independiente (COPEI), which was then headed by President Rafael Caldera. While AD promoted a secular form of government that planned to use oil rents to boost basic development projects throughout the country, COPEI promoted similar development policies, but sought to offer more institutional power to the Catholic Church and overtly promoted Christian values (Hellinger 2003).[1] Under the leadership of these two parties, corporatist political practices characterized much of Venezuelan life. This involved the development of youth groups, women's groups, unions, and student organizations affiliated with each of the two parties.

Similar to other Latin American countries during the mid-twentieth century, Venezuela contained a small presence of revolutionary leftist groups, or guerillas, that sought to overthrow the Venezuelan government, establish a newfound communist state, and align the country with both the Cuban and Soviet governments (Miller 2016; Velasco 2011, 2015). However, these groups failed to garner an extensive support base throughout the country, and were heavily targeted by the Venezuelan military, which received aid and support from the US government, and, even more specifically, the Central Intelligence Agency (CIA), in their anti-communist efforts (Miller 2016; Velasco 2011, 2015). Though the groups had some small successes, the government largely neutralized their threat and imprisoned many of their members.

Yet despite the perceived stability of the Venezuelan political model to many outsiders, Venezuelan citizens began to lose interest in their political system all together and/or demand serious political and economic change (Buxton 2001). Beginning in the late 1970s and early 1980s, citizens came to view the two-party system with much cynicism, as national politicians became embroiled in a multitude of corruption scandals (Crisp 2000; Crisp and Levine 1998; Gates 2010), corporatist political practices buried demands from increasingly diversified citizen groups (Pilar Garcia-Guadilla 2003; Salamanca 2004), a hierarchical political-institutional system rewarded party loyalty over local accountability (Crisp 2000; Gates 2010), and oil revenue dwindled, having a deadly impact upon the provision of social services (Karl 1997).

Citizen frustrations reached a crescendo in 1989. In that year, the administration of President Carlos Andres Pérez attempted to alleviate growing economic frustration by enacting a series of neoliberal economic reforms aimed at generating economic growth and overcoming the deficiencies of a political-economic model that remained tethered to the international price of oil. After meeting with representatives from the International Monetary Fund (IMF) following his election, Pérez enacted several economic reforms, including tax reform to solicit foreign investment, the partial privatization of state industries, and the elimination of state subsidies for gasoline, all in order to free up state revenue that might serve outstanding international debt. As a result of the latter reform, citizens faced public transportation price hikes, which disproportionately affected working-class populations who rely upon public transport to move across Caracas, often from their respective barrios and into more upper-middle-class areas for places of work (López Maya 2003). After years of citizen frustration and citizen concern with a political-economic model that seemingly no longer served them, Caracas exploded.

On the day that the government raised the price of gasoline, public transportation vehicles also raised their prices for travelers. Instead of responding by begrudgingly paying higher costs, working-class populations rioted throughout the capital. Caracas witnessed burning vehicles, looting, and widespread protests against the government's decision to work with the IMF, a decision which, during his campaign, Pérez explicitly stated he would not undertake. Instead of calmly attempting to assuage the violence, meet with citizen groups, and/or potentially reverse the government's decision, the Venezuelan government ordered the military to violently repress the protests by indiscriminately firing upon crowds of citizens out in the streets of Caracas. In the end, the Venezuelan military's domestic offensive left over a thousand Venezuelans dead and, not surprisingly, further radicalized the political-economic imaginary of the populace. These events also left a deep and traumatic impact on many Venezuelan military members—many of whom, at the time, resisted and refused to fire upon their fellow citizens. It was at this time that Chávez served in a Venezuelan military group located in the capital region.

Not long after these events, Chávez, then a military commander, personally led a dissident military group named the Movimiento Bolivariano Republicano-200 (MBR-200) in a failed coup d'état effort that landed him in jail for two years. Prior to his imprisonment, Venezuelan leaders allowed Chávez to speak on national television for a brief moment. Sporting a red beret, Chávez claimed that the struggle to achieve political power was over *por ahora* (for now), and he asked his fellow conspirators to lay down their weapons. After taking responsibility for the coup d'état efforts before a national audience, Chávez gained countrywide prominence and became the public face of political-economic frustrations within Venezuela. In addition, the phrase *por ahora* would become his and his supporters' political battle cry and signal that he was not ultimately defeated—only just for the moment.

Following a commutation of his sentence and his release from prison, Chávez and the MBR-200 chose to pursue legal channels of political change, focusing their efforts on grassroots mobilization throughout the country.

Although the MBR-200 initially rejected participation in national elections, Chávez was convinced by the support he received throughout the country to run in the 1998 presidential election, tailoring to his campaign to the plight of Venezuela's popular and increasingly marginalized social classes (Lander and López Maya 1999; López Maya and Lander 2000; Smilde 2011). David Smilde (2011, 4–5) describes the socioeconomic divides that had come to characterize Venezuelan society during the late twentieth century.

> Economic decline of the 1980s and 1990s . . . spurred a fundamental realignment in social-class identity political cleavages. In effect, Venezuela moved from a modern conflict between Right and Left, to a postmodern clash between those with a place in organized, formal society and those without . . . The former work in jobs with benefits and legal protections, have legally recognized property, and enjoy municipal services such as water, telephone, and police protection; the latter lack formal employment, live in barrios and rural areas not fully recognized by the state, and do not enjoy full access to the benefits of modern citizenship: job security and protections, professional health care, municipal services, and professional police protection.

Unlike T. H. Marshall's (1949) famous conception of national societies as evolving together and his description of citizens securing equal rights, citizenship rights in Venezuela evolved in an uneven manner and, for many individuals, had regressed throughout the 1980s and 1990s, with inclusion in "organized, formal society" becoming the privilege of only some Venezuelans (Smilde 2011).

Recognizing this situation, Chávez campaigned for the 1998 presidential election on the idea of convoking a constituent assembly and drafting a new constitution that would emphasize, above all else, what Chávez termed a protagonistic and participatory democracy—that is, a new model of governance that would include all members of society in decision-making processes regardless of one's location in the social-class hierarchy (Lander and López Maya 1999; López Maya and Lander 2000; Smilde 2011). Other candidates in the 1998 election included Irene Sáez, the mayor of the upper-class Caracas neighborhood of Chacao, who received endorsement from COPEI, and Henrique Salas Römer, the governor of Carabobo and leader of the newly developed political party Proyecto Venezuela, but who formerly remained part of COPEI. After several setbacks for the initial leading candidates, as well as some confusing last-minute changes by then-dominant political parties, the opposition threw all of its support behind Römer. Despite this final attempt to back one candidate against Chávez, Chávez emerged victorious and took office in 1999.

Since 1999, scholars have observed that "a steady radicalization process" characterized Chávez's time in office (Ellner 2008, 109). After his transition into the presidency, his programmatic efforts began with a push toward a more participatory mode of governance and a pursuit of citizen inclusion. In his first year in office alone, Chávez held three national elections, including a referendum for the convocation of a Constituent National Assembly to write a new constitution, for members of the Constituent National Assembly, and, finally, for a new constitution to replace the 1961 Venezuelan constitution that AD and COPEI leaders had drafted and passed following the Pact of Punto Fijo. In all three endeavors, the Chávez government was victorious: a Constituent National Assembly was convened; 125 of the 131 members elected to the Constituent National Assembly supported Chávez, and a newly drafted constitution was ratified, which explicitly promoted the development of a protagonistic and participatory democracy. While opposition political parties claimed that Chávez wanted to consolidate his grip on power, Chávez and aligned politicians claimed that they were simply putting more decisions before the Venezuelan populace and following the will of the people above all else.

Although President Chávez's intentions and the political-economic path he desired were not entirely clear at this point, an anti-neoliberal, economic agenda became evident by 2001. In April 2001, at the Summit of the Americas conference in Quebec, Canada, Chávez registered his objections to neoliberal capitalism by objecting to the Free Trade Area of the Americas and, specifically, the trade liberalization policies it promoted. In the same year, the Chávez government enacted a series of forty-nine new laws, two of which signaled the beginning of Chávez's anti-neoliberal, economically nationalist, and redistributive approach, including the Land Law and the Organic Hydrocarbons Law. For its part, the Land Law permitted the government to expropriate unused lands held by large, rural property owners, with the intent of breaking up land concentration and using idle lands for national food production. For its part, the Organic Hydrocarbons Law annulled the opening of the oil sector to increased foreign ownership and reestablished the national government as the owner-operator of the Venezuelan oil industry.

In addition to revamping some domestic economic policies, Chávez began to use the Venezuelan military for new purposes, namely the provision of social services for citizens throughout the country. One of President Chávez's political-military initiatives, for instance, included Plan Bolívar 2000. As Daniel Hellinger (2003, 44) points out, this plan "was a bold attempt to fuse military capabilities with those of other public institutions to attack social problems with programs of sanitation, health, indigent care, public transport, housing, and the like. The programs delivered immediate, short-term relief to many and demonstrated how the military could aid and not simply repress the population." These efforts were highly controversial, however, and government opponents claimed that Chávez was attempting to militarize society and use military forces for strictly his own partisan gains.

It is within these early years, too, that Chávez witnessed the beginnings of a historically tense relationship with the US government, as his domestic and international policies clashed with US government expectations for the country. At this point, however, it is important to note that while the US and Venezuelan governments formerly maintained a strong relationship, this relationship deteriorated quite intensively under the Chávez administration. At the center of these disagreements, Chávez criticized US military action in both Afghanistan and Iraq, and the US global war on terror more broadly; he refused to allow the US government to use Venezuela as a base for counter-narcotics operations and kicked the Drug Enforcement Agency (DEA) out of the country; he rejected free trade agreements and neoliberal economic policies encouraged by the US government in international fora; and rendered far less criticism of the Revolutionary Armed Forces of Colombia (FARC), a US-designated terrorist organization, than previous administrations (Gill 2016, 2019). For their part, US political leaders exacerbated deteriorating relations by demanding that Chávez retract his criticism of its war of terror, often referred to Chávez as a despotic leader and in other unflattering terms, and funded and established relations with opposition political parties and opposition-oriented nongovernmental organizations (NGOs) that sought to displace Chávez from power (Gill 2016, 2019).

On the domestic front, Chávez's new political-economic policies irritated many sections of the Venezuelan business community, including large agricultural landowners and oil executives; the Venezuelan Federation of Chambers of Commerce (Fedecámaras), the country's largest business organization; and the Confederación de Trabajadores Venezuela (CTV), the country's largest union, which includes many of the workers in the national oil industry. In April 2002 an opposition protest led by Fedecámaras united with private media groups and dissident factions within the Venezuela military to stage a coup d'état that removed Chávez from office for nearly two days. Following Chávez's detention, the head of Fedecámaras, Pedro Carmona, became the president of the transitional government. During his brief time in Miraflores Palace, Carmona suspended the new Venezuelan constitution, removed the word *Bolivarian* from the country's name as was included under the new constitution (the Bolivarian Republic of Venezuela), and disbanded the Venezuelan legislature and judiciary. This series of anti-democratic and unconstitutional missteps led many individuals who formerly supported the overthrow to retract their support for the transitional government. More significantly, though, a mass of Chavistas took to the streets of Caracas and demanded that the Venezuelan military return Chávez to power. During this time, many military members and politicians feared that more violence might ensue between Chávez's supporters and transitional government supporters, and that the situation might quickly devolve into a civil war. After Chávez-supporting military members—namely, the Presidential Guard—regained control of Miraflores Palace and sent Carmona into hiding, the Venezuelan military returned Chávez to Caracas from a military base off the coast of the country, and Chávez resumed the presidency.

In the aftermath of the coup d'état, much confusion developed surrounding its development and execution, including the shooting deaths of several citizens, whether or not Venezuelan groups had planned to stage the coup in advance or if it spontaneously developed, whether or not US government leaders knew in advance that Venezuelan groups were preparing to stage the coup d'état, and whether or not US government leaders had funded Venezuelan groups that they allegedly knew were planning to stage the coup d'état for these specific purposes. In its aftermath, both the Venezuelan and US government investigated and supplied their own interpretation of the details surrounding these events. Venezuelan government leaders largely understood and publicly discussed the coup d'état in the same way that Eva Golinger (2006, 2008) wrote about the events surrounding the affair. Golinger, a Venezuelan American lawyer by trade, would become one of Chávez's advisors following her investigative work on this subject. In both Golinger's and the Venezuelan government's perspective, the US government under the Bush administration actively supported the individuals and organizations that executed the coup d'état, and they primarily did so through US democracy assistance. From their perspective, democracy assistance was not passively provided to the coup d'état plotters at random intervals, but was actually accelerated in the months and weeks directly prior to the coup d'état (Golinger 2006). For them, the US government decisively plotted with the opposition to overthrow Chávez and the Venezuelan government, and the US government's decision to immediately recognize the transitional government as a legitimate government, as well as the decision to blame Chávez and his supporters for street violence that ensued, reveal that the Bush administration had assisted opposition forces in bringing down the government and possessed prior knowledge that this series of events was to unfold against Chávez.

On the US government's end, the inspector general of the Department of State and the Broadcasting Board of Governors conducted its own investigation into the coup d'état events. In contrast with Golinger and the Venezuelan government, the investigation concluded that while "it is clear that NED, Department of Defense (DOD), and other US assistance programs provided training, institution building, and other support to individuals and organizations understood to be actively involved in the brief ouster of the Chávez government, we found no evidence that this support directly contributed, or was intended to contribute, to that event" (Office of the Inspector General 2002, 3). The report thus acknowledged that US government leaders worked with and met with opposition NGOs, political parties, and their leaders, but it found that they did not approve the use of undemocratic and violent channels to remove Chávez from power, and, as a result, were not to blame for the coup d'état efforts.

In the aftermath, suspicions and tensions between the Chávez government and opposition groups persisted. In fact, the opposition quickly moved on to new strategies to oust to the Chávez government. First, the opposition unsuccessfully subjected the country to a damaging oil strike in 2002–2003 and, second, unsuccessfully pursued a 2004 recall election, both of which aimed to remove President Chávez from office. During these years, claims also persisted that the opposition groups behind these campaigns continued to receive democracy assistance in order to carry out these activities. For example, Golinger (2006, 2008) claimed that those Venezuelan NGOs that were actually collecting signatures to recall Chávez from office received US democracy assistance for precisely this purpose, including, for example, the civic group Súmate. William Robinson (2006) also claimed that, in general, in the aftermath of the failed 2002 coup, the US government switched from a policy of overt government overthrow to a policy of strategically and legally removing Chávez from office. After Chávez's victory within a 2004 recall referendum election, though, Robinson (2006) and Golinger (2006, 2008) claim that the US government allocated funds and guidance for the political opposition in an effort to consolidate opposition fractions and develop a unified front against Chávez—a strategy that Robinson (1996, 2006) argues the US government had also employed in Nicaragua in the late 1980s in order to remove the Sandinistas from office. Despite all opposition efforts, though, Chávez and his supporters continued to consolidate its hold on all formal institutions of political power before and after the 2002 coup d'état. Chávez and his party accomplished this through the aforementioned convening of the Constituent Assembly in 1999 and elections for the new Venezuelan National Assembly; the appointment of dozens of new judges to the Supreme Tribunal of Justice, albeit to much criticism; and, finally, through Chávez's own 2006 and 2012 presidential electoral victories.

As noted earlier, Chávez's time in office was marked by a process of radicalization in his political-economic views (Ellner 2008). Most notably, while Chávez initially focused on participatory democracy and social missions to enhance the livelihoods of the poor, he gradually moved toward an emphasis on socialism. Yet, while Venezuela is most closely identified with socialism more than anything else within the public imaginary, Chávez's emphasis on socialism only began in 2005—after a full six years into his presidency. In 2005 Chávez replaced his earlier emphasis on participatory democracy with a newfound emphasis on what he specifically termed "twenty-first-century socialism." At the World Social Forum in Brazil, Chávez proclaimed an imminent need to rejuvenate such a leftist economic model. He asserted that there "is no solution within capitalism, one must transcend capitalism. Nor is it about statism or state capitalism, which would be the same perversion of the Soviet Union, which was the cause of its fall. We must reclaim socialism as a thesis, as a project and a path, but a new socialism" (Wilpert 2007, 238). Thereafter, Chávez rebranded his political party as the Partido Socialista Unido de Venezuela (PSUV), and, in keeping with this emphasis on twenty-first-century socialism, he intensified and expanded social services, which included bringing substantial amounts of education, housing, food, and medicine to the country's poorest populations; developing policies and laws promoting communal councils and communes as bastions of participatory democracy; and, at least discursively, encouraging the devolution of state power unto these popular power bases so that citizens might increasingly render more decisions over their lives and resources without any more need for direct state intervention (Ciccariello-Maher 2013, 2016; Kingsbury 2018; Fernandes 2010). Subsequently, Gabriel Hetland (2017) documents how Chávez generated a new form of socialist and Chavista hegemony within the country, with even right-wing, opposition politicians recognizing some of the advances of community councils and other socialist initiatives.

Throughout 2007 and 2008, Chávez pushed further with land redistribution and nationalization efforts, which included exerting state control over banks, cement industries, foreign energy firms, and telecommunications firms. Yet, it was also during this period that the Venezuelan government suffered its first major setback. In 2007 Venezuelans voted against a referendum that, for one, would have abolished presidential term limits and permitted Chávez to run for a third presidential term in 2012. The referendum included an additional sixty-eight constitutional amendments, which Chávez stated would permit him to move ahead with the country's socialist agenda. Although citizens rejected this package in 2007 in a nationwide vote, portions of it were still passed through the National Assembly, and in 2009 an entire new referendum was successfully passed that allowed Chávez to run for the presidency in 2012.

Several scholars claim that President Chávez's emphasis on twenty-first-century socialism and popular power corresponded with an increasingly contentious relationship between the national government and private media, journalists, and NGOs (Corrales 2011; Corrales and Penfold- Becerra 2011; Hidalgo 2009). Throughout Chávez's time in office, conflicts between the Venezuelan government and opposition media sources and opposition leaders indeed persisted. These tensions heightened following Chávez's 2006 presidential victory. For instance, in 2007 the Venezuelan government refused to renew the contract of the television station RCTV, taking it off public airwaves, and in 2010 another six television stations were found in violation of national laws and removed from public airwaves. In 2010 the Venezuelan government arrested the owner of the remaining publicly televised, opposition news media source, Globovisión, on what some viewed as fabricated claims used to intimidate a key opposition source. Additionally, in 2010 the Venezuelan government arrested Governor Oswaldo Álvarez Paz for, among other issues, referring to Venezuela as a lawless haven for drug smugglers and terrorists.

Although the national government recovered from its 2007 defeat with victories in 2009, the PSUV faced a more serious setback in the 2010 parliamentary elections. The results of this election reduced the PSUV's supermajority within the National Assembly and illustrated that many Venezuelan citizens, particularly in urbanized states such as Zulia and Miranda, had grown frustrated with Chávez and the PSUV. The PSUV faced continual accusations that government members were corrupt and skimmed money from public projects in order to enrich themselves, that the party had grown too bureaucratic and less responsive to local needs, and that Chávez was becoming more repressive and less democratic. In the wake of the PSUV's constitutional setback, the Venezuelan National Assembly pushed through several pieces of legislation, before the new National Assembly with stronger opposition membership would begin in January 2011. During this period, the PSUV passed several pieces of legislation that sought to consolidate the communal state and deliver more power to community councils. In addition, in December 2010 the Venezuelan National Assembly successfully passed the Law for the Defense of Political Sovereignty and National Self-Determination, in two quick discussions in just over a week (Gill 2016). This legislation, which is discussed in more depth in chapter 9, prohibits political parties and politically oriented organizations from receiving funds from abroad. It also prohibits organizations from inviting individuals into Venezuela that offend Venezuelan government leaders or attack Venezuelan national sovereignty. With the passage of this legislation, Chávez made it clear to civil society actors that the government was more willing than ever to prosecute groups that linked up with foreign countries, particularly the United States, and received funding and technical assistance from them.

Despite the 2010 parliamentary setback, Chávez defeated Henrique Capriles, governor of Miranda State, in presidential elections in October 2012 by over ten percentage points. As a guide for his upcoming term, Chávez laid out a six-year socialist plan that aimed for a full transition toward socialism through the cultivation of a communal state. Under this plan, Chávez embraced the idea that community councils could link up with one another to develop larger communes, wherein they might produce all the resources required to meet community needs (Ciccariello-Maher 2016; Kingsbury 2018). Not long after Chávez's victory, though, his new term was cut short. In March 2013 Chávez passed away from cancer, and he designated Foreign Minister

Nicolás Maduro as his successor. The government organized new presidential elections, and, while Maduro delivered a second electoral defeat to Henrique Capriles, this time the margin of victory was much narrower. While Chávez won by over ten percentage points in October 2012, President Maduro won by less than two points six months later in April 2013. As of this writing, Maduro continues as president of Venezuela.

Antinomies under the Chávez Administration

The recent, historical trajectory of US-Venezuela relations since the mid-twentieth century, in many ways, remains rather straightforward. Following Venezuela's transition to a two-party democratic system in 1958,[2] the US and Venezuelan governments maintained a strong and harmonious relationship, and the United States could generally count on Venezuela as a reliable ally in the region, with few exceptions (Kelly and Romero 2002). For US government leaders, Venezuela represented the possibility that a functioning, liberal democracy could persist without the threat of Soviet-inspired parties taking power—either through the ballot box or through violent revolution (Miller 2016; Velasco 2011, 2015). In keeping with their support, the United States served as Venezuela's largest trading partner, and the US government supplied Venezuela with a wealth of economic aid for agriculture and education, among other areas, through programs such as the Alliance for Progress and through state organizations such as the US Agency for International Development (USAID). What is more, the US government provided Venezuela with much military aid to assist the government in its elimination of what presence of leftist guerillas existed in the country in the mid-twentieth century (Miller 2016).

With the election of Chávez in 1998, such historically warm relations between the two countries began to wither. Initially, as noted earlier in this chapter, President Chávez traveled to the United States during one of his first overseas visits, meeting with President Bill Clinton, seeking to garner business investment (Kelly and Romero 2002). Differences between the countries, however, became increasingly manifest in the years to come, and continue to characterize relations into the present. In these early years, Chávez rendered several foreign policy decisions that irritated the US government. In 1999, for instance, Chávez refused to accept aid for floods that destroyed hillside housing from US military boats that were already traveling across the Caribbean Sea en route to Venezuela. US officers were flabbergasted to find that they would need to return back home without successfully delivering any support to the Venezuelan government. Chávez also refused to provide the US government with any airspace for counter-narcotics missions throughout South America, namely in neighboring Colombia. Instead, Chávez emphasized Venezuelan national sovereignty and expressed that the United States could not simply use any territory that it demanded for any purpose it demanded. In 2001, as mentioned earlier, Chávez also criticized and rejected the ideas of free trade and representative democracy, asserting that both were a detriment to the poor and working classes of Venezuela, and, as a result, a new political-economic vision was required for the region. Such assertions directly challenged US hegemony and made clear that Chávez would not take unilateral direction from the United States.

During his foreign travels, President Chávez greatly irritated the US government. Chávez made no secret that he was willing to visit with US foes, including Saddam Hussein in Iraq, in order to discuss oil and energy policies. The US government attempted to stop Chávez from traveling to Iraq, but the Venezuelan government openly defied these attempts. What is more, Chávez lambasted the United States' decision to invade not only Iraq but also Afghanistan. Despite US criticism of Venezuela's position on the war on terror and its diplomatic visits abroad, Chávez and other Venezuelan leaders continued to emphasize their country's national sovereignty and their desire to render decisions based on their own—and not a US—calculus.

US government leaders have focused the bulk of their public criticism of Venezuela on democracy and human rights, but Venezuelan government leaders and their supporters, as well as many scholars, have attributed US government differences to other issues. Golinger (2006), for instance, attributes much of the US government dismay with the Venezuelan government to economic and security interests, rather than any genuine regard for democracy and human rights. Golinger (2006) has argued that since the Venezuelan government has sought more control over its energy resources and has refused to support anti-terrorist and counter-narcotics missions, this remains the basis as to why the US government has promoted the continual overthrow of the Venezuelan government. She has argued that the US government has aimed to accomplish this feat by supporting opposition political parties and opposition-oriented NGOs in their quest to unseat to President Chávez.

Golinger (2006) has generally portrayed democracy assistance programs in Venezuela under the Chávez administration in the same manner that William Robinson (1996, 2006) and others such as Neil Burron (2012) have depicted democracy assistance programs elsewhere. Golinger (2006), like Robinson (1996, 2006), argues that the US government possesses no true interest in promoting human rights and democracy, as the United States has maintained strong relations with countries, such as Azerbaijan and Saudi Arabia, that possess authoritarian, and, in the instance of Saudi Arabia, dictatorial governments, which demonstrate no genuine regard for human rights. Golinger (2006) has thus depicted the US government as seeking to engineer Venezuelan civil society in a manner most conducive to US economic and security interests.

At the heart of these interests in Venezuela, Golinger (2006, 4–6, 31–32) argues that US government leaders want to secure unimpeded access to Venezuelan oil, and, in addition, that they would prefer a national government that supports the war on terror, US counter-narcotics missions, and other US foreign policy endeavors. It is clear that the Venezuelan government has contravened such US government interests—that is, by criticizing US intervention in Afghanistan and Iraq; maintaining close relations with US opponents such as Belarus, China, Cuba, and Russia; enacting the Hydrocarbons Law, which restricted the extent of foreign ownership over Venezuelan oil ventures; "focus[ing] on policies to reduce poverty and promote a participatory democracy, ideas repulsed by diehard market economists"; and denying airspace for counter-narcotics missions and removing the DEA from the country (Golinger 2006, 4–6). As a result of these policies, Golinger (2006, 6) argues that the US government has sought to "penetrate[e] all sectors of civil society, political parties, and the Venezuelan Armed Forces . . . to facilitate several attempts to overthrow Venezuela's democratic government." She also alleges that the US government will not cease these efforts until the Chavistas are out of power.

Golinger (2006) also claims that the cornerstone of US government efforts to overthrow the Venezuelan government includes its use of the National Endowment for Democracy (NED) and its associated groups, USAID, and Department of State–led democracy assistance programs to destabilize the Venezuelan government and build a coalition of political and civil society forces to replace the Venezuelan government. What is more, she argues that the NED and USAID ultimately serve the CIA in their pursuit to intervene into Venezuelan civil society. That is, Golinger links US democracy assistance programs with a history of CIA involvement in Latin America, as it has historically involved events such as the Cuban Bay of Pigs invasion, support for General Augusto Pinochet's overthrow of the Allende government in Chile, the destabilization of the Sandinista government in Nicaragua, and other unconstitutional and undemocratic assaults on Latin American governments across time. Robinson (2006) and others make the same connection between US foreign policy past in Venezuela present.

Concretely, scholars such as N. Scott Cole (2007) and Christopher I. Clement (2005) claim that US government functionaries have explicitly selected particular Venezuelan politicians to lead the opposition against the Chávez government. They, alongside Golinger, allege that the International Republican Institute (IRI), one of the NED's four core grantees, had specifically been charged with organizing opposition political parties to challenge the former Chávez government throughout its early years. For instance, Golinger (2006, 38) writes that the "IRI was ready to back any party capable of beating Chávez," including Union para El Progreso, Proyecto Venezuela, and

Movimiento al Socialismo. In doing so, she points out how the IRI brought Republican Party representatives from the United States to Venezuela to discuss political communication efforts, platform building, youth activism, and training for party activists. What is more, she claims that the US government, and specifically the IRI, has taken special interest in the political party Primero Justicia, an opposition party largely composed of young conservatives, such as former opposition presidential candidate and Miranda State governor Henrique Capriles, and asserts that the IRI "has been able to form and mold party leaders and determine and shape the party goals, strategies, and platform, essentially building the party from scratch" (Golinger 2006, 42). In addition to political party training, she discusses how Republican Party members, such as Mike Collins, a press secretary for the Republican Party, met with local libertarian journalists in Venezuela to discuss how to report on and frame political events. In doing so, Golinger argues that the IRI linked Venezuelan opposition politicians with US government leaders in order to help opposition politicians develop a plan to defeat the Chavistas and achieve institutional political power.

While the IRI trained and molded opposition political parties, Golinger (2006) points out that the National Democratic Institute (NDI), another one of the NED's four core grantees, supplied funding and a platform for the views of opposition NGOs, including Fundación Momento de la Gente. In particular, she has argued that this NGO "was one of the leading civil society groups in the growing opposition movement to President Chávez" and that NDI funding allowed this group to take on a leadership role within the opposition movement (Golinger 2006, 50). And so, while the IRI worked with opposition politicians, she has argued that the NDI has worked with NGOs in order to bolster the Venezuelan opposition and their abilities to unseat Chávez. In addition to NDI, Golinger has argued that the NED directly funded several NGOs all "with one characteristic in common: a public aversion to President Chávez" (51). These funding efforts included groups focused on combating Chávez's education reforms and other Chávez-supported legislation, opposing military involvement in politics during a time when the Chávez government sought to involve the military in social projects, and other groups that aligned with the opposition in their attempts to overthrow Chávez and bring a new government to power. I examine some of these same US initiatives in ensuing chapters and find that much of this is indeed correct.

In the early years of the Chávez government, Golinger also argues that these NGOs and political parties, alongside business and labor groups also funded by NED core grantees, played prominent roles in the 2002 coup d'état that temporarily removed Chávez from power. Upon returning to power, she argues that the NED and its associated groups continued funding some of the very same groups and individuals, who supported Pedro Carmona's transitional government and were even named to positions within the new government. Other forms of democracy assistance that persisted included the Center for International Private Enterprise (CIPE), one of the NED's four core grantees, funding the Center for the Dissemination of Economic Knowledge for Liberty (CEDICE), whose leader endorsed and signed the Carmona Decree, and the IRI's continued work with Primero Justicia, Proyecto Venezuela, Movimiento al Socialismo, and other opposition parties, some whose members endorsed the temporary transition. Altogether, she argues that these groups continued to attempt to displace the Chávez government, in the wake of the failed coup d'état efforts, and that US political leaders and agencies assisted these groups, despite their anti-democratic behavior.

In the aftermath of the coup d'état, Golinger (2006, 88) draws attention to how USAID set up an Office of Transition Initiatives (OTI) in Venezuela, and she argues that OTI "was a way to penetrate civil society even further than the NED... [and that] its ultimate goal had always been to facilitate the removal of President Chávez from office." USAID and OTI, to make matters even murkier, did not directly carry out their projects in Venezuela. Instead, USAID contracted with Development Alternatives, Inc. (DAI), a private contracting firm, which manages USAID contracts in countries throughout the world. In chapter 8, we will indeed meet some of the folks who worked for USAID/OTI and DAI during these years and hear directly from them about what they sought to accomplish in Venezuela and how they precisely pursued their objectives.

Golinger (2006) claims that through USAID/OTI programs, alongside the NED and its counterparts, the US government continued to finance groups that had participated in and supported the coup d'état efforts. She also argues that DAI assisted the opposition with creating anti-Chávez radio and television ads, in the aftermath of the coup d'état and leading into a period when opposition activists were leading a general strike against the government (94). Following the failure of this strike, as mentioned in the previous section, she argues that USAID/OTI and the NED and its counterparts helped organize the Coordinadora Democrática (CD), an opposition coalition of business groups, civil society groups, and political parties that now sought the premature electoral defeat of President Chávez through a recall referendum.

To further pursue this goal, Golinger (2006, 107) points out that the NED and USAID provided immense financial support for Súmate, "a technologically advanced, elections-focused non-profit led by opposition-aligned wealthy Venezuelans," and an organization with the explicit mission statement of recalling Chávez from power. Although she acknowledges that US government funds were not given with the express mandate to gather signatures to recall Chávez, Golinger shows that the funds were delivered for "electoral observation, voter registration monitoring, and training of poll site officials—activities that when conducted at the behest and supervision of a foreign government are *sure signs of intervention*" (110; my emphasis). In all, Golinger argues that the US government worked on all fronts through its democracy assistance programs to lead a successful recall effort against Chávez in order to legally remove him office. Despite all of this, however, these efforts failed, and Chávez won his recall election in 2004 and nearly every subsequent election that he and his supporters would participate in, with few exceptions, until his death in 2013.

Golinger's thorough account is one among similar accounts of the objectives of US democracy assistance programs in Venezuela, which became the primary foreign policy piece that the US government used within the country to achieve its goals (Cole 2007; Clement 2005; Robinson 2006). Through such programs, US government leaders walked back their celebration of the failed 2002 coup d'état and decided to pursue a more democratic route—that is, by supporting a recall election and continuing their efforts to funnel money to opposition NGOs and opposition political parties, so that the latter group could more effectively compete in elections. According to these accounts, US democracy assistance programs remain reminiscent and quite similar to mid-twentieth-century CIA efforts in places such as Guatemala and Chile at the height of the Cold War, wherein the US government worked to unseat democratically elected, leftist leaders. The same anxieties concerning leftist leaders and popular politics that drove CIA efforts during the mid-twentieth century are also now understood as driving US foreign policy toward Venezuela.

Outside of democracy assistance efforts, US-Venezuelan relations incrementally deteriorated under the former Chávez government for a host of reasons. Indeed, despite some attempts at rapprochement throughout Chavez's years of governance, with more serious efforts developing under the Obama administration, relations between the Chávez government and the US government continued to generally plummet. While Chávez maintained somewhat of a working relationship with President Clinton, the Chávez and Bush administrations developed a highly acrimonious relationship. On the Venezuelan end, aside from criticizing the war on terror, Chávez often engaged in personal insults of Bush. On his weekly television show, for instance, Chávez often referred to Bush as an alcoholic, a drunk, and a donkey. During the 2006 United Nations General Session, Chávez performed the sign of the cross and proclaimed that the podium reeked of sulfur from its recent visit from "the devil," a reference to Bush.

Under the Bush administration, Chávez also made considerable efforts to cultivate an anti-US nexus of allies, which included Belarus, China, Cuba, Iran, and Russia (Gill 2016). This also included regional allies such as Bolivia,

Ecuador, and Nicaragua, countries that also criticized neoliberal economic policies as well as US hegemony writ large. What is more, Chávez even cultivated relationships with some highly isolated nations throughout the world system, such as Syria and Zimbabwe, seemingly as a result of their anti-US dispositions (Corrales and Romero 2013).

Above all, the Venezuelan government asserted that it alone controlled its sovereign decisions, and that it would cultivate relations and trade with any country of its own choosing, regardless of their relationship with the US government. Throughout the years of the Bush administration, President Chávez recurrently alleged that Bush was plotting to overthrow him, and that the Venezuelan government would need to take precautions in order to ensure the safety of the president. In 2008 these accusations reached a new height when Chávez expelled US ambassador Patrick Duddy from the country for allegedly fomenting plans to destabilize the government and overthrow Chávez. The US government denied the existence of these plans, but, following suit, the United States expelled Venezuelan ambassador Bernardo Alvarez. Since these events, the two countries have yet to fully reinstate an ambassador and normalize their relationship. Instead, the relationship has been characterized by recurrent removals of diplomats from both countries in shared demonstrations of just how far down the relationship has sunk.

Under the Obama administration, which remained in power for the last four years of Chávez's presidency, Chávez publicly wished for a more productive and respectful relationship. Shortly after coming to power, Chávez provided Obama with a copy of the *Open Veins of Latin America: Five Centuries of the Pillage of a Continent*, a neo-Marxist, dependency theory classic that details colonial and neocolonial efforts to economically exploit the people and resources of Latin America, at the Summit of the Americas in Trinidad and Tobago in April 2009. Despite the hope that the United States and Venezuela could resume normal diplomatic relations, they would not, and relations would reach even new lows.

In 2010, following the Summit of the Americas, President Obama nominated a new ambassador, Larry Palmer, to the country to replace Patrick Duddy, in pursuit of a resumption of relations. On the Venezuelan end, Chávez remained open to these developments. During Senate nomination hearings, however, Palmer claimed that there was low morale within the Venezuelan military and that the Venezuelan government allowed FARC members to receive safe haven within the country (Buitrago). Palmer also claimed that Venezuelan officials were themselves involved in extensive narco-trafficking. Chávez unsurprisingly rejected Palmer's nomination and said that he would not allow Palmer to assume an ambassadorial position in Caracas. Chávez also asserted that Palmer and his claims represented the same sorts of imperialist visions that the Bush administration embraced, and that under no circumstances would he accept Palmer as ambassador to the country. For his part, Obama put forth no new ambassador, and, as a result, their embassies, though open, remain empty of such a high-level presence.

At other points under the Obama administration, there were brief moments of dialogue between the United States and Venezuela, but, similar to Palmer's nomination process, these openings were corroded by one statement or another from a US government functionary, which, in turn, upset the Venezuelan government and pushed them to terminate communications. For instance, in June 2013 Venezuelan law enforcement arrested a US filmmaker at the airport outside of Caracas before he departed the country. Venezuelan law enforcement claimed that the filmmaker had provided funding for student groups seeking to destabilize the Venezuelan government. In the meantime, US Secretary of State John Kerry and Venezuelan Foreign Minister Elias Jaua initiated a dialogue over this episode and other long-standing issues. Although the two agreed to start high-level communications, these efforts would not last through July. In late July 2013 Susan Rice, then-nominee to become the US ambassador to the United Nations, stated, that as ambassador, she would contest "the crackdown on civil society" that persisted in countries such as Venezuela (Neuman). As a result, the Venezuelan government terminated the dialogue, stating that it would not accept interference from external powers into its domestic affairs and that it could not maintain a dialogue with countries that make such claims.

Despite the hope that the US and Venezuelan governments would normalize their relationship under President Obama, this did not happen. Indeed, the Venezuelan government, now under the Maduro administration, continued to render the same claims as Chávez regarding US activity in and involving Venezuela: that the United States is attempting to destabilize the Venezuelan government by funding and providing assistance to opposition political parties and opposition NGOs, despite 2010 legislation that prohibits the practice, and that ultimately the US government wants to depose the socialists and assist a new set of actors in coming to power who follow US global leadership and embrace the same economic and security interests as the United States.

Though the focus of this text concentrates on relations between the United States and Venezuela under Chávez, I will note here briefly that US-Venezuela relations hit a new low under the Obama administration in 2015, when it passed an executive order deeming Venezuela an "unusual and extraordinary threat to the national security and foreign policy of the United States" (White House). After facing much criticism over this designation, Obama and other US government leaders slightly walked the designation back, stating that it remained a mere formality in order to sanction Venezuelan government officials. As a result, though, this designation has persisted through the

Trump administration and into the Biden administration. What is more, following the death of Chávez, the US government became the only country that refused to recognize the electoral results after the election between Maduro and Capriles, charging that the electoral context was possibly manipulated. No evidence, however, ever appeared that this vote was manipulated following the collection of ballots. Far from rapprochement, then, US-Venezuelan relations appeared nearly as worse as they ever were under Obama.

Though it became difficult to envision how relations between the United States and Venezuela could plummet any further, they have indeed worsened under the Trump administration. Under President Trump, the United States enacted both individual sanctions against Venezuelan government members, in addition to sectoral sanctions disallowing the Venezuelan government to profit from any oil sales to the United States. Given that the United States has remained one of the country's primary oil purchasers, this decision has had a highly deleterious effect on an already disastrous economic situation facing the country, as oil prices have dropped and corruption has eaten away at the country's would-be monetary reserves. What is more, the Trump administration recognized opposition leader Juan Guaidó of the Voluntad Popular party as the rightful president of the country and sought to instigate several military overthrows. Following Maduro's decision to prohibit the opposition from initiating a recall referendum on his presidency and a 2018 presidential election which saw Maduro defeating Acción Democratica leader Henry Ramos Allup, many in the international community concluded that this election was neither free nor fair, and they have refused to recognize the legitimacy of the election and of the Maduro government.

In January 2019 the opposition initiated the claim that since there was no rightful election in the country, the head of the country's legislature, Juan Guaidó, would become interim president until free and fair elections could be held. Within moments of this declaration, the Trump administration recognized him as the Venezuelan president and shortly thereafter several countries throughout Europe and Latin America followed in their recognition. Into the present, the world remains split in their recognition of either the Maduro or Guaidó government.

In August 2021 renewed talks hosted in Mexico emerged to help move Maduro and the opposition toward a negotiation on fair elections. The Biden administration has supported the efforts and, unlike the Trump administration, has sought to mute extensive criticism of the Maduro government and to signal its willingness to remove some sanctions against his government. In the end, although Guaidó continues to lay claim to the presidency, Maduro and his allies control the Venezuelan state and its institutions, including the military, and, in reality, Guaidó possesses very little power.

The United States and Venezuela formerly remained strong allies throughout the twentieth century. With the election of Chávez in 1998, however, relations between the two countries incrementally plummeted due to a multitude of reasons. With the exception of a military invasion, it is difficult to envision how more tenuous relations could become. Though President Donald Trump openly floated this idea on several occasions, it does not appear that an invasion will transpire. Nonetheless, the two countries remain without ambassadors, trade has largely stopped, and Venezuela remains characterized by a political crisis wherein two individuals have placed claims on the presidency for over two full years. In the latter instance, the United States has recognized Juan Guaidó, the current leader of the opposition as the rightful president of the country.

As this text is focused on US foreign policy during the years of the Chávez administration, I discuss the ways that the US government sought to dislodge Chávez from power through democracy assistance efforts in the ensuing chapters. It remains possible, of course, that the US government sought additional methods through which they might have sought to depose the former president, such as through the CIA or other US government agencies. Democracy assistance, however, has played a central role in the US foreign policy approach toward the country over the past two decades. Before moving into how the US government precisely sought to embolden the Venezuelan opposition and undermine President Chávez, I discuss the broader use of democracy assistance in theoretical terms in the following chapter, discussing existing perspective on the practices and thereafter delineating my own perspective.

Chapter 2

THEORETICAL PERSPECTIVES ON US DEMOCRACY ASSISTANCE

Two prominent sociological perspectives on democracy assistance exist: a neo-Marxist and a neo-Tocquevillian perspective. While I find the neo-Tocquevillian perspective generally lacking, in this chapter I build upon the neo-Marxist framework by taking influence from postcolonial work and critical-historical work on US foreign policy in Latin America. In doing so, I aim to build a theoretically accurate understanding of this prominent component of contemporary US foreign policymaking, particularly as it involves its usage in contemporary Venezuela. Such usage of US democracy assistance, however, persists far beyond Venezuela and Latin America, into most areas of the world, and my hope is that this work might thus provide insight its operations elsewhere.

For their part, neo-Marxists generally view US democracy assistance as the political counterpart to the promotion of neoliberal economics. Such scholars argue that the US government provides support to nongovernmental organizations (NGOs) and political parties that promote capitalist class interests—namely, neoliberal economic policies. In their perspective, US democracy assistance is a highly partisan endeavor that prioritizes only certain groups, including those that promote neoliberal economic policies. Neo-Tocquevillian scholars, on the other hand, claim that US democracy assistance for NGOs and political parties supports a healthy democracy and promotes democratic pluralism. In this perspective, democracy assistance is understood as a neutral form of aid that prioritizes no one group over any other group, but rather enhances democracy for all citizens. These scholars assume that US democracy assistance efforts are thoroughly beneficent endeavors. Subsequently, they fail to seriously grapple with the history of US racism, paternalism, and neocolonialism in US foreign policymaking, particularly in Latin America and the Caribbean, and they fail to offer any sort of critical assessment of these efforts abroad.

These two perspectives are starkly at odds with one another. Neo-Tocquevillian scholars fail to critically interrogate the objectives and consequentiality of US interventionist measures, including the use of democracy assistance abroad. Such scholars seemingly assume that these efforts necessarily promote a multiplicity of democratic actors and generate a pluralist democracy. They do not consider the range of competing understandings of democracy, and they do not recognize that US interventionist efforts might favor particular political parties and particular groups to the detriment of other groups and parties that promote differing versions of democracy. Neo-Marxists, however, understand these issues.

My aim, then, is to build upon their insights and to link US democracy assistance with a history of US racist and imperial policies toward Latin Americans and a history of US colonial and neocolonial efforts in the region. Throughout this history, US foreign policymakers have depicted Latin American and other foreign leaders as uncivilized, irrational, anti-democratic, and unfit to govern their citizens. Such depictions have often historically justified interventionist behavior in Latin America dating back to the Monroe Doctrine of 1823 and the Mexican-American War two decades later. US democracy assistance efforts indeed represent an attempt to alter the Venezuelan political landscape in a manner that US policymakers deem appropriate for "a modern democratic society."

While the Venezuelan government has promoted a participatory democracy that has in some ways curtailed the absolute right to private property, US policymakers have promoted policies and groups that seemingly share the same vision of liberal democracy that US political elites possess. My work thus recognizes that a continuing, neocolonial effort characterizes US foreign policymaking. These efforts parallel late nineteenth-/early twentieth-century colonialist endeavors in places such as the Philippines and Puerto Rico, as well as US interventionist efforts in Latin America during the twentieth century, which sought to destabilize governments that espoused ideologies distinct from the US emphasis on liberal democratic capitalism. Much like these earlier US efforts, US policymakers deploy racist tropes, depicting Venezuelan government leaders and their citizen-supporters as irrational and uncivilized, and thus in need of US government tutelage so they might make the appropriate political decisions in their selection of leaders to guide their country.

A Brief History of US Democracy Promotion and Democracy Assistance

Scholars point out that international efforts to promote democracy have a lengthy history within US foreign policy circles, dating back to the inception of the United States. Jeff Bridoux and Milja Kurki (2014, 3) write that it "is difficult not to consider the United States as the cradle of democracy promotion." They argue that since the very beginning, US government leaders championed a basic desire to promote democracy throughout the world. Tony Smith (2013) similarly observes that the US government has subscribed to a liberal internationalist foreign policy framework since its founding, albeit with varying moments of emphasis on democracy promotion throughout its history and, of course, with racist, sexist, and classist limitations on the practice at home. The US-led liberal internationalist framework has involved the championing of liberal democracy, an embrace of economic openness and economic interdependence, the promotion of some multilateral institutions, and an acceptance of US government leadership across the world. Smith (2013) points out that liberal internationalists disagree with both realists and Marxists. Liberal internationalists believe that government type matters in terms of cooperation and conflict. They expect democratic governments to possess particular qualitative properties that authoritarian regimes do not possess, and which make cooperation among democracies more likely. Liberal internationalists also disagree with Marxists in that they believe that capitalism does not necessarily result in antagonistic and exploitative relations between countries. Rather, they believe that economic interdependence through a capitalist system diminishes rather than facilitates conflict.

Smith (2013), among other international relations scholars and historians, claims that US government leaders have promoted some form of democratic governance since the establishment of the United States as country, and he views early US leaders as promoting a preclassical form of liberal internationalism. We must recognize, though, that while early US political leaders rhetorically embraced democracy, they maintained a white racial dictatorship, only extending democracy to white, male, property holders. With such serious limitations on the practice, early US political leaders championed an anti-monarchical form of governance, and leaders, including George Washington and John Adams, conceived of the United States as an example that might inspire other revolutionaries throughout the world (Bridoux and Kurki 2014; Horsman 1981; Smith 2013). When individuals developed national movements to free themselves from monarchical, European governments, as in Latin America during the early nineteenth century, US government leaders rhetorically supported them and looked the other way as US citizens provided weapons to Latin American revolutionaries (Fitz 2017). Smith (2013, 21) argues that this tendency to serve as an example and support burgeoning democratic movements continued until the presidency of Woodrow Wilson, who, then, ushered in a period of classical liberal internationalism. President Wilson endorsed the creation of the multilateral League of Nations and sought to "make the world safe for democracy," thus ostensibly becoming the first president to actively pursue democracy promotion in both word and deed (Smith 2013).

In the early twentieth century, economic support became the primary means through which US government leaders purported to cultivate democracy abroad. While US government leaders had formerly offered rhetorical support for developing democracies and sought to lead by example, the US government began to institutionalize and provide foreign aid to developing countries in order to assist them with "economic modernization" in the twentieth century, particularly following World War II. Influenced by theorists and scholars embracing a modernization perspective such as W. W. Rostow and Talcott Parsons, US government leaders believed that political development—that is, the development of a stable liberal democratic system devoid of communist influence—could only be achieved after a certain level of economic development had been reached (Carothers 1999; Latham 2000; McCarthy 2009). Thomas Carothers (1999, 21) writes that at this time "aid was expected to produce economic development, which was in turn expected to foster democracy. Aid was not directly targeted at political institutions and processes and thus was not democracy assistance in the sense the term has come to be used in recent years." In keeping with this perspective, the Truman administration furnished the Greek and Italian governments with several hundreds of millions of dollars of economic aid, as well as military aid, in order to stifle communist movements and political parties in the wake of World War II (Miller 1983). In addition, the US government established the European Recovery Program, also known as the Marshall Plan, in order to supply several European countries, including France and Great Britain, with economic aid following the decimation of their infrastructure, and to ensure that communist movements did not develop.

The modern bureaucratization of US economic assistance ensued under the Kennedy administration in the 1960s. Under President Kennedy, Congress passed the Foreign Assistance Act of 1961 and established the US Agency for International Development (USAID) as the government's unified organization for the delivery of economic aid. During this time, USAID "focused on budgeting, project development, and personnel management... [with] no specific democratic focus" (Carothers 1999, 21). In 1966, though, Congress added a new portion, Title IX, to the Foreign Assistance Act of 1961 in order to explicitly charge USAID with promoting democracy abroad. Nonetheless, USAID primarily remained focused on economic aid and economic development, as "assistance for political parties, elections, and political education sounded to many USAID officers like out-and-out meddling in politics, something they were disinclined to do" and something that the Central Intelligence Agency (CIA) was already covertly engaging in (Carothers 1999, 26; Rid 2020).

Carothers (1999, 19) points out that while "foreign aid became a major component of US foreign policy toward the developing world in the 1950s, democracy promotion was not a priority," due to the US government's prioritization of anti-communist policy. Social scientists coming from a range of perspectives agree on this point. Michael Mann (2013), for instance, argues that as the United States garnered the largest portion of world GDP and manufacturing following World War II, it displaced Great Britain as the global hegemon. In doing so, he argues that the US government began to rely upon an informal form of empire to maintain global domination. Informal empire involved developing client—often dictatorial—regimes through economic and military assistance, and covertly supporting counterrevolutionary groups where alleged or actual socialist-communist sympathizers had gained control of foreign governments, such as in Nicaragua under the Sandinistas throughout the 1980s (Grandin 2006; Schoultz 2018; Mann 2013; Robinson 1996. In other words, where democracy and anti-communism simultaneously existed, the US government did not interfere. What is more, even where authoritarian governments existed side by side with anti-communist forces, the US government did not interfere. However, where democracy brought groups that allegedly or actually sympathized with or endorsed socialist-communist practices, the US government worked to undermine them, such as in Guatemala in the early 1950s and Chile in the early 1970s (Grandin 2006; Mann 2013; Robinson 1996, 2006; Poznansky 2020).

Julian Go (2011) also points out how the US government developed an informal form of empire due in part to several additional dynamics beyond its embrace of anti-communism. Go (2011) shows that due to consolidated nation-state structures across the world in the post–World War II context, a nearly ubiquitous discourse of anti-colonial nationalism in formerly colonized territories, and support from the Soviet Union for liberation movements throughout the formerly colonized world, US government leaders could not colonize territories as the British Empire and other European powers formerly had during the nineteenth and early twentieth century. As a result, Go (2011) argues that informal imperial modalities became best suited for US imperialism in the post–World War II period.

Several researchers are not as thoroughly critical as these aforementioned scholars in their assessment of early to mid-twentieth-century US foreign policy. Kathryn Sikkink (2007) argues that US foreign policy toward Latin America mostly involved "mixed signals" rather than an across-the-board embrace of anti-communist dictatorship during this time period—that is, as a result of the disparate emphases that different administrations and diplomats placed on anti-communism, human rights, and democracy promotion. Sikkink (2007) argues, for instance, that while the US government supported some efforts to depose democratically-elected governments in Latin America, such as in Chile under Salvador Allende, there were also moments when US government leaders and diplomatic representatives pushed authoritarian governments to enact stronger democratic and human rights policies. For example, she points out that the Carter administration moved human rights policies to the forefront of its foreign policy agenda and, at times, suspended foreign aid to the Somoza government in Nicaragua due to human rights concerns. Nonetheless, she acknowledges the intermittent support for dictatorial regimes and the implicit and often explicit support that government officers, such as Secretary of State Henry Kissinger, gave for the brutal policies enacted by anti-communist leaders in places such as Argentina, Chile, and Uruguay.

Democracy Assistance at the End of the Cold War and in the Post–Cold War Period

While the US government had provided economic and military aid, as well as offered rhetorical support, to some foreign governments throughout the early to mid-twentieth century in their attempts to establish democracy, albeit under a flawed conception of "modernization," it was not until the 1980s that the US government began to explicitly provide what is now understood as democracy assistance. Even more, it was not until the 1990s that we see a striking increase in the provision of democracy assistance throughout the world (Burnell 2000; Carothers 1999). While democracy promotion includes all those efforts taken by the US government in any capacity to ostensibly promote democracy, including military invasion, democracy assistance specifically involves providing government institutions, political parties, and NGOs with financial and technical support for advancing democratic political systems. In comparison with negative efforts to promote democracy including sanctions and more violent policies such as direct military intervention, Peter Burnell (2000, 9) writes that "democracy assistance occupies the positive terrain, comprising elements of support, incentive, inducement and reward. The provision of advice and instruction, training, equipment and other forms of material support to institutional capacity building are typical examples, as are financial subventions to pro-democracy bodies and subsidies to cover costs of certain democratizing processes."

Democracy assistance explicitly came to the fore of foreign policy discussion under the Reagan administration. President Ronald Reagan believed that the US government should actively cultivate democracy as an ideology throughout the world in order to combat the Soviet Union (Carothers 1999, 30–31; Grandin 2006; Robinson 1996). Under Reagan, Congress agreed to provide initial funding for the National Endowment for Democracy (NED), which then provided funding for four associated groups: the International Republican Institute (IRI), the National Democratic Institute (NDI), the Solidarity Center (SC), and the Center for International Private Investment (CIPE). Reagan and his allies conceived of the NED and its associated groups as organizations that could lead the ideological battle on behalf of the US government against the Soviets. Carothers (1999) also argues that new thinking about the relationship between democracy and development began to arise in many policy circles: no longer were politicians and government functionaries allegedly wedded to the idea that "economic modernization" must necessarily precede democracy. Rather, they had begun to realize that they might promote both democracy and economic development at once.

William Robinson (1996), however, disputes this account of the origins of democracy assistance and argues that it developed in response to the visibly unstable nature of US-sponsored anti-communist, authoritarian regimes. Such regimes in places such as Iran and Nicaragua, for instance, had unified populations in their resentment, and, in several instances, groups that rejected US global leadership and remained partially inspired by socialism/communism came to power. Robinson (1996) argues that the programs that developed under the Reagan administration were designed to ensure that political leaders came to power who generally championed free market capitalism and did not threaten US global leadership. Robinson's perspective on democracy assistance is dealt with in more detail shortly.

Although dispute remains concerning the origins of democracy assistance programs, scholars have noted several reasons why democracy assistance as a new modality of US foreign policymaking eventually took off in the 1990s, and why it continues as a modality into the present. Carothers (1999, 44–45), for one, claims that by the 1990s a new consensus developed within the US foreign policymaking community, due to "the global trend towards democracy, the end of the Cold War, and new thinking about development," which placed democracy assistance firmly on the US foreign policy agenda. First, many social scientists point out—and some US government leaders acknowledge—that the US government supported many dictatorial governments throughout the mid-twentieth century due to the threat of communism. In many places throughout the world, communism as an ideology influenced both insurgents and political parties. However, during the Cold War, US government leaders were willing to forgo their alleged commitments to democracy in order to suppress any socialist/communist governments, should they achieve power through revolution as groups did in Cuba and Nicaragua, or through the ballot box as official political parties did in Chile and Guatemala (Grandin 2006; Robinson 1996, 2006). Even when governments did not openly champion socialism or communism, land redistribution programs, nationalization programs, and trade with the Soviet Union could be enough to warrant covert intervention by the US government in order to destabilize apparent socialist-communist sympathizers (Grandin 2006; Kinzer 2006; Poznansky 2020). With the alleged discrediting of communism and the absence of the Soviet Union to prop up socialist/communist sympathizers, US government leaders now seemingly need not worry about socialist/communist-inspired governments taking power either by bullets or the ballot box. Consequently, the US government could now ostensibly embark on a full-fledged mission to truly promote democracy worldwide.

Second, during this time, the idea of promoting civil society organizations garnered much attention. Carothers (1999) attributes this focus to the euphoria produced by the success of NGO-led movements throughout Eastern Europe, as well as Asia and Latin America, during the 1980s. Carothers (1999, 207–8) writes that the "current keen interest in [the] venerable but for many generations almost forgotten concept [of civil society] was stimulated by the dissident movements in Eastern Europe in the 1980s, particularly in Poland and Czechoslovakia. The rise of these movements, and their triumph in 1989, fostered the appealing idea of civil society as a domain that is nonviolent but powerful, nonpartisan yet prodemocratic, and that emerges from the essence of particular societies yet is nonetheless universal." Civil society is quite an expansive concept that includes a multiplicity of groups, from sports clubs to human rights organizations, and from groups that champion animal rights to those that endorse libertarian values. In terms of democracy assistance, though, the US government has "focused on a limited set of the broad fabric of civil society in most recipient countries: nongovernmental organizations dedicated to advocacy for what aid providers consider to be sociopolitical issues touching the public interest—election monitoring, civic education, parliamentary transparency, human rights, anticorruption, the environment, women's rights, and indigenous people's rights" (210).

Lastly, modernization perspectives that formerly governed thinking about development began to give way to newfound conceptions regarding how development could ensue. Many US government leaders and academics formerly believed that democratic transitions could only take place after countries had reached a certain level of economic development (Almond and Verba 1963; Bhagwati 1966; Lipset 1959; Parsons 1966; Rostow 1960). If particular countries were not yet understood as "economically developed," US government leaders and academics believed that such aid aimed exclusively at constructing democratic systems would lead to futile results. However, this perspective has changed since the mid-twentieth century, and government functionaries, as well as academics, have largely come to believe that both economic and political development could be simultaneously promoted abroad (Carothers 1999; Diamond 2009; Mitchell 2016). Indeed, while many scholars formerly identified as "modernization theorists," such thinking and such monikers have fallen out of favor within government, academia, and beyond.[1]

The Democracy Bureaucracy and Its Main Players

Thomas Melia (2006) describes the present-day US democracy assistance community as "the democracy bureaucracy," wherein an array of government and private actors promote democracy throughout the world with little direct coordination between them. Melia (2006, 9) observes that although the US secretary of state is generally understood as the US government's head of foreign affairs, "there is ... no 'command and control center' of the democracy promotion community, no single place where overarching strategy is developed or coordinated." Rather, a variety of US government organizations, US government-funded semi-autonomous organizations, US government-funded private contractors, and US private organizations and foundations, deliver democracy assistance. This primarily includes USAID, the Department of State, the NED and its associated groups, but also a smattering of additional organizations.

USAID remains the most prominent, contemporary agency involved with providing democracy assistance. As noted earlier, the Kennedy administration established the group with the Foreign Assistance Act of 1961. Prior to this act, several government agencies provided economic aid to foreign governments. The Foreign Assistance Act of 1961, however, unified economic foreign assistance under one agency: USAID. At this time, its mission was to provide developing countries with economic assistance in order to bolster national industry and national capacity. In doing so, much assistance was contingent upon the purchase of US material goods, including machinery, products, and vehicles for agriculture and industry.

In the present period, however, USAID provides economic aid, as well as democracy assistance, for a range of countries. USAID (2016) specifically describes its mission as "invest[ing] in ideas that work to improve the lives of millions of men, women and children by: investing in agricultural productivity so countries can feed their people, combating maternal and child mortality and deadly diseases like HIV, malaria and tuberculosis, providing life-saving assistance in the wake of disaster, promoting democracy, human rights and good governance around the world, fostering private sector development and sustainable economic growth, helping communities adapt to a changing environment, [and] elevating the role of women and girls throughout all our work." More specifically concerning democracy assistance, USAID (2016) reports that it is "focused on: supporting more legitimate, inclusive and effective governments, so that they are responsive to the needs of their people; helping countries transition to democracy and strengthen democratic institutions, capitalizing on critical moments to expand freedom and opportunity; and promoting inclusive development, so that women, minorities and vulnerable populations benefit from growth, opportunity and the expansion of rights."

The US Department of State, for its part, has served as a crucial element of the US government since its inception. The Department of State generally engages in foreign diplomacy, and the secretary of state leads its efforts. Below the secretary, the Department of State contains several bureaus relating to various regions of the world as well as its different objectives. Within the Department of State, the Bureau of Democracy, Human Rights, and Labor (DRL) is charged with delivering democracy assistance. The DRL (2016) defines its purpose as "promot[ing] democracy as a means to achieve security, stability, and prosperity for the entire world; assist[ing] newly formed democracies in implementing democratic principles; assist[ing] democracy advocates around the world to establish vibrant democracies in their own countries; and identify[ing] and denounc[ing] regimes that deny their citizens the right to choose their leaders in elections that are free, fair, and transparent." The Department of State sometimes provides its own direct funding to groups abroad, and, in some places, such as Venezuela, distributes funding directly to the NED and/or USAID to strengthen their efforts.

The final, primary component of the US democracy bureaucracy is the NED and its associated groups (the NDI, IRI, CIPE, and SC). In later chapters, I discuss the origins and history the NED and each of its associated groups. The NED and its associated bodies receive nearly all of their funding from Congress and must inform Congress of their activities on an annual basis. However, the NED and its associated groups possess independent boards of directors and consider themselves semiautonomous entities that ultimately render their own decisions as to how and where they will provide assistance. Interestingly, though, much like USAID and the Department of State, citizens can submit a Freedom of Information Act (FOIA) request in order to examine NED documents. Given this possibility, it appears rather clear that the NED and its agencies act on behalf of the US government. Private agencies, by contrast, are not subject to FOIA requests.

In the private sphere, a number of groups provide funding and technical support to NGOs abroad, including the Ford Foundation, the Open Society Foundation, the Rockefeller Foundation, Freedom House, and the Pan American Development Foundation. These private organizations are similar to the NED in that they retain independent boards of directors. However, while these organizations often receive much government funding and sometimes contract with US government agencies, they also receive some private funding for their pursuits. In addition, there are also several private groups that directly serve as government contractors including Development Alternatives, Chemonics, and Creative Associates International. Like the NED, they retain private boards of directors and receive their funds from the US government, but unlike the NED, they possess next to no autonomy in terms of where they provide assistance. In addition, one cannot directly submit a FOIA request inquiring into their activities.

Sociological Theory and US Democracy Assistance

Democracy assistance, and democracy promotion, more broadly, have largely flown under the radar of most sociologists. Indeed, very few sociological analyses deal with any US democracy promoting agencies—USAID, the NED, or otherwise. Throughout the social sciences as a whole, though, we can stitch together two overarching perspectives on the practice. These include a neo-Tocquevillian perspective and a neo-Marxist perspective, both of which I describe in the following sections. Thereafter, I move into a description of how I aim to build upon the neo-Marxist perspective and rectify any existing limitations found therein. In doing so, I bring in the work of critical historians and postcolonial scholars to illustrate additional dynamics involving the US provisioning of democracy assistance.

The Neo-Tocquevillian Perspective

Alexis de Tocqueville (2003 [1835]) claimed that the practices of early nineteenth-century US citizens and their political-institutional arrangements generated favorable prospects for a new modern period where citizens could truly experience individual liberty. Tocqueville, in fact, pioneered the US exceptionalism thesis, an idea that remains prominent within contemporary social scientific research and, of course, US government and political discourse into the present. In his journeys throughout the United States from which he composed *Democracy in America*, Tocqueville found that unlike France, the United States did not contain a powerful national government, and, unlike England, the United States did not contain a historically enfranchised aristocracy. Instead of relying upon a strong national government or a philanthropic aristocracy, Tocqueville found that US citizens often worked through local associations to accomplish community projects. He (2003 [1835], 596) fondly observed that "Americans of all ages, all conditions, and all dispositions, constantly form associations. They have not only commercial and manufacturing companies, in which all take part, but associations of a thousand other kinds—religious, moral, serious, futile, extensive, or restricted, enormous or diminutive." Yet, it was not only the capability of citizens to self-sufficiently complete their objectives that inspired Tocqueville but also the social solidarity produced by engaging in associational life. He believed that through associations, citizens cultivated a sense of cooperativeness and ultimately wove the moral fabric that unified society. In doing so, he believed that US Americans had created a truly exceptional society that might provide inspiration for other countries, including France.

Tocqueville viewed the state and civil society as engaged in a zero-sum struggle. By entrusting the government with societal responsibility, he believed that citizens necessarily forfeit some of their liberty. As a result, he assumed that citizens might subsequently pave way for totalitarian rule. Tocqueville believed that "the progress of [all society] depends upon the progress [that associational life] has made. Amongst the laws which rule human societies there is one which seems to be more precise and clear than all others. If [individuals] are to remain civilized, or to become so, the art of associating together must grow and improve in the same ratio in which the equality of conditions is increased" (598). Indeed, for Tocqueville, the health of entire societies rested upon the development of civil society groups. If such groups did not proliferate, we might expect to see societies wherein citizens no longer possess liberty and the ability to guard against government domination. Tocqueville assumed that associational groups were an inherently virtuous aspect of society, and he believed that it was morally correct for citizens to handle all societal affairs without government intrusion. Governments, in his opinion, should only possess a minimal role, by providing order, ensuring the rule of law, and providing an arena in which groups might contend for political power. Beyond these features, he believed that citizens must limit government as much as possible.

Neo-Tocquevillian Theory

While most scholars do not explicitly use the neo-Tocquevillian moniker to describe their perspective, many scholars work with many of the same assumptions that Tocqueville himself worked with. That is, many scholars assume the natural beneficence of civil society writ large, and they do not, for instance, recognize the range of anti-democratic groups that might exist within civil society. In addition, many scholars do not critically evaluate the nature of US democracy assistance efforts—efforts that have promoted various civil society groups abroad. Rather, such scholars direct attention to how the US government can enhance its programs, and they attempt to show how such programs have historically assisted groups in bolstering democratic transitions and buffering against authoritarian leaders. And so, while some of the scholars I discuss later might object to the neo-Tocquevillian heading, it is clear that they work with many of the same conceptual underpinnings that Tocqueville also worked with, thus rendering this title useful for conceptually mapping out the perspectival terrain.

Many US government functionaries, democracy assistance practitioners, and social scientific researchers agree that the prospects for enhancing democracy through foreign assistance, including democracy assistance, remain quite feasible. Laurence Whitehead (1996), for instance, estimates that nearly two thirds of democracies existing near the end of the twentieth century achieved democracy through some form of foreign intervention. Whitehead, however, refers to all forms of democracy promotion, including democracy assistance, but also military intervention and warfare, including, for instance, efforts taken during World War II. The main distinction between forceful impositions of democracy and the modality of democracy assistance is that democracy assistance providers recognize that "the primary motive force for democratization is and must be internal to the country in question. Outsiders lend support to a process that is locally driven" (Burnell 2000, 9).

Like their predecessor, neo-Tocquevillian scholars emphasize how NGOs contribute to well-functioning democracies throughout the world (Carothers 1999; Diamond 2009; Fung 2003; McFaul 2004; Putnam 1993; Wiarda 2003). For them, a symbiotic relationship exists between an expansive civil society and a well-functioning democracy. For example, Robert Putnam (1993) has demonstrated how in contemporary Italy, the presence and strength of civic communities—from political groups to choral societies—has resulted in more responsive local governments that perform better than those located in areas that lack an expansive civil society. In northern Italy, where individuals join together with great frequency for both social and political ends, citizens report more trust in one another. In addition, governments respond to the demands of citizens with more efficiency and their economy is much more developed and diversified than in southern Italy, where individuals do not join organizations with great frequency.

Neo-Tocquevillian scholars also believe that democracy should no longer exist as the privilege of high-income societies. Rather, they believe that all world citizens should enjoy the benefits of democracy, and, where democracies do not exist or where they are still consolidating democratic gains, they believe that foreign actors should promote them (Carothers 1999; Diamond 2009; McFaul 2004, 2009; Mitchell 2016; Wiarda 2003). Scholar and former ambassador Michael McFaul (2004, 153) argues that "as new international norms protecting the human rights of individuals have gained strength, the sanctity of state sovereignty as an international norm has eroded." McFaul (2004) observes that the proliferation of global treaties, covenants, and declarations, including the United Nations Declaration on Human Rights Defenders and the International Covenant on Civil and Political Rights, illustrates how a norm promoting the global spread of democracy and human rights now trumps earlier norms supporting national sovereignty. Claims to national sovereignty, he argues, should not deter government and NGO leaders from promoting democracy throughout the world. Similarly, borrowing from Emile Durkheim, Wade Cole (2012) describes the amalgamation of global treaties, covenants, and declarations that champion democracy and human rights as comprising a new, global totem of world cultural values, which are increasingly coming to replace nation-based laws and values. Neo-Tocquevillian scholars thus argue that it is the responsibility of the international community to promote these world cultural values and ensure that governments respect them.

In this regard, neo-Tocquevillian scholars agree with US government leaders who also encourage democracy promotion. While chairing a 2010 congressional hearing on democracy, for instance, Representative Howard Berman (D-CA) proclaimed a view highly indicative of such thinking within Washington, DC, political circles on the role of democracy in the world and how a core American principle is that all people should enjoy freedom of speech, expression and religion, and freedom from tyranny, oppression, torture, and discrimination. U.S. foreign policy should reflect and promote those core values, not only because it implicates fundamental human freedoms, but also because it serves U.S. national interests. Violent extremism that threatens U.S. national security flourishes where democratic governance is weak, justice is uncertain, and legal avenues for change are in short supply. Efforts to reduce poverty and promote broad-based economic growth are more effective and sustainable in a political environment in which fundamental freedoms and the rule of law are respected, government institutions are broadly representative, and corruption is held to a minimum (US Congress 2010).

Democracy is thus expected not only to internally benefit those populations that should enjoy it as a "fundamental human freedom," but it is also expected to benefit the United States by producing a more safe and secure world, conducive to broader "US national interests." In this chapter, I mostly examine existing literature, and I do not yet examine any empirical data from this case study. However, in an interview with the author, a high-ranking former member of the Department of State and the National Security Council relayed a relevant sentiment regarding US democracy promotion, telling me: "We have these totems that we all worship in Washington. One of them is: we support democracy." In saying so, this particular US foreign policymaker portrayed US democracy promotion with a religious sort of zeal, a sentiment common to many of the individuals within US foreign policymaking circles who I interviewed during the course of my research.

US political leaders also present the use of democracy assistance as involving constructive rather than coercive relationships between democracy assistance providers and newly developing political parties and NGOs throughout the world. Lorne Craner and Kenneth Wollack (2008, 9), as presidents of the IRI and NDI, respectively, claimed that "'regime change' is not a goal or objective of democracy assistance. Incremental improvements and democratic reform—at a pace that each body politic sets—define the mode of operation . . . [democracy] cannot be orchestrated or imposed by outside forces. Dictatorship is an imposition; democracy is about choice." Instead of regime change, Craner and Wollack (2008, 10) argue that democracy assistance is about "building political parties that are internally democratic, open, and responsive to constituencies; helping parliaments conduct pluralist political debate that includes public input and leads to legislation and executive oversight; assisting civil society organizations that engage in policy advocacy and accountability activities; and supporting journalism, the rule of law, civic education, and citizen participation." According to them, democracy assistance is not aimed at strengthening particular political parties or NGOs to the detriment of others. Rather, it is aimed at increasing the overall quality of democracy within a particular national context by supporting an array of political parties and NGOs in order to cultivate a pluralist democracy where many voices thrive in the public sphere. They thus present such assistance as nonpartisan.

Social scientific researchers have also both quantitatively and qualitatively sought to demonstrate some of the apparent successes of US democracy assistance efforts in supporting democratic transitions and consolidations throughout the world. In South Korea, for example, Lorenzo Fioramonti and Antonio Fiori (2010, 90) point out how a democratic transition would not have transpired without the presence of aggressive, foreign-funded NGOs. They describe how a

> window of opportunity for civil society opened in late 1983, when the military regime led by Chun Doo-hwan decided to adopt some liberalization policies in order to strengthen its legitimacy. Not only did this decision provide some oxygen to a hitherto agonizing civil society, but it also allowed for the reemergence of political opposition. These two forces grew over time, giving birth to a large anti-authoritarian movement, which gradually began to involve also those members of the urban middle class that had refrained from taking a firm political stance up until then. Finally, on June 29, 1987—despite the numerous attempts by the government to sideline the opposition—mass mobilizations forced the regime to restore democratic elections in the country.

In South Africa, the same authors discuss how foreign-funded NGOs and social movements helped to catalyze the demise of the apartheid system. Similarly, in Taiwan, Yun Fan (2004) has argued that foreign-financed NGOs were primarily behind the push for a democratic transition, and that without such NGOs a democratic transition would not have ensued.

Elsewhere, scholars note the critical role specifically played by the US government in promoting democratic transitions and assisting in the consolidation of existent yet weak democracies. In Romania, Thomas Carothers (1999) underscores the role played by USAID and the NED in helping newly established Romanian political parties run campaigns, develop political platforms, and conduct elections during their transition to democracy. In addition, USAID and the NED helped Romanian citizens to establish NGOs and cultivate democratic leadership among youth and students. In Poland, Janine Wedel (2000) points out that the US government helped several NGOs network with other groups throughout the country and pave way for the demise of the communist system.

Finally, some quantitative work has attested to the importance of US democracy assistance programs in effecting democratic advances throughout the world. Steven Finkel et al. (2007, 406) have generated "the first comprehensive examination of the effects of US democracy assistance on democratization worldwide over a large portion of the cold war period." They examine the effect of USAID's assistance on democratization as measured by Freedom House and the Polity IV indices. Finkel et al. (2007, 414) find that between 1990 and 2003, USAID's democracy assistance generated "consistent positive impacts . . . on overall levels of democracy in recipient countries, as measured by the Freedom House and Polity IV indices over time." The authors argue that international pressure and support can lead to democratic advancement in two ways: "Indirectly, by transforming some of the structural conditions that serve as prerequisites for regime transition or survival, and directly, by empowering agents (individuals, political institutions, and social organizations) that struggle for regime change in the domestic arena" (410). Such direct empowerment primarily involves funding for NGOs including women's rights groups, Indigenous rights groups, and groups that monitor attacks on journalists. James Scott and Carie Steele (2011, 65) echo these earlier findings and show how USAID expenditures on democracy assistance sometimes play "a consequential role . . . as external sources of democratization." Taken together, both sets of researchers provide some support for the claim that US democracy assistance might assist in the enhancement of democracy in some countries throughout the world.

Neo-Tocquevillian Expectations and Criticisms

Based on what I have termed a neo-Tocquevillian perspective on US democracy assistance, we might expect US democracy assistance in contemporary Venezuela to be characterized by several features. First, we might expect that the US government will provide assistance in a nonpartisan manner that shows no favoritism for any particular types of democratic policies and democratic actors. Neo-Tocquevillian scholars, of course, hope that this is the case, but their analyses have also largely assumed that this is the case. They have generally praised US government endeavors to promote democracy throughout the world, and they have cast little serious criticism upon the practice, viewing it as a thoroughly beneficent practice.

Second, based on this perspective, we might expect that the US government will provide democracy assistance primarily to organizations that strive for nonpartisan ends, such as electoral monitoring, government transparency, and the rights of minority groups, rather than primarily for partisan ends such as removing President Hugo Chávez from office, recalling Chávez from office, and mobilizing opposition groups against Chávez and his administration's policies. Third, we might expect that they might fund some NGOs that identify with the opposition, but mainly organizations that do not identify with any particular partisan endeavor beyond the promotion of democratic features of governance. Lastly, we might expect that the US government will provide democracy assistance to a multiplicity of political parties, including some that promote neoliberal and free market policies, and other parties that do not promote these measures.

Neo-Tocquevillian scholars are not mistaken for emphasizing how the US government supports and promotes liberal democratic policies abroad. However, they are normatively suspect due to their inability to offer any serious criticism of contemporary US democracy assistance practices. Neo-Tocquevillian scholars have not seriously disentangled the variety of democratic policies that governments throughout the world have pursued, and they have not seriously addressed how views of US exceptionalism continue to characterize the US government approach to promoting democracy across the world. They have failed to consider alternative democratic visions that differ from the standard liberal democratic features that the US government often promotes abroad.

Finally, neo-Tocquevillian scholars, as well as representatives from US democracy assistance agencies themselves, depict US democracy assistance programs as generally inclusive of a multiplicity of democratic actors. They claim that US government programs do not favor any particular political party or any particular group over others. Rather, they portray the US government as only promoting programs that enhance democracy writ large, such as rule of law, pluralism, and the rights of minorities. Such scholars fail to consider whether or not US government programs favor some particular parties and some groups over others. That is, these scholars fail to consider whether we can understand US democracy assistance as, in fact, involving partisan endeavors that only provide support for some organizations. What is more, such scholars fail to consider whether or not US government funding might flow to groups that have actually supported anti-democratic measures, such as coup d'état efforts in Venezuela and other unconstitutional practices. Within recent Venezuelan history, a number of actors indeed supported the violent removal of President Chávez from power. Neo-Tocquevillian types of scholars seemingly do not have much to say on these sorts of practices, but rather they praise US government efforts and only minimally offer any criticism. This deeply differs from the neo-Marxist perspective, which offers much criticism of US foreign policy and US democracy assistance efforts more specifically.

The Neo-Marxist Perspective

While scholars debate continuity and consistency within Karl Marx's writings, there is no question that Marx recurrently condemned capitalism. Despite his contempt, however, he believed that capitalism was a necessary terminal en route to a truly egalitarian future. Since the bourgeoisie had developed the industrial machinery and production techniques that allowed for the possibility of providing for nearly all human needs, Marx understood that the bourgeoisie was indeed a revolutionary class. He believed that the industrial powers that capitalism unleashed should be harnessed to produce a just and equitable society that would place human need and human dignity over the quest for private profit, which, in his opinion, inevitably resulted in monopoly, alienation, extreme inequality, and premature death for working-class folks.

Despite Marx's inaccurate prediction of where and how socialism/communism would develop,[2] Marx accurately predicted that economic inequalities come to pervade nearly all aspects of capitalist society, including its accompanying political system. Under capitalism, Marx (1978, 475) argued that the state acted "as an executive committee for managing the common affairs of the entire bourgeoisie"—that is, as an instrument of the capitalist class. He believed that state functionaries were beholden to the interests of capitalists.

With the rise of democratic political systems and the promotion of civil liberties throughout parts of Europe and the Americas, liberal philosophers, such as Alexis de Tocqueville, John Locke, and John Stuart Mill, lauded the development of civil society and political freedom, believing that it would rectify existent inequalities and provide all citizens with a political voice. Marx (1978, 35) agreed that "political emancipation certainly represents great progress . . . [but he also believed that] it is not the final form of human emancipation . . . [Rather,] it is the final form of human emancipation within the framework of the prevailing social order." The "prevailing social order"— the capitalist order—encourages political emancipation in some instances, but Marx asserted that it places individual liberty and the pursuit of private interest above all else, and allows capitalist interests to dominate the state. Although Tocqueville believed that liberty and freedom from government formed the basis of an ideal society, Marx argued that liberal democracy fell short of encouraging the full development of citizens and societies. Instead, Marx believed that a preoccupation with liberty alone encouraged selfishness, placing the individual over the collective, and the private pursuit of profit over the welfare of the populace.

In his critique of several US state constitutions, as well as *The Declaration on the Rights of Man and of the Citizen*, set by France's National Constituent Assembly in 1789, Marx (1978, 45) wrote that "none of the so-called rights of man [*sic*] . . . go beyond egoistic man, beyond man as a member of civil society—that is, an individual withdrawn into himself, into the confines of his private interests and private caprice, and separated from the community . . . Political emancipation is the reduction of man . . . to a member of civil society, to an egoistic, independent individual." For Marx, a liberal democratic civil society could not accomplish "the final form of emancipation." True emancipation would only take place within a socialist and then communist society. This final form of emancipation would include emancipation from the anti-humanist confines of the capitalist system. Liberal democratic practices surely advanced human possibilities beyond what had previously existed, but for Marx true human progress could not stop at the door of liberal democracy, but most move beyond in order to truly enhance human possibilities.

Neo-Marxist Theory

Although Marx analyzed Great Britain's Industrial Revolution, the French Revolution of 1848, and other current international events of the time, Marx's analysis of capitalist systems largely involved analyses of class relations within particular, national societies. Marx made reference to the global expansion of capitalism, and at times he discussed British imperialist efforts in India and Ireland, and slavery within the United States. However, the extension of his mode of analysis to include relations between and beyond nation-states has fell to later scholars, including V. I. Lenin, Nikolai Bukharin, Rosa Luxembourg, and Karl Kautsky. Elsewhere, social scientists, including W. E .B. Du Bois, Oliver Cromwell Cox, Walter Rodney, and dependency theorists, such as Eduardo Galeano and Samir Amin, advanced and broadened Marxist forms of analysis, taking into consideration an increasingly interconnected world. Into the present, social scientists such as Leslie Sklair, William Robinson, and Immanuel Wallerstein have continued the neo-Marxist focus on globalization and have sought to account for transnational capitalist practices and transnational capitalist interlockings through acquisitions, mergers, and boards of directorships.

Writing at the beginning of the twentieth century, V. I. Lenin (1917) became one of the first observers to broaden Marx's class analysis to incorporate relations between countries and regions of the world. Lenin (1917) began his analysis of imperialism by observing that within the most industrialized countries of the world, monopolies and cartels had developed that controlled a majority of industrial production. However, corporate control did not end at the national borders of Germany, the United States, and Great Britain. Corporate leaders were now extending their economic domination into the developing world and partitioning it among themselves, albeit while also cultivating interimperialist rivalry and pushing such countries closer toward war. Unlike Marx, Lenin believed that revolutionaries could no longer wait on the working class of the industrialized world to catalyze a worldwide socialist revolution. Instead, he saw the working class of the industrialized world as increasingly benefitting from an international division of labor that exploited labor in places with little industrialization, such as Russia, and, as a result, benefiting from global imperialism. Consequently, he believed that the working classes of the nonindustrialized world would have to construct socialist/communist systems without the assistance of those socialist/communist states that were expected to arise in, for example, France and Germany.

Within Russia, Lenin (1902) proposed that a professional revolutionary class, or a professional vanguard, would have to develop that could accurately interpret Marxist theory and understand precisely how and when to carry out revolutionary acts. On the ground, Lenin's Bolshevik Party and the Red Guard played a prominent role in forcing the Russian czar out of power, but they did not initially achieve power with the czar's abdication. It was only when the Bolsheviks dissolved the Russian Constituent Assembly in January 1918, after having suffered an electoral defeat against the Socialist Revolutionary Party, that they took control of Russia and eventually established the Soviet Union. Although many international socialist groups aligned with the newly named Communist Party of the Soviet Union, others also had misgivings with the way in which the Soviet communists maintained power. In Italy, for example, Antonio Gramsci, a Marxist intellectual and leader of the Italian Communist Party, made a habit of practicing "cultural messianism," whereby he lectured to workers and youth, and created Marxist and socialist study circles (Davidson 1974, 126–27). Gramsci (1971) believed that socialists developed through both class struggle and cultural education. He believed that parties were necessary, but he did not believe that change would ultimately ensue as a result of party directives, especially from abroad.

In his theoretical work, Gramsci (1971) argued that capitalism dominates individuals not only at the point of production but also through culture and ideology. More than sheer economic domination, Gramsci advanced that culture and ideology enabled the capitalist class to perpetuate their domination. For Gramsci, culture and ideology remained autonomous entities to the extent that individuals retained the ability to alter and challenge them. As a result, culture and ideology are "no longer the thing to be explained but . . . now a thing that does the explaining" (Bergesen 1993, 13). Gramsci distinguished between two forms of domination wielded by state and class powers: coercive domination and hegemonic domination. While the former refers to the use of the military and police to forcefully dominate and subdue populations, the latter refers to domination achieved through culture and ideology wherein masses of people actually consent to their domination. Within societies with little industrialization, Gramsci argued that political power is largely maintained through coercive domination. In such societies, political conditions necessitate wars of maneuver—or forceful assaults directed against the state, such as in Russia. In liberal democratic societies where civil societies have expanded and developed, however, Gramsci maintained that political power is largely exercised through hegemonic domination. In such societies, socialist/communist revolution necessitates a war of position, whereby socialists/communists aim to undermine cultural and ideological domination, and to convince workers and other individuals of the rightfulness of developing a socialist society. In doing so, Gramsci believed that a new consciousness could develop, one that understood the contradictions of capitalism and could allow citizens to undermine it.

Neo-Marxism

Throughout the mid-twentieth century, neo-Marxist sociologists examined how capitalism led to uneven development across the world and how countries in the colonized and formerly colonized world remained trapped in a situation of dependency upon the United States and Western Europe. In particular, dependency school theorists such as Fernando Henrique Cardoso, Eduardo Galeano, and Andre Gunder Frank led these scholarly endeavors. Their important work continues to shape thinking and research on the relations between high-income and low-income societies, as well as the extent of global corporate power. Other social scientists such as Kwame Nkrumah (1966) conceptually moved the discussion into the realm of "neocolonialism" and thinking through how as formal colonialism evaporated, neocolonial relations persisted—both in the realm of economics and in politics.

Indeed, during the mid-twentieth century, US methods of political control remained quite crude. In particular, the US government bolstered authoritarian, anti-communist regimes with economic and military support and sought to undermine governments that rejected US global leadership, possessed socialist/communist leanings, and/or worked with the Soviet Union (Bevins 2020; Booth 2020; Grandin 2006; Mann 2013). In some ways, then, scholars and theorists had little work to do concerning the conceptualization of how and why the US government engaged in such tactics. The answer remained fairly clear: break socialism/communism any way possible, even if this is involved contravening democratic practices. It was clear that the US government often supported coercive rather than hegemonic forms of domination abroad. Yet, as the Cold War wound down, and the Soviet Union withered away, the threat of communism could no longer seriously justify support for authoritarian governments. As noted earlier in this chapter, this is when US government functionaries developed democracy assistance as a modality within its battery of foreign policymaking.

Since US democracy assistance remains a relatively new practice, we cannot entirely fault scholars for failing to describe or theorize the practice in much depth. As it stands, only a few serious forms of engagement with the practice exist within neo-Marxist social science. The most prominent social scientist who has written about the origins of US democracy assistance and how it has unfolded in practice includes sociologist Willian Robinson. In his work, Robinson (1996, 2006) widens the Marxist lens of analysis to include, like Gramsci, the provinces of civil society, and he, too, understands democracy assistance as an effort to achieve hegemonic domination abroad. Robinson (1996, 2006) adjusts Lenin's imperialist focus to capture not only the workings of the capitalist mode of production and the use of force within the developing world but also what he understands as historically novel, transnational forms of hegemonic domination. Like Lenin and other internationally minded scholars, such as world systems analysts (Bergesen 1980; Boswell and Chase-Dunn 2000; Chase-Dunn et al. 2000; Wallerstein 1974), globalization theorists (Castells 2000; Ritzer 2000; Robertson 1992), and theorists of global capitalism (Beck 2005; Robinson 1996, 2001; Sklair 1995), Robinson (2001, 2007) claims that globalization has rendered state-centric analysis obsolete. Robinson (2006, 101) "stress[es] the collective nature of [transnational domination], [and] disagree[s] with the prevalent notion that the emergent global capitalist order is based on US hegemony" alone. Rather, he understands global capitalists as working together to ensure access to cheap labor and raw materials.[3]

Robinson (1996, 2006) claims that two new transnational forms of economic and political practices define our current epoch, and these include neoliberal economics and the promotion of polyarches through democracy assistance, respectively. Robinson (2006, 97–98) "suggest[s] . . . that not only are these two linked, but that what Washington refers to as 'democracy' has become a functional imperative of economic globalization . . . The promotion of 'free markets of democracy' is intended to make the world both available and safe for global capitalism by creating the most propitious conditions for the unfettered operation of the new global production and financial system." By neoliberal economics, Robinson refers to a political-economic ideology that encourages the removal of government from business and citizen affairs, through policies such as "deregulation, [trade] liberalization, privatization, social austerity, [and] labor flexibility" (102). By democracy, Robinson observes that "what [transnational elites and state bureaucrats] . . . mean is the promotion of polyarchy . . . a system in which a small group actually rules, and mass participation in decision making is confined to choosing leaders in elections that are carefully managed by competing elites" (99). Robinson asserts, though, that polyarchy "do[es] not . . . [fill] the lives of ordinary people with authentic or meaningful democratic content, much less . . . social justice or greater economic equality" (100).

Further, Robinson (2006, 100) argues that the promotion of polyarchy is the political counterpart to neoliberal economics in that it provides national economic stability by "co-opt[ing], neutraliz[ing], and redirect[ing] . . . mass democratic movements . . . [and] reliev[ing] pressure from subordinate classes for more fundamental political, social, and economic change in emergent global society." Within many low- and middle-income countries, Robinson (1996, 2006) points out that the US government has historically supported dictatorial regimes so long as they destroyed socialist/communist movements. This coercion-based political model embodied by brutal anticommunist dictators increasingly proved unstable, though, for two reasons. First, according to Robinson (1996, 2006), dictators became rather anachronistic, given the imperative for increased global economic integration. Dictatorial regimes, like the one maintained by the Somoza family in Nicaragua during the mid-twentieth century, regularized the practice of crony capitalism, whereby businesses were often awarded to individuals on the basis of familial relations. According to Robinson (1996, 2006), these practices ultimately impeded the spread of neoliberal capitalism. Second, and more importantly, popular mass movements had begun to unseat many dictators. In places like Cuba, Iran, and Nicaragua, revolutionaries succeeded in toppling dictatorial regimes and, in some instances, ushering in socialist/communist systems. Robinson (2006, 104) observes that the US government sought, instead, to promote carefully managed polyarchic systems in order to placate the demands of citizens for extensive political-economic change and to provide "a more efficient, viable, and durable form for the political management of socioeconomic dictatorship in the age of global capitalism."

Like Carothers (1999), Robinson (1996, 2006) writes that the promotion of polyarchy through democracy assistance involves support for a multiplicity of organizations. However, he argues that US government functionaries select only certain political parties and NGOs to receive democracy assistance. These organizations include groups that are "expected to generate ideological conformity with the elite social order under construction, to promote the neoliberal outlook, and to advocate for policies that integrate the intervened country into global capitalism" (Robinson 2006, 108). Similar to Manuel Castells's (2000) conception of the network society, wherein only certain international economic units, corporations, and cities are keyed into the global economy, democracy assistance keys only particular groups into its complex, and these include only those groups that promote neoliberal capitalism. Based on the work of Robinson (1996, 2006), among others, we might expect to see several sorts of practices under the banner of US democracy assistance.

Based on existing neo-Marxist work, then, we might expect US democracy assistance in contemporary Venezuela to be characterized by a number of features. We might expect that the US government will primarily grant democracy assistance to NGOs that strive for partisan ends such as removing Chávez from office, recalling Chávez from office, and mobilizing opposition groups against Chávez, rather than for nonpartisan ends, such as electoral monitoring, government transparency, and the rights of minority groups. This might include support for NGOs that define themselves as part of the opposition and thus do not cooperate with the Chávez administration on projects and programs. These efforts might also include providing support for political parties and political leaders that oppose the Chávez government and build coalitions to defeat it. In addition, we might expect that the US government has primarily funded groups that support neoliberal economic policies.

Such expectations clearly diverge from neo-Tocquevillian expectations that funding flows to groups primarily focused on nonpartisan endeavors.

Advancing Critical Theory on Democracy Assistance

Throughout this text, my aim is to build upon the insights of neo-Marxist scholars and underscore further dimensions at play in the provisioning of democracy assistance abroad, particularly as it involves racism and paternalism linked with a continuing history of US neocolonialism throughout the world, but intensively within Latin America. Neo-Marxists who have examined US democracy assistance have rightly emphasized the economic interests of US state actors, but we also need to highlight these additional aspects involving US foreign policymaking. Indeed, the precise nature of US interests involving its foreign political endeavors requires more a bit more unpacking.

Democracy is, of course, an essentially contested concept, and there remains much debate concerning how government leaders should engage in democratic politics (Held 1997; Gallie 1956; Robinson 1996, 2006; Ryan 2012). Early US government leaders founded the United States based, in part, on a liberal democratic vision, which has continued to shape the country's approach to promoting democratic political systems abroad. I write "in part," because although in theory democratic participation should ostensibly extend to all under a liberal democratic framework, this did not ensue in practice, and many early liberal philosophers justified restrictions to the practice (McCarthy 2009; Mill 1997). Within the United States, early leaders deployed a rhetoric of liberal democracy, but in practice established a patriarchal, racial dictatorship led by white male property owners. Regardless of such obvious restrictions and obvious contradictions, however, what has remained consistent—from the days of the American Revolution into the present—has been an overt emphasis on liberal democratic politics above all other variants of democratic politics.

Liberal philosophers and political theorists initially developed their ideas in contrast with monarchical and aristocratic power. Synthesizing many of their ideas, Alan Ryan (2012, 23, 28) defines liberalism "as the belief that the freedom of the individual is the highest political value," and writes that "the history of liberalism is a history of opposition to assorted tyrannies." Among these "assorted tyrannies," Ryan writes that liberal advocates have opposed all forms of absolutist authority, including monarchical rule, totalitarianism, despotism, and theocracy. Instead, what proponents of liberal democracy have promoted is for the government to engage in "as little coercion as possible in its dealings with its citizens" (38–39).

Indeed, many of the early liberal democrats laid out the precise contours of what a liberal democracy should involve. While Thomas Hobbes set the philosophical stage for a justification of the modern state, John Locke argued that the modern state must also have limitations on its sovereign power. Locke believed that all citizens possessed natural rights to life, liberty, and property, and he believed that possession of the latter provided the basis for true freedom, a view held by more recent liberal thinkers such as Ludwig von Mises (Held 1997; Kurki 2013; Ryan 2012). Similar to Hobbes, Locke claimed that governments remained necessary to protect citizens from other individuals who may not respect their private property rights in the state of nature. He argued that "government exists to safeguard the rights and liberties of citizens who are ultimately the best judges of their own interests; and that accordingly government must be restricted in scope and constrained in practice in order to ensure the maximum possible freedom of every citizen" (Held 1997, 81). Locke thus believed that citizens must limit government and allow it only to preserve law and enforce contracts over a given territory. In his view, a liberal democratic government must abide by rule of law and enforce order in a non-biased manner that respects the freedom of the individual. Although Locke did not specifically detail what a modern state should precisely look like in its operations, he embraced not only rule of law but also some citizen control over government. In addition, Locke set the stage for a conception of decentralized state structures, where most governance would transpire at the local level rather than derive from dictations from a centralized national state.

While Locke urged individuals to consider citizen control over government, the work of laying out what this might entail fell to other liberal philosophers, including Montesquieu. For Montesquieu, liberal democratic governments must include the separation of powers (Held 1997, 85–86). This would involve a separate executive, legislative, and judiciary branch of government. In this way, a legislative body accountable to the populace through periodic election and a court system governed by law could balance the executive branch of government and allow for citizen restrictions on the unrestrained use of state power. Altogether, then, both Locke and Montesquieu advocated for some form of representative democracy where citizens would select individuals to represent their interests within the government and to curtail the centralization of executive power.

Beyond rule of law and popular sovereignty, many early liberal democrats espoused support for a free market capitalist system, including John Locke, but most namely Adam Smith. Locke, as noted earlier, made the right to private property a cornerstone of his perspective on freedom and citizenship. In addition, he supported the ideas of colonialism and more specifically settler colonialism, believing that only Europeans knew how to properly cultivate land and render it private. Smith, for his part, thoroughly championed the idea of free market capitalism. For Smith, free markets provided the basis for the cultivation of a healthy civil society. He saw free markets as drawing individuals together, producing economic interdependence, and allowing for individual freedom. He also saw liberal democratic governance as tightly connected with the development of free markets. For Smith, "rule of law and representative systems of government [arose] from the needs of market . . . to ensure efficient grounds for economic interaction" (Kurki 2013, 35). That is, the purpose of governments generally derived from the necessities of a free market economy.

In their totality, liberal democratic proponents have rhetorically championed civil and political rights—or the rights of the individual. Their vision of democracy deeply contrasts with socialist-inspired perspectives on democracy, which have their origin in the work of Karl Marx and Friedrich Engels, and have received endorsement from recent Venezuelan leaders, including former president Hugo Chávez and current president Nicolás Maduro. For Marx and those influenced by him, representative democracy serves to enfranchise the capitalist class above all, and, in their opinion, leads to a dictatorship of the bourgeoisie. For Marx and those he has influenced, true democracy entails social and economic rights, including widespread redistribution of income and wealth, and universal access to important resources, such as universities, medical facilities, and childcare. Instead of representative democracy, Marx and his adherents have promoted direct forms of democracy, including worker and citizen control over resources, including land, water, factories, and mines.

It should come as little surprise that liberal democratic ideas might infuse US democracy assistance efforts throughout the world, and Robinson (1996, 2006) has also discussed some of these dynamics involving the promotion of liberal democracy in his own work on democracy assistance abroad. In some ways, US democracy assistance indeed embodies the idealistic side of US governance. Milja Kurki (2013), for one, has recognized how US foreign policy and, more specifically, US democracy assistance efforts remain conceptually underpinned by the ideas of classical liberal democracy. Kurki (2013, 135) underscores how the US government "seems to be unable to move away from a democracy promotion paradigm that puts liberal democracy and free markets at its centre." To support her claim, she examines US reconstruction efforts in Japan after World War II, as well as recent reconstruction efforts in Iraq, in addition to NED, the Department of State, and USAID programmatic statements. She concludes that classical liberal conceptions undoubtedly continue to shape US democracy assistance efforts more than any other vision of democratic politics. In keeping with this work, and the importance of liberal democratic politics throughout US history, we thus might certainly expect to find similar patterns within contemporary Venezuela.

US Empire and Its Racist-Imperial Modalities

Since Tocqueville published his observations of US society in the early nineteenth century, several scholars have pointed out, for better or worse in their opinion, that the United States allegedly possesses an exceptional nature (Go 2011; Fischer 2010; Lipset 1997). Some of the early features of US exceptionalism purportedly include its revolutionary origins and absence of a feudal aristocracy. Although some scholars—and certainly most US politicians—still commend the United States for its exceptional character, many contemporary observers have not been as celebratory of the country's alleged exceptionalism. For example, in comparison with other high-income countries, researchers have directed attention to the continued use of capital punishment, absence of a socialized medical system, and political disenfranchisement of Black and Brown folks (Alexander 2012; Behrens et al. 2003; Uggen and Manza 2002). In keeping with the tradition of the US exceptionalism thesis, several social scientists and policymakers have also claimed that the United States has maintained an exceptional empire due to its allegedly distinctive set of values in contrast with former European colonial powers and thus possesses the moral clout to lead the contemporary world (Boot 2001, 2003; Ferguson 2005; Ignatieff 2003; Kaplan 2014, 2020). In comparison with previous European empires, some scholars and policymakers have designated the United States as the first liberal empire. They allege that while previous European empires maintained colonies throughout the world, the US government has never seriously pursued colonial efforts. What is more, they argue that the United States has based its empire on liberal democratic principles that have encouraged political and economic freedom, and the advancement of all peoples. In one recent iteration, Robert Kaplan (2020) praises US imperialism, writing that the US-led

> liberal international order has comprised the most advanced form of imperialism the world has ever known: so advanced that it really represented a sort of benign afterlife of empire—a solution to empire that provides for the stability once afforded by imperialism but without its cruelties. Indeed, simply because a foreign policy has imperial tendencies does not automatically mean it is irresponsible or unenlightened. The key is not to denounce imperialism per se, but to recognize that it, as the most common form of political order throughout human history, comes in an infinite variety of forms, from the morally chilling to the morally edified, from the overt to the subtle.

Altogether, such scholars understand the US Empire as a benevolent and often necessary global force that effectively promotes liberty and freedom where it often formerly did not exist.[4]

Other social scientific scholars, however, have strongly disagreed with the notion that the US Empire remains exceptional and distinct from previous empires—or that it ever was (Go 2007, 2011; Du Bois 1920, 1947; Grandin 2006; Horsman 1981; Jung 2011; Steinmetz 2005). In particular, Julian Go (2007, 2011) has taken issue with this particular variant of the US exceptionalism thesis and has shown how the US Empire has, in many ways, mimicked many of the policies and dynamics deployed by the British Empire and British citizens, including the use of colonialist policies, the subordination of outside territories to US political-economic power, and the public denial of empire. For Go (2011, 7), empires are "sociopolitical formation[s] wherein a central political authority (a king, a metropole, or imperial state) exercises unequal influence and power over the political (and in effect the sociopolitical) process of a subordinate society, peoples, or space." Empires also involve an array of strategies to exert control over subordinate territories. While empires may engage in formal colonialist policies—or directly control the political-economic arrangements in a particular area, empires may also deploy informal modalities of power (Mann 2013). Kwame Nkrumah (1966) and others have also described such informal modalities as neocolonialism. Such informal modalities of power include "money, protection, access, or other resources in exchange for deference . . . [and they also include] financial aid or market control, temporary military occupation or deployments of military power, covert operations to topple recalcitrant regimes, or just the threat of military assault" (Go 2011, 11). Altogether, empires deploy a multiplicity of imperial modalities in order to ensure that dependent territories operate in a manner that imperial leaders deem appropriate. Such strategies have differed, though, depending on the apparent recalcitrance of governments abroad.

Yet, even aside from the creation of newfound imperial modalities, many social scientists take exception to the notion that the US government never pursued colonies. Go (2007, 2008a, 2011) has contested the US exceptionalism thesis and pointed out how that during the late nineteenth and early twentieth centuries, the US government maintained several colonies, including the Philippines, Puerto Rico, and several areas of North America that would eventually acquire statehood, such as California, Louisiana, and New Mexico. Far from a liberal empire devoid of colonies, Go (2007, 2008a, 2011) has shown how colonial policies shaped the incipient years of US hegemonic ascendancy, before it surpassed the British Empire during the early twentieth century and became the lone global hegemon. During the late nineteenth century, for example, US diplomatic elites attempted to export democracy to the Philippines and Puerto Rico. Go (2000, 333–34; 2008b) argues that US government functionaries often treated local citizens as children engaged in a political form of education and attempted to set up local government structures that could, in the words of US diplomats, serve as a "sort of kindergarten" and allow local populations the chance to "demonstrate a fitness for self-administration." In the end, US government functionaries primarily offered support to domestic political and economic elites that it perceived as appropriate harbingers of liberal democratic principles, and only allowed certain members from mostly elite Filipino and Puerto Rican families to engage in the political process.

What is more, Go (2008a, 2011) has shown that the US government did not pursue additional colonies following its consolidation of global hegemony in the wake of World War II due to developments that transpired beyond the United States. While some scholars have argued that a distinctive liberal value system precluded the US government from maintaining colonies during the twentieth century, Go (2008a, 2011) has pointed out that many formerly colonized countries had by this point consolidated their state structures, and that a discourse of anti-colonial liberation and nationalism had now pervaded global society. In addition, he points out that the Soviet Union challenged US global supremacy and encouraged anti-colonial revolutionary movements. Due to these particular dynamics—and thus not to an allegedly anti-colonialist and liberal US essence, US government leaders recognized that they could not even attempt to colonize nations, lest such nations potentially embrace the Soviet Union and thus threaten US global supremacy.

Since such dynamics precluded US colonialism in the twentieth and twenty-first centuries, scholars have pointed that the US government has deployed alternative imperial modalities in order to maintain control throughout the world. In doing so, many scholars have conceptualized the United States as engaging in an informal—rather than formal form of—empire (Bulmer-Thomas 2018; Go 2011; Mann 2013). In Latin America during the twentieth century, for instance, Greg Grandin (2006) has shown how the US government has used both overt and covert tactics to destabilize governments that possessed leftist sympathies, vowed support for socialist and communist policies, and sometimes worked with the Soviet Union. Grandin links US foreign policymaking with a racist-imperial and White Anglo-Saxon Protestant (WASP) history of paternalist policies in the region. Grandin, among others, has demonstrated how early US government elites have continually depicted Latin American citizens as unable, and often unwilling, to understand what is truly in their best interest (Fitz 2017; Krenn 2006; Schoultz 2018). As a result, US government leaders have continually depicted Latin Americans as requiring US tutelage (Fitz 2017; Go 2008a; Grandin 2006; Horsman 1981; Krenn 2006). Grandin additionally claims that similar US government policies continue to govern US government behavior in the Middle East, and, in fact, received their training ground in Latin America during the mid-twentieth century.

Throughout Grandin's work on US foreign policy in Latin America, his findings remain consistent with and parallel the work of pioneering sociologist W. E. B. Du Bois, as well as the postcolonial work of Edward Said and Aníbal Quijano. For his part, Du Bois (1903) recognized how "the color line" remained a key component of international relations moving into the twentieth century. Though many scholars often make use of "the color line" with reference to domestic dynamics within the United States, Du Bois (1903) intended his phrasing to apply to the broader, global world, writing that the "problem of the twentieth century is the problem of the color-line—the relation of the darker to the lighter races of men in Asia and Africa, in America and the islands of the sea." Du Bois (1920, 1945) saw how the US government had become the primary beneficiary of the European colonial system set up by the British, French, and other colonial powers. Du Bois (1945, 275) pointed out how US "government and economic organization, have already built a tremendous financial structure upon the nineteenth-century conception of race inferiority. This is what the imperialism of our day means." Indeed, Du Bois became one of very few sociologists to critically examine the rise and nature of US global power during the early and mid-twentieth century, and how it was indeed built upon a racist-imperial edifice. In doing so, he connected these two dynamics.[5]

In addition to US economic domination throughout the world, Du Bois (1920, 1945) also saw how US foreign policymakers manipulated its vision of democracy to achieve the results it wanted to see throughout the world: subservient governments that combated socialist and communist groups. Du Bois (1920, 28) connected these dynamics with earlier instances of US westward expansion into Mexican and Native American territory, with US slavery, and with US intervention abroad, writing that for "two or more centuries America has marched proudly in the van of human hatred,—making bonfires of human flesh and laughing at them hideously, and making the insulting of millions more than a matter of dislike,—rather a great religion, a world warcry: Up white, down black; to your tents, O white folk, and world war with black and parti-colored mongrel beasts!" Du Bois (1920) understood white US policymakers as embracing whiteness as "a great religion" and viewing nonwhite, non-European populations as uncivilized and generally unfit to govern. Edward Said (1978) similarly saw how European elites often bestowed denigrating characteristics upon nonwhite, non-European populations beyond "the West." This involved portraying nonwhite, non-European populations as uncivilized, lawless, intellectually inferior, and prone to emotional outbursts, and thus requiring Western tutelage in order to properly pursue civilization.

Likewise, Aníbal Quijano (2000) has shown how white European colonial elites used the rhetoric of modernity and a tightly linked cultural binary involving "modernity" in order to epistemologically dominate peoples and cultures they viewed as inferior, including Africans and indigenous peoples throughout the world. In doing so, Quijano (2000, 542) points out how such elites portrayed "modernity and rationality as exclusively European products and experiences. From this point of view, intersubjective and cultural relations between Western Europe and the rest of the world were codified in a strong play of new categories: East-West, primitive-civilized, magic/mythic-scientific, irrational-rational, traditional-modern—Europe and not Europe . . . underneath that codification of relations between Europeans and non-Europeans, race is, without doubt, the basic category. This binary, dualist perspective on knowledge, particular to Eurocentrism, was imposed as globally hegemonic in the same course as the expansion of European colonial dominance over the world." Du Bois, Said, and Quijano all converge upon the idea that white Europeans and their WASP descendants in the United States and other settler colonies embraced a view of cultural superiority and acted upon such a view through genocide, displacement, slavery, and exploitation of non-European, nonwhite populations throughout the world. All the while, they justified their actions with reference to alleged cultural superiority and an allegedly true understanding of rational, logical behavior, often with reference to the works of liberal democratic thinkers such as Locke.

In Latin America, for example, Grandin (2006, 125) points out how even in more recent years, US government policymakers have used "perception management" strategies from the public relations industry in order to portray leftist governments as anti-democratic and uncivilized. He writes that during the 1980s US policymakers depicted the Sandinistas in Nicaragua as "'evil,' Soviet 'puppets,' 'racist and repress human rights,' 'involved in US drug problems.' [By contrast] the Contras were 'freedom fighters,' 'good guys,' 'underdogs,' 'religious,' and 'poor.'" The Contras were the counterrevolutionary forces that the US government supported to undermine the Sandinista government, who committed widespread human rights violations, including murder, rape, and arson (Grandin 2006). Even with such knowledge in hand, however, US government leaders, including President Ronald Reagan, continued to depict the Contras as engaged in an epic struggle to liberate Nicaragua and usher in a free and democratic system.

Similar to Grandin (2006) and Go (2008a, 2011), Michael Mann (2012b) has shown how US government leaders continue to possess what he terms an imperial arrogance, and how such leaders have attempted to demonstrate US global supremacy by unseating leaders who ostensibly challenge US national security interests, including Saddam Hussein in Iraq, the New Jewel Movement in Grenada, and the Sandinistas in Nicaragua. What is more, Stephen Krasner (1978) has shown how US government interest in maintaining national security—in this instance, understood as undermining and destroying leftist governments—has often trumped short-term economic concerns and domestic stability issues. For example, Krasner (1978) has pointed out how US military involvement in the Vietnam War undermined domestic stability and financially cost the US, to say nothing of human casualties.

Altogether, these scholars draw attention to two important cultural-historical aspects of US foreign policymaking. First, they show how US foreign policymakers often depict foreign citizens and foreign leaders in a racist-imperial manner—that is, as irrational, uncivilized, and backwards individuals who require instruction from abroad on how to properly select leaders and how to govern a society. Such scholars point out how US government leaders evidenced such a disposition in their genocidal approach towards Native Americans throughout what is now North America since the 15th century, towards Latin Americans since the early nineteenth century and the development of the Monroe Doctrine of 1823, and towards the Middle East leading into the contemporary period characterized by the global war on terror. These scholars, however, have not fully explored the issue of US democracy assistance programs amid many of these violently interventionist forays. Of course, as a new modality, we cannot entirely fault such scholars, but, rather, we can work to extend their important work on US imperialism and US foreign policymaking to include this practice.

Second, some scholars, such as Grandin (2006) and Krasner (1978), among others, point out that US policymakers' concerns with national security interests have frequently overrode short-term domestic and economic considerations. On no shortage of occasions, the US government has pursued militaristic overseas endeavors, in addition to less intensive forms of intervention abroad. In doing so, US foreign policymakers have targeted governments and countries that often pose little serious threat to the existence of the United States and to those residing in the United States.[6] Instead, many countries where the United States has intervened have only posed symbolic threat to US global supremacy and US national security interests. Indeed, countries such as Cuba, Nicaragua, and Grenada could not conceivably threaten the United States on their own. However, the symbolic, and, potentially, influential threat they posed to the US government generated enough attention in Washington to provoke violent reactions. Overall, these two particular facets direct us to the fact that a racist-imperial disposition to provide tutelage to Venezuelan citizens, and an overzealous focus on destroying all threats to US global supremacy, might strongly factor into US democracy assistance programming in contemporary Venezuela. What is more, they might factor into the equation to intervene in a seemingly more consequential manner than economic interests alone.

Based on the work of postcolonial scholars and historians of US foreign policymaking in Latin America, we might expect US democracy assistance efforts in contemporary Venezuela to be characterized by several features. First, similar to the neo-Tocquevillian perspective, we might expect that the US government will mainly provide democracy assistance to NGOs that develop programs in line with liberal democratic principles, such as support for civil liberties, rule of law, decentralization efforts, and the rights of the individual. However, in contrast with the neo-Tocquevillian perspective, we can expect that the US government will primarily distribute funding to NGOs and political parties that expressly oppose the Chávez government. Indeed, this perspective remains silent on the partisan nature of democracy assistance, but my analysis brings these dynamics to the fore.

Second, while the neo-Tocquevillian perspective uncritically assumes that US government funding promotes democratic actors, my analysis leaves open the possibility that US government funding might also flow to Venezuelan civil society actors who have not absolutely prioritized democratic policies. For example, US government agencies might promote NGOs and political parties that legitimized the 2002 coup d'état efforts in Venezuela, which temporarily deposed President Chávez from power. What is more, my analysis links these types of dynamics with a continuing history of paternalistic and neocolonialist US foreign policymaking, which involves the depiction of Latin American leaders as uncivilized, anti-democratic, and unfit to govern over its citizens should they veer from liberal democratic politics and reject US global leadership. It centralizes these racist-imperial dimensions of US foreign policymaking that date back to the inception of the US government as an independent entity.

The purpose of this chapter has been to lay out the dimensions of two theoretical perspectives on contemporary US democracy assistance. Serious disagreements between the neo-Marxist and neo-Tocquevillian perspectives are apparent. The purpose of the ensuing chapters is to build upon these perspectives in order to make the most sense of contemporary US democracy assistance in places such as Venezuela.

In doing so, I aim to link contemporary US democracy assistance efforts with a continuing history of US imperialism in Latin America. Indeed, we can fruitfully conceptualize US democracy assistance efforts as an imperial modality that allows the US Empire to exert political control over areas that it has historically designated as its proverbial backyard. From this perspective, we might also recognize how depictions of Venezuelan government leaders and citizens as uncivilized, irrational, and backwards justify US government intervention into the country. That is, we can link such racist-imperial views of Venezuelans with US democracy assistance efforts, showing how visions of US global supremacy in the realm of democratic thinking justifies such intervention and justifies attempts to impose liberal democracy abroad.

Chapter 3

UNDERSTANDING VENEZUELANS, UNDERSTANDING CHÁVEZ

The Endurance of Racist-Imperialist Mentalities

Since the origins of racial capitalism and capitalist imperialism, European and thereafter US imperial efforts have recurrently involved justifications for their exploitative practices. This is not surprising given that cultural and racial justification for political-economic domination precedes capitalism (Robinson 1983). For instance, during the feudal period and into the capitalist period, the English developed racist views toward the Irish, depicting them as uncivilized, lazy, and barbarous. European colonial powers enslaved Africans and forcibly relocated them to formerly colonized territories, including within the Caribbean and North America. Though the United States achieved independence from Great Britain in the late eighteenth century, a racist-imperial mind-set persisted among its leadership just as it had among British political leaders. Much like the British, early US government leaders embraced a vision of White Anglo-Saxon Protestant (WASP) supremacy and believed that they were destined by Providence to create a WASP-dominated society in the proverbial New World. This racist-imperial mind-set provided the justification for slavery, settler colonialism and westward expansion toward to the Pacific, land annexation from Mexico, and land annexation from and genocide of Native Americans (Du Bois 1920; Fitz 2017; Horne 2020; Horsman 1981; Krenn 2006). For early US political leaders, their alleged God-given destiny and their alleged chosen-ness outweighed any humanitarian concern for non-WASP individuals.

Early US government leaders encouraged a break from continental European domination in the New World and, as a result, supported Latin America's liberation from Spain, but they also viewed the region as their unique sphere of influence and codified these views under the Monroe Doctrine in 1823 (Fitz 2017; Grandin 2006). Under this policy, US government leaders self-appointed the United States as the guardian and manager of the Americas. US leaders annexed land from Mexico and developed a racist-imperialist view of Latin America and its inhabitants, viewing Mexican citizens as uncivilized, corrupt, childlike, and irrational, and thus in need of continual US tutelage (Fitz 2017; Horsman 1981; Krenn 2006). Though such views might appear outmoded and perhaps no longer prevalent among US government leaders, analysis of US foreign policy toward contemporary Venezuela reveals otherwise. In this case, US government leaders continue to view Latin American leaders and citizens as uncivilized and irrational, and, once again, in need of US tutelage in order to properly understand what is in their best interest.

I detail such views among US government elites through an analysis of US diplomatic cables emanating from the US embassy in Caracas, and through interviews with former US government elites who devised policy toward Venezuela during the years that Hugo Chávez maintained the Venezuelan presidency and recurrently challenged US global leadership, embracing what he termed twenty-first-century socialism (Ellner 2008). In doing so, President Chávez sought to chart an equal and independent path in his foreign policy approach. Chávez aligned with US foes such as Belarus, Cuba, Iran, and Russia, and opposed major US foreign policy objectives, such as the invasions of Afghanistan and Iraq. As a result, US government leaders sought to undermine the Chávez government and assist the political opposition in coming to office. I show how US government elites deployed racist and Orientalist depictions of Chávez and his supporters in an effort to justify US intervention into the country. Such intervention aimed to support a political opposition that has also embraced racist depictions of Chávez and his supporters (Cannon 2008; Gottberg 2011; Herrera Salas 2005; Gonzalez 2021). In doing so, I show how US government elites believed it was their duty to educate Venezuelans in the true ways of democracy, and, as a result of such US intervention, they believed Venezuelan citizens might thereafter reject Chávez and his allies in favor of the US government-supported opposition. Far from evaporating, a racist-imperialist mentality continues to characterize the thinking of US government elites, as it has since the inception of settler colonialism in the Americas.

Defining US Imperial Relations

The existence of US Empire remains unacknowledged by some. Such terminology is more regularly used to describe former European colonial powers, including the British Empire, which early US revolutionaries distanced themselves from and ultimately rebelled against (Bulmer-Thomas 2018; Go 2011; Immerman 2010). When the existence of the US Empire is explicitly acknowledged, it is sometimes depicted as a benevolent force destined to usher in an era of peace and democracy, instead of chaos and authoritarianism (Boot 2001; Kaplan 2020; Ignatieff 2003; McFaul 2004, 2009). Indeed, many US government leaders have taken great pains to proclaim how the US government is not an imperial force, but rather seeks to promote sovereignty and self-determination for countries throughout the world (Amin 2001; Go 2011; Immerwahr 2019).[1] The reality, however, is that many consistencies exist between the British Empire and the US Empire. For one, as Julian Go (2011) has demonstrated, government elites and journalists within both empires were initially resistant to identifying their respective powers as empires. Instead of emphasizing power, control, and self-interest, individuals within both areas often emphasized goodwill, selflessness, and the supposed humanitarian nature of their global endeavors. Many British citizens and elites, much like those in the United States, believed in the beneficence of their respective countries and believed that their global might resulted in a more peaceful and "more civilized" world (Go 2011; Horsman 1981; Vucetic 2011).

Some social scientists,[2] as well as formerly colonized subjects, have been much less celebratory of British and US foreign relations and the alleged benevolence that has characterized such relations (see, e.g., Amin 2001; Du Bois 1920, 1947, 1951; Jung 2011; Mills 1956; Nkrumah 1966; Robinson 1996. Many colonized individuals, for instance, became revolutionary agents and revolutionary intellectuals focused on abolishing colonialism from their territories, and, subsequently, influenced further anti-colonial and anti-imperial efforts into the present day. Revolutionaries actors and thinkers such as Simón Bolívar in Venezuela, James Connolly in Ireland, Amílcar Cabral in Guinea-Bissau, George Padmore in Trinidad, and Aimé Césaire and Frantz Fanon in Martinique wrote from the colonial world and provided broad expression for anti-colonial sentiments and anti-colonial rebellion against the Spanish, British, Portuguese, and French imperial powers, respectively. Bolívar was influenced by US revolutionaries who had defeated the British and won independence for their settler colony turned newfound country in the late eighteenth century.[3] In their own work, such anti-colonial thinkers and revolutionaries drew attention to the dehumanizing aspects of colonial rule and how, under European control, colonial rulers drained native resources and established settler colonies with privileges awarded to European expatriates. They encouraged anti-colonial rebellion, and many—such as Connolly, Padmore, and Fanon—rejected capitalism and championed socialist and communist alternatives.

Though parallels remain between British and US imperial power, there are clear divergences. The US government has not pursued widespread colonial efforts in the same manner as European colonial powers—that is, since the US rise to global power following World War II. Instead, the United States has largely operated what scholars describe as an informal form of empire (Bulmer-Thomas 2018; Gill 2019; Jung 2011; Mann 2013; Appleman Williams 1959). Rather than systematically pursuing formal colonies, the US government has used alternative imperial strategies in an effort to maintain global domination and achieve its will throughout the world. In Venezuela, these efforts have primarily included the use of democracy assistance in order to buttress the efforts of like-minded political parties and nongovernmental organizations.[4] Yet, as with the British Empire, imperial force requires justification regardless of its modalities. Since feudalism gave way to capitalism and, thereafter, to capitalist imperialism, such domination has recurrently involved a rationale for its existence (Cox 1959; Doty 1996; Horsman 1981; Robinson 1983). What is more, such justifications for political-economic domination have historically involved racist components designed in order to naturalize arbitrarily created hierarchies between groups of individuals (Cox 1959; Doty 1996; Horsman 1981; Robinson 1983; Rodney 1972). As a result, many social scientists describe the formation of capitalism as, more accurately, the formation of racial capitalism.

As Cedric Robinson (1983) describes, while taking influence from sociologist Oliver Cromwell Cox, among others, racialist thinking involving human hierarchy developed in Europe during the feudalist period, and, as capitalism developed, it shaped its creation and came to justify slavery, colonialism, and imperialism in areas of the world beyond continental Europe. The English, for instance, racialized the Irish and portrayed them as lazy, uncivilized, and savage (O'Callaghan 2013; Horsman 1981; Mac an Ghaill 2000; Robinson 1983). In doing so, the English colonized Ireland, confiscated land, conscripted individuals to join their army, and forced the Irish to learn the English language. England also imported Irish individuals to work in their developing cities and sent Irish individuals abroad to work as indentured servants in additionally colonized territories, such as Barbados, Canada, and the United States (O'Callaghan 2013). European powers also moved toward the enslavement of Africans and introduced chattel slavery wherein the children of enslaved Africans were born into slavery with very little possibility for liberation (Cox 1959; Horne 2020; Rodney 1972; Williams 1944). Much like the English, additional European colonial powers justified such relations with reference to an alleged scientific racial hierarchy situating white Europeans at the top, evidently deserving of the political-economic domination that they possessed in territories throughout the world (Christian 2019; Du Bois 1920, 1947; Horsman 1981; Rodney 1972). For their part, the English embraced their own particular vision of WASP superiority, which placed the English above all other groups as the world's chosen people. Under this vision, the English believed that they reserved the right to rule over the world and to establish colonial rule wherever they decided (Horsman 1981; Hunt 2009; Parmar 2013; Vucetic 2011).

Though US independence emerged out of resistance to British colonial power, US political-economic elites had long developed an imperial, colonial, and oppressive relationship with Native Americans, Africans, African Americans, and Latin Americans (Du Bois 1915, 1947; Horne 2020; Horsman 1981). Indeed, the philosophical ideas and beliefs among early US government elites and settlers remained rooted in the same WASP vision that prevailed among the English—a view rooted in WASP chosen-ness to rule the world as God's elite representatives and which placed WASPs above all other groups (Horsman 1981; Vitalis 2010; Vucetic 2011). Michael H. Hunt (2009, 91) identifies how "Americans of light skin, and especially of English descent, shared a loyalty to race as an essential category for understanding other peoples and as a fundamental basis for judging them . . . As Americans came into closer contact with an ever-widening circle of foreign peoples in the last decade of the nineteenth century, racial assumptions continued to guide their response. Those crying for a strenuous foreign policy invoked the need to enhance the racial vitality of the Anglo-Saxon stock and to honor the tutelary obligations superior races owed lesser ones." Going further, US Americans developed an enhanced vision of their supremacy over and above the English, particularly after the success of the American Revolution. Reginald Horsman (1981, 81) describes that though "many of America's leaders believed that, with the exception of the United States, England was the happiest and most democratic country under the sun. The belief that the Americans were the most distinguished descendants of the Anglo-Saxons grew rather than diminished in the decades after the Revolution."

Yet while US Americans pledged to create a new society based on freedom and democracy in distinction with the British Empire, a racist-imperialist, WASP mentality persisted within the newly independent settler colony. Richard Immerman (2010), for instance, as well as Hunt (2009), documents the existence of a racist-imperialist mentality among early US government elites such as Benjamin Franklin and Thomas Jefferson—two individuals still widely venerated by many US citizens. Both Immerman (2010) and Hunt (2009) show that Franklin and Jefferson held plainly racist-imperialist views, justifying the existence of the enslavement of Black Americans and war with Native Americans. Indeed, Jefferson held enslaved individuals on his property. Many of these government leaders also intensely believed that US Americans were a chosen people, and that they were destined by God and by Providence to "move westward" toward the Pacific Ocean and to begin a historically superior Anglo-Saxon society in the New World.[5] Religious bigotry also thoroughly remained parcel to this project with anti-Catholic sentiments, shaping early government elites' vision of Protestant domination and Catholic inferiority (Horsman 1981; Hunt 2009; Immerman 2010; Vucetic 2011).

Even more, Horsman (1981, 83) documents how as US "settlements advanced outward, the Puritans not only saw God's kingdom moving to the West, but also thought of America as the place from which the renovation of the world would begin." Some early government elites even envisioned a unified New World led by WASPs, with their accompanying customs and language extending throughout nearly the entirety of what is understood as the Western Hemisphere. Horsman (1981, 87) documents how John Quincy Adams

> was willing as early as 1811 not only to support expansion to the Pacific Coast, but also to urge political unity across the whole breadth of America. "The whole continent of North America," he wrote to his father, "appears to be destined by Divine Providence to be peopled by one nation, speaking one language, professing one general system of religious and political principles, and accustomed to one general tenor of social usages and customs. For the common happiness of them all, for their peace and prosperity, I believe it is indispensable that they should be associated in one federal Union."

Such thinking contained obvious racist views and remained buttressed by European pseudoscientific thought. As Horsman (1981, 4–5) writes, "The process by which the long-held beliefs in the superiority of early Anglo-Saxon political institutions became a belief in the innate superiority of the Anglo-Saxon branch of the Caucasian race was directly linked to the new scientific interest in racial classification . . . Americans had long believed they were a chosen people, but by the mid-nineteenth century they also believed that they were a chosen people with an impeccable ancestry." Early US government elites thus tethered their whiteness to an alleged superiority over all other peoples, even the British. Such a vision surely involved religion, but it also involved an emphasis on white racial ancestry that, in their view, naturally distinguished them from other peoples, particularly nonwhite, non-European peoples.

The United States Confronts Latin America

Racist-imperialist mentalities directly extended into US government elite thinking on Latin America. Such ideas were not imported into Latin America from the United States, but rather had long suffused relations between European colonial powers, and Indigenous and Afro-descendants in the region (Galeano 1971; Herrera Salas 2005). Jesús María Herrera Salas (2005, 72) traces contemporary racism in Venezuela to the period of European colonization, writing that the contemporary period "is nothing more than the historical continuation of the long process of conquest and slavery of the indigenous and Afro-Venezuelan populations that began in 1496." Indeed, such ideas of white racial domination permeated societies all throughout the Americas and persist into the present. Yet, US government leaders exclusively believed it incumbent upon them to take a paternalistic approach to the region writ large and even to annex land when believed necessary. In addition, US government leaders thought themselves racially superior to all Latin American peoples, regardless of European ancestry, and, in making these arguments, often emphasized the Indigenous and African "blood" of Latin Americans (Horsman 1981).

Indeed, within several decades following US independence, the US government developed the Monroe Doctrine in 1823 (Booth 2020; Fitz 2017; McPherson 2016). While US government leaders claimed a desire to protect Latin American nations from foreign invasion, they primarily wanted to prohibit European powers from encroaching upon the United States' new sphere of influence (Fitz 2017). US government elites had nearly always expressed geopolitical and economic interests in Latin America (Fitz 2017; Horsman 1981; Hunt 2009). These interests clearly manifest in the decades that followed. Instead of safeguarding the sovereignty of Latin American territory, US military forces annexed land from Latin America, particularly large portions of Northern Mexico, in the mid-nineteenth century. In a similar vein, and following US involvement in the Spanish-American War in 1898, the McKinley administration formally colonized Cuba, Guam, the Philippines, and Puerto Rico, demonstrating that at one point there was, in fact, a desire among US government elites to engage in colonialism in much the same manner as European imperialists.

All the while the US government engaged in imperialist efforts, US government leaders justified these efforts with reference to cultural inferiority, backwardness, childlike immaturity, and a need for US tutelage (Baldoz 2008; Cottam 1994; Fitz 2017; Horsman 1981; Krenn 2006). By this point, US American social scientists had also come aboard the mission. Robert Vitalis (2010) has demonstrated how prominent US American political scientists and sociologists, such as Franklin Giddings and Edward Ross, intellectually supported these efforts and championed the same racist-imperialist mentalities that US government leaders embraced. Both sets of actors believed it had become the US government's duty to manage the region as a result of the WASP superiority of US leaders. In Northern Mexico, Horsman (1981, 210) reveals how US government elites deployed such racist-imperialist thinking: "Americans, it was argued, were not to be blamed for forcibly taking the northern provinces of Mexico, for Mexicans, like Indians, were unable to make proper use of the land. The Mexicans had failed because they were a mixed, inferior race with considerable Indian and some black blood. The world would benefit if a superior race shaped the future of the Southwest ... the Mexicans who stood in the way of southwestern expansion were depicted as a mongrel race, adulterated by extensive intermarriage with an inferior Indian race." Horsman demonstrates how US government leaders believed in both the racial and cultural superiority of WASP, US Americans. Though US government leaders recognized that Europeans, namely the

Spanish, had colonized much of Latin America, they presented Mexicans and other Latin American nations as "a mongrel race" with impure blood. Indeed, W. E. B. Du Bois (1920) references this line of thinking in his essay "The Souls of White Folk," relaying how the US government had "whetted [its] sword for mongrel Mexico and mulatto South America" in its march towards becoming an imperial power. Tomás Almaguer (2008) has similarly detailed how US racist-imperialist schemas shaped policy in California in the decades following the Mexican-American War. Although land annexation and attempts to colonize new territories in Latin America ended in the aftermath of the Spanish-American War, US imperialism has visibly persisted beyond this moment. What is more, the racist contours of such imperial projects have also persisted.

Into the twentieth century, Du Bois became one of the first social scientists to recognize how racism continued to shape US foreign policy toward the formerly colonized world, including Latin America. In his most renowned phrase, Du Bois (1903) famously described how the most prominent issue confronting the twentieth century world remained the problem of "the color-line," which resulted in extreme disparities in access to resources between white citizens and persons of color at a domestic level but also resulted in disparities between white-dominated countries and the formerly colonized world, largely composed of Black and Brown individuals. While many surely remain familiar with the first half of Du Bois's famous passage, the full phrasing of it reads: The "problem of the twentieth century is the problem of the color-line the relation of the darker to the lighter races of men in Asia and Africa, in America and the islands of the sea" (Du Bois 1903, 12). Strangely enough, however, despite Du Bois's global focus, scholars have more regularly used his work to make sense of dynamics at the domestic level, with very few exceptions (Anievas et al. 2014; Itzigsohn and Brown 2020; Weiner 2018).

Du Bois clearly saw continuities between European empires and the US Empire. He identified how European imperial leaders promoted ideas of racial inferiority with assistance from European pseudoscientists and journalists, who depicted white Europeans as "the heaven-sent rulers of yellow, brown, and black people" (Du Bois 1947, 12). Thereafter, he saw how US government leaders continued to champion WASP superiority (Horsman 1981; Hunt 2009; Vucetic 2011). Du Bois (1947) also recognized how the US Empire garnered the benefits of former European colonial rule. At the turn of the twentieth century, he pointed out that "modern life ... was built around colonial ownership and exploitation" (Du Bois 1947, 22). Du Bois (1945, 275) documented how the US government increasingly came to displace the former European powers and inherited the benefits of the financial edifice erected by European colonialism, writing that "government and economic organization, have already built a tremendous financial structure upon the nineteenth-century conception of race inferiority. This is what the imperialism of our day means."

Indeed, Du Bois made the connection between the transfer of global power between Europe and the United States, and how a similar imperial vision and set of mentalities continued to characterize newfound US global domination. Though he made these connections, he never fully fleshed out the relationship between the United States and Latin America, and how US imperial efforts remained in some ways continuous but also divergent from earlier imperial policies. However, he surely recognized the existence of US global machinations, writing that colonialism had "not disappeared, even though its back is broken in India and China ... American business is desperately trying to restore the essentials of colonialism under the name of free enterprise and western democracy; and are plunging the world into destruction for false ideals and misleading fears" about communism (Du Bois 1951, 3). Du Bois thus began to glimpse the disjuncture between US government leaders' public praise for democracy and freedom and the ugly realities of their policies abroad. What is more, he saw how the US government cloaked its racist-imperialist vision with discussions of free market economics and democracy promotion, all the while it stifled any movements that sought to move beyond capitalism and liberal forms of democracy.

Just as Du Bois (1951) noted how colonial policies had not entirely disappeared, scholars more focused on the particularities of US imperialism in Latin America describe the relationship between the United States and Latin America as a neocolonial relationship. Indeed, this is the sort of relationship that Du Bois had begun to describe in his prescient work in the early twentieth century. Thereafter, in the mid-twentieth century, scholars influenced by Du Bois, as well as the work of Marxist thinkers such as V. I. Lenin, Nikolai Bukharin, Karl Kautsky, and Rosa Luxembourg, drew attention to the ways the US government continued to economically dominate Latin America, developing what became known as dependency theory (Cardoso and Faletto 1979; Frank 1966; Galeano 1971; Nkrumah 1966; Rodney 1972). Dependency theorists illustrated how the United States set prices for primary products such as foodstuffs and minerals, but resold manufactured goods at elevated prices, cultivating economic dependency and, what some termed *underdevelopment* within the formerly colonized world. In addition, corporations headquartered in the rich core countries utilized labor and resources in poor countries, engaging in a form super-exploitation wherein local workers were poorly remunerated—a process that further encouraged deindustrialization and off-shoring from what was understood as the First World to the Third World at the end of the twentieth century. In the end, dependency theorists claimed that so long as Latin American countries remained dependent on the United States for trade relations and employment, their respective economies would fail to diversify and develop, and most of its people would remain impoverished. Though some scholars have took issue with some of the finer points of the dependency school of thought, many contemporary social scientists are in agreement that US-based corporations and US financial capital continue to dominate the economies of many Latin American countries (Robinson 2001, 2003; Tuman and Emmert 2004).

As with earlier instances of European and US imperial projects, the exertion of global power does not solely include control at the point of production, but it also includes attempts at geopolitical control as well as ideological justifications for such political-economic domination in the first place. Unlike colonial rule, countries now nominally possess independence and territorial sovereignty. As a result, the US government must either rely upon some form of consent from abroad or make use of interventionist strategies to achieve its objectives. To characterize these dynamics, scholars make use of the concept of neocolonialism to thread the theoretical needle between earlier colonial projects and postcolonial US imperial projects leading into the present day.

Former Ghanaian president Kwame Nkrumah (1966) initially developed the concept of neocolonialism and used it to make sense of imperial projects following the formal collapse of colonialism. Nkrumah argued that neocolonialism remained "the main instrument of imperialism . . . The essence of neo-colonialism is that the State which is subject to it is, in theory, independent and has all the outward trappings of international sovereignty. In reality its economic system and thus its political policy is directed from outside" (ix). Further, Nkrumah pointed out that the "ideal neo-colonialist State would be one which was wholly subservient to neo-colonialist interests" (xiv). According to Nkrumah, neocolonial interests involved both geopolitical and economic domination. While economic domination involved continued corporate profiteering and exploitation of labor and resources, geopolitical domination required subordination to broader US foreign policy interests. Throughout his book, Nkrumah spotlights various modes through which the US government has sought to perpetuate its global domination during the mid-twentieth century, including the periodic use of military warfare, the provision of foreign aid, the application of interest rates on multilateral bank loans, the encouragement of government overthrows, and the use of the Peace Corps to surveil foreign societies. Nkrumah updates existing theories of imperialism and moves beyond a reductive focus on economic intervention alone. Though some scholars solely focused on the economics of the US Empire, Nkrumah drew much needed attention to some of the geopolitical modalities of US imperialism, such as coups d'etat and the use of seemingly benign US agencies, such as the Peace Corps. In later chapters, I discuss how the US government has also primarily worked through such political modalities in an attempt to effect political-economic change in contemporary Venezuela.

Similar to colonial policies, neocolonial policies require justification for their existence. However, while early US government elites openly broadcast their embrace of a WASP ideology, such overt forms of racism have become socially recognized as, in the least, impolite. Indeed, while many US government elites in decades past appealed to phrenology and racist scientific classification, such crude, biological appeals no longer remain prevalent. Still, a racist-imperialist mentality persists and takes the form of cultural racism. In Venezuela, such mentalities continue to pervade discussions and depictions of citizens and leaders in the country. This is not entirely surprising. Depictions of Latin American individuals as uncultured, lawless, and criminal persist within mainstream US media and continue to characterize the thinking of many non-Hispanic, white US Americans (Berg 2002; Lacayo 2017; Ramirez and Peterson 2020). Celia Olivia Lacayo (2017), for instance, has shown how white US Americans believe in what she terms the "perpetual inferiority" of Latinos. In her interviews with white US Americans, she finds that they "subscribe to the racial ideology of perpetual inferiority because they believe that Latinos are unable to change and progress (i.e., 'become white') because they pass down a 'deficient' culture to the next generation" (569). Indeed, over 90 percent of her participants reported "overwhelmingly negative" characterizations of Latinos (571). But while such research has examined how citizens writ large view Latin Americans, an analysis of recent US foreign policy toward Venezuela shows how these views remain tethered to contemporary US foreign policymaking. Some might believe that such thinking remains a relic of an unfortunate past. This, however, is far from the case.

In the sections below, I show how the justification for US democracy assistance efforts in contemporary Venezuela remains linked with a racist legacy of US foreign policymaking in the region since the early nineteenth century and the enforcement of the Monroe Doctrine. Since this time, US political elites have exercised a form of paternalism that envisions Latin American leaders and citizens as uncivilized, lawless, and unfit to govern, should they veer from the political-economic vision that the US government has encouraged within the hemisphere. Such paternalism continues, and it continues to involve a racist-imperial understanding of Latin American leaders who, in this instance, challenge the US government, as well of the Venezuelan citizens who support them. For US foreign policymakers, it remains unacceptable that Latin American citizens would elect a leader who criticizes US foreign policy, adopts divergent political-economic policies (e.g., anti-neoliberal and socialist policies), deeply aligns with US foes such as China and Russia, and seeks to diminish US global power. Given that Venezuelans voted Chávez into office on multiple occasions, US foreign policymakers believed it was their duty to intervene into the country in order to change the minds of Venezuelans. Their justifications involve racist-imperial schemas, and this chapter examines them, before moving onto an analysis of the actual efforts themselves in ensuing chapters.

Racist-Imperial Depictions of Chávez and His Supporters

Throughout the course of my research, I interviewed US government elites directly involved in formulating and/or carrying out US foreign policy toward Venezuela. This included individuals who formerly worked within the Clinton, Bush, and/or Obama administrations, and it included individuals who worked for agencies such as the US Agency for International Development (USAID), USAID's Office for Transition Initiatives, the Department of State, the International Republican Institute (IRI), and the National Security Council, among other US foreign policymaking agencies. In my interviews, I asked individuals about topics such as their view of President Chávez and his supporters, what the US government sought to accomplish in Venezuela, and how they sought to accomplish their goals. Interviews were tailored to many of the specific individuals and the agencies they worked with, and our conversations often focused on particular periods wherein such individuals directly worked on issues related to Venezuela. In addition, in order to examine the mentalities and thought processes governing US foreign policy decisions in the country, I examined thousands of pages of US diplomatic cables, which were initially gathered by Private Chelsea Manning and delivered to Julian Assange, and I also examined various policy documents describing US government efforts in the country, particularly from USAID and the National Endowment for Democracy (NED) and its associated groups.

Depicting Chávez the Man

US government functionaries rarely portrayed President Chávez in any positive light—either in conversation or within their diplomatic cables. Instead, their depictions of him were nearly always disparaging and negative. More specifically, US government functionaries often exhibited patronizing and racist views of Chávez, derived from white racial mentalities that have historically portrayed Latin Americans as uncivilized, emotional, and irrational (Feagin 2009; Gómez 2020; Horsman 1981; Krenn 2006). Such US government functionaries rarely expressed any consideration of a serious logic behind Chávez's actions and the support that he received from Venezuelan citizens. Indeed, many of these depictions dovetail with the same racist depictions that were often deployed by Chávez's domestic opponents. Salas Herrera (2005), for one, has documented how the political opposition often referred to him as a "mixed-breed" and a "monkey" (see also Cannon 2008; Gottberg 2011; Gonzalez 2021).[6] Despite Chávez claiming that he wanted to enfranchise the poor and working classes of Venezuela, and despite many poor Venezuelans voting for Chávez, there was never any serious consideration that such concerns might have driven both Chávez and his supporters. In addition, there was never any serious consideration of socialist ideas and their domestic appeal to Venezuelan citizens. Instead, US government functionaries engaged in other sorts of speculation concerning Chávez and his support base.

Within embassy cables, various US government elites describe Chávez as "bizarre," "hot-headed," "a megalomaniac," and "rambling"—instead of attempting to understand any sort of existing logic behind Chávez's policies and why citizens might support him. In addition, many diplomats expressed a dismissive view of Chávez and his actions, nearly always presenting him as foolish, unintelligent, and irrational. For instance, following US government criticism of Venezuelan legislation, Ambassador William Brownfield describes Chávez as "lash[ing] out" against the United States for its criticism, asserting that Chávez engages in a "thin-skinned and hot-headed response to any criticism, no matter from whom it emanates" (Cablegate 2007d). Another former US government functionary who worked on the White House's National Security Council recounted to me that "I remember joking with people. No one could figure out Hugo Chávez, whether he was dangerous or a clown. Then they realized he was a dangerous clown." In both of these instances, US government functionaries display Chávez as an irrational individual who responds in inappropriate ways to criticism and remains a fool—or "a clown." In both instances, these functionaries caricature Chávez and seemingly never take him and his ideas seriously.

US government diplomats continually depicted President Chávez not only as a fool but also as a mentally unstable individual. In May 2006 Ambassador Brownfield wrote a lengthy cable from the US embassy in Caracas titled "Is Chávez Losing It?" In the cable, Brownfield writes that Chávez "has flown off the handle in front of international microphones" by criticizing former President Bush, neoliberal policies, and alleged US government support for the 2002 coup d'état that temporarily deposed him (Cablegate 2006f). Brownfield remarks that he is unsure about "whether Chávez's job is getting to him, but his public antics are making him appear increasingly on edge. Whatever the cause, we can take advantage of his volatile behavior" (Cablegate 2006f). Brownfield concludes that "Chávez's narcissism cannot be overestimated. Part of his self-worth derives from the amount of international attention he receives... With this in mind, we should not respond to every one of his nutty remarks" (Cablegate 2006f). In this cable, Brownfield clearly attempts to show that Chávez is mentally unstable, erratic, and deploys "nutty remarks" that are unworthy of a US government response. Regardless, though, the ambassador says that they want to take advantage of Chávez's allegedly "volatile behavior," perhaps by highlighting dynamics that they believe would further contribute to an image of Chávez as unhinged.

Other diplomats also routinely described Chávez as unstable and unpredictable. In January 2007 Deputy Chief of Mission Kevin Whitaker wrote that Chávez "has gained a well-deserved reputation for being a predictably unpredictable megalomaniac . . . [who] appears increasingly thin-skinned and confrontational" (Cablegate 2007a). Indeed, diplomats continually draw attention to Chávez's sensitivity to criticism. In May 2006 Ambassador Brownfield cabled that the Venezuelan government reacted to a US government report that criticized the Venezuelan government's lack of support for anti-terrorist policies with a "communiqué . . . the hysterical contents [of which] have become commonplace" (Cablegate 2006a). What is more, he writes that Chávez "lashed out at [the report] . . . and began accusing the USG of harboring terrorists for not extraditing accused Cuban airline bomber Luis Posada Carriles" (Cablegate 2006a). Similarly, in January 2007 Whitaker wrote that Chávez "lashed out at two actors who urged reconsideration of the [the decision not to renew an opposition-oriented television station's public broadcasting license, RCTV], OAS Secretary-General Jose Miguel Insulza and the church, churlishly insulting Insulza and calling for his resignation, and telling the church to mind its own business" (Cablegate 2007b). In another cable, Chargé d'Affaires John Caulfield portrays Chávez as "hypersensitive to any opposition, particularly perceived criticism from the United States . . . [and] quick to react to criticism with irrational counter-arguments" (Cablegate 2009b).

All of these cables remain emblematic of the racist-imperial mentalities US diplomats possess. Such individuals present Chávez as an "irrational" individual who cannot control his "hot-headed" emotions, and, instead, he hysterically "lashes out" against any criticism from the US government. By contrast, there is no attempt to understand why Chávez might have become sensitive to US government criticism of his strategies and actions, even after a coup d'état that the US government applauded and, of course, a lengthy history of US intervention in the region. From these US diplomats' perspective, sensitivity to US government criticism remains seemingly pathological and should not receive such strong rebuke. However, it is not clear how they believe that Chávez should respond to their criticism—that is, whether with acquiescence or otherwise—but, in the least, that he should not condemn such criticism emanating from abroad with so much intensity. Rather, he should seemingly accept it quietly.

US government diplomats have also been quick to describe the policies of the Chávez administration as "outlandish," "bizarre," and "stupid." In September 2007 Ambassador Patrick Duddy composed a cable titled "We aren't Making this Up: The BRV's Bizarre Policy Highlights." In this cable, Duddy reported on a series of changes, which included moving the country's time zone thirty minutes backwards so that individuals could travel to work and school in the daylight, in addition to limiting alcohol sales over a holiday weekend. Duddy cabled that these "outlandish policies . . . clearly illustrate the arbitrary and capricious nature of Chávez's regime" (Cablegate 2007h). In an earlier cable, Whitaker also described Chávez as "untethered by voices of restraint or even reason . . . [and that an] untethered Chávez presents a rather brittle situation" (Cablegate 2007c). In another example, a former US ambassador to Venezuela described to me how Chávez embraced "neo-stupid economics" and how the ambassador had tried to push Chávez in a different economic direction. As the former ambassador told me, though, this was an unsuccessful endeavor.

Once again, in these instances, US government diplomats present President Chávez in unflattering and negative terms. Throughout all of these cables, he is depicted as a clown, a fool, irrational, and "untethered by voices of restraint or even reason." US diplomats have also depicted Chávez as immature, "juvenile," and "unstatesmanlike." Indeed, Whitaker described Chávez as "untethered" in the aforementioned passage because he believed that Chávez was "without a mature advisor" that could provide him with some reason, suggesting that he believed that Chávez possessed a rather immature mind on his own that required much counseling (Cablegate 2007c). In February 2007 Ambassador Brownfield also wrote that "Chavez lashed out at President Bush . . . [and] invoked the names of more than one historical figure in his juvenile damnation of President Bush," which included Alexander Hamilton and Thomas Jefferson, following President Bush's criticism of the Chávez government (Cablegate 2007b). In doing so, Chávez allegedly acted like a "juvenile" or, more simply, a child.

In another indication of Chávez's immaturity, US government diplomats also recurrently noted that they believed that President Chávez behaved in a manner unfitting for a world leader. Following Chávez's criticism of the Organization of American States and the Catholic Church for their commentary of the Venezuelan government's refusal to renew RCTV's license, Whitaker reminded his audience about Chávez's speech before the United Nations General Assembly just a few months earlier when Chávez referred to President Bush as the devil. Following this criticism, Whitaker wrote that "Chávez once again has engaged in outrageous, vulgar personal attacks, and unstatesmanlike rhetoric" (Cablegate 2007a). In addition, Whitaker has described Chávez's speeches as "long and rambling," "semi-coherent," and "at times laughable," and describes Chávez as possessing "mastery of bovine scatology" (Cablegate 2006c).

Throughout their cables and our conversations, such depictions of Chávez became commonplace. Individuals expressed incredulity at his behavior and his success. They continually portrayed their own selves as calm, collected, and rational. They displayed Chávez, however, as irrational, unpredictable, unintelligent, and juvenile. Despite lengthy educations, US government diplomats offered little attempt to understand Chávez outside of such crude caricatures. Instead, they quickly dismissed him and "laughed at" at his behavior from the sidelines. Nonetheless, they believed he was motivated by nefarious and self-serving purposes, and they believed he cared very little for the Venezuelan citizens he purported to represent through his public policies throughout the country.

Depicting Chávez's Ultimate Motivations

Throughout cables and within conversations with me, diplomats and functionaries never presented President Chávez as truly driven by social justice, compassion, socialist ideals, or any sort of positive, selfless motive. Such motivations include what Chávez often spoke about in his speeches before both domestic and international audiences. Rather, US diplomats and government functionaries often speculated about his true motivations and generally ascribed nefarious and self-serving motives to his behavior. Many US government elites possessed a rather simplistic and reductive understanding of Chávez and his motivations. They viewed him as primarily interested in maintaining power for its own sake. The reasons behind this desire varied, however, among different individuals. Some attributed Chávez's alleged hunger for power to the historical lack of democracy in the country or to machismo. US diplomats and functionaries also depicted Chávez as manipulating ideas about racial inequality in order to achieve and maintain power in Venezuela. In the end, US diplomats and government functionaries all searched for an understanding of Chávez, but never on the terms that he presented himself. Rather, they always sought to uncover perverse motives behind his allegedly irrational and bizarre behavior.

Indeed, diplomats continually depicted President Chávez as a dangerous authoritarian that desired power alone. In June 2006, for instance, Deputy Chief of Mission Kevin Whitaker cabled that like "many autocrats intent on maintaining power, [Chávez] uses rhetoric as a blunt political weapon that seeks to vivisect society along class, political, social, and race lines" (Cablegate 2006c). Whitaker claimed that Chávez does not truly care about such social divisions, but that he only attempted to underscore such divisions in order to stir up resentment and somehow politically benefit from it. In June 2009 Chargé d'Affaires John Caulfield similarly wrote that Chávez's preference for "loyalty over competence, creation of parallel Bolivarian institutions, efforts to forge a one-party state, and chest-thumping nationalism also smack of creeping totalitarianism" (Cablegate 2009e). Here and elsewhere, US government functionaries recurrently portrayed President Chávez as an opponent of democracy gravitating toward totalitarianism all in an effort to solidify his time in office. This, of course, does not mesh with the reality that Chávez continually participated in elections that included numerous opposition political parties as well as domestic and international electoral monitors. What is more, in their descriptions of Chávez and his allegedly undemocratic ways, diplomats often deployed animalistic and racist terms, depicting Chávez as rather beastly: "chest-thumping," "hot-headed," and continually "lashing out." Such depictions are also consistent with how members of the Venezuelan opposition often depicted Chávez in darker hues than his actual skin color and even likened him to a gorilla (Gottberg 2011).

While US government diplomats described Chávez in inhuman and beastly ways, some claimed that he specifically manipulated race in order to win support. One former USAID employee suggested that perhaps Chávez had played "the race card" in order to garner support and achieve power. When asked about his understanding of Chávez's rise to office, he said, "You know how Latin America works . . . he comes from a less elite, Indian family. He excels in the military, becomes a paratrooper. For whatever reason [he] becomes outraged about the state of politics in Venezuela, which is not bad and corrupt. [He believes] the darker you are, the less you matter to the state. Is this an MLK or Benito Juárez? A guy who loves liberty? Or is this a guy that says this would be a great vehicle to ride? This is a guy like others that wanted power." For this individual, who devised policy in Washington toward Venezuela, Chávez manipulated citizens by suggesting that racial/ethnic minorities were oppressed by a corrupt, white elite minority. Despite much evidence to the contrary and even a prosecution of a former president for corruption, this individual denies the corrupt nature of pre-Chávez politics. According to this US government official, Chávez only deployed such a narrative of rampant corruption and racial/ethnic inequality to achieve power, and he suggests that Chávez might not have even believed that racial/ethnic oppression existed, but only wanted to push a particular perspective in order to use it as "a vehicle" to reach the Venezuelan presidency. In doing so, he contrasts Chávez with Martin Luther King Jr. and his apparently true concern with racism.

Subsequently, US government officials, including Chargé d' Affaires John Caulfield, depicted President Chávez as an individual who "craves attention and influence abroad" (Cablegate 2009e). Despite Chávez's ambitions, however, Caulfield labeled Chávez a "world leader wannabe" (Cablegate 2009b). In his attempts to become a world leader, Caulfield wrote that "Chávez travels extensively and doles out substantial foreign assistance in an effort to achieve international status as Latin America's foremost leader. He jealously guards his exaggerated self-perception, and reacts negatively to other Latin American countries' receptivity to [US] initiatives and [US] attention focused on other Latin American heads-of-state" (Cablegate 2009b). Caulfield thus presents President Chávez as a highly jealous leader, and he hypothesizes that Chávez would be jealous of all the attention paid to President Obama at an upcoming Summit of the Americas conference (Cablegate 2009b). In this high-ranking diplomat's opinion, Chávez wanted power at home and, thereafter, he wanted to project power around the world, to the detriment of the United States. In his perspective, it might have been the case that Chávez provided foreign aid to countries abroad. However, in his opinion, these endeavors appear as vanity projects designed only to serve Chávez's ego.

Despite his attempts to capture international attention and to become a prominent global actor, diplomats disparaged Chávez in their cables. Such cables show how US government diplomats aimed to annoy him on this particular issue, by illustrating apathy and indifference to his comments on the United States. Indeed, while Caulfield, an Obama appointee, referred to Chávez as a "world leader wannabe," Stephen McFarland, deputy chief of mission to Venezuela under the Bush administration, dismissed Chávez's international ambitions. Under a section of an embassy cable ironically titled "The World Revolves around Caracas," McFarland wrote that Chávez's speeches on his weekly television program "demonstrated a typical, exaggerated view of Venezuela's geostrategic importance and of US media coverage of Venezuela" (Cablegate 2005a). In a nonchalant response to Chávez, McFarland claims that the US chargé d'affaires under the Bush administration told local radio "that '[the US embassy] didn't know if President Bush was aware of Chávez's comments,' a statement calculated to annoy President Chávez" (Cablegate 2005a). US officials thus attempted to convey that Venezuela is rather unimportant to the United States, and that Chávez is delusional about the significance of his country. Bush, of course, knew very well that Chávez disagreed with his foreign policy. US officials, however, tried to signal to Chávez that he could care less what the Venezuelan president thought. These signals, however, are at odds with how much energy successive US administrations devoted to the country.

US government diplomats and functionaries indeed often pointed out how they believed Chávez was only interested in power, and sometimes they even connected such a disposition to cultural elements in Chavez's background. In doing so, they denigrated Venezuelan and Latin American culture, and plainly evidenced culturally racist views. One individual who worked for the National Security Council claimed that "Chávez was the failure of the two-party system [in Venezuela], and he knew how to use symbols, take advantage of symbols, demagoguery." In doing so, this US government functionary expresses a sort of sympathy for Chávez and said that due to Chávez's upbringing in Venezuela he could not possibly, truly understand the ways of democracy: "People used to say how undemocratic Chávez was. His idea of democracy was kind of warped by living under Venezuela under the previous regime. It was clear that it was a democracy in name before Chávez. He almost couldn't be blamed for not understanding democracy, because he grew up in this undemocratic society." While this individual asserted that Chávez could not understand democracy because he grew up in a deficient location, another US government functionary who worked with USAID in Venezuela personally opined to me that perhaps machismo lay behind Chávez's support for, what the functionary saw as, the failed ideology of socialism. *Machismo* refers to the hypermasculine, arrogant behavior that is allegedly characteristic of Latin American men. In both instances, such US government functionaries make reference to Chávez's apparently deficient heritage in order to make sense of, from their perspective, his presently deficient views.

Yet, though many US government functionaries and diplomats viewed Chávez as "a clown," they also saw him as capable of successful manipulation. Indeed, this is how they largely understood his capacity to win the support of the Venezuelan masses and regularly succeed at the ballot box. Similar to how they often depicted Chávez, US diplomats and functionaries also depicted Chávez's supporters as irrational and generally unintelligent, and thus susceptible to Chávez's "demagoguery." In embassy cables, diplomats described Venezuelans as a "frenzied" mass of Chávez supporters that eschew free thinking for unwavering support for their leader. In June 2006 Whitaker wrote that while to "outsiders Chávez's long and rambling speeches are semi-coherent and at times laughable. To the average Venezuela[n], however, Chávez's words have meaning, offering hope or fear, depending on the message" (Cablegate 2006c). In this cable, Whitaker presents Venezuelans as unlike US Americans, who have the apparent capacity for discernment. In his understanding, individuals like Whitaker and seemingly other US Americans can easily see the allegedly ridiculous nature of Chávez's incoherent "rambling." Yet, according to him, Venezuelans, for some reason, cannot see Chávez's incoherence, and they cannot see him for the apparently "laughable" fool that he is.

As a result of Chávez's manipulation, Whitaker claims that such rhetoric results in "a frenzied and fearful, or at best intimidated, population incapable of resolving basic conflicts... [and this] frenzied populace [is] afraid to express anything other than support, genuine or not" for Chávez and the Venezuelan government (Cablegate 2006c). From this vantage point, Whitaker generally depicts Venezuelan citizens as automatons who follow Chávez's lead and possess no critical thinking capabilities. In addition, he presents Chávez's supporters as under the emotional control of their leader's oratorical skills and incapable of independent thought. In other words, Whitaker paints Chávez's supporters as irrational individuals that are incapable of utilizing any type of reason to understand that Chavista policies are not beneficial to them or to Venezuelan society. From the outside, US government officials argue that Chávez's speeches are "laughable," but to the rather simple minds of the Venezuelans, they insinuate, these speeches potentially offer hope. And, indeed, this understanding of Chávez and Venezuelans provides the basis from which

US government diplomats and functionaries justify their intervention into the country.

The US Duty to Intervene in Venezuela

Such depictions of President Chávez as a tyrant who manipulates his supporters and seeks power alone provide the justification for US government intervention into Venezuela. US diplomats and functionaries indeed believed it was their responsibility and their duty to intervene in order to show Venezuelans their true interests and to bring real democracy to the country, which, not unsurprisingly, involved supporting political parties and groups opposed to Chávez and his allies. During the years that Chávez maintained the presidency, the US government operated a multiplicity of democracy assistance programs within the country, primarily through USAID and the NED and its associated groups, including the International Republican Institute (IRI) and the National Democratic Institute for Foreign Affairs (NDI). Through these programs, the US government assisted the Venezuelan opposition in its efforts to unseat Chávez and his allies. In doing so, the United States sought to transgress the judgments of Venezuelan citizens, who supported Chávez, and attempted to cultivate opposition to him by assisting groups also opposed to him with funding and support.

Indeed, this represents the sort of neocolonialist and paternalistic pattern in the realm of politics that remains evident elsewhere today, wherein the US government privileges some political actors over others, regardless of whether they actually retain public support (Burron 2012; Gill 2019; Robinson 1996). Unlike former European colonial powers, US political leaders do not select a domestic citizen to rule over foreign countries in a dictatorial manner. Instead, the US government aims to shape the electoral playing field by supporting only those actors that the United States deems to be the political players that should operate governments throughout the world. In Venezuela, this has included center-right politicians who challenged Chávez during presidential elections and who displayed visible affection for the US government. For instance, during the 2006 presidential campaign, the IRI provided opposition presidential candidate Manuel Rosales with several technical specialists to assist with his campaign (Cablegate 2006m). The US government also continually urged opposition members to unite behind one opposition candidate, so that they would not splinter their vote. One former ambassador told me that she continually met with political party leaders and urged them to do this. She said that she had "met with the opposition—I can't tell you how many times. I told them they need to come up with a plan and needed to unite. There were fifty opposition parties registered!" In doing so, high-ranking diplomats strategized with opposition leaders so they could possibly defeat Chávez and his allies when elections arose. While Rosales was unsuccessful in the election, this did not deter the United States from supporting the opposition in later years.

Throughout the mid-2000s, for instance, USAID had the explicit aim of tearing supporters away from Chávez, particularly within poor urban neighborhoods, where darker-skinned Venezuelans primarily live. Into the present, Venezuela, a former European colony marked by African and Indigenous slavery, remains an intensively segregated society (Gottberg 2011; Smilde 2011; Wright 2013). Before Chávez, Venezuela contained a light-skinned political-economic elite whose members could often directly trace their roots back to Europe.[7] In poor, urban neighborhoods, USAID established community programs that seemingly sought to promote community ideals like participatory democracy. However, they established these programs with opposition political parties, who helped them locate opposition activists in the area. Thereafter, they helped opposition activists create seemingly neutral organizations, so that they did not appear to be linked with the opposition and thus could attract Chávez supporters to their meetings. The ultimate purpose of these community groups was to slowly introduce Chávez's supporters to opposition viewpoints and to put them into direct contact with opposition activists, who would attempt steer them into the opposition camp. One of the individuals who directly worked on these programs in Venezuela recalled that USAID and its local contractors

> developed new NGOs that were looking very neutral in the eyes of the government... They looked neutral because they had no affiliation with no political party. They were people from the neighborhood, even though they were opposition. They create the organizations with no past relation to political parties. So when they work in the [poor neighborhoods], they looked very neutral. So we gave them money ... They were pulling people away from Chávez in a subtle manner. We were telling them what democracy is and showing them what democracy means. We developed very nice materials and took care of every word to give them, so it didn't look like we were sympathizing with the opposition ... We wanted to spread liberal democratic values. Not what the government said.

Throughout all of these programs, the US government's message was rather clear: "The politician whom you have supported, you really shouldn't support." Instead, the US government through USAID sought to convert Venezuelans into anti-Chávez voters. US government functionaries believed that Chávez was manipulating the populace, buying them off with social development projects, and offering them false promises of participatory democracy and socialism. They believed it was the United States' responsibility to show Venezuelans their true interests, and that they should support center-right politicians, who represented a different sort of politics than what Chávez offered.

US government functionaries who designed these programs often depicted Venezuelan citizens as unable to think for themselves, and, as a result, in need of US tutelage. In 2006, for instance, Whitaker described the US government's vision of foreign assistance for the country and its people: "Chavez also cannot control the fact that his revolution is resulting in a slow process of political maturation (in which people are deeply confused as to what they should be doing). He has unleashed forces that will eventually escape his control. Millions have internalized the message that everyone must participate in their own governance. A new generation of social activists wants to get involved but doesn't know how. Venezuelan civil society needs partners like OTI [an office within USAID] to help build and strengthen the democratic institutions necessary to move the country beyond its deeply flawed past" (Cablegate 2006k). In this instance, Whitaker presents Chávez's apparent manipulation of Venezuelan citizens as possessing unintended consequences that the US government might harness to build, in this diplomat's vision, real democracy. Whitaker presents Venezuelans as "deeply confused" and stuck in a developmental process of "maturation." Indeed, this is the same sort of language that US foreign policymakers used in earlier instances of imperialism abroad—that they could help, for instance, Puerto Ricans, Filipinos, and Nicaraguans move forward in a developmental process toward true democracy albeit only with US tutelage (Fitz 2017; Horsman 1981). In much the same way, Whitaker presents the United States as capable of alleviating Venezuelans' "deep confusion" and showing Venezuelans how to get involved in politics.

Whitaker, however, moves beyond simply involving Venezuelans in politics but also involving them in a clearly partisan manner against Chávez. He writes that while "Venezuela's institutions have always been deeply flawed... Chavez continues to loudly define and distort what democracy is all about" (Cablegate 2006k). As a result, and "to provide some balance—primarily in low-income neighborhoods—OTI has developed five highly inter-active training modules that focus on: rule of law, separation of powers, political tolerance, the rights and responsibilities of citizens, and the role of civil society. In the two months since this project launched, over 40 NGOs around the country are using the materials to push back on the *Bolivarian brain-washing effort*" (Cablegate 2006k). In these passages, Whitaker clearly depicts Chávez as distorting democracy and "brain-washing" Venezuelans, who apparently cannot think for themselves. As a result of such manipulation, US diplomats like Whitaker believe it is the United States' duty to counter Chávez's ideas and develop training modules and materials designed to properly educate Venezuelan citizens, particularly citizens in "low-income neighborhoods," where support for Chávez historically remained high.

This sort of interventionist and neocolonial thinking turned up in many conversations with additional diplomats and functionaries. An individual who contracted with USAID to operate programs in Venezuela said that he believed it was the United States' duty to show Venezuelans how to do democracy properly. He stated that it was the United States' duty to spread "Jeffersonian democracy" throughout the world. This vision of politics is derived from Thomas Jefferson, who himself owned slaves, embraced "westward expansion," and advanced a liberal vision of democratic politics primarily rooted in the rights of the individual, albeit only applying to white male property owners. This vision deeply contrasts with the more collective form of economic and participatory democracy encouraged by the Chávez government. Similarly, a former US ambassador to Venezuela during the years of Chávez's presidency asserted that Chávez routinely attacked what the United States sought to cultivate abroad: "A conventional Western-style democracy." In this phrasing, this individual contrasts President Chávez with "the West," and, in doing so, presents him as somehow anti-Western. Such a distinction is similar to the sort of Orientalism described by Said (1978) and Quijano (2000), among others, in their work examining how Europeans often depicted non-European individuals and societies.

Taken together, US government leaders and functionaries in Venezuela generally sought to establish US supremacy in the realm of politics. Although there are many variants of democracy (e.g., direct, participatory, representative, Jeffersonian), the US government wanted to impart its own vision and promote those actors who embraced it. Though these practices are not formally colonial, they embody a neocolonial sort of paternalism that continues to characterize US foreign relations with many Latin American countries (Burron 2012; Robinson 1996; Schoultz 2018). US diplomats and functionaries depicted Venezuelans as "deeply confused," easily manipulated by an irrational and anti-Western leader, and thus in need of US direction and US tutelage. In doing so, US government leaders embraced a form of cultural racism, ultimately viewing Venezuelans and Venezuelan society as undeveloped and "immature." Indeed, some government functionaries have spoken and written quite plainly in culturally developmental terms, presenting Venezuelans as culturally lagging behind US Americans. In the end, these depictions of Venezuelans, as well as their president, provided the justification for US intervention and the US government's accompanying democracy assistance programs.

Since the inception of settler colonialism within what is now the United States, a WASP elite dominated the country's political institutions. Individuals such as Benjamin Franklin and John Quincy Adams believed that WASP Americans were a chosen people destined to usher in a new era of global prosperity. They believed it was their duty and God-given responsibility to cultivate a new world. In doing so, US American leaders displaced and murdered

Indigenous populations from the Atlantic to the Pacific Oceans, enslaved African and African American peoples, and engaged in colonial efforts by annexing land on both the American continent and beyond, such as in Hawaii and Puerto Rico. In doing so, US government leaders deployed racist understandings of non-WASP, nonwhite populations to justify these endeavors. Yet although formal land annexation and efforts toward direct colonialism have ended, the US government has still pursued imperial endeavors, all the while using the same racist justifications as earlier US political elites.

In contemporary Venezuela, US foreign policymakers became disturbed by the challenge President Chávez posed to US global hegemony. As a result, they sought to unseat him and his allies within the country. However, in doing so, US policymakers deployed racist and neocolonialist schemas designed to justify intervention into the country. US policymakers depicted Chávez as an irrational and uncivilized leader who sought to manipulate the Venezuelan populace. They portrayed Chávez as ultimately interested in power, rather than the welfare of the Venezuelan population. Some policymakers even attributed Chávez's alleged motivations to machismo and ostensibly deficient cultural traits within Venezuela. US policymakers thus claimed that it was their duty to intervene into the country in order to essentially save the Venezuelan population from Chávez and his manipulation. Indeed, US diplomats and government functionaries portrayed themselves as easily able to see the "laughable" and absurd nature of Chávez's policies, but they depicted Venezuelans, particularly poor Venezuelans, as unable to see through Chávez's manipulation. Such dynamics thus necessitated US intervention and US tutelage through democracy assistance programs.

Such thinking and such ideas remain consistent with a history of racist-imperial US foreign policy writ large, and, more specifically, toward Latin American populations. Since the mid-nineteenth century, US foreign policymakers have portrayed Latin Americans as corrupt, backwards, and uncivilized, and thus in need of tutelage and intervention. Such thinking guided land annexation and continual intervention in places such as the Dominican Republic and Nicaragua in the early twentieth century. Parallels run deep with regards to contemporary US foreign policymaking in Venezuela. As we have seen, US foreign policymakers continue to believe in a sort of "civilizing mission" throughout the world, wherein they might instruct and show citizens what their true interests are. There is no doubt that many such policymakers indeed believe in the supremacy of US American thinking and US American culture. Regardless of what is in their heart of hearts, it is clear that they use such racist-imperial thinking in order to justify their geopolitical aims, which, in the instance of Venezuela, includes the cultivation of domestic leaders who embrace or at least do not threaten US global leadership.

Chapter 4

COACHING OPPOSITION POLITICAL PARTIES I

The International Republican Institute

The International Republican Institute (IRI) is one of four core grantees of the National Endowment for Democracy (NED), and has, at times, received additional funding from the US Agency for International Development (US-AID) and the US Department of State. Despite its affiliation with the US Republican Party, the IRI considers itself "a nonprofit, nonpartisan organization committed to advancing freedom and democracy worldwide by helping political parties to become more issue-based and responsive, assisting citizens to participate in government planning, and working to increase the role of marginalized groups in the political process—including women and youth" (IRI n.d.). Similar to the NED, the IRI was established in 1983, and it has maintained programs in Venezuela since 1994, which it claims "supported the efforts of Venezuelan citizens to strengthen the country's democratic institutions, with particular emphasis on increasing youth participation in the political system" (IRI 1998, 20).

While the IRI lightly worked with some pro-Chávez political parties at some points in time, it has primarily offered funding and technical support for an array of opposition political parties in the country. This has included prominent opposition parties such as Acción Democrática, Comité de Organización Política Electoral Independiente (COPEI), Primero Justicia (PJ), and Proyecto Venezuela. Indeed, the IRI, as well as the National Democratic Institute (NDI), has been instrumental in helping opposition parties actually get off the ground and become formidable anti-Chávez opponents, such as Primero Justicia, a party formed in 2000, and Voluntad Popular, a party formed in 2009. The IRI has provided opposition parties will several forms of support. First, the IRI has facilitated high-level exchanges between Republican officials and opposition party members. The IRI has continually sponsored Republican visits into Venezuela, so that high-ranking members might lead seminars and workshops on campaign-related efforts, such as unification among opposition groups. Second, the IRI has provided opposition party leaders with a range of tools to allow them to strengthen their parties and attract members. IRI officials, for example, have worked with opposition party leaders on issues such as crafting campaign messages, attracting members, and using new technologies. Finally, while the IRI initially engaged in some electoral monitoring work, it did not continue these endeavors in later years. Instead, the NDI came to manage this facet of US democracy assistance within the country.

What is also striking about the IRI is how the group provided vocal support for the 2002 coup d'état that displaced President Hugo Chávez and paved way for a transitional government led by the head of the Venezuelan Federation of Chambers of Commerce, Pedro Carmona. Indeed, it was not until the NED director demanded that George Folsom, former IRI director, retract his statement and assume a more neutral position that their support was withdrawn. In this instance, we find clear indication that the IRI opposed the Chávez government and was elated to see Chávez's departure. From the NED and its other associated groups, we do not find a similar outburst of support for the Venezuelan opposition. This is not to say that behind the scenes, individuals who worked for these organizations did not, at least rhetorically, support the coup d'état, but unlike the IRI, they were not publicly outspoken in their support.

The IRI at Work in Venezuela

The IRI's work in Venezuela during the early years of the Chávez administration begins with electoral monitoring for regional and national elections, a seemingly innocuous manner of support, in late 1998. While Chávez would take serious issue with the IRI and similar groups, acrimonious relations had yet to develop under the previous administration of President Rafael Caldera. In November 1998 the IRI sent a nine-person delegation to monitor regional elections—for the Senate, Chamber of Deputies, and state legislatures. The IRI deployed their team to six Venezuelan states and analyzed both automated and manual vote counts. This program was funded by the NED, who "also supported the efforts of IRI and two Venezuelan civic groups to increase youth participation in the elections by organizing a series of candidate forums and conducting a 'get out the vote' campaign" (IRI 1998, 1). On top of the electoral monitoring efforts, the IRI focused on youth participation in politics, as it often has elsewhere in the world. In Venezuela, this latter project involved the creation of media spots, including television and radio ads, designed to increase youth participation in the elections (13).

The seemingly welcome relationship between the IRI and the Caldera administration is also apparent given that in December 1998 the Venezuelan National Electoral Council (CNE) provided the IRI with accreditation to monitor upcoming national elections. To do so, the IRI received funding from the US Department of State's Economic Support Fund for a team of twenty-seven individuals, headed by former US ambassador to Venezuela Otto Reich, to visit the country. On both occasions in 1998, IRI reports commended the Venezuelan electoral system, but noted some room for improvement in its electoral reporting (IRI 1998). At this point in time, the IRI's recommendations centered on technical aspects that might strengthen Venezuela's electoral model—including the allocation of more resources for poll worker training, simplifying the ballot to avoid confusion, and consideration of presidential run-off elections (IRI 1998).

Following Chávez's presidential victory in the 1998 elections, however, the IRI began to strategize for a physical and more intensive presence in the country. IRI members initiated plans to open a field office in Caracas in 2000, where they could broaden their efforts and begin trainings for political parties, specifically for parties opposed to the Chávez government and for leaders who might challenge him and his allies in future elections. At the time, the IRI website described how such training would "be developed in close cooperation with party representatives and particular effort [would] be made to identify and reach out to new and/or emerging party leaders" (IRI n.d.). The IRI established its office in Caracas in 2000 and spent much of their time and efforts that year establishing contacts with opposition party leaders throughout the country. In doing so, they initiated plans on how they might work with such political leaders to rejuvenate interest in their parties and combat President Chávez and his allies in the National Assembly.

Following the initiation of party contacts, in 2001 the IRI received a $340,000 from its parent organization, the NED, for a project called Strengthening Political Parties. The IRI (2001a) reported that the program's goals were threefold: to help develop internal, democratic structures for selecting party leaders; to enhance two-way communication with the electorate in order to better represent constituent concerns, especially those coming from young Venezuelans; and to help civil society groups and citizens to work with political parties and attend their events. The IRI (2001a, 1) also reported that "many unanswered questions remain, however, about the roles of various existing and newly created government institutions and the prospects for continued decentralization. The coming months will be instrumental in determining Venezuela's path and its chances for success as it attempts to reform."

In an interview with the author, an IRI contractor directly affiliated with the Republican National Committee (RNC) opined to me that after the successful election of President George W. Bush in 2000, and the constitutional changes and increasingly harsher rhetoric from President Chávez and other government members, IRI and RNC leaders believed they could alter the political landscape of countries that did not seemingly have the same national security interests as the US government. The contractor revealed that the IRI hired him due to his family's historical affiliation with the US Republican Party as well as their historical connection with Latin American politics and diplomacy. The former contractor said that the IRI asked him to come to Venezuela to assist with their Strengthening Political Parties program and its general party-building efforts within Venezuela. The contractor claimed that IRI leaders believed that IRI staff could use the same "ground-swelling tactics" that activists used to get George W. Bush elected to the US presidency in 2000.

The IRI contractor revealed to me that during this period he felt that the mission of the IRI was to unite opposition parties so that they could develop a unified message and begin efforts to field one candidate against Chávez in upcoming presidential elections. In blatant terms, he said that he felt their overall message for the opposition was to "get your shit together, so you can defeat Chávez." The representative pointed out that this, however, was an exceedingly difficult task as the opposition was fragmented and not entirely receptive to fielding only one opposition candidate against him. According to the contractor, the political opposition possessed a high degree of infighting, and he suggested that individuals were often little inclined to put their personalities aside in order to pursue one approach against the new government.

Under the Strengthening Political Parties program, the IRI sought to link the Venezuelan opposition not only with like-minded individuals from the United States but also from other parts of Latin America. In 2001, for example, the IRI sent Rogelio Carbajal from Mexico's National Action Party (PAN), a conservative Christian Democratic party whose leader—Vicente Fox—was recently elected president, to Venezuela to lead political party training sessions. In other words, the IRI brought in a representative from a conservative Mexican political party that had recently achieved electoral success—similar to the Republican Party in the United States. Carbajal met and worked with leaders from several parties that actively opposed the Chávez government, including Acción Democratica (AD), one of Venezuela's longest-running political parties, but had recently experienced diminishing support throughout the country; Proyecto Venezuela (PV), a centrist opposition political party that fielded Henrique Salas Römer against Chávez in the 1998 elections; and Unión para el Progreso, which, at the time, contained Francisco Arias Cardenas, a former Chávez supporter who would run against him in the 2000 presidential elections, but, interestingly enough, eventually returned to his side several years later and became a United Nations ambassador.

Consistent with the IRI's historical focus on youth politics, Carbajal focused on how party leaders might appeal to and attract youth voters during his meetings with Venezuelan party leaders. He also discussed how to organize youth structures, bring in qualified youth staff, and hold youth party leader elections (IRI 2001a, 1–2). In addition to meeting with party leaders, the IRI also worked with local youth-oriented NGOs to organize training sessions involving Carbajal. In Caracas and Valencia, Carbajal met with university students and NGO members where participants discussed youth participation in social movements and likeminded political parties (1–2). Altogether, his work sought to enhance the electoral possibilities of opposition parties and to help them understand how they might best incorporate youth constituents.

Back in Washington, DC, in February 2001 the IRI worked together with the NDI to host two events. First, the NDI hosted Eduardo Fernandez from Fundación Pensamiento y Acción, and also former secretary-general of COPEI and presidential candidate, to discuss the political situation in Venezuela. The IRI (2001a) reported that Fernandez spoke before some twenty individuals from media groups, think tanks, NGOs, and the US and foreign governments. Although IRI reports do not provide specifics, Fernandez was at the time a vociferous critic of the Chávez government and its policies. Second, the two groups hosted two National Assembly representatives, Tarek William Saab from the Movimiento Quinta Republica (MVR)—Chávez's political party before it transformed into the Partido Socialista Unido de Venezuela (PSUV), and Pedro Díaz Blum from PV, at the IRI's Washington offices to talk about a range of issues facing Venezuela. While Blum discussed the National Assembly and its current composition, the IRI documents that "Saab read a statement outlining Venezuela's foreign policy priorities, including the importance of cultivating a relationship of mutual respect with the United States," showing that Chávez was not opposed to positive, working relations with the country (IRI 2001a, 5).

In the following month, the IRI "organized a series of individual and collective training sessions with Venezuelan political parties, university students, and members of civil society," which included 110 participants and centered on political communication (IRI 2001a, 2–3). George Fondren, former College Republican National Committee field director and then-executive director of the Mississippi Republican Party, led these training sessions, which incorporated leaders and members from eight parties, including Saul Ortega from the MVR, the 1998 presidential candidate Henrique Salas Römer and his son Henrique Fernando Salas Feo from PV, and Julio Borges from Primero Justicia, a recently founded political party that primarily included and trained young politicians, including Henrique Capriles, then mayor of Baruta, future governor of Miranda, and future presidential candidate in the 2012 and 2013 elections, as well as Leopoldo López, the former mayor of Chacao, who would start and lead his own party, Voluntad Popular, in 2008, and become imprisoned for his role in the 2014 protests against the Maduro government.[1] Other opposition parties included AD, COPEI, Convergencia, and

Venezuela Posible. While individual sessions involved political leaders from a range of parties, collective sessions involved national committee members, state party coordinators, and university students, including a "special session on inter-party dialogue and democracy" with party leaders from across the groups at the events (IRI 2001a, 3).

The IRI recounts that before the training sessions, Fondren assessed each political party's strengths and weaknesses. With the exception of PV, Fondren "generally concluded that all the parties have a weak political infrastructure, no political plan, no message, internal tension, and a tendency to blame the ruling party MVR for their problems . . . and that serious reform of the parties must be undertaken in order to reestablish themselves" (IRI 2001a, 3). In order to illustrate how parties might reestablish and reinvigorate themselves, Fondren used the example of the Republican Party's 1992 presidential loss, during which time Fondren worked with the College Republican National Committee. He bluntly claimed that the GOP was simply out of touch with citizens. He pointed out that the Republican Party underwent serious reform in order to rebuild its political infrastructure and develop new messages that would resonate with the population. Fondren underscored campaign communications and how party leaders and representatives must tap into emotional issues and "basic human values" that Venezuelan citizens subscribe to, so that they might convince voters that they too care about the same issues (IRI 2001a, 3). Fondren also argued that these values could only be uncovered through extensive research into Venezuelan society. In addition, he discussed how to debate opponents and establish debate terms, how to deal with the media, and how to advertise their political campaign properly.

During these meetings, the IRI also organized a roundtable discussion solely for opposition leaders. This included leaders from AD, COPEI, Convergencia, Fundación Pensamiento y Acción, and PJ, and centered on working out personal rivalries in order to create "a common vision for the country" (IRI 2001a, 4). The roundtable modeled itself after recent negotiations within the Dominican Republic that had sought to establish an agreement for a common economic, cultural, and social vision among the political opposition in their own country. Similarly, IRI leaders believed that it would serve the Venezuelan opposition well if they too could work out their rivalries and put forward a common solution to the situation facing the country: Chávez's electoral success. The IRI reports that many of these leaders heavily criticized former President Chávez for generating country-wide problems; however, some participants claimed that the opposition was also partially responsible for some issues. IRI representatives emphasized that the purpose of the roundtable was not to target former President Chávez, "but to create a framework allowing the parties to work together and discuss future challenges" (4–5). Representatives also pointed out that they could provide technical assistance to the opposition, such as campaign training and other types of instruction, but "the parties themselves must take certain initiatives for such efforts to be truly effective" (5).

The IRI says that much of the last quarter of 2001 "was dedicated to making fresh contact with various political parties, building on IRI's relationships with them, assessing their situation and needs, and setting up training workshops" (IRI 2001b, 1). In October the IRI took Francisco Arias Cárdenas, a political party leader and former opposition presidential candidate with Unión para el Progreso, to Washington to speak before members of the international community, where he discussed "the shortcomings of President Chávez's administration and the desperate need for change in Venezuela" (2). Back in Venezuela, IRI members met with members from Unión para el Progreso, including Arias, who requested training in grassroots mobilization and media relations. IRI representatives also met with Caracas mayor Alfred Peña, an opposition mayor and potential presidential candidate, and his staff, and offered guidance on how Peña might develop a political party. The IRI ultimately agreed to assist Peña with his plans for party development as long as his party was "based on ideology, not personality" (2).

The IRI continued to develop its relations with other opposition groups during these months. In November, IRI staff met with leaders from COPEI, AD, and PJ. With COPEI, the IRI discussed conducting a training seminar that could assist in reunifying its membership in light of increased fragmentation. Similar to AD, COPEI remained one Venezuela's longest-running parties, but since the 1980s it had suffered from perceptions of ossification, corruption, and obsolescence (Hellinger 2003; Lander and López Maya 1999). With AD, the IRI discussed media relations and "proposed holding a youth summit in Washington for young party leaders" (IRI 2001b, 3). And with PJ, the IRI discussed training new party members and developing technology in order to reach out to potential supporters.

In December 2001 the IRI brought Darryl Howard, executive director of the Oregon Republican Party, to Venezuela to lead several workshops and offer his advice to several Venezuelan political parties. Members from PJ, AD, COPEI, Unión para el Progreso, and supporters of Mayor Peña attended the workshops, which focused on "grassroots development, political party structure, and political negotiation" (IRI 2001b, 3–5). Howard also attended a new member training seminar for young PJ party leaders. While there, Howard provided participants with College Republican recruiting materials and demonstrated how the Oregon Republican Party used a computer program to help identify and canvas potential GOP supporters. With supporters of Mayor Peña, Howard discussed how to develop a political party structure and a platform based on how the Oregon Republican Party developed ideas from its members and supporters—that is, by reaching out to them and understanding their concerns. Howard also met with leaders from Unión para el Progreso to discuss how to develop party support, assign tasks to party members, establish demographic chapters, and raise funds for the party. With COPEI members, Howard emphasized party unity and the development of a single platform, given increased fragmentation within COPEI's ranks. And with AD, Howard spoke to young party leaders about reaching out to other civil society groups in order to maintain strong support networks.

Later in December, the IRI organized meetings between opposition party leaders and Mike Collins, former Republican Party press secretary (IRI 2001b, 6). Collins met with youth members from PJ and supporters of Mayor Peña to discuss developing messages and images for their party; he met with leaders from Union para el Progreso, including Francisco Arias Cardenas, to discuss how to better attract press attention by holding weekly conferences in the streets in order to be seen with the people; and he spoke with journalists at an event hosted by the libertarian nongovernmental organization CEDICE, which also continually received US government funding and will be discussed in a later chapter, on how to report on political events and conduct media relations with political parties (IRI 2001b). On his final two days in Venezuela, Collins met with leaders from COPEI and AD, Venezuela's longest-running political parties. He suggested that COPEI find a new, young spokesperson to combat their elitist and outdated image, and, with AD, Collins spoke with young leaders about how to recruit individuals in universities and elsewhere to rejoin the party as many had left them for Chávez.

In March 2002 the NED awarded the IRI with another $340,000 for their Strengthening Political Parties program (IRI 2002a, 1). This program would run until May 2002 and involve workshops for political party delegates throughout the country in areas such as negotiation training, political communications, and campaign strategies. During this time, though, problems between the government and the opposition became pronounced, and in April 2002 a collection of dissident actors, including military members and business leaders, removed President Chávez from power in a coup d'état. At the time, the IRI (2002a) reports that the organization remained in contact with political party and civil society leaders in order to stay informed about ongoing political problems and the nature of the coup d'état efforts. For example, an IRI representative attended regular meetings with Consorcio Justicia, an NGO receiving funding from the NED, in preparation for an upcoming NED-sponsored conference on the political situation facing the country.

Under this new program, IRI representatives decided to prioritize and establish intensive long-term plans with opposition parties AD, PJ, and PV, and to maintain dialogue with COPEI and Unión para el Progreso. To strengthen relations, IRI representatives met weekly with members from AD, PJ, and PV. In its meetings with AD, the two groups discussed training in the area of internal structure and reforming internal bylaws. The IRI also planned a visit for AD leaders to meet with political leaders in Washington. With PV, the two groups discussed focusing on the issue of decentralization and developing plans to help PV achieve an impact outside of its traditional stronghold in Carabobo State. With PJ, which the IRI described as "the most significant new political party in Venezuela," the group planned to help the new political party with future support in the areas of decentralization, grassroots training, outreach, and political communications (IRI 2002a, 3). During these years, these three organizations became the primary political parties that the IRI worked with and offered guidance to on a regular basis. As we have seen, this largely included workshops and training seminars with IRI leaders, but it also included sponsoring visitors such as Republican Party leaders to provide personal advice to these parties and their leaders.

On April 11, 2002, Venezuelans were jolted by the temporary coup d'état that removed President Chávez from power. This was indeed the most significant instance of wide-scale violence that Venezuelans had witnessed since the 1989 *caracazo* and subsequent coups d'etat in 1992, one of which was, in fact, led by Chávez. Following Chávez's removal and military detention on April 12, IRI president George Folsom released a statement titled "IRI President Folsom Praises Venezuelan Civil Society's Defense of Democracy." In his statement, Folsom commended Venezuelan citizens' efforts following what he called "systematic repression by the Government of Hugo Chávez" (OIG 2002, 31). Folsom applauded the "the bravery of civil society leaders—members of the media, the Church, the nation's educators and school administrators, political party leaders, labor unions, and the business sector—who have put their very lives on the line in their struggle to restore genuine democracy to their country" (31). IRI's parent organization, the NED, however, was not pleased with such affirmation of the coup d'état (32). After NED president Carl Gershman criticized Folsom's response, Folsom released a second statement on May 6. In his statement, Folsom appears most concerned with the behavior of interim Venezuelan government leaders who took over following the coup d'état efforts. Folsom argued that the IRI felt compelled to release a statement on behalf of "calls from Venezuelans asking for international support to rebuild the country's fractured political system and restore elected democracy" (33). In addition, he wrote that his statement was "not an endorsement of extra-constitutional measures to forcibly remove an elected President, and IRI never contemplated the notion that the will of the Venezuelan people would be circumvented by extra-constitutional measures, such as the closure of the National Assembly and the Supreme Court" (33).

In the IRI's second quarterly report in 2002, the group stated that the IRI issued their initial statement because of "its close relationship with the victims of the violence," which included a PJ member who was shot in the head but recovered (IRI 2002b, 1). The report also stated that it remains important to recognize that the IRI issued their initial statement before the National Assembly was dissolved, and that the IRI had called on the transitional government and legislative branch to hold elections as soon as possible (1). And so, while the IRI did not endorse the ways in which the transitional government proceeded, it did not entirely object to Chávez's departure from the presidential office. Instead, the group suggested that had the interim government ruled in a democratic manner, that its ouster of Chávez would have generally been appropriate and commendable. Such a move, however, whether in support of Chávez or not, runs entirely contrary to the ideas of liberal democracy rhetorically espoused by the IRI and its leaders. Nonetheless, such ideas would not get in the way of an opportunity to rid the country of Chávez, perhaps illustrating an ends-justifying-the-means calculation among IRI staff.

From April 22 to 25—in the weeks following the coup d'état—the IRI sent their regional director and their program officer to look into the recent coup d'état events and how the IRI might assist groups in the future. The two-party delegation first met with Aurelio Concheso, president of CEDICE, who told the group that the coup d'état was spontaneous and Venezuelan political party members played no part in the events (IRI 2002b). Concheso also stated that the coup d'état efforts began with a spontaneous uprising that was then betrayed by interim president Pedro Carmona and those around him who hijacked the coup d'état efforts for their own benefit (IRI 2002b). The two individuals also met with several political leaders, including former Caracas mayor Antonio Ledezma, then leader of a newly developed opposition political party called Alianza Bravo Pueblo, who stated that he would like to work with the IRI in the future, and Eduardo Fernandez, former COPEI leader and close friend of Carmona, who said that he was surprised by Carmona's decision to dissolve the National Assembly (IRI 2002b). In addition, the delegation met with PJ and AD leaders to discuss their future plans in Venezuela (IRI 2002b). AD leaders argued that they should push ahead with a referendum to legally remove Chávez from office, and PJ leaders discussed long-term plans to enhance their party's stature. Finally, the two met with leaders of the Venezuelan-American Chamber of Commerce, who agreed that the opposition currently lacked a leader and that the opposition had ultimately foiled its own attempt to unseat President Chávez, and with representatives from the periodical *El Nacional* and the television station Globovisión, who claimed that the media could play an instrumental role in pushing the opposition to field one candidate to challenge Chávez in the ensuing years (IRI 2002b). The ultimate IRI strategy remained uniform: unify the opposition to defeat Chávez.

In the aftermath of the coup d'état, the IRI recounted that it began to assist several political parties in developing negotiation techniques (IRI 2002b).

These exercises were led by Dr. Elsa Cardozo, a professor from the Central University of Venezuela, who held a two-day workshop for AD members in May 2002. The IRI (2002b, 2–3) reported that the purpose of the training was to show AD members how to develop win-win situations when negotiating with members from other parties. IRI members also met with AD members to discuss how they could decentralize their party structure in order to appeal to voters, and they provided them with US Republican Party materials to assist them in this endeavor. In the post–coup d'état period, the IRI also continued to work closely with PJ. IRI members met with PJ deputy Carlos Ocariz and a Venezuelan communications specialist to assist the party in developing better contact between Venezuelan citizens and political parties. IRI members sought to push PJ to promote citizen communication with newly developed congressional staffs that could pass concerns to deputies, governors, and other high-ranking politicians, rather than having citizens attempt to directly address their governors. IRI members also met with PJ leaders, including their secretary general, to discuss how they could expand their party's base. In their quarterly report, the IRI commends PJ for their media exposure and talented spokespersons. At this point in time, however, IRI members continued to emphasize that they "lack a product" as well as definite solutions to the country's problems, beyond opposition to Chávez, which PJ members also agreed with (IRI 2002b, 4).

In late 2002, the IRI contended that its ability to help strengthen political parties had been largely hindered (IRI 2002c). Instead of dealing with internal issues, opposition groups had mostly engaged in verbal sparring with the Chávez government. Indeed, one of IRI's perennial concerns with the opposition remained its inability to carefully design campaign platforms laying out clear policies, instead of vague anti-Chávez messaging. Because of this, the IRI refocused its efforts on identifying young party leaders, who they might work with, and training party leaders in negotiation techniques in order to foster an atmosphere of dialogue amid political polarization and conflict. The IRI again contracted with Dr. Cardozo to work with COPEI on negotiation training (IRI 2002c, 3). In addition, the IRI recognized that COPEI understood that it would require new lifeblood in the party in order to remain relevant within the country, as the party had been unable to overcome its perceived obsolescence. The IRI also held similar training sessions with PJ. The organization reports that it began a new relationship with youth leader Oswaldo Perozo, who ran PJ's Justicia y Democracia recruitment and training arm of the party, and it placed renewed emphasis on reinvigorating the party with young members (IRI 2002c, 3). Similarly, IRI representatives met with AD youth leader Alexandra Belandia to discuss the importance of bringing youth back into the party, and overcoming its image as an outdated organization (IRI 2002c, 3). During this period, while the IRI mostly met with opposition members, IRI officials also met with Venezuelan Foreign Minister Roy Chaderton at the IRI's Washington headquarters, where they primarily report that Chaderton complained of the US media's poor treatment of President Chávez (IRI 2002d).

In the final months of 2002, the IRI worked with the Instituto Zuliano de Estudios Políticos, Económicos y Sociales (IZEPES), a political academy whose mission is to train public servants, in order to help "local political party leaders on negotiation techniques in Maracaibo, Zulia state" (IRI 2002d, 2). The IRI worked with delegations from nine political parties, including MVR, COPEI, AD, MAS, PJ, and PV (2). The IRI claims that seven of the delegates were affiliated with the Chávez government, and that government members worked with opposition members during their negotiation training on developing dialogue between the two groups. This is indeed one of the few instances where we find MVR members participating in events sponsored by the IRI and attended by a multiplicity of opposition parties, albeit in a locality outside of the capital city of Caracas.

In its first 2003 quarterly report, the IRI (2003a) documents that it continued to view political party building as the long-term solution to the political crisis facing Venezuela. In January, in keeping with this perspective, the group conducted three training workshops in Caracas for members from various political parties, including the MVR as well as AD, COPEI, PJ, and the Communist Party of Venezuela (PCV), all with an IRI representative from Guatemala and a member of the Colombian Conservative Party. These workshops focused on "communicating constructively with constituencies in crisis environments, strategic analysis methods, coordinating effective organizational structures, and political party experiences in Central America and Colombia" during these countries' respective political crises (IRI 2003a, 2). Due to extreme polarization, however, the IRI held two days of sessions for opposition party members and one day of sessions for primarily pro-government PCV members. Although the IRI reported that more than thirty-five members from opposition parties attended the sessions, only four members from PCV and one MVR member—and future Venezuelan diplomat in the United States—Calixto Ortega, attended the sessions designated for pro-government individuals (2–3). And so, while there is some semblance of participation among pro-government parties, this involvement is marginal to the many instances of involvement from a range of opposition parties, including, namely, AD, COPEI, PV, and PJ.

In March the IRI brought their political party training workshops to Anzoátegui State and worked with members from AD, COPEI, and PV with a focus on external communication and conflict resolution (IRI 2003a, 2). Their report reveals that IRI leaders emphasized the need to find common ground between opposing political parties. Despite participants placing blame on the Chávez government for political polarization and domestic conflict, the report states that IRI leaders avoided the tendency to place blame and emphasized finding common ground with their political counterparts.

Back in Caracas that same month, IRI leaders held separate training sessions in the headquarters of COPEI, PV, PJ, and AD. With COPEI, the IRI documents that it discussed strategic analysis of how COPEI could consolidate its base and strengthen its position as a political party (IRI 2003a, 3). At PJ headquarters, the IRI said that it worked on simple tasks with youth leaders, such as defining what a political party is and what the importance of political parties are in a democracy (4). With PV, IRI leaders discussed the importance of internal democratic measures such as internal elections, which it reports that such suggestions were met with defensive statements (4). And with AD, IRI leaders worked with a contingent of youth leaders, discussing the importance of political parties and particular ideologies. IRI reports that AD members were frustrated by a lack of discussion on the political problems between the government and opposition, but states that IRI members told them "that this is not IRI's role, but instead to provide them a broader perspective on the long term sustainability of parties in any political circumstance" (5). In many instances, we see that opposition leaders continually condemn the Chávez government to IRI staff. At least in their documentation, IRI representatives claim that they sought to refrain from this sort of Chávez-bashing in order to push opposition parties to generate more productive changes to their electoral approaches and to find ways that they might focus on long-term solutions to the apparent political problems facing the country.

In the following month, the IRI co-hosted a public forum with NDI that featured Calixto Ortega (MVR) and Pedro Diaz Blum (PV) in Washington. The IRI (2003b) reports that both members expressed the need to reconcile their political differences and move past politically polarizing obstacles. The aim of the forum also sought to illustrate how moderate elements exist within both pro-government and opposition groups, and that many members aspired to work together to solve the political problems facing the country.

For the coming period, NED president Gershman signed off on an extended $116,000 grant for the IRI's Strengthening Political Parties program, which would run until January 2004. The program would focus on regions beyond the capital city, including Zulia, Carabobo, and Anzoátegui, and its core objectives were to strengthen communication between regional parties and their counterparts in Caracas, in addition to its recurrent focus on bringing young individuals into political parties. The grant describes this program as "encourage[ing] a more decentralized organizational structure ... to allow for more inclusive recruitment, stronger bi-directional communication, more constituency-reflective platform development, and broader and more innovative party reform" (IRI 2003b, 4). The IRI program also sought to encourage the participation of working-class individuals, students, women, and youth, in order to combat the parties' elitist images (5).

Under this grant, the IRI held a training seminar attended by seventy-seven deputies from seven political parties throughout the country. Although the IRI report notes that the MVR was invited, only opposition members attended the seminar, demonstrating how Venezuelan government went from minimal to no interest in these programs. The training featured two guests, including Sergio Cedeño, secretary general of the Reformist Party in the Dominican Republic, and Jarryd Gonzales, the California Republican National Committee political director. Cedeño discussed designing and developing campaign strategies, and Gonzalez presented campaign management techniques that were used during the 2000 US national elections, including door-to-door efforts, fundraising, and final Election Day strategies. The new IRI program also sought to bridge the gap between political parties and universities as well as political parties and youth. The IRI program recognized that many Venezuelan political parties were losing support due to their ossified perception: "Reconstructing a political party system that was not long ago repudiated by many voters is difficult without the addition of new blood" (IRI 2003b, 5). In keeping with this perspective, the IRI sought to link up with local universities for training seminars, and, in doing so, to attract university students to their training sessions and into these political parties.

Finally, in 2003 IRI staff worked again with IZEPES to train politicians on effective external political communications. This training session was run by US-based communications specialist Steven Elena, who once received a political communication award from the Anti-Chávez Political Coalition of Venezuela for his work on Venezuela. The IRI reports that Elena trained both pro-government and opposition politicians in how to craft political messages, construct press releases, and other forms of political communication.

In the aftermath of the 2002 coup d'état, US democracy-promoting agencies received more attention than they might have ever as journalists and academics began to look into their role in the country. As a result, organizations such as USAID and the NED and its subgroups became more closeted with regards to their activities in the country. While in earlier years, the groups released unredacted documents concerning their funding and programming. In subsequent years, these groups have only slowly released documents—some of which are so heavily redacted that they remain almost useless. The remainder of this section pieces together what is indeed possible to piece together through 2010—through the use of documents released to the author through a Freedom of Information Act (FOIA) request, interviews with US government elites, and with diplomatic embassy cables released by Private Chelsea Manning to Julian Assange and thereafter posted on the Cablegate/WikiLeaks website.

In February 2004 former US ambassador to Venezuela Charles Shapiro revealed in a diplomatic cable that USAID and its Office for Transition Initiatives (OTI) had now begun to directly fund the IRI for its Strengthening Political Parties program in the country, in addition to an IRI program designed to have local volunteers monitor elections. Shapiro wrote that the objectives of these programs were "to provide training to political parties in 1) execution of electoral campaigns with emphasis on developing campaign strategies and communicating party platforms effectively to voters; and 2) observation of electoral processes, focused on assessment, reporting, and establishment of a volunteer trainer network" (Cablegate 2004b). Two days later, Shapiro cabled that USAID/OTI would provide the IRI with $450,000 for its political party training program (Cablegate 2004c). Shapiro described how the training was aimed at campaign managers in order to help them "develop viable campaign strategies and effectively communicat[e] party platforms to voters." In addition, the IRI offered training in several largely populated areas throughout the country, including Caracas, Zulia, Anzoátegui, and Carabobo, which also served as regional hubs for campaign managers from other nearby states. Shapiro does not mention what parties campaign managers came from; however, given immediately previous relations, we can expect that this included opposition parties, such as AD and PJ.

In July 2004 US diplomat Stephen McFarland reported that the IRI was continuing its campaign schools for campaign mangers throughout the country. However, he reports that only opposition parties participated and that "participation by government-leaning parties has been insignificant despite IRI's efforts to encourage government participation" (Cablegate 2004c). In the same cable, McFarland reveals that the IRI maintained a joint program with the NDI to train poll watchers for elections. In doing so, the groups linked up with the domestic organization Hagamos Democracia to conduct their activities. Similar to their campaign schools, though, pro-government groups did not participate in these sessions. Instead, he reports that the groups have worked with COPEI and Bandera Roja, an officially communist-inspired party that supported opposition candidates, for their trainings thus far.[2]

Throughout 2005, the IRI discusses similar work with the Venezuelan opposition under both a Strengthening Political Parties, and Venezuela Elections Assistance program. In one diplomatic cable, US ambassador William Brownfield describes the year as focused on the second phase of their campaign training school (Cablegate 2005c). He describes the foci of the workshops as including "campaign strategy and organization, message development (including working with focus groups), outreach (including public speaking), fund-raising, public relations, get-out-the-vote techniques, and candidate selection" (Cablegate 2005c). Participating groups included AD and PJ, who Brownfield says the IRI helped to assist in conducting polls by phone. In their first quarterly report from the year, the IRI laments that the opposition appeared "weak and fragmented," and that "it remains to be seen whether these parties will be able to effectively address their weaknesses, forge alliances and restore competitiveness to Venezuelan democracy" (IRI 2005a, 1). During this period, the group primarily focused on assisting opposition parties in the area of "external communication." In their third quarterly report, the IRI documents how they have continued their trainings and encouraged the opposition to unify around particular candidates. The group further laments opposition electoral losses, but it indicates that "one positive development" is that such defeats have forced the opposition to move towards reunification (IRI 2005b, 7). In their final report of the year, the IRI makes clear that they are "working with state opposition coalitions . . . to help them consolidate common objectives and strategies, organize effective campaigns, communicate strong and consistent messages that resonate with the electorate, mobilize voters and challenge fraud" (IRI 2005c, 1). In doing so, they discuss how they have sought to help the opposition unify around one particular candidate in elections throughout the country and how they should develop policies and "concrete alternatives to . . . the theft of private property and the assault on the rule of law now the norm in Venezuelan society" (10).

Venezuelan presidential elections transpired in 2006 and galvanized much of the IRI's efforts in the country for the year. In this election, opposition candidate Manuel Rosales, a member of the Un Nuevo Tiempo (UNT) party, competed against President Chávez. This election followed a last-minute effort by the opposition to boycott parliamentary elections in late 2005. As a result, Chávez and his supporters came to totally dominate all government institutions—a move that the IRI says it intensively disagreed with. In a revealing note, however, Ambassador Brownfield suggested that if this move "marginalizes the opposition's leadership dinosaurs and the grassroots retains its voice" that this could be a big win for the opposition "at least in the long run" (Cablegate 2005e). Such an assertion remains entirely consonant with the IRI and NDI focus on the cultivation of young party leaders within US-led programs instead those they perceived as "dinosaurs." US government elites continually underscored just how necessary youth members were for rejuvenating their parties. In August 2006, for instance, Deputy Chief of Mission Kevin Whitaker writes that the IRI, as well as the NDI, "Continue to work on political party renovation, primarily with young(er) leadership, primarily outside of Caracas. They are also identifying potential future political leaders who are not affiliated with a political party. Those identified will participate in a program to prepare them for a run at local council seats and/or mayorships in 2008" (Cablegate 2006j).

During the 2006 presidential campaign, the IRI provided Rosales with five technical specialists to assist him with exit polling and interactions with government institutions, particularly on Election Day (Cablegate 2006m). In addition, the IRI trained hundreds of individuals from opposition political parties to monitor voting locations all throughout the country in order to detect any foul play from the government. Chávez, however, handily defeated Rosales, awarding him with another six-year term to run until 2012. One contractor who worked with IRI recounted to me that he had thought that the opposition decision to field Rosales was failed from the start. The contractor said that the opposition was at the same time "led by elitist conduction ... USAID [was funding] all these white people from the US who were not democratic at all ... I'd say 'I'm not saying you're racist, but you need to do something about it.' They didn't want to talk about it. The reaction was so brutal that they accused me of supporting Chávez." In terms of Rosales himself, the contractor said when the "they chose Rosales, I thought forget it! His baby looked like a Gerber baby."

On the day after Rosales's defeat in December 2006, Ambassador Brownfield sent a cable to Washington, titled "Time to Re-Double Our Pro-Democracy Efforts in Venezuela" (Cablegate 2006j). In particular, this cable responded to a request from the National Security Council Deputies Committee concerning resources for the US mission in Venezuela. Brownfield began his cable to Washington stating that "we are grateful for all resources made available, but in light of Chavez' triumph, his aggressive post-election approach to the opposition, the incipient efforts of the opposition to build long-term infrastructure, and Chavez' own long-term vision, we need more. Embassy strategy is to strengthen democratic institutions, *penetrate and divide Chavismo*, and build independent society" (Cablegate 2006j; emphasis mine). While at times and, in public, US diplomats asserted that they were not opposed to Chávez, diplomatic cables make clear their intentions if they were not already clear: the defeat of *chavismo*. In his request, Brownfield asked for increased funding for an array of programs, including funds for "NDI and IRI to expand their party-building efforts toward 2008 local and state races" (Cablegate 2006j).

From 2007 to 2010, when the Cablegate database begins to conclude, US government diplomats discuss very little of what the IRI sought to accomplish within the country. However, based upon IRI's own documents, they continued their Strengthening Political Parties program within the country through the end of 2010 with increased involvement from USAID/OTI as well as an organization that USAID/OTI contracted with: Development Alternatives, Inc. (DAI). Though the database ends and many of these released documents are replete with redactions, I conducted interviews with several members of USAID/OTI and DAI who were involved in working with the IRI on their programming within Venezuela.

In the ensuing years, and leading into the present, US democracy promoting agencies took more concerted interest in parties with a more youthful leadership, primarily including PJ but also youthful members of Rosales's UNT party, such as Leopoldo López. Relations with AD also persisted, but with far less interest from US government functionaries and their contractors. Indeed, in the first IRI report in 2007, the agency failed to redact PJ in one area within their quarterly report. In this report, the IRI described how they continued conducting workshops with opposition parties to help them "to reengineer messages, platforms and to implement outreach strategies" (IRI 2007a, 3). In their second report, the IRI lamented the Chávez government's closure of the television station RCTV, but the group praises the "new student-led opposition" movement that had begun to protest against Chávez in the streets (IRI 2007b, 1). In the same report, the IRI also noted that their main objectives at this point include consensus-building within the opposition and the development of opposition political party platforms. At the time, PJ faced much internal strife as López had begun to publicly criticize high-ranking PJ leader Julio Borges. In addition, some opposition parties had also begun to contest Rosales's leadership within the UNT, including members from AD and COPEI. To help unify the opposition, the IRI planned to bring in representatives from opposition movements in other countries to discuss how they unified against government leaders. The countries from which these individuals traveled, however, is redacted. In the past, though, this included party representatives from the Dominican Republic, Mexico, and Spain, as well as the United States.

One individual who helped devise these programs back in Washington during these later years told me that USAID/OTI "maintained relationships with people who had a more positive outlook towards the US," in contrast with Chávez and the Venezuelan government. He said that USAID/OTI "kept the faith with them, we were there for them in their darkest hour. In their minds, with how much the opposition was looking to the US for help, we know Europeans give aid, but [there is] no supplanting the US in the minds of these people who were struggling against these new governments that sought to suppress the opposition," including the Venezuela government, but he also referenced the Nicaraguan government under President Daniel Ortega. Other US functionaries also referenced working with such groups "during their darkest hour," illustrating a sort of religious rhetoric among these actors and their activities in the country.

Multiple members of USAID/OTI, however, often downplayed the consequentiality of these programs and claimed they were more symbolic than anything else. The same individual who devised programs in Washington claimed that USAID/OTI did not aim "to organize an overthrow, but it was more of a political bond or a political signal to people who shared a lot of the ideals with us about how a society should operate—openness, tolerance, etc." He said that these were "very nuts and bolts program, not sexy . . . [They were the] nuts and bolts of good governance, civic organization, message managing, how do you recruit, how do you organize." A USAID/OTI Venezuelan team member who worked on the ground in the country recounted to me that the US government wanted to work with "good-faith, democratic actors," and that such programs were certainly "useful if Chavez woke up and knew that there were democratic movements around opposing him." Another USAID/OTI administrator spoke in similar terms, saying that USAID/OTI "are vexing dictators. As long as Chavez wakes up and is angry with what we're doing, that's good, that's good for freedom . . . For our foreign policy, it's good that they know they have hostile forces."

In the post-2006 electoral period, though, USAID/OTI in relation with the IRI had a clear change of interest in terms of the parties they wanted to embrace and enhance. One USAID administrator said that that the previously dominant opposition "parties were horrible and corrupt, and should have went away. We couldn't work with AD and COPEI. The only people to work with were youth, and then [Leopoldo] López [from VP], and then with [Henrique] Capriles [from PJ]." US government agencies and their functionaries seemed to particularly sour on COPEI. One member of the DAI team in Venezuela told me that for a time he "participated with COPEI for instance . . . I was good friends with Eduardo Fernández [the former leader of the party]. They don't talk to you if you don't have a bottle of whiskey on the table. Everything runs on whiskey." Instead of these older parties and seemingly elitist party leaders, one administrator said that USAID/OTI "wanted to identify new politicians, so they didn't have the taint of the old system . . . [Chávez] understood the two-party system [led by AD and COPEI] was corrupt. Elites in power were so corrupt in the old system. Chavez was the failure of the two-party system." Indeed, members of both USAID/OTI and DAI continually referenced their particular interest in Leopoldo López and Henrique Capriles, as new, youthful leaders, who the US government believed could seriously challenge Chávez.

Through the end of 2007, IRI documents continually reference their support for consensus-building activities among the opposition parties, and they lament the activities of Chávez and the Venezuelan government, including their push for a constitutional referendum and the creation of a new time zone. Opposition leaders and their members had indeed remained fractured and had continued to grow irritated with Rosales's leadership among the opposition. While the IRI had continued to work with his party, interest in López and Capriles continued and would eventually outpace interest in Rosales. Nonetheless, in the wake of the defeat of Chávez's constitutional referendum, several opposition parties had begun to unify and agree on fielding one candidate among them in many regional elections. This included UNT, PJ, and COPEI. Still, US ambassador to Venezuela Patrick Duddy commented that "opposition parties still have not clearly staked out comprehensive alternative programs for voters to consider. They have done even less to sell their political programs to Venezuela's poor, the vast majority of voters and Chavez's traditional, extensive electoral base" (Cablegate 2007e).

In 2008 and 2009, the IRI continued many of its same programs, including assisting the opposition in their crafting of public messages and in their amplification of particular leaders. Such training also had begun to involve the creation of social media profiles, websites, and intensive use of the internet. Indeed, the IRI reported on its website at the time that they had helped Primero Justicia, in particular, to create their websites and online profiles. For Rosales's part, he decided to lower his profile and run again as mayor of the western Venezuelan city of Maracaibo, an election which he would win. Yet, he still wanted to maintain leadership among the opposition. Internally, however, he had begun to confront more challenges, both from activists affiliated within the party and other opposition leaders, including Leopoldo López, who had been serving as the mayor of Chacao, an upper-middle-class neighborhood in Caracas. One UNT activist reported the growing sentiment among the opposition to US diplomat John Caulfield, saying that Rosales and his older allies in the opposition remained "only interested in claiming power for themselves, rather than grooming rising stars in the party who may generate broader public appeal. One young UNT activist told [a US diplomat] that while Rosales had connections and power in Zulia State, Lopez was far more charismatic and popular. She added that the Primero Justicia mayor of the Sucre Borough of Caracas had made an effort to communicate directly with the poor residents of the densely-populated Petare slum, and they had responded by voting across party lines for him in November 2008" (Cablegate 2009a).

Setbacks, however, also faced López. The Venezuelan government banned him from running in the late 2008 elections after he was charged with corruption. Internally, too, some opposition members reported frustrations with him, leading Caulfield to report that opposition party members "appear frustrated with his uncompromising approach and do not trust his motives. Ponte [a member of PJ,] said that for the opposition parties, Lopez draws ire second only to Chavez, joking that 'the only difference between the two is that Lopez is a lot better looking'" (Cablegate 2009f). Amid the court case and accusation, López eventually began his own party, Voluntad Popular (VP), and has continued to lead the opposition, albeit from eventual prison, house arrest, and relocation to Spain. Although he has not officially led the opposition, he has served as the mentor of current opposition leader Juan Guaidó, leading some to believe López is ultimately the one who has decided opposition strategies against the Maduro government.

Following the formation of a new opposition umbrella unit, the Mesa de la Unidad Democrática, the IRI primarily worked with the group to keep the opposition unified so that they might best compete against Chávez. In the remaining years of Chávez's life, Henrqiue Capriles from PJ became his final competitor as well as the first electoral competitor of Chávez's successor, Nicolás Maduro. Indeed, by 2012, the year in which Capriles ran against Chávez, he and his party had maintained a relationship with nearly all US democracy assistance agencies: the IRI, NDI, NED, and USAID/OTI. One USAID/OTI contractor in Venezuela even remarked to me that he had met with "the two boys, López and Capriles ... but preferred Capriles better than López," who he found "too moody." Another USAID/OTI contractor said that Capriles was much more sympathetic to what USAID/OTI tried to accomplish in the country by visiting poor neighborhoods and reaching out to Chavistas, much more so than other politicians. In contrast, he said that Julio Borges, another PJ leader, displayed too much elitism and "wouldn't shake hands with people and so forth."

IRI programs continue into the present, and, although the content of these programs is not entirely clear under President Donald Trump and now President Joe Biden, we can be assured that much US government funding is flowing to Guaidó and his allies. Members of the former Trump administration certainly made that much clear. In earlier years, though, it is evident that the IRI allocated much training and funding for a range of opposition political parties, particularly PJ, VP, and AD. In other instances, the IRI lost interest in particular parties and actors over time, such as COPEI, Rosales, and Peña. Altogether, the bulk of IRI activities were designed to help the opposition defeat Chávez and his allies at the ballot box. Though the IRI at times met with some government members, IRI and USAID personnel revealed to me in interviews that they were much consumed by efforts to unseat Chávez and his allies. Over time, too, Venezuelan government members stopped meeting with them.

Such dynamics run contrary to neo-Tocquevillian assertions that the US government acts in a nonpartisan manner abroad, but, as we see here, the IRI clearly sought to assist opposition groups defeat Chávez for over a decade, through a range of activities. Indeed, the IRI sought to assist like-minded opposition parties that accepted US foreign policy aims, broadly speaking, and accepted US global hegemony. Such parties were quite eager to work with the United States and cultivate relations, particularly with members of the Republican Party. These dynamics illustrate the importance of a theoretical perspective that foregrounds explicit US support for a particular set of actors—that is, those actors that the US government deems worthy of leading the country instead of, in this instance, Chávez and his allies.

Chapter 5

COACHING OPPOSITION POLITICAL PARTIES II

The National Democratic Institute

Alongside the International Republican Institute (IRI), the Reagan administration also assisted in the formation of the National Democratic Institute for International Affairs (NDI). Into the present, the NDI remains a foundational sub-grantee of the National Endowment for Democracy (NED) and ostensibly acts as the international arm of the US Democratic Party. Despite its historical affiliation with the Democratic Party, the NDI describes itself in similar terms as the International Republican Institute (IRI), as "a nonprofit, nonpartisan, nongovernmental organization working to support and strengthen democratic institutions worldwide through citizen participation, openness and accountability in government" (NDI n.d.). The group possesses more than sixty field offices throughout the world, and the group has primarily received funding from the NED but also the US Agency for International Development (USAID) and the US Department of State (NDI n.d.). In addition, it has often worked alongside the IRI on the same sorts of political party strengthening programs and with the same political parties within Venezuela.

In its public relations materials on its website, the group reports that it maintains several objectives in its work in other countries. First, the NDI (n.d.) reports that it is focused on involving citizens in political life and providing them with tools to hold elected officials accountable. Second, the NDI has aimed to utilize technology to advance democracy, including ways to track legislation and help political parties effectively reach constituents. Third, the NDI has sought to work directly with government leaders to address constituent needs and improve their performance. Fourth, the group has monitored elections and assisted domestic organizations in their own electoral monitoring projects. Fifth, the NDI has sought to strengthen political parties in a variety of ways, "from internal democratic procedures and candidate selection to polling, platform development and public outreach." Finally, the group claims that it has pushed for more involvement of women in politics.

During the years of the Chávez administration, the NDI worked both with political parties and assisted with the establishment of a nonpartisan, domestic electoral monitoring group, Ojo Electoral. Similar to the IRI, the NDI primarily worked with opposition political parties, but it made a more consistent effort to work with and include the Movimiento Quinta República (MVR), particularly during the early years of the Chávez administration. For instance, the NDI conducted research with government supporters, and it also provided research on political parties to MVR members. Unlike the IRI as well, the NDI and its leadership did not publicly voice support for the 2002 coup d'état efforts that deposed President Hugo Chávez. Finally, the group has placed much emphasis on assisting in the development of a credible, domestic electoral monitoring group that received accreditation from the national government to periodically monitor elections. On multiple occasions, this group validated the electoral victories of the Chávez government and its supporters through 2004 and beyond.

As years went on, relations between the NDI and the government generally frayed, mimicking broader dynamics involving the US-Venezuela relationship. While it is true that the NDI sometimes reached out to the government, the lion's share of their work went into training, strategizing, and enhancing the capabilities of prominent opposition political parties, such as Primero Justicia (PJ), Acción Democrática (AD), and Un Nuevo Tiempo (UNT). Training was directed at national party leadership, regional leadership, youth and student wings of the party, and, in more recent years, for the cultivation of women leaders in these parties. NDI staff trained opposition members with an eye toward respective electoral cycles and offered workshops on a range of issues, such as platform development, media engagement, and member recruitment. In the end, analysis of NDI programs generally reveals that their initiatives were highly partisan and geared at assisting the opposition and their electoral prospects.

Strengthening Opposition Political Parties

In 2001 the NDI opened an office in Caracas and began "to implement a project that hope[d] to promote and facilitate the re-engagement of Venezuelan citizens in state-level politics" (NDI 2002a, 1). The rationale behind the NDI's mission included alleged lost "faith in the democratic process," as reflected by the "political rise of former coup leader Hugo Chávez and the demise of traditional political parties" (1). Indeed, this is a striking interpretation of contemporary Venezuelan political life, as Hugo Chávez's candidacy led many formerly disenchanted Venezuelan citizens to come out to the polls in larger numbers than in any recent election. Nonetheless, the NDI called its initial project Re-Engaging Citizens in Local-Level Politics, and, in its program description, NDI reports that "the long-term stability of democracy in Venezuela is under threat [due to] the increasing concentration of executive power, the rise of political violence, and dropping oil prices" (2). In addition, the NDI lamented the inability of new political parties and movements to provide successful alternatives to Chávez's Bolivarian vision. The NDI reported that to "help salvage democracy, an effective political party system must be rebuilt" (2). For the NDI, President Chávez represented a political-economic problem that required rectification from abroad. In order to contend with these issues, the NDI proposed implementing programs where political parties would work with NGOs to reenergize citizens and help to bring new members into their parties, an objective similar to much of the IRI's work in Venezuela.

Under its first program, the NDI initiated projects with mayors in two municipalities, Baruta and Naguanagua. The NDI signed agreements with Mayor Henrique Capriles (Primero Justicia) in Baruta and Mayor Julio Castillo (Proyecto Venezuela) in Naguanagua. Indeed, this program initiated a long-term relationship with Capriles through to his presidential runs in 2012 and 2013. Altogether, this plan shows how many US government agencies have overlapped in their cooperation. In the instance of both Capriles and Castillo, the IRI and NDI worked with these individuals and their respective parties. In their two municipalities, the NDI planned to increase transparency and citizen participation in local government. In its program report, the NDI (2002a, 3–4) claims that due to their work in Baruta, the local government began conducting its first public hearings regarding zoning laws. The NDI also reported that it planned to help Naguanagua with similar efforts in the future to host public hearings.

In 2002, similar to the IRI, the NDI established a program called Strengthening Political Parties. The NDI (2002b, 1) writes in its program description that Venezuelan political parties have witnessed considerable disapproval and diminishing public confidence. The NDI argues that the only way that traditional political parties in Venezuela can move forward is by understanding why disillusionment continues. In doing so, the group lamented the lack of attention to internal issues within political parties and their diminishing public appeal. Under this program, the NDI conducted focus group research in order to provide Venezuelan political parties with public perceptions of their organizations. Thereafter, the group expected that their research "would then be used to guide party leaders in the modernization and renewal of their organizations" (2). The IRI similarly used this same language to describe their efforts in working with parties: modernization and renewal.

In administering their research, the NDI hired an Argentine organization, Graciela Romer & Associates, to carry out ten focus group interviews involving an equal number of Chavistas and non-Chavistas. The group also conducted fifty interviews with leading journalists and academics concerning the state of political parties in the country. Following the collection of data, the NDI met with the research group in Washington, DC, and then made plans to present the group's research findings to Venezuelan political party leaders. The research group found that polarized political sentiments indeed existed; political parties exacerbated the polarized sociopolitical climate rather than assuaging it, and a sense of fear and apprehension due to societal tension as well as a desire for social order also existed among most Venezuelan citizens (NDI 2002b, 3–6).

Their findings, however, showed that Chavistas and non-Chavistas differed in terms of what sorts of social order they preferred. Generally, while opposition supporters demanded that order remain based around freedom of speech, property rights, and other civil and political rights, Venezuelan government supporters prioritized social and economic rights, such as the encouragement of social justice (NDI 2002b). Despite these divisions between government supporters and the opposition, the research group reported that Venezuelans agreed on a basic belief in democracy as a legitimate form of government. However, these two groups, again, differed in their view concerning democracy, with government supporters emphasizing participatory democracy and opposition members endorsing a more limited political democracy involving rule of law and pluralism. Finally, many supporters and opposition members both viewed a presidential referendum on Chávez as a way out of the polarizing crisis following the 2002 coup d'état and a path forward for the country.

The research group presented their findings to members from each of the national parties, including both government and opposition groups, such as PJ, AD, and COPEI. In addition, their presentations involved suggestions from Genaro Arriagada, former Chilean ambassador to the United States and a former Chilean minister, who held consultations with opposition party leaders and potential opposition presidential candidates. During these consultations, Arriagada pointed out that polarization helps only the government, as it makes the opposition appear petty and unconcerned with moving the country forward in a productive manner (NDI 2002b, 7). He also underscored the importance of building party structures and trying to reach out to Chavistas rather than ignoring them. Similar to IRI activities linking Venezuelan opposition political parties up with esteemed international politicians, the NDI also sought to connect political parties with prominent politicians from abroad, particularly from Latin America.

In the years following the coup d'état, and similar with the IRI, the NED censored the contents of its NDI program descriptions in its Freedom of Information Act (FOIA) releases much more intensively than in years prior. In doing so, the group attempted to shield its activities from public scrutiny and cloak many of their funding recipients. In particular, NDI representatives had become quite upset with the writings of journalist Eva Golinger, who wrote extensively on some of the activities of the NDI around the time of the 2002 coup d'état. In a 2012 meeting with an NDI representative involved in developing programs in Latin America, this individual expressed what I could most accurately describe as disgust, as I had cited Golinger (2006) in my previous written work, which the representative had perused. In fact, I thought the individual might terminate our meeting all together at the outset, due to this citation. This is rather consistent with the positions exhibited by other US state functionaries when this journalist's name arose in other interviews, including one USAID member who described her as "fucking crazy." Nonetheless, we can piece together much of the group's activities from such documents, even though they remain replete with redactions.

Continued Training for Opposition Party Members

In the post–coup d'état period, the NDI continued its Strengthening Political Parties program, wherein the group primarily worked and strategized with the Venezuelan opposition. In their final quarterly report of 2003, for instance, the NDI describes that while they had sought to reach out to both the government and opposition during such heightened times of polarization, the NDI had "played an important role in helping the opposition to become a credible alternative to Chávez" (NDI 2003, 2). All the while, NDI staff encouraged President Chávez to work on rendering his tone more peaceful—that is, in the wake of the coup d'état that temporarily removed him from office.

NDI documents continue to label Chávez's government as characterized by authoritarianism, demonstrated by the pursuit of "controversial land reform measures, politiciz[ing] the judiciary, and attack[ing] his critics in the media" (NDI 2003, 2). As a result, the NDI offered specific recommendations for the opposition amid their push to electorally recall Chávez from office. Similar to the IRI, these recommendations included ensuring internal unity, perhaps through the use of a primary election, focusing on broader issues rather than simply an anti-Chávez discourse, reaching out to young and poor voters during the recall election in order to defeat Chávez, and, most importantly, that they "not return to projecting an image of disunity, disarray, and petty squabbling" (NDI 2003, 3). The latter remained an issue that perpetually plagued the opposition under Chávez, even into the present, with different parties and leaders suggesting different sorts of paths to depose the government. It also remained a continual conversation between US ambassadors and diplomats and Venezuelan opposition politicians (Cablegate 2004a). Under its ensuing programming, the NDI planned to host workshops for opposition members to show them how parties in other countries worked together and formed a coalition against governments in power.

In 2004 the NDI continued to describe the Venezuelan government as characterized by "the populist policies and authoritarian leadership of Hugo Chávez," and, as a result, the NDI planned new programming for the ensuing year (NDI 2004a, 1). In a diplomatic cable, though, Ambassador Charles Shapiro notes that NDI projects "got off to a late start given that the project manager did not assume his position until January, 2004" (Cablegate 2004c). Nonetheless, the NDI embarked upon several initiatives involving its Strengthening Political Parties program. It remains technically true that the group reached out to members of Chávez's party, but much of this work involved asking the government to tone down its rhetoric and attempt to reduce polarization. One high-ranking NDI staff member told me that the NDI indeed had built some forms of relationships with some members in the Chávez government, but there was not much interest in continuing to meet with them after 2003.

Instead, the NDI continued to work with opposition parties who were trying to remove Chávez from office either through a recall election in 2004 and a presidential election in 2006. NDI technical staff continually met with political parties comprising the opposition umbrella group the Coordinadora Democrática (CD) to help strategize with them on their moves toward unity and in their citizen outreach. In addition, NDI staff held seminars with opposition members "present[ing] party renewal experiences, highlighting electoral successes" (NDI 2004b, 3). What is more, the group began assisting the opposition in the development of the technical "preparation for the 2005 legislative elections" (3). At the outset of 2005, the NDI sought to work with opposition parties on their outreach strategy and on how they might grow their membership, including "an internal grassroots training initiative" beginning with a national meeting followed by localized meetings for party members (NDI 2005a, 1).

At the same time, Ambassador William Brownfield cabled back to Washington, describing precisely what the NDI was up to in the country:

> Another component of NDI's strategy is to animate the process of party renovation through rebuilding / strengthening ties between affiliated political blocs in Europe and Venezuela, primarily the Christian Democrats and the Social Democrats. As an example, NDI recently sponsored a visit by Elena Flores, the Latin American Director for the Pablo Iglezias Foundation of the Spanish Workers' Socialist Party. Ms. Flores visited three regional workshops organized by AD whose purpose was to discuss future training plans and party membership. NDI reported that the response by attendees to Ms. Flores motivational discourse was overwhelmingly positive—occasionally tearful—in large part because of her affiliation with the European Social Democratic movement and the sense given to AD membership that they had not been forgotten by their European counterparts. (Cablegate 2005c)

In addition, while the NDI linked Venezuelan parties with likeminded parties in Europe, Brownfield's cables also reveal that the NDI continued to work with many of the same parties it had in recent years: Acción Democrática ("a focus on party organization and political values—such as internal democratization—as a move to reinvigorate AD's once robust but now moribund training program"), COPEI ("an NDI consultant spent a week working with party membership to begin a process of party restructuring"), and Primero Justicia ("possible collaboration on modern techniques of message development and diffusion") (Cablegate 2005c).

Throughout 2005, leading up to the legislative elections, much of the NDI's work remained uniform: working with opposition parties to better enhance their electoral strategies, particularly through party unification, and engaging in a process of party renewal to assist in helping opposition parties broaden their appeal and chip away at Chávez's base of support throughout the country. More specifically, the NDI urged opposition parties to develop "a clear, targeted message to constituents and potential supporters, with particular attention to underrepresented and poor sectors of the population" in their training sessions regarding party platform development (NDI 2005b, 5). Despite all of this, however, the opposition chose to boycott legislative elections in 2005, in an effort to portray Chávez as an authoritarian ruler—a move discouraged by many US government functionaries.

In the wake of the opposition's legislative boycott, the NDI dedicated more efforts to working with the youth and student wings of opposition political parties, such as Acción Democrática and Primero Justicia. In doing so, the group sought "to respond to the need for long-term ... reform and renewal" (NDI 2006a, 3). The NDI developed a three-module program in its work with opposition youth and "to help [them] become catalysts for change ... and revitalize parties' connection with the population" (3). In their first module, the NDI focused on basic issues such as communication, public speaking, and negotiation. In the second module, the NDI emphasized project development, and, in the third module, the group focused on strategic planning (1, 3). Offering more insight into the long-term goals of the program, US Deputy Chief of Mission Kevin Whitaker cabled Washington, writing that the NDI, alongside the IRI, is working with youth, who "will participate in a program to prepare them for a run at local council seats and/or mayorships in 2008" (Cablegate 2006k).

This period also led to the recognition among NDI staff that the political party Un Nuevo Tiempo (UNT) had become the leading group among the opposition. Indeed, it was their member, Governor Manuel Rosales, who had unsuccessfully run against Chávez in the presidential election in 2006. Following Chávez's presidential reelection, the NDI reveals it had more intensively began to work with UNT as well as PJ (NDI 2007). Youth leadership workshops continued during this period but also more general work with opposition parties. NDI conducted leadership workshops with UNT and PJ members, and, as an apparent result of their work, the NDI reported that "UNT had approved new ... structures aimed at improving internal democracy and transparency," and that both "UNT and PJ ... took concrete steps to improve internal communications through the development of a communication network" (NDI 2007, 4). The NDI also reports that opposition youth improved their internal democratic structures and began to develop more concrete policy proposals to bring to their parties' attention (4).

All of these efforts, while seemingly mundane, align with the NDI's strategy of long-term renewal and growth of opposition political parties to help them to enhance their infrastructure and better connect with constituents. That is, the NDI and opposition parties worked together to better enhance their capacity to undermine Chávez and his allies. Such interest was not only confined to the ballot box, either. Deputy of Chief of Mission Kevin Whitaker, for instance, reports that UNT member Gerardo Blyde told several US diplomats stationed in Venezuela that UNT was seeking "IRI and NDI leadership training for popular network members that they want to insert into community councils ... [which might] give the UNT a foothold within poorer neighborhoods ... they believe they can best disrupt Chavez's plans from inside, rather than by not participating" (Cablegate 2007g). Whether or not, the NDI and the IRI explicitly agreed to this sort of training, however, is not clear, but work with UNT and other opposition groups surely persisted.

In late 2007 the NDI reports that many political parties remained focused on defeating Chávez's then-proposed constitutional amendments, and, as a result, they postponed their scheduled workshops with the opposition for early 2008. Indeed, the referendum in late 2007 became the only real electoral loss Chávez faced throughout his time in office. With the end of the electoral cycle, the NDI continued much of the same, long term–oriented work that it had previously committed to—both with students and youth, and national party leadership among the opposition. The NDI reports that it "conducted a multiparty youth leadership workshop" in early 2008 to help youth members become familiar with their parties' history and ideology, as well as to help them establish communications networks (NDI 2008a). In addition, the NDI helped opposition youth develop press releases so that they might use them moving toward state and municipal elections in 2008, the electoral cycle that the NDI had long had its eye on with regarding the development of its youth leadership programs.

In the lead up to the November 2008 elections, the NDI (2008b) also helped to work with opposition members on their media outreach and their message development. The group reviewed media guidelines with them and then held, taped, and reviewed mock interviews with opposition members to help train them for upcoming elections. From April to July, the group hosted four of these particular workshops with opposition members. During this same period, the NDI also reports that it continued to work with youth members from PJ, in addition to other opposition parties, on internal democratic reforms within their respective parties. While workshops did not include government members, the NDI reports that it reached out to members of the government to discuss what sorts of projects it had undertaken within the country. However, the year 2008 would become a turning point in US-Venezuela relations as it featured the beginning of such relations becoming characterized by the absence of respective ambassadors, after Chávez expelled the US ambassador in a display of solidarity with the Bolivian government, who had also claimed there was recent US intervention in the country.

As the November elections concluded, the NDI notes that many opposition members succeeded in elections, and, as a result, "many political parties now face an increased need for practical assistance on local governance best practices" (NDI 2008c, 5). Moving into 2009 and 2010, the NDI reports that it planned on working with opposition parties to enhance their governance strategies. In addition, given that recent legislation mandated 50 percent participation of women candidates on political party lists, the NDI planned "to help parties identify and develop women candidates" (5). Still, many of the workshops the group reported conducting appear relatively similar to previous years, including workshops on leadership, political participation, and communications strategies (NDI 2009, 4). However, some of their political participation workshops expressly involved women from opposition political parties (4).

In the final document released to me from 2010, the NDI continues to claim that Chávez's actions have led to "the erosion of democratic institutions and processes" (NDI 2010, 1). Consistent with previous programming, NDI workshops continued to focus on communication, outreach, leadership, and public management (2). Workshops helped participants craft press statements, recruit new party members, and identify party leaders in order to assist the opposition in the development of their organizational infrastructure. As in earlier periods and even more increasingly, government interactions also remained minimal through 2010. Yet, one NDI staff member told me in an interview that while relations were generally tenuous, some government members, such as Calixto Ortega, a Venezuelan diplomat stationed in the United States, maintained some dialogue with the United States. In particular, when the Venezuelan government pursued legislation placing limitations on foreign funding for NGOs in 2010, the subject of a later chapter, some members of the Venezuelan government allegedly told NDI staff that they were not necessarily concerned with NDI funding. Indeed, one high-ranking NDI staffer told me that he believed Venezuelan government criticism of the NDI did not arise out of fear of the consequentiality of this funding, but to drum up nationalist support. Nonetheless, the NDI decided to close their Venezuelan offices in 2011 because, as one high-ranking staffer told me, they were going to trust the law over an informal conversation and did not want to become subject to fines and penalties while in the country. In the end, though, these developments have not resulted in the absolute termination of their funding for programs inside Venezuela. Instead, the NDI developed a virtual program to engage with members of the Venezuelan opposition from abroad.

Training the Opposition in the Use of Social Media and Technology

Following the death of President Hugo Chávez in 2013 and the election of President Nicolás Maduro, the NDI received nearly $300,000 for a project called Improved Training and Communication Skills for Political Activists, a project which has seemingly persisted into the near present. The program description begins by stating that "Political activists in Venezuela confront increased threats, intimidation, and abuses of power by state institutions, as well as restrictions on their ability to present alternative views to citizens" (NDI 2013, 1). Instead, the NDI report notes that social media has offered an alternative outlet for activists opposed to the government; however, the issue remained, according to NDI, that many "local activists have limited exposure to ICT [information and communications technologies] best practices and are in need [of] additional technical assistance and support in order to effectively use of [sic] social media and other information and communications technologies (ICTs) to overcome the challenges they face in Venezuela" (1). The report moves on to claim that Chávez "dismantled democratic principles" including by passing constitutional referenda allowing for indefinite reelection, concentrating power in the executive, and "us[ing] state funds in support of his Bolivarian partisan agenda" (1). In addition, the NDI reports that Maduro's recent presidential victory remained "slim and disputed," a claim only advanced by the US government and the Venezuelan opposition.

This particular program was established specifically in the lead-up to municipal elections in 2013 in order to assist activists in developing and crafting their messages. The NDI reported that they would "host a seminar outside Venezuela on the use of technology and social media for citizen outreach and engagement" for a number of its participants from the country that "would take place prior to the December 8 municipal elections" (NDI 2013, 2). Thereafter, the group reports that their Venezuelan participants would be introduced to the NDI Virtual Toolbox hosted on a particular website (redinnovacion.org), offering "online customized capacity-building courses on a range of issues relating to political innovation. After the seminar, this platform would allow participants to review the course materials, interact with one another, and solicit feedback from the instructor" (2–3). The ultimate purpose of the seminar, however, "would include strategic planning sessions facilitated by NDI consultants during which all the seminar participants would design strategies for online citizen outreach, engagement, and information disseminator for the December municipal elections" (3).

In an area of the program, Red Innovación encouraged participants to write short papers on the importance of transparency throughout Latin America. In one submission, youth opposition activist Gerardo López, a member of the opposition party Primero Justicia, authored a piece titled "Ideas para mejorar la Transparencia y accountability de la gestión pública, caso Venezuela." While the content of the submission remains vague and generally denounces widespread political and judicial corruption, Lopez's submission indicates how NDI/Red Innovación programs featured involvement of members from prominent opposition parties within Venezuela.

Following municipal elections in December, the NDI sought to continue working with opposition activists through its Red Innovación virtual forum. NDI members hosted another session with "seminar participants in Venezuela to develop longer-term strategies to maintain contact with citizens and improve their ability to communicate and disseminate information using ICTs" (NDI 2013, 4). The NDI specifically planned to work with eight participants and to provide them with individualized virtual coaching and regular access to NDI staff and NDI-hired consultants in order to best provide them with the tools requested by the participants. Perhaps most telling of all, the NDI featured an article on its Red Innovación website detailing the NDI's specific initiatives involving ICT assistance for political parties abroad. Within the article, the NDI presents a case study involving the Venezuelan opposition's use of ICT technologies. Again, this was the express purpose of the NDI/Red Innovación program in Venezuela: to train opposition activists in the better use of social media and information technology in order to reach voters. In their article, the NDI details how the Mesa de la Unidad Democrática (MUD), Venezuela's opposition coalition founded in 2008, made significant advances within the country through their use of social media and technology, particularly in 2015, just shortly after this NDI program commenced and developed.

In its case study, the NDI underscores how the MUD developed a new voter database and a new outreach strategy using social media (NDI 2015). Specifically, the MUD plan included:

1. Creating a database of voters to identify soft Partido Socialista Unido de Venezuela (PSUV) supporters and swing voters;

2. Organizing the voters in the database into specific categories for targeted messaging to more effectively use limited financial resources;

3. Using social media campaigns for outreach and voter mobilization to respond to closing access to traditional media outlets such as newspapers, radio and television;

4. Building greater consensus among the parties that make up the MUD regarding a multiparty communication platform to help design common strategies, information and messages within the framework of a unified communications strategy; and

5. Training the mid-level and regional communications structures of the parties that make up the MUD in the use of new technologies for political communications (NDI 2015).

In doing so, the group calculated the probability that an individual might vote for the opposition, the government, or remain undecided, and, thereafter, created their voter database. Following this initiative, the NDI reports that the MUD worked through Facebook to contact voters. For voters already aligned with the opposition, the MUD simply sought to target them with a get-out-the-vote type of message. For those aligned with the government, they sought to target them "with information about PSUV candidates designed to draw them across the aisle" (NDI 2015). The NDI also notes that these efforts were developed across two years, since 2013, the year in which NDI developed their Red Innovación program.

In later years, this same forum continued to broadcast opposition initiatives and provided a platform for opposition activists. In March 2017, for instance, the site hosted a presentation titled "Estrategia y organización electoral de una coalición política" from opposition activist Juan Mijares. Throughout 2012 and 2013, Mijares served as opposition candidate Henrique Capriles's campaign coordinator, primarily tasked with examining and using polling data. In the wake of Capriles's defeat, Mijares also headed an opposition initiative termed Comando Venezuela to try to make sense of the October 2012 electoral defeat of Capriles in its aftermath. In his 2017 presentation, Mijares detailed successful and unsuccessful opposition strategies to combat the Chávez government for participants, particularly within the Capriles campaign. Although no presentation remains of the event, the NDI also featured Marino Gonzalez, a former technical coordinator of the MUD, to discuss coalition-building strategies among the opposition within the Venezuela.

Electoral Monitoring

In 2003 USAID provided the NDI with $770,000 for a program called Ensuring Credible Elections, with aims "to support the establishment of a domestic electoral observation organization that [would be] widely perceived as credible and impartial by a majority of Venezuelans" (Cablegate 2005d). Ojo

Electoral, which the US embassy described as "a consortium of individuals and groups affiliated with both the government and the opposition," became the group that the NDI would work with (Cablegate 2005d). The group established a board composed of members that spanned the political spectrum, including former Chavista minister Carlos Genatios, as well as two columnists from the opposition-leaning newspaper *El Nacional*. Ojo Electoral, however, limited the NDI's assistance to the group due to concerns that might arise regarding their credibility. The group feared that too much assistance from a US government group might make their organization appear biased in their approach to Venezuelan politics. Instead of direct financial funding for office equipment, the group decided only to receive consultation and training on electoral monitoring from the NDI.

The Venezuelan National Electoral Council (CNE) accredited Ojo Electoral to first observe the August 2004 recall referendum on President Chávez. During this election, the group deployed 110 observers and provided a quick count of the electoral results that favored Chávez (Lean 2012, 100). Following this, the CNE provided Ojo Electoral with credentials to monitor the October 2004 regional elections and worked with them on verifying the final results. The CNE allowed over 400 Ojo Electoral observers to participate in conjunction with the NDI in seven states throughout the country (Cablegate 2005d). Observers qualitatively monitored polling stations and polling practices, and, again, audited the results and provided a quick count of them, verifying the success of pro-government parties in the regional elections.

USAID provided funding for this program through June 2007; thereafter, retitling the program Supporting Transparent Electoral Processes, a program that ran until at least October 2010. USAID released documents to the author, but, as with many other releases, these documents were heavily redacted. Nonetheless, they seemingly show that the NDI continued funding Ojo Electoral to receive training to monitor elections and thereafter to take on a primary role in electoral monitoring throughout Venezuela. US diplomat Stephen McFarland cabled that the NDI planned to host a workshop for Ojo Electoral participants in April 2005 with specialists from several countries, including Colombia, Guatemala, and Mexico, reporting that they were developing a "workshop in Caracas with Latin American political specialists—including the participation of Ojo observers from around the country. Topics will include: electoral observation in general, issues related to recent Venezuelan electoral events, electronic voting, experiences with dialogue in highly polarized environments, and experiences of organizations that have come under attack by their governments. In addition to the exchange of technical information, this event is also intended to motivate / encourage members of Ojo, as well as serve as a forum for publicizing the presence and work of Ojo" (Cablegate 2005b). Publicizing Ojo Electoral's work was particularly important so that they might receive additional funding. McFarland reports that the NDI sought to assist the group in securing additional funding from foreign state sources, such as the European Union, Canada, and Norway, asserting that "even symbolic donations would be useful both for providing political cover as well as priming the pump for other donations" (Cablegate 2005b). In doing so, McFarland suggests that while the United States became a key ally and force behind the group, it would help if they could demonstrate that they were not a US government puppet, by demonstrating how they had received funding from a multiplicity of international sources.

While many IRI and NDI programs primarily involved the Venezuelan opposition and even sought to undermine government efforts, we find quite a different outcome in the instance of Ojo Electoral. In this instance, we find that the NDI helped to establish an organization that verified electoral results that bolstered the legitimacy of the Venezuelan government. And so, in some instances, if we take the premise that US democracy-promoting agencies have sought to undermine the Venezuelan government, their efforts have not always had their intended effect. By contrast, some of these efforts have had the reverse effect of strengthening the Venezuelan government, its democratic credentials, and its claims to legitimacy.

Beyond Ojo Electoral, however, the NDI primarily worked with opposition groups in their quest to undermine Chávez and his allies at the ballot box. Although some dialogue existed between NDI staff and the Venezuelan government, this proved the exception to the rule that the NDI primarily funded and worked with opposition political parties such as AD and PJ. As with the IRI, the NDI is thus in no way acted as a nonpartisan force within the country. Rather, it worked to embolden the opposition and assist in their success at the ballot box. What is more, both IRI and NDI efforts show that US government efforts are not always success. In Venezuela, President Chávez regularly succeeded and only faced a serious defeat during a constitutional referendum in 2009.

Chapter 6

PROMOTING FREE MARKET ECONOMICS AND TRADITIONAL LABOR UNIONS IN CHÁVEZ'S VENEZUELA

During the years of the Chávez government, the US government worked on many fronts to boost the capabilities of domestic actors opposed to President Hugo Chávez's public policies, including within the country's business and labor communities. While the International Republican Institute (IRI) and the National Democratic Institute (NDI) worked with opposition political parties and to a lesser extent on issues of electoral observation, the US government also sought to enhance the efforts of groups opposed to the Chávez government and its policies within the business and labor community, too. Traditionally, the US Agency for International Development (USAID) has operated as the premier US foreign policy arm focused on economic development. However, on account of its oil wealth, Venezuela has existed as a middle-income country and has not required much bilateral or multilateral assistance, until recently, facing a severe economic crisis under the current government of Nicolás Maduro, Hugo Chávez's successor.

Instead of working through traditional economic development programs, the US government has worked through the Center for International Private Enterprise (CIPE), a subgrantee of the National Endowment for Democracy (NED), to promote free market, capitalist policies in the country. Indeed, the promotion of free market economics plays an integral role in what the US government promotes abroad. Through CIPE, the US government has sought to promote such ideas through, for example, support for a large think tank and its initiatives, including the use of radio programs and legislative analyses, as well as through training programs for poor Venezuelans so that they might embrace free market economics. I show how the US government through the Solidarity Center (SC)—the international arm of the American Federation of Labor and Congress of Industrial Organizations (AFL-CIO)—has worked with labor groups expressly opposed to Chávez government policies, including worker councils and worker cooperatives. Indeed, the SC provided groups with training in ways to push back against Chávez and even provided funding for a conference to help a newfound, seemingly nonpartisan labor group establish itself.

Before analyzing CIPE and SC programs, however, I briefly describe how some US government functionaries, including former ambassadors to Venezuela, actively lobbied Venezuelan government members to abandon state interventionist policies and implement free market reforms similar to other US-aligned countries throughout Latin America. US diplomats continually sought to encourage President Chávez to follow policies promoted by the US government in earlier years, falling under the umbrella of the Washington Consensus. These recommendations included an emphasis on trade liberalization, privatization of industry, and deregulation of markets. Nonetheless, as former diplomats revealed to me, Chávez remained uninterested in such US policy recommendations and, as a result, this rendered CIPE and SC programs all the more important for US government functionaries to assist Venezuelan domestic actors in pushing back against Chávez government policies.

Diplomatic Interactions

Throughout President Hugo Chávez's tenure in office, and in interviews with the author, high-ranking US government elites discussed how they urged President Chávez to follow a free market rather than state interventionist or socialist path. Although economic development programs were largely absent from the country, US government elites still sought to promote economic reforms during their meetings with Venezuelan government officials. This included former US ambassadors and other diplomats who operated out of the US embassy and the US Department of State.

For instance, several US government elites claimed that they continually lobbied successive US presidential administrations to take the perceived threat that Chávez posed seriously. One former high-ranking Department of State official told me that the "more capitalist countries there are, the better it is for the US I had to remind people of this. We were using taxpayers' money, and I had to remind them." For him, the problem was clear: given the middle-income nature of Venezuela, "one of the major problems was that [the United States] couldn't promote economic policies. We had no economic growth programs." As a result, the Department of State was limited in its capacity to promote economic reforms in the country, and this Department of State official recognized this as a serious problem: "If [Chávez] didn't have any money, fine. But he was sitting on the oil, and this was a problem for us . . . We would say [to the administration]: 'It's not the Middle East, but it's not good to have that problem in our backyard.'"

This official quite plainly uses the same language deployed by early US government members who understood Latin America and the Caribbean as the proverbial "backyard" of the United States (Fitz 2017; Grandin 2006; Horsman 1981). Within such imagery, the region, understood as "the backyard" of country, becomes something that requires US government tutelage lest it become unmanageable. For this official, there is no consideration of the fact that Venezuelans voted Chávez and his allies into power perceivably in part as a result of the political-economic policies promoted by them. Instead, the only considerations that matter include the threat posed by the Venezuelan government to US global hegemony. Given that Venezuela contains vast supplies of energy resources, this US government official recognized that Venezuela could potentially influence other countries, both with its economic supplies and its counter-hegemonic project to create, in the words of Chávez, a multipolar world. For this individual, these were serious problems that demanded the attention of the US president.

Yet, while the Department of State could not work through technical programs to promote reforms in Venezuela, high-ranking diplomats, including US ambassadors, directly pressed for reforms in their conversations and interactions with Chávez and other high-ranking Venezuelan state members. One former US ambassador during the Chávez years explained his understanding of US policy in the country to me quite clearly in a personal interview. This individual pointed out that "economic and trade interests, obviously they're there . . . I don't know how to tell you this, but the US is a capitalist system, and that what's we do, and that's what makes our country great."

More specifically, I asked the former ambassador about the promotion of economic reforms, and, whether or not, it remained true that the US government promoted free market policies in Venezuela under President Chávez. In response, he told me that it was "abso-fucking-lutely true . . . [The Venezuelan government] uses neo-stupid economics . . . You bet. You damn, ass bet that US embassies around the world are trying to encourage developing world countries and host countries to follow economic policy which is sound and attracts foreign investment and makes the GDP grow and achieves economic inclusion and social inclusion. Those that followed the Washington Consensus are better, and poverty rates are dropping." Though economic and social inclusion does not necessarily correspond with free market reforms, the former ambassador references the Washington Consensus here, which refers to the economic policies that the United States encouraged throughout Latin America during the 1980s and 1990s. In a word, the Washington Consensus is simply shorthand for free market economic policies, such as privatization, trade liberalization, and deregulation of markets—or even, more parsimoniously, as little state intervention into the economy as possible.

Given Chávez's antipathy for the US government and its paternalism, though, the former ambassador pointed out that as a point of strategy he did not pressure Chávez to imitate US economic policies. Instead, he said that he "met Chávez and spoke for hours. I encouraged Chávez to please go to Chile and see how they brought down poverty. Don't mimic the US, look at Chile, talk to them . . . [but he had] zero interest." Despite all efforts, he said that the Venezuelan government remained undeterred by US admonitions to follow a more free market–oriented path. Instead, Chávez remained intent on a path moving toward what he termed *twenty-first century socialism*, even intensifying such efforts until his death in 2013.

Indeed, this former ambassador, similar to the previous former Department of State official, expressed incredulity and even anger regarding Chávez and his political-economic vision. Both individuals, as one might infer from their commentary, grew heavily animated in these discussions to the point of seeming fury with the direction of Venezuela under Chávez. Such dispositions were common among US government elites who I interviewed throughout the course of my research. For them, it seemed apparent that US government functionaries understood the proper and correct way to run an economy and to run a government. In discussions, there was no attempt to understand why Chávez and why Venezuelan citizens might believe in the possibility of socialist economic reforms. Among US political elites working in and on issues of Venezuela, there was no mistaking the nature of their true belief in the rectitude of US policy recommendations. In the instance of Venezuela, Chávez pursued "neo-stupid" economics, and, in the least, presented a regional "problem" for the US government that required intervention beyond diplomatic conversation and urgings.

Enter CIPE

Alongside the National Endowment for Democracy (NED), the Center for International Private Enterprise (CIPE) was founded in 1983 as the international arm of the US Chamber of Commerce. The US Chamber of Commerce (n.d.) describes itself as the "world's largest business organization representing the interests of more than 3 million businesses of all sizes, sectors, and regions," as well as an "advocate for pro-business policies that create jobs and grow our economy." Among the ideas they promote, the group has championed private enterprise, trade liberalization, global trade, and deregulation of the economy—all of which are hallmarks of free market capitalism. Indeed, the US Chamber of Commerce exists solely to advocate for private sector business interests.

CIPE delineates the organization's core objectives on their website in a similar manner. CIPE reports that it remains governed by "the idea that economic freedom and political freedom are intertwined and that progress and development comes through a combination of political and economic liberalization" (CIPE n.d.). In addition, the group contends that "countries need to build market-oriented and democratic institutions simultaneously, as they are essentially two sides of the same coin. Without a functioning market system, democracies will remain weak. Likewise, without a democratic process, economic reforms are unlikely to succeed" (CIPE n.d.). CIPE thus links the concepts of democracy and market economies together and claims that the two are inextricably bound. In CIPE's vision, democracy and capitalism cannot exist without the other. In other words, democracy will fail if free market economics are not simultaneously pursued. In keeping with this perspective, CIPE has provided assistance to business groups and other organizations that promote private enterprise, trade liberalization, and, in general, less state intervention into domestic economies. In doing so, the congressionally funded organization asserts that they are also promoting democracy alongside these free market economic policies.

CIPE remains the one US democracy-promoting agency fully focused on economic reforms. Through CIPE, the US government has continually promoted free market economic policies throughout the world, such as trade liberalization and privatization of formerly nationalized industries within the former Soviet Union. In the view of CIPE, free market societies should enhance the well-being of all societal inhabitants by providing them access to an array of goods and services. That is, free market societies are expected to benefit all individuals, not exclusively one particular class. For CIPE functionaries, economic freedom and political freedom will bolster one another, and, in doing so, strengthen broader possibilities of freedom throughout entire societies. To promote these ideas, CIPE has historically provided funding to civil society groups abroad to internally encourage them within respective countries.

Under the Chávez government, CIPE primarily worked with el Centro de Divulgación del Conocimiento Económico para la Libertad, or the Center for the Dissemination of Economic Knowledge for Liberty (CEDICE). CIPE funded CEDICE for a range of projects that generally championed the promotion of private property rights and free market capitalism. CEDICE representatives, for example, criticized a number of pieces of legislation and policies enacted by President Chávez, including the 2001 Land Law, which allowed the Venezuelan government to expropriate unused land held by large rural land owners; the 2001 Hydrocarbons Law, which allowed for greater executive control over the oil industry; and price controls for basic commodities. In later years, though, from which I received documents from a Freedom of Information Act (FOIA) request, CIPE diversified its recipients and began to fund additional groups also focused on promoting free market economic thought in the country, including one project involving training explicitly for poor Venezuelans so that they, too, might embrace free market economics.

CIPE at Work in Venezuela

Since the beginning of Hugo Chávez's presidency, CIPE partnered with CEDICE, a Venezuelan nongovernmental organization (NGO) whose stated mission is to "disseminate, train, investigate and defend the principles of the free market and individual liberty, [and] to construct a society of free and responsible people" (CEDICE n.d.). From its office in Caracas and through its website, CEDICE sells books and pamphlets from free market luminaries. When I briefly visited CEDICE's headquarters while in Caracas, a glass case at the entrance of its offices featured available titles from libertarian economists, including Friedrich Hayek and Ludwig von Mises. On its website heading, too, CEDICE features a quotation from Hayek: "La única forma de cambiar el curso de la sociedad será cambiando las ideas." This quote encapsulates CEDICE aims in the country: alter the ideological landscape of Venezuela so that individuals and policymakers embrace the free market.

Much of CEDICE's funding is derived from foreign entities, such as CIPE. Over the past several years, CIPE has provided CEDICE with a number of grants for a range of projects focused on the promotion of free market policies. Given continuity between the US democracy assistance community and its recipients, it remains highly probable that funding continues into the present as relations have further deteriorated and as the United States has increasingly allocated more funding for democracy promotion within Venezuela.

Since nearly the inception of the Chávez government, CIPE funded projects in Venezuela designed to impede its agenda. From July 2000 until November 2001, CIPE provided CEDICE with nearly $100,000 for a project called Recasting Liberty: Constitutional Reforms (CIPE 2001). In its trimestral report detailing CEDICE's efforts in Venezuela, CIPE lays out its understanding of Venezuela under Chávez. CIPE describes Chávez as "extremely interventionist in nature [and] limiting individual freedoms," and the group claims that he is "repressing any residual hopes that a transition to a modern, market-oriented economy might yet occur" (CIPE 2001, 58). In this passage, we thus see open criticism of "interventionist" efforts and much praise for a "market-oriented economy." In addition, we also find CIPE using the language of "modernity" and suggesting that Venezuela under Chávez is somehow regressing into an unmodern or unenlightened state of existence. As a result, CIPE seemingly believes that the country requires assistance and support, and even tutelage, from CIPE in order for Venezuela to advance toward "modernity" and away from the path preferred by Chávez.

Given this situation in Venezuela, CIPE explains why it has elected to fund CEDICE in the first place. The organization claims that CEDICE's overarching aim has been to shift "the debate away from populist rhetoric and toward concrete reforms that will encourage individual initiative, private enterprise and participatory democracy" (CIPE 2001, 58). Interestingly, CIPE deploys the same language of "participatory democracy" as the Venezuelan government, but instead of policies involving community councils, nationalization of industry, and the redistribution of income and wealth, CIPE talks about "individual initiative" and "private enterprise"—two classic, ideological hallmarks of free market economic thought.

CIPE more specifically identifies its objectives in working with CEDICE, writing that their objectives were designed "to encourage members of the new Congress to ensure all economic reform legislation be carefully studied and that they seek *expert opinion of private sector groups* as part of their review process; to encourage participation in a framework of democratic governance and foster community support for *market oriented economic reforms*; and *to increase the effectiveness of these private sector participants* in implementing a new legislative agenda by inviting regional and international guests to attend project activities and observing their outcome" (CIPE 2001, 58; my emphasis). CIPE and CEDICE objectives are nowhere more explicit. What these two groups pushed for through their joint initiatives was to promote a free market–based economy, in contrast with an economy in which the Chávez government heavily intervened, and they wanted to ensure that private sector elites possessed access to decision-makers and decision-making processes within the country. In the end, in an attempt "to shift the debate" and achieve these objectives in Venezuela, CEDICE organized several national and regional forums on particular pieces of Venezuelan legislation, namely those related to labor, the Venezuelan tax code, social security, and unused rural lands, and, within these forums, CIPE included Venezuelan legislators from both the government and the opposition, local and foreign experts, local business persons, and local NGO representatives during its discussions.

During these forums, CEDICE advocated for a number of reforms largely in line with its political-economic ideology. However, not all their recommendations contained the standard free market economic bend toward privatization and deregulation. Some of CEDICE's proposed changes to the Venezuelan tax code included intensifying penalties against tax evaders and against individuals that assist with tax crimes as well as a recommendation to develop clear tax rules to alleviate any ambiguity concerning how taxation works in Venezuela (CIPE 2001, 60). In doing so, CEDICE, in part, sought to rectify a perpetual problem in Venezuela: individual tax collection. As the Venezuelan government has historically relied upon oil and energy rents, it has not prioritized the taxation of its individual citizens and other domestic businesses as a primary source of revenue.

Elsewhere, though, CEDICE proposed recommendations boasting the importance of the free market, with as little state intervention as possible. Concerning rural land holdings, for instance, CEDICE called for the "full respect for private property," and the group rejected the government's mission to expropriate rural lands from large landholders under the 2001 Land Law (CIPE 2001, 60). CEDICE, for example, sponsored a forum with the National Federation of Cattle Owners to discuss government legislation. In the forum, CEDICE leaders emphasized the importance of private property rights in the face of government attempts to expropriate properties, and its members encouraged cattle owners to contest these policies. CEDICE also sought to meet with and lobby Venezuelan legislators "on the fundamental values of freedom, democracy, the market, and legal security as the basis for preparing sound reforms" (59). Interestingly, these meetings included not only visits with opposition legislators but also a visit with President Nicolás Maduro, who was then head of the National Assembly's Social Security Commission, demonstrating that the Chávez government maintained at least some level of dialogue with groups critical of their policies during the early years of his presidency.

During 2000–2001, CEDICE produced regular bulletins and newsletters for legislators, businesspeople, and the media, detailing their positions on particular legislative issues. This is a practice that continues into the present and involves recurrent critique of the Venezuelan government's now explicitly socialist economic model. Similar to the present, CEDICE bulletins critiqued the Venezuelan government's economic policies during the early years of Chávez's presidency. CEDICE bulletins, for instance, possessed titles in keeping with the group's views on particular pieces of legislation, including "Land Ownership Bill: A Trustworthiness Problem," which criticized the 2001 Land Law for violating private property rights, as well as other titles such as "Property Rights a Key to Development" (CIPE 2001, 33). What is more, CEDICE reprinted articles and ideas from CIPE leaders such as John Zemko, regional director for Latin America and the Caribbean, who authored a piece on reducing the Venezuelan informal economy and stimulating investment "directly linked to private property" (33).

In addition to its bulletins, CEDICE targeted national and local media and engaged in what it termed an "Op-Ed Campaign," wherein it mobilized its resident experts to provide analysis in line with their political-economic perspective (CIPE 2001, 61). These analyses included articles in national media outlets, including *El Universal* and *El Nacional*, condemning the Land Law, urging pension reforms similar to those established in Chile in the 1980s under right-wing military dictator General Augusto Pinochet, and criticizing President Chávez's general style of governing and his inclination toward intervention into the economy. Local Venezuelan businessman and CEDICE leader Aurelio Concheso authored several of these opinion pieces as well. Into the present, Concheso remains a cherished member of the extended US foreign policy community. CIPE, for instance, has featured an interview with him on their podcast, and the group has also included him as a member within their Free Enterprise and Democracy Network. In addition, the NED and CIPE have continued to invite Concheso to speak alongside NED president Carl Gershman at events hosted in Washington, DC, with titles such as "Defending Liberal Democracy in Emerging Markets: The Role of Free Markets and Rule of Law" in January 2017, illustrating CIPE's continued support for free market reforms (CIPE 2017).

The April 2002 coup d'état that temporarily deposed President Chávez from office paralyzed much activity in Venezuela throughout 2002 and leading into 2003. Amid the tumult, CIPE provided CEDICE with over $50,000 for a project called Building Consensus on a National Agenda, which would run from September 2002 until September 2003. CIPE reports that its programmatic objectives included "develop[ing] a viable agenda for Venezuela to solve its current national political and economic crisis, to engage business groups and civil society organizations in the development and advocacy of this agenda before public policymakers, [and] to educate local leaders, entrepreneurial organizations, and labor unions to gain their support for the national agenda" (CIPE 2002a, 20). CEDICE planned to host several meetings with business leaders from Fedecámaras—the Venezuela Federation of Chambers of Commerce; labor leaders from the Confederación de Trabajadores de Venezuela (CTV), a national union historically linked with opposition political parties and receiving US government funding from the Solidarity Center; several Catholic Church leaders; and several media and civil society leaders to devise policy papers describing their recommendations for the advancement of the country. Altogether, CEDICE planned to consult with leaders from various organizations affiliated with the Venezuelan political opposition. Indeed, leaders from both Fedecámaras and the CTV played an active role in the protests and eventual coup d'état. In fact, Pedro Carmona, head of the Fedecámaras, served as interim president of Venezuela until loyalist soldiers and citizens brought Chávez back to power.

Following CEDICE-led meetings with these leaders, the group planned to distribute its findings through several media outlets, including national newspapers *El Nacional* and *El Universal*, and cable television station Globovisión (CIPE 2002a, 21). In addition, CEDICE planned to host ten workshops throughout the country in order to share its findings and recommendations on the Venezuelan economy, and it planned to have several individuals that helped to devise their policy documents lobby the Venezuelan legislature on its behalf. The organization linked up with Fedecámaras to host six of these workshops on their documents throughout several regional states and included around one hundred participants in each workshop (CIPE 2002b, 47).

Experts from CEDICE ultimately prepared three documents written by three university professors focused on political-economic changes within

Venezuela. These policy papers included "Reconstruction of the Republic of Venezuela" by Emeterio Gómez, "A Programmatic Agenda of National Reconstruction" by Maxim Ross, and "Bases for a Pact to Rescue the Republic" by Thaelman Urgelles. In his report, Gómez, an economics professor at the Central University of Venezuela, applauded free market reforms and linked their contributions to liberal democracy (CIPE 2002a). Specifically, he advocated for limiting government intervention into the control of natural resources, he criticized protectionism and financial policies such as price controls, and he generally promoted private enterprise as well as free markets in lieu of state interventionist policies. In addition, Gómez recommended that Venezuela should embrace the macroeconomic stability policies promoted under the Washington Consensus, but he added that more attention should be paid to reducing poverty and inequality (CIPE 2002a). Similarly, Ross, also an economics professor, promoted several standard free market policies: decentralization of political-economic power and individual liberties (CIPE 2002a). The guiding thread throughout all of these documents included the reduction of government involvement in the economy and the promotion of private enterprise as a way to eliminate poverty and inequality in Venezuela. In all instances, these scholars criticized government involvement in the economy, and asserted that free market policies would best serve the country.

CEDICE's policy document and its plans were monitored and closely read by members of the Venezuelan Coordinadora Democrática (CD), an overarching opposition organization composed of CTV, Fedecámaras, civil society leaders, and political parties opposed to the Chávez government. In other words, the CD was composed of those same groups and individuals that partook in organizing CEDICE's general plans—with the exception of opposition political parties. And while CEDICE formulated policy recommendations for the future of Venezuela, the CD itself became a key organization behind mobilization efforts to push Chávez into a recall referendum election on his presidency in 2004. Indeed, following the completion of CEDICE's policy proposals, the CD released a 117-page booklet as a plan for a transitional government should Chávez lose the 2004 referendum election. The CD titled their document *Consenso País* (Country Consensus), a title quite similar to CEDICE's originally titled document: *Building Consensus on a National Agenda*.

In addition to these efforts, in 2002–2003 CIPE provided CEDICE with over $73,000 for a project called Reducing the Informal Sector in Venezuela. In its program description, CIPE declares that due to President Chávez's "harmful attempt to control Venezuelan civil society institutions through the imposition of economic laws that hamper financial and social development. It is therefore imperative to seek consensus among civil society groups that will help build an alternative vision for Venezuela that will be characterized by greater democratic participation and input" (CIPE 2002c, 70). Since the informal sector composes a large portion of the Venezuelan economy, as it composes a large portion of many Latin American economies, CIPE claimed that informal workers must assist in moving the country forward. What is more, CIPE believed that the existence of the informal sector illustrated that Chávez had enacted laws and regulations that damaged the formal sector, thus leading to a burgeoning informal sector. Altogether, CIPE and CEDICE wanted to call attention to the informal sector as evidence of failed Chavista policies, and, thereafter, the groups wanted to reach out to informal sector leaders, demonstrate how Chávez had failed them, and assist them in joining the formal economy. All the while, they aimed to illustrate the pitfalls of Chávez's policies and encourage informal workers to join the opposition.

In order to reach informal workers, CEDICE reported that it would host ten regional workshops in the states of Lara, Carabobo, Aragua, and Zulia, with twenty-five to thirty informal entrepreneurs. During these meetings, CEDICE leaders planned to present them with their programmatic documents that critiqued Chávez's political-economic policies and pointed the path forward. In addition, CEDICE planned to measure the extent of informality in Venezuela, and, thereafter, the group planned to disseminate information on how informal entrepreneurs could formalize their businesses, and, in doing so, remove themselves from the informal sector of the economy. Finally, CEDICE planned to host several meetings with members from the Venezuelan National Assembly's Commission on Economic and Social Development to discuss their perspective on the informal sector.

In the years following the coup d'état and with the public release of documents detailing the NED and its associated groups' efforts in the country, US state agencies more intensively redacted and guarded their documentation of their activity in the country. However, much as with the IRI and the NDI, it remains possible to see the broader purpose of their funding in Venezuela, and, most certainly, the conceptual politics undergirding their activities. The NED personally released to me documents involving their funding and activities in Venezuela between 2006 and 2013, the subject to which I now turn.

Free Market Education for Poor Venezuelans

In 2006 CIPE supported a newfound program in the country called Venezuela: Educational Program for Community Leaders. Through this program, CIPE planned a six-month-long series of workshops for dozens of citizens in the country with a local partner. In earlier years, Chávez carved out a larger role for the government in Venezuelan society. Beginning in 2005, however, Chávez began to embrace the idea of twenty-first-century socialism. Unsurprisingly, CIPE (2006, 1) took notice, writing in the first paragraph of its program description that

> Venezuela is going through one of the most challenging times in its history. The current government has twenty-first century socialism as its ideological orientation and expanded the role of the state to all realms of social and economic life. The nature of private property is being questioned and there have been a series of property invasions and confiscations. Businesses must operate with price controls, payroll freezes, and many other regulations that create a very difficult environment. The government has instituted an intensive information campaign that challenges concepts of capitalism, free trade, markets, decentralization, and many other fundamental components of modern, prosperous democracies.

As a result of these developments, CIPE believed that it must fund programs to combat Chávez's socialist moves, and, once again, helped to place the country on a "modern" path toward prosperity.

Under this program, CIPE explicitly sought to provide alternatives to socialism and "to educate" individuals in Venezuela about the ills of socialism, particularly individuals "with limited formal education who nevertheless have an important impact in poor and middle income communities" (CIPE 2006, 2). CIPE specifically notes elsewhere that they expect participants will not have completed high school. In doing so, CIPE presents itself and its partner as a sort of savior who will properly educate the uneducated and help them to lead fellow Venezuelans out of the blindness imparted by President Chávez and his socialist propaganda. Indeed, the group makes this explicitly clear, writing that "with this battle of ideas taking place in the country, it is unclear to the average Venezuelan how to improve his or her economic situation without relying on the state. Venezuelans must find a way to rise to this challenge by seeking out new concepts, ideas, information, and examples of what a better world can be. A way must be found to define and present a new vision for the country that incorporates a different set of values, practices and policies" (CIPE 2006, 2). More specifically, CIPE declares that the values that they seek to impart to Venezuelans include "a set of critical values for the development of Venezuela as a nation, including liberty, justice, democracy, free enterprise, individual responsibility and government accountability" (2). In doing so, once again, CIPE presents Venezuelans as incapable of understanding alternatives to Chávez's vision, despite the fact that Venezuela had only embarked on an explicitly socialist path just one year prior. Nonetheless, CIPE presents itself and its partner as working to show Venezuelans the correct and modern path to pursue within the country.

Throughout its course, CIPE's partner held sessions with titles such as "A Long Term Vision for Venezuela," "Company Models," and "Policies to Build a Better Future for Venezuela." The focus of the latter's session reads as follows: "This module concentrates on some of the critical decisions the country must make to establish a sustainable path of sound growth. Some of the policies discussed here include: a) redistribution of power in society to assure appropriate checks and balances; b) integrating into global markets; c) creating an appropriate business climate; d) opening the oil sector to all Venezuelans; e) reforming the social security system; f) imposing fiscal discipline; h) restructuring the state." Altogether, it is quite evident how intensive these sessions, or modules, belabored the superiority of free market economics, including tenets such as "fiscal discipline." Although CIPE planned only "to educate" thirty-five people, they also planned to connect them with "local partners" in their neighborhoods and, in doing so, they claim that "30,000 additional people [will] benefit from this program in the communities where the participants live as they bring to bear what they have learned in the course" (CIPE 2006, 4–5). The group thus believed that this program would become a catalyst for developing support for free market capitalism throughout Venezuela and eventually lead individuals to part from Chávez's base of support and his move toward twenty-first-century socialism.

Free Market Analysis of Legislation

In 2009 CIPE initiated another program seemingly again with CEDICE. In CIPE's newly released documents, however, the group has redacted its recipients' names. Nonetheless, the content of the program coheres quite closely with previous CIPE-CEDICE programming, and CIPE notes that they have worked with this particular group recurrently throughout the early 2000s. CIPE called their new program Venezuela: Promoting Democratic Dialogue through a Legislative & Economic Analysis Program, and allocated funding of nearly $150,000 to run, with future funding, until at least mid-2010. CEDICE for its part indeed maintains a project called Observatorio Económico Legislativo, leaving little doubt about the identity of the recipient. Even more, within its own description, CEDICE uses much of the same language as CIPE in describing its purpose: "Como objetivo contribuir a mejorar *el diálogo democrático*, a través del monitoreo, seguimiento y análisis de las leyes económicas y su impacto, incidir en políticas públicas y dar a conocer la metodología costo-beneficio como instrumento para abogar por una mejor legislación que benefcie [sic] a los ciudadanos" (CEDICE 2015; my emphasis). In its program description, CIPE claims that President Chávez has "push[ed] through laws that threaten the basic rights to freely elect government authorities, the right to own property, the freedom to form associations, and the freedom to pursue individual economic activities" (CIPE 2009, 1). What is more, CIPE claims that "without proper analysis, Venezuelan society has no knowledge of the economic consequences that these laws will have on individual and property rights" (1).

As a result of this perceived situation, CIPE's grantee promises to analyze Venezuelan legislation and to "educate and empower legislators, regional and local authorities, academics and policy experts; the media, student movements, and society in general, by warning against the risk of negative legislation and proposing viable alternatives in a controlled economy" (CIPE 2009, 2). Thus, once again, we find among CIPE's programming that there is a central focus on "educating" Venezuelans on the realities and ills of socialist economic policies. As with the previously described program, CIPE insists that Venezuelans do not really understand what socialism involves, and, as a result, it is up to CIPE and its partners to impart real, true knowledge to them so they can make the correct decision of pushing back against Chávez's political-economic policies and demand a free market economy instead of state interventionist programs. CIPE, in fact, praises the group for how it "has worked to develop strong links with teachers, students, and journalists with a free market philosophy" (2).

With CIPE funding, their recipient specifically planned to release bulletins and analyses, organize periodic events and seminars, and even planned on "establishing a weekly radio program to discuss economic issues" (CIPE 2009, 3). Through its bulletins and analyses, the group planned to communicate its findings to its "database of legislators, regional and local officials, academics, policy experts, student movement representatives, and the media, with the goal of reaching the general public" (3). CIPE also planned to help the group translate their materials into English so that they might also transmit them to the United States. They also planned to host events throughout the country to inform citizens of their findings and to work with a radio station to host a weekly program where they would also discuss their findings. Not coincidentally, during this same timeframe, CEDICE generated *boletíns* (bulletins) on economic-legislative analysis, and hosted events and seminars throughout Venezuela wherein CIPE planned to supply some of their speakers and guests.

CIPE renewed this program with their grantee in both 2011 and 2012 to run through at least through July 2013. In its 2011 program description, CIPE claims that since the program developed, many legislators have used these analyses in their arguments within the National Assembly in an attempt to develop a free market economy (CIPE 2011, 1). They also note that their grantee's "analyses have been widely distributed through events and the media, helping shape public opinion" (1). As under the previous program, CIPE's grantee planned to send analyses "by email to all members of the National Assembly, officials from regional and local governments, public policy experts, business leaders, trade unionists, NGOs, and the media," as well as post them on their website and social media pages (3). CIPE also planned to host conferences and roundtable discussions all throughout the country to publicize and disperse their findings. Lastly, they planned to continue its weekly show with "a radio station serving the greater Caracas area with an approximate listenership of 25,000 people ... broadcasted during rush hour, ensuring high levels of listenership" (3).

In its 2012 program description, CIPE continues to praise their grantee's ability to shape the public conversation, to provide legislators with economic analysis, and to push back against Chávez government policies. CIPE describes their grantee's initiatives as particularly important throughout 2012 as Chávez and opposition candidate and governor Henrique Capriles ran for the presidency. As in previous iterations, CIPE objectives remained unchanged: publication of analyses, public events, and the maintenance a weekly radio show. However, in this cycle, CIPE also planned to help their grantee to train journalists and news editors on economic cost-benefits analyses and how to report and discuss their results. They also planned workshops for "legislative staffers, business leaders, and representatives of civil society organizations to teach them policy advocacy techniques" (CIPE 2012, 2). What is more, CIPE also planned to help their grantee work with "national and international newspapers and magazines" to publicize their ideas (5). Finally, CIPE planned to underscore their work on the economic problems facing Venezuela on CIPE's newfound blog.

In 2012 CIPE published two specific posts on their blog regarding Venezuela. In the first, CIPE's Latin America director John Zemko (2012) reveals that he was asked by the Capriles campaign to join a group of international observers to travel to Venezuela for the presidential election. Zemko claims that Chávez paid motorcyclists to bring voters to the polls because Chávez had sensed he was losing the election by the afternoon of Election Day. In the end, although Chávez won by ten percentage points, Zemko concluded that "Chavez would be well advised with these results to listen to the opposition and the 6 million voters they represent who really do want another path for their country." In the second post following the election, Zemko praised the work of Fedecámaras for its work in trying to promote free market economic policies in Venezuela.

Perhaps more telling, in April 2013, following the death of Chávez and Maduro's defeat of Capriles, former CEDICE president and at the time president of Fedecámaras' Labor and Legislative Relations Committee, Aurelio Concheso, also authored a post on CIPE's blog titled "The Venezuelan Election." In his post, Concheso (2013) renders unsubstantiated claims about why Maduro had now defeated Capriles, including widespread "voter intimidation" marked by "armed paramilitary gangs intimidating voters in poorer neighborhoods to keep them away from the polls." Concheso makes his position on Chávez and Maduro clear, writing that Venezuela "now enters a transition phase which hopefully will end with its recovering its democratic traditions after 14 years of increasing authoritaniarism [sic] bolstered by Chavez's charisma and popularity." As in earlier years, CIPE and (former) CEDICE members continued to openly oppose Chávez, with no serious attempt to appear nonpartisan or objective.

Establishing Newfound Business Organizations

Not only did CIPE work with a large think tank and with like-minded actors to "educate" poor Venezuelans about free market economics, but the US group also helped to found new business organizations for Venezuelan business owners. In 2013 CIPE developed a program called Venezuela: Fostering Entrepreneurship in Defense of Democracy & Free Markets, totaling nearly $150,000 and set to run until nearly 2015. In doing so, CIPE hoped that these groups would place pressure on the Venezuelan government to pursue free market initiatives. Although the name of the organization is redacted, CIPE planned to fund "Venezuela's most important business organization and provide it with an even larger platform to promote democratic and market oriented reform" (CIPE 2013, 2). This quite likely refers to Fedecámaras and its program of setting up Club de Emprendedores (Entrepreneurship Clubs) across the country.

With funding, CIPE (2013, 2–3) planned to help the business organization establish three new Entrepreneurship Clubs in three cities in Venezuela, located in the cities of Maracaibo, Zulia; San Cristobal, Táchira; and Mérida, Mérida, and to help them monitor the progress of four additional clubs else in the country. To promote their establishment, CIPE planned to help the business organization link up with national and regional media outlets to air interviews with the organization's member. CIPE (2013, 3) also planned to help the group publish advertisements in national and regional newspapers, including "the highest selling newspaper in the country with an approximate daily circulation of 210,000." Indeed, in 2014, for instance, Fedecámaras helped to establish an Entrepreneurship Club in Maracaibo, which remains in existence to this day.

Throughout its eight-week training program, the group maintained four objectives:

> To develop skills to ensure the effectiveness of citizens starting a business,
>
> To improve the chances of success of the business endeavors, helping owners enhance their business models, refine their business scope and development projections,
>
> To facilitate networking of program participants, especially among themselves, with institutions and business associations, universities and organizations in the communities,

> To instill the values of democracy, free initiative and free market, as well as ethical responsibility that should characterize all business formation. (CIPE 2013, 4)

The group also sought to develop political advocates for a free market economy in the country. Throughout its training, CIPE sought to "to ensure that participants understand the importance of supporting democratic development, participants will also receive courses on leadership and democracy" (4). Further, CIPE claims that "Entrepreneurship Clubs offer the possibility of functioning as space to strengthen the private sector's voice to create democratic dialogue with the government" (6). As a result, CIPE did not simply envision its programming as helping individuals to start businesses, but rather as political entities that might advance a particular political-economic vision with the country—and one clearly opposed to the Chávez government's vision of twenty-first-century socialism.

The Solidarity Center and Its Work to Undermine Chávez's Vision of Socialism in Venezuela

The AFL-CIO founded the Free Trade Union Initiative (FTUI) in 1978 in order to assist ideologically allied labor movements abroad. In 1983, with the development of the NED, the Reagan administration nominated FTUI as one of the NED's core grantees and dramatically increased its funding levels. Throughout the 1980s, FTUI funded and provided assistance to a range of labor movements throughout the world. In 1997, however, FTUI was reorganized as the American Center for International Labor Solidarity, or the Solidarity Center (SC) for short, with continued intentions to assist labor movements abroad.

The SC (n.d.) describes itself as "a non-profit international worker rights organization that assists workers around the world who are struggling to achieve safe and healthy workplaces, family-supporting wages, social protections and a voice on the job." Similar to the NDI and the IRI, the SC states that it works in approximately sixty countries with over four hundred labor unions to promote worker rights. In Venezuela, the organization has specifically worked with the Confederación de Trabajadores de Venezuela (CTV). During the early years of the Chávez administration, this work primarily included assistance with internal elections and organizing informal sector workers. The CTV, however, recurrently opposed the Venezuelan government, and its leadership offered strong support to the 2002 coup d'état efforts that deposed President Chávez as well as the subsequent strikes that paralyzed the country.

The Solidarity Center at Work in Venezuela, 2000–2002

The SC continually funded and worked with the CTV, the largest federation of labor unions in Venezuela, representing laborers in a number of sectors, throughout the early years of the Chávez administration. The union was founded by Acción Democratica (AD) leaders in the 1940s during the struggles to transition toward a democratic system and continued to remain affiliated with AD, as well as COPEI, leading into the twenty-first century. Because of this affiliation, President Chávez lambasted the union during his 1998 campaign for the presidency, and, unsurprisingly, relations between the two groups declined following his election. Indeed, the CTV came to align itself with the country's political opposition. During the early years of the Chávez government, Carlos Ortega, a vocal critic of the Venezuelan government, headed the CTV and took a leading role in opposition marches that culminated in the April 2002 coup d'état and subsequent strikes that sought to destabilize the government. While SC programs with the group did not entail funding for these endeavors, they did involve assistance with internal elections, and attempts to organize formerly unorganized areas of labor; namely, the informal sector. And so, while we cannot claim that the SC funded the CTV in order to destabilize the Venezuelan government, we might certainly recognize that the US government funded a known element of the Venezuelan opposition that continually critiqued the Venezuelan government.

In 2000 the SC assisted the CTV in its plans to hold upcoming elections for various positions within the organization (SC 2000). The primary objectives included increasing awareness and participation in the upcoming elections and monitoring the elections with both national and international observers, in order to alleviate any concerns that the elections were tampered with (SC 2000, 1). In July 2000 the SC held seven three-day courses across Venezuela with regional CTV federations in order to increase awareness about the elections and its general process, and how to participate in them. Following the elections, the SC assisted the CTV with developing and hosting a national conference in March 2002 alongside Fedecámaras and the Catholic Church to discuss national development plans and attempt to initiate a dialogue with the government. To do so, SC hosted meetings between Miranda governor Enrique Mendoza, who was affiliated with COPEI, and Fedecámaras, and also brought a labor-business coalition consultant from the Chicago-based Center for Labor and Community Research. In addition, the SC organized regional meetings to prepare regional union members for this conference. In the end, the groups developed a ten-point initiative for dialogue. As a result, SC (2000, 2) reported that this "joint action further established the CTV and Fedecámaras as the flagship organizations leading the growing opposition to the Chávez government."

Following the April 2002 coup d'état, the SC began assisting mid-level union leaders to understand how internal democracy works and what the role of trade union leaders should be in a democracy. In its documentation, the SC (2002) reports that mid-level union leaders were generally caught off guard by the coup d'état, despite the CTV leader's support for the events, and they were unsure how to respond to the escalating series of events that characterized the coup and its aftermath. The SC (2002) reports that its programs evidenced success when in July 2002 the CTV president attempted to call a general strike, but regional federations demanded an internal, democratic consideration of the issue. And so, while SC assistance has appeared to help an organization that sought to unseat President Chávez, there is also some indication that SC funding helped the organization become a more internally democratic organization as well.

The SC (2002) also supported the CTV in developing a plan for and organizing informal sector workers. Throughout Venezuela, the informal sector remains an area in which many citizens earn their income, through endeavors such as selling bootlegged DVDs and CDs, providing services such as shoeshining, and selling food that they have prepared. The SC first held seminars with a team of CTV representatives and informal sector worker representatives to discuss strategies for organizing informal sector workers (SC 2002, 11–12). The group held a three-day course led by a local sociologist and lawyer, and it involved informal worker leaders as well as several police officers, concerning legal requirements, ordinances, and redress for problems. The group also focused on how informal workers' groups can organize members and how to successfully conduct meetings and affairs within their organizations. Altogether, the SC assisted CTV members with networking with informal sector workers, informing such workers about how they can legalize their work, and informing them about how they can organize to more effectively address their demands.

Later Years

In later years beyond the coup d'état period and its aftermath, the AFL-CIO continued to support CTV efforts to confront the Venezuelan government, in addition to assisting in the establishment of a newfound labor organization expressly opposed to the Chávez government. In documents obtained from a FOIA request, it remains clear that the SC continued its challenge to the Chávez government and actively sought to undermine labor efforts pursued by the socialists as recently as 2014.

In their program descriptions, the SC portrays the Chávez government as a brutally authoritarian regime that limited freedom of expression and cracked down on opposition activities. In many of its program descriptions, the SC

(2006, 2) claims that the Chávez "government has increased measures to limit political opposition activities, curb freedom of expression, and increase control over popular organization and participation." Still, the SC seemed to recognize the reality that President Chávez did indeed retain much support, reporting that he had "come to command such control over the institutions of the country precisely because his message keys into the deep resentment of many of the poor and marginalized working people of the country" (2).

Yet, under the Chávez government, opposition members routinely criticized the president and his view of socialism within multiple media outlets, and they continually participated in elections and won electoral contests— that is, when they actually decided to participate in elections rather than boycott them. For instance, though the opposition pulled out of the 2005 legislative elections in an attempt to demonstrate how authoritarian the Chávez government was, elections went forward with international monitors guaranteeing that the elections were free and fair. Nonetheless, the SC (2006, 2) depicts the Chávez government as rigging the vote in its reporting during this period and as systematically destroying any opposition movement, writing that "the presence of opposition parties was completely eliminated from the National Assembly," and then claiming in a footnote that "opposition parties pulled out of the parliamentary elections . . . due to unfair elections conditions." In later legislative elections in 2010, though, when the opposition chose to participate, they won 65 out of 165 seats.

Throughout 2006–2014, the SC generally sought to combat two efforts pursued by the Chávez government: the building of workplace cooperatives and the move toward worker councils. From the SC's perspective, these moves were designed to displace the power of traditional unions, such as the CTV, and to exercise control over labor in a top-down manner. For instance, the SC (2013, 2) claims that while councils were "meant to 'empower' . . . they are actually tied to the government and political parties." Yet, much of this information presented within SC program descriptions remains replete with inaccuracies. In particular, their rationale for their involvement in the country in the first place is justified with plainly false information. The group, for instance, references legislation titled the Law of Popular Participation, which allegedly mandates that only Partido Socialista Unido de Venezuela (PSUV) members or socialist supporters may participate in and found community councils throughout the country. Throughout several years, the SC documents claim that as "defined in the Law of Popular Participation, community councils cannot be formed by or include general assembly participants that are not members of the United Socialist Party of Venezuela, or who are not 'known members' of 'Twentieth Century Socialism'" (2). The group also alleges that the labor legislation was modeled after this piece of legislation— allowing only PSUV members to form worker councils.

There are a couple issues with this. First, Venezuela never saw the introduction of any legislation titled the Law of Popular Participation. It remains possible that the group is making reference to the Law of Community Councils, which formalized the existence of neighborhood community councils. Indeed, Chávez viewed the councils as the engine of Venezuelan democracy, wherein community members could propose projects, discuss community efforts, and request funding from the state (Ciccariello-Maher 2013; Kingsbury 2018). The SC, however, alleges that only PSUV members or known supporters of socialism can participate in the community councils. This is absolutely false. As Gabriel Hetland (2017) has shown, opposition supporters also formed community councils within areas wherein the opposition retained support, and they, like Chavistas, recognized the importance of these groups.

SC reports from this period reveal that their efforts were primarily directed at hosting conferences and workshops wherein they might train individuals to directly challenge the Chávez government's proposed activities. In their 2012–2013 report, for example, the SC (2012, 2) describes how the group "will support industrial unions' efforts to resist the imposition of undemocratic workplace organizations." Within their training workshops, they pledged to help individuals confront "the imposition of 'worker councils' charged with usurping representation functions and subjugating workers to politicized, undemocratic organizational structures" (4). Specifically, the group describes how their workshops would help to "coordinat[e] concerted resistance actions" to the government's move towards workers councils and cooperatives, as well as helping raise "basic awareness of these issues among rank and file membership, mounting legal defense strategies . . . building coalitions among unions and broader civil society where possible, advocating policies [to] political leaders in government and National Assembly, and developing broader community support" (4).

In their development and hosting of workshops and conferences, the SC bused Venezuelan oppositionists-in-training in from throughout the country for events funded, catered, and rented with US taxpayer funding. They also funded legal/technical advisors to help their allies in their confrontations with the Chávez government. In particular, their programs focused on workers within the formal sector, including the petroleum industry and mining and metals manufacturing, as well as support for journalists. In coordination with their allies in the country, the SC sought to provide the infrastructure to bring local allies from across Venezuela together in order to devise and implement strategies to combat Chávez's move toward worker councils and cooperatives. With US taxpayer funding, the SC (2013, 5) "cover[ed] catering, venue rental, training supplies and transportation for participants from Caracas and immediate surrounding areas, as well as travel costs and per diem for participants from other parts of Venezuela."

While it appears that the SC continued to work with the CTV, they also began to work with the Movimiento Solidaridad Laboral (MSL), which formed in 2009 as a seemingly nonpartisan labor group opposed to Chávez's labor policies and devoid of any of the former anti-Chavista baggage associated with the CTV and Fedecámaras following the 2002 coup d'état and its aftermath. While the SC redacted most of the areas where its recipients were listed in the documents they released, they failed to redact in all locations, confirming its work with the MSL in one area where it failed to redact their name. In its 2010 program description, the SC (2010, 2) bluntly states that it helped form the coordinating body, which was "launched in an [SC]-supported national conference in July 2009," and that it would continue to help the group in the "development of... its labor rights platform." Still, while setting out to appear nonpartisan, many of its main figures, including Rodrigo Penso and Froilán Barrios, formerly held positions within the CTV and/or remained formerly affiliated with them. Its national leader and spokesperson, Orlando Chirino, also had been recently fired from his position within Venezuela's state oil company, PDVSA, and had become a vocal opponent of President Chávez, even running against him in the 2012 presidential election.

After its formation, the SC appears to have continually funded MSL meetings and training sessions as well as conferences in which they devised their approaches to combating Chávez's labor policies. The group's largest effort included a march with the CTV against the Chávez government in 2011. The explicit purpose of SC events was to assist these organizations to "coordinat[e] concerted resistance actions" against the Chávez government, and it remains quite possible that the SC helped to plan this march, or at least provided a venue to help them plan such an event. Yet, while the SC remained exuberant about the group in its infancy, the organization seems to have fizzled out within a few years of its formation and shortly after its 2011 march alongside the CTV, with little public presence to speak of thereafter. This is not surprising given that the organization's leader, Orlando Chirino, unsuccessfully ran against Chávez in the 2012 presidential elections under the Partido Socialismo y Libertad. With the seeming dissolution of the MSL, it appears that the international arm of the AFL-CIO continued its work with the CTV and sections of the labor movement expressly opposed to Chávez and now Maduro, as in documents from years beyond 2011, the SC continues to condemn Venezuelan government policies and note its efforts with a large anti-Chávez labor group.

CIPE maintained several initiatives within Venezuela over the past several decades. First, the US government through CIPE supported CEDICE and its efforts to combat public policies enacted by President Chávez. During the early years of the Chávez administration, two major pieces of legislation that

Chávez passed include the Land Law and the Hydrocarbons Law, both of which allowed for greater state intervention into the economy. CIPE provided CEDICE with funding to engage in a number of activities, including hosting forums and distributing newsletters throughout the country that condemned such government policies. Second, while many of these projects took place in the lead up to the 2002 coup d'état that displaced Chávez, CEDICE continued to work with many of the same groups that supported and played key roles in the coup d'état, including Fedecámaras and the CTV. Indeed, Fedecámaras head Pedro Carmona briefly served as the interim president of the transitional government following Chávez's displacement. Thereafter, CEDICE worked with Fedecámaras and other organizations affiliated with the opposition to put together documents that might provide the infrastructure for a post-Chávez, opposition-led government. At the same time of these activities, the SC worked the CTV, the primary labor group opposed to Chávez, whose leadership took part in the 2002 coup d'état and a subsequent 2003 lockout strike designed, no less, to bring down the Chávez government.

In the post–coup d'état period, both CIPE and the SC continued to work with opposition actors and to develop programs designed to combat Chávez government policies. CIPE, for its part, funded low-income Venezuelans to attend courses promoting free market capitalist policies as well as newfound business organizations throughout the country, in addition to radio shows and press releases denouncing the Chávez government. The SC, for its part, seemingly continued work with the CTV, and it helped to create a new labor organization also opposed to the Chávez government. In particular, the SC funded groups to develop actions against the government's move towards worker councils and cooperatives.

It is clear that through CIPE and the SC that the US government has aimed to promote free market capitalist policies, albeit with some labor representation therein. However, the groups it has selected have all openly opposed the socialist policies of the Chávez and Maduro governments. Indeed, these two units include some of the primary agents through which the US government has sought to promote free market capitalism within Venezuela and beyond. There is no question that through these groups the US government has promoted capitalist policies in Venezuela and has sought to undermine Venezuelan socialism. This is clearly a partisan endeavor that neo-Tocquevillian scholars have remained silent on in their discussions on the nature of democracy assistance. In fact, there is very little social scientific, scholarly work that even engages in any discussion of these particular groups and their recent activities abroad (for exceptions, see Robinson 1996; Scipes 2005, 2010). This chapter clarifies these organizations' commitments, at least in the instance of Venezuela, to combat particular governments and their policies.

Chapter 7

FUNDING ANTI-CHÁVEZ VOICES IN CIVIL SOCIETY

The National Endowment for Democracy

While the National Endowment for Democracy (NED) provides direct funding to its four core grantees—the International Republican Institute (IRI), the National Democratic Institute for International Affairs (NDI), the Solidarity Center (SC), and the Center for International Private Enterprise (CIPE), the NED also provides direct funding for many nongovernmental organizations (NGOs) in countries throughout the world. Much like broader democracy promotion efforts, though, since its inception in the 1980s, controversy has surrounded the NED and its operations abroad. I systematically document and discuss NED funding during several years of the Chávez administration throughout this chapter.[1] The NED has assisted NGOs in Venezuela since the early 1990s. Since this time, the NED has supported an array of groups largely focused on civil and political rights; namely, the diminution of executive power and government intervention into the lives of citizens. The group has also focused on organizations that reduce conflict and offer human rights training for law enforcement officers. In doing so, the NED has shown a disposition toward liberal democratic, rather than radical democratic, features. These emphases diverge from what the Bolivarian government of President Hugo Chávez championed during his tenure in office—the prioritization of the rights of socially and economically oppressed Venezuelans through measures that sometimes ran counter to, but mostly sought to exceed, many liberal democratic features of governance.

These findings demonstrate that NED funding practices are in no way neutral and nonpartisan, and that the US government has indeed provided funding and support to groups and parties that have encouraged and supported anti-democratic behaviors. This includes some groups whose representatives supported coup d'état efforts against Chávez in 2002, and, in the instance of one group that has continually received US government support, even accepted a position within the transitional government's presidential cabinet. These findings show that their efforts clearly remain opposed to the Chávez government. Yet, as I discuss in a later chapter, US government programs ultimately failed to undermine the Venezuelan government. Instead, Chávez used the opportunity to shore up nationalist sentiments and to demonstrate that the US government had sought to manipulate domestic political affairs by lavishing opposition political actors with funding and support. In response, he developed legislation to counter the activities of the NED and other groups within Venezuela.

The NED in Venezuela

Until Hugo Chávez's death, funding priorities largely remained the same with the NED continuing to work with many of the same organizations for many years. In its operations, NED funding largely centered on two distinct areas: funding for civil liberties issues and funding for conflict and law enforcement reform. In the first area, the NED provided much funding for groups that have actively contested and organized around pieces of legislation and policies pushed or enacted by the Chávez government. This has included, for example, the Land Law, which allowed the government to expropriate rural lands left idle; legislation on education that would allow the government more control over national curricula; and the involvement of the military in national government and its implementation of public policies, such as food distribution. This has also included funding to enhance to basic abilities of NGOs to persist and raise funding. The NED's second area of focus concerns conflict and law enforcement reform. The NED has allocated much funding and attention to reducing conflict and crime, and to supporting groups that train Venezuelan law enforcement members. In particular, this has included supporting NGOs that work with neighborhood groups on conflict mediation, groups that train justices of the peace and promote the justice of the peace system, and groups that provide human rights training for police officers.

We will see that NED operations are in no way unbiased and instead champion a liberal democratic vision of governance. This vision clashes with the Venezuelan government's radical, socialist democratic vision of government. Second, US democracy assistance efforts remain linked with a history of paternalist and neocolonial US foreign policymaking in the region that dates back to the Monroe Doctrine in 1823. Since this time, US government elites have envisioned Latin American leaders as uncivilized, lawless, and unfit to govern, should they veer from the political-economic vision that the US government has encouraged within the hemisphere. Such visions involve a racist-imperial understanding of Latin American leaders and the citizens that support them. For US government elites, it is unacceptable that Latin American citizens would elect a leader who criticizes US foreign policy, adopts divergent political-economic policies from the United States, and seeks to create a multipolar global system.

Third, US government agencies have supported an array of actors who have consistently sought to block Chavista policies, such as education reform and land reform. In addition, the US government supported several groups that openly championed the 2002 coup d'état that temporarily deposed President Chávez and empowered a transitional government to take his place. As a result, the US government does not demonstrate an absolute commitment to democratic actors. By contrast, it shows a tendency to support groups that have engaged in and supported anti-democratic and unconstitutional behaviors. Even though US government agencies might not have funded these groups to engage in these specific policies, it continued to furnish them with assistance following their support for such anti-democratic policies. In addition, such agencies also supported NGOs that openly aligned themselves with the opposition, including Súmate, which urged Venezuelan citizens to vote against President Chávez in a recall referendum in 2004.

Fourth, US government efforts are in no way omnipotent. Instead, the Venezuelan government seized upon US government efforts in order to discredit its opponents, muster nationalist sentiment, and build support for legislation affecting NGO operations throughout the country. In other words, US government support ultimately had the unintended effect of bolstering the Venezuelan government. Finally, several groups that received US government funding and technical support, actually legitimized the Venezuelan government, including groups that monitored elections, in addition to some of its social policies, and some groups even worked with the Chávez government on particular projects. While this cooperation does not characterize the trend of US government funding, it does indicate that each instance of US government funding does not always have its intended effect of tarnishing that group that it seeks to destabilize.

The NED and Its Civil Liberties Focus

During the Chávez administration, the NED provided much funding for groups that combated particular pieces of legislation and policies initiated by the Venezuelan government. At the general level, the Chávez government promoted a radical, direct, and participatory form of governance during its early years, and, beginning in 2005, introduced the idea of socialism. In many instances, President Chávez placed the rights of the majority of socially and economically dispossessed Venezuelans over the rights of the country's social and economic elites. As discussed in earlier chapters, some of these policies included exerting greater control over the national oil industry and its managerial staff; using oil revenues to fund programs involving higher education, medical missions, and subsidized food; and nationalizing formerly privatized industries, and expropriating unused, rural landholdings from large landowners.

These policies unsurprisingly irritated many members of the Venezuelan middle and upper classes. In addition, several civil society groups formed in order to combat such policies, and the US government supported them through its democracy assistance programs. What is more, some groups that openly aligned with the opposition, and whose leaders would sign the Carmona Decree legitimizing the transitional government, received US government funding and support for their projects. This demonstrates that the US government regularized support for groups that clearly aimed to undermine the Chávez government.

Under its auspices, the NED funded a number of groups to monitor societal changes that ensued as a result of Chavista policies. Some of these policies included land reform, education reform, and broader inclusion of military members into political life. The NED, for instance, provided continual funding for Fundación Momento de la Gente (FMG), a civic group founded in 1999 focused on monitoring elections, policy, and legislation. In its program description, the NED (2001a, 4) reports that the FMG "has figured prominently among Venezuelan civil society organizations and opposition political leaders, for its leadership and expertise on key democratic issues." The NED thus takes no efforts to distinguish the FMG from the Venezuelan political opposition. Instead, it readily admits that this group "has figured prominently" within the opposition on account of the group's "leadership and expertise on key democratic issues." Within its first agreement with the NED in 2001, the FMG received $40,000 "to organize Venezuelan civil society groups to monitor the National Assembly and provide policy input on key pieces of legislation pertinent to civil liberties" (4). In doing so, the FMG provided analysis on legislation, such as the Law on Municipal Governance, which encouraged decentralization efforts and a reduction of state power to local governments. For some time, under the Chávez administration, the political opposition indeed directed much of its attention toward building anti-Chávez forces at the state and local level, and cultivating potential presidential candidates at these levels, including future presidential candidates Manuel Rosales, former mayor of Maracaibo and governor of Zulia, and Henrique Capriles, who formerly served as a mayor of Baruta and currently remain one of the opposition's primary leaders.

In 2002 the NED granted an additional $64,000 to the FMG, and, in its program description, the US government agency openly critiqued the Chávez government on several grounds. These critiques covered a number of issues, including general aspects of governance, private property rights and investment, and the treatment of civil society groups. First, the NED (2002a, 4) criticized the passage of Chávez's "pet 'Bolivarian' constitution, [which] despite the concentration of power that it ceded to the executive, appears to have done little [to] help the government actually govern." In this passage, the NED describes the Venezuelan constitution as a lowly, "pet" accomplice to former President Chávez's inability to govern the country. This contrasts with the reality that many members of Venezuelan civil society actually assisted in the construction of the new Venezuelan constitution, and, thereafter, Venezuelan citizens voted on and successfully passed this document.

Second, the NED (2002a, 4) criticized the Venezuelan government's passage of forty-nine laws in 2001 by executive decree that "threaten to undermine the protection of private property and discourage international and domestic investment." This emphasis on issues of private property rights illustrates the discrepancy that exists between US agencies like the NED and the Chávez government concerning the importance each placed on an absolute commitment to private property rights. Chávez recurrently argued that such moves were necessary given the situation that many rural Venezuelans experienced: a landless and dispossessed state, while large rural landholders possessed so many tracts of land that they had not even the ability to maintain it all. And third, the NED claimed that Chávez attacked civil society groups and NGOs as they "have emerged as an effective and constructive counterweight to the government... and played an important role in defending important political rights, highlighting specific policy issues, and mobilizing popular opinion" (4). Based on these assessments, the NED funded the FMG to continue to provide legislative analysis, as well as to train municipal authorities in twenty municipalities on issues of budgeting, transparency, and citizen involvement in administration (5). Similar to its policy analyses, these measures were promoted in a general effort to push for more decentralization and municipality control over resources, in contrast with centralization of power within the executive branch.

In 2003 the NED supplied nearly the same critiques of the Chávez government as it did in its earlier program descriptions. In 2003, however, it actually applauded the Venezuelan National Assembly as "one of the only the institutions in which parties and civil society organizations across the political spectrum come together in a constructive dialogue" (NED 2003a, 4). It also applauded the efforts between opposition and pro-government legislators to amend and approve a new election law, an initiative that the FMG had assisted with. And so, while the NED largely critiqued the Venezuelan government in its program descriptions, it sporadically praised some aspects of the Venezuelan political system, such as, in this instance, the National Assembly, which, at the time, remained dominated by Chávez and his supporters. In the 2003–2004 funding cycle, the NED approved another $64,000 grant to assist the FMG with the development of three new legislative initiatives. During this time, the FMG represented civil society on commissions devising a new law on municipal governance, citizen participation in governance, and financing for political parties and voting regulations. The FMG received funding to study these pieces of legislation, contract specialists when necessary, and hold public seminars to update the public and other NGOs on the development of the law.

Outside of its work with the FMG and its general emphasis on decentralization efforts, the NED focused efforts on the effects of the 2001 Land Law. During these early years, the NED funded Asociación Civil Acción Campesina (ACAC), "a social and political actor [established in 1976] that promotes sustainable agriculture in correspondence with other actors, privileging the participation of rural people and their organizations in the rural development of the country" (NED 2002b, 1). From September 2002 until November 2003, ACAC received $35,000 from the NED to monitor land reforms that were taking place throughout the country after the Venezuelan government passed the Land Law in November 2001.

As the NED's program description for its ACAC funding reports, the Land Law "gives the government authority to seize and redistribute private property that is not being put to productive use. The law, in effect, sanctions land invasions of private property which will then be recognized by the government . . . the law is dangerously vague on how the land distribution program will be carried out and grants the government a great deal of discretion in selecting which private land is to be distributed" (NED 2002b, 2). With NED funding, ACAC's objectives were to provide alternative proposals to the recently passed law and to provide a new proposal for a law to the National Assembly that would replace it. In addition to this, the NED describes ACAC "as a source of information to policy makers, political parties and civil society on the implementation of the law and its effects" (3). While the new law did indeed allow the Venezuelan government the ability to expropriate landholdings from large landowners, the law hardly sanctioned arbitrary land invasions. The Venezuelan government continually negotiated with large landholders regarding what land it would, in fact, expropriate, and, in many instances, these expropriations involved the least tenable and least arable pieces of land that large landholders possessed (Enríquez and Newman 2015).

Using the funding, ACAC held several discussions and meetings with activists, farmers, peasants, and educators to discuss the Land Law, and how it would affect rural communities, in order to generate a public information campaign. ACAC developed an advisory team with several experts to develop a document publicizing information on land seizures, their legality, and the effects of land redistribution. The organization also trained several state-based representatives to analyze the situation in nine states throughout Venezuela and report back to its branch in Caracas on land conflicts. At the culmination of its meetings and monitor reporting, ACAC drew up plans to contact local and national media and disseminate information on these issues.

The group's final document became titled "Agro-Food Security and Rural Development." Within it, ACAC "call[ed] for a legal instrument that gives priority to the farmers in the resolution of the agrarian problem, which we believe involves solving two major problems... access of farmers to ownership of productive assets, including land... [and] the legal security of farmers on full ownership of these assets" (ACAC n.d.). In addition, ACAC called for a new law that would generate a new framework for encouraging small and medium-level farmers, eliminate structural problems such as a price controls and access to foreign currency, establish "a coherent system of property rights (individual and collective)," and strengthen the role of local governments in executing a new lands law (ACAC n.d.) Thus, the ultimate objectives of ACAC were to enact a new land reform law, but one that included more clarification and established a more comprehensive framework for redistribution of land. In addition, the organization called on the government to tackle what it deemed to be the structural problems concerning agriculture and food security facing Venezuela—price controls and access to foreign currency.

In addition to rural land issues, the NED provided funds for groups to contest Venezuelan government initiatives on education, including the Asociación Civil Asamblea de Educación (ACAE). In its program description for its funding for ACAE, the NED describes how the Chávez government had sought to advance new education plans under its Bolivarian Revolution. The report states that at

> issue is a plan by President Chávez to overhaul the nation's school curriculum by granting the central government powers of oversight by directly monitoring and managing teachers, principals and material used in classes... the government has sought to incorporate leftist teachings in school curriculum and supervise principals and teachers in the nation's schools... newly written textbooks referred to the use of violence as an effective means to achieve rapid political and economic changes, portrayed Ché Guevara and other leftist leaders as heroes of modern history and suggested that Venezuelans must be taught to reject individualism and competition. (NED 2000b, 4)

The program description likens Bolivarian initiatives to "Soviet-sponsored citizen brigades... [including] government plans to form neighborhood Bolivarian youth committees, revitalize a largely dormant pre-military training program for elementary school children, and promote intelligence gathering on the political party affiliation of neighbors through the use of polls and surveys" (NED 2000b, 6). In this excerpt and commentary on Venezuelan affairs, we garner much insight into what sorts of issues and policies NED leaders found unfit for a democratic society. First, the group objects to youth organizations that promote Bolivarian values, and, in doing so, likens these projects to Soviet-sponsored citizen brigades, rather than similar groups that exist within, for example, the United States, such as the Young Democrats or Young Republicans. Instead, the Soviet Union operated as a one-party state that violently suppressed dissent from its citizens. What is more, most political parties throughout Venezuela possess a lengthy history of developing political organizations for its youth members, including Acción Democratica, the Comité de Organización Política Electoral Independiente, and more recently developed parties, such as Primero Justicia and Voluntad Popular. Far from a Chavista development, Bolivarian youth organizations are rather consistent with Venezuelan political history.

This excerpt also finds it unfitting that a government would promote the rejection of individualism and competition. These two values, of course, have a central location within US American civil religion, which has championed risk-taking, the existence of an alleged meritocracy, and private and corporate business pursuits (Fischer 2010). The promotion of collectivism and cooperation seemingly runs anathema to the apparent virtues of US American civil religion. In addition, the program description highlights the alleged influence of the Cuban government on Venezuela and its school system, and it laments the upcoming passage of the National Education Law, which would allow for the establishment of Bolivarian-oriented schools. Lastly, the NED description illustrates an aversion to positive depictions of leftist leaders such Che Guevara, who condemned US imperialism. In doing so, the NED indicates that both US citizens and Venezuelan citizens should agree on what individuals should receive veneration and what individuals should receive scorn within elementary and secondary school teachings. Given that Chávez wanted to depict critics of US imperialism in a positive light, the NED funded ACAE to, in part, push back against these efforts.

Teacher and parent groups headed by Leonardo Carvajal, former director of the National Council of Education, a group that formerly advised the Venezuelan Ministry of Education throughout the 1990s, formed ACAE in November 1999. The NED underscores some of the earlier successes of ACAE in its program description, including holding rallies in a majority of states throughout the country to reject Chávez's proposals, developing their own alternatives to the reform law, and seeking to nullify government efforts "to revolutionize" the education system (NED 2000b, 6). As the Venezuelan government prepared to introduce legislation to develop new schools and universities, the NED provided $55,000 to ACAE from 2000 to 2002 for a four-pronged strategy that the group had developed to combat these government objectives.

The first part of the strategy included monitoring the government's education reform efforts. The group promised to survey parents, students, community members, and educators about their perception of the education system as well as track the progress of reform efforts and their outcomes. The group also reported that it would link up with media outlets and publicize relevant and factual information concerning the realities of the reforms. This included the creation of a website, the development of several brochures on the reforms, and preparation of annual reports on the state of education reform in Venezuela. Second, the NED funded the group to organize over a dozen public forums in over a dozen major cities throughout the country to discuss their perspective on the education reforms. The group planned to bring in representatives from the American Federation of Teachers to discuss the government's reforms and to host interviews with media outlets to publicize its views.

Third, ACAE planned to hold twenty working meetings with academics from several universities to draft alternatives to such legislation allowing the government greater control over institutions of higher education as well as several forums to discuss the draft legislation with civil society leaders, teachers, students, and citizens. Thereafter, the organization reported that it planned to garner signatures and present the legislation to the National Assembly. Lastly, ACAE planned to work with 1,200 individuals, including 600 students and 600 parents and representatives, in order to train them as education leaders. The group planned sixty workshops across the country in order to work with these individuals on issues such as the role of education in democratic societies (NED 2002b, 7–8).

In October 2002 ACAE received an additional grant for $57,000 for projects that would last until October 2003. Since its initial grant, the Venezuelan government had failed to pass its education reforms; however, the future of such reform remained in question. During this cycle, the NED funded ACAE for three objectives, including the collection and monitoring of policy changes at all levels of government and budget levels; convening fifty public forums involving academics, students, and teachers to discuss education reform in Venezuela; conducting a public information campaign by maintaining a website and working with the National Assembly on education bills; and finally, the group planned to continue training local leaders on education reform and the state of education in Venezuela. Overall, NED funding for ACAE aimed to combat policies pushed by the Chávez government, which included more national government control over educational institutions throughout the country. With its funding, ACAE sought to undermine the advancement of these policies by training individuals throughout the country to contest these policies at the local level and pressure the Venezuelan legislature to reconsider its objectives.

Aside from receiving NED funding to combat the Venezuelan government's educational reform plans, Carvajal played a central role in the 2002 coup d'état that temporarily deposed President Chávez from power. Following Chávez's detention on a military base on an island off the coast of the country, the transitional government headed by the former head of the Venezuelan Federation of Chambers of Commerce, Pedro Carmona, dismissed Chávez's entire presidential cabinet, in addition to dissolving the legislature and the judiciary branches. In their place, Carmona appointed a new presidential cabinet. Indeed, this new cabinet included Carvajal as the new government's minister of education. Carvajal agreed to the new minister position, and signed the Carmona Decree, which was a document that gave support to the transitional government. Such actions demonstrate that ACAE's leader fully supported Chávez's removal from power and the institutionalization of the transition government. What is more, Carvajal became part of the transitional government. While the US government might surely claim that it had no knowledge that Carvajal intended to join a transition government that was constructed in the wake of an unconstitutional transition of power, the NED continued to fund the group following the coup d'état events. As illustrated earlier, the NED provided funding to the group both before and after these events, and for projects would run at least until October 2003, up until over a year after Carvajal joined the transitional government.

In addition to rural lands and education-based issues, the NED funded programs focused on social programs in Venezuela. From July 2002 to July 2003, the NED provided the Centro al Servicio de la Acción Popular (CESAP) with $63,000 for a program called Monitoring Social Programs. In its program description, the NED points out that extreme political polarization had come to characterize Venezuelan political life, as evidenced by the April 2002 coup d'état. The NED (2002c, 4), however, strongly lamented how there have been many individuals who have "pointed to the socioeconomic and racial makeup of the interim government and the background of the protestors that took to the street to call for Chávez's return. The interpretation is unfortunate as it ignores the multi-class opposition to Chávez, and because it mistakenly lumps together the broad-based coalition that participated in the original protest with the interim government. This interpretation discredits the diversity and legitimacy of those opposing the anti-democratic government." From this statement, we can clearly see that either the NED believed that opposition to President Chávez possessed a pronounced cross-class, cross-racial bend, or that they, at least, wanted to portray it this way. While it is true that members from all classes and racial groups both supported and opposed Chávez, there have been clear geographical, racial, and class patterns involving opposition and support for Chávez.

Indeed, Chavistas have largely drawn support from the poor Venezuelan barrios, which primarily contain darker-skinned citizens in comparison with Venezuelans that live in, for example, western Caracas. In fact, opposition members recurrently depicted President Chávez and his supporters with racialized features, and they often presented him with darker skin than his own (Gottberg 2011). In addition, eastern Caracas, which has long served as an anti-Chávez bastion and recurrently elected anti-Chávez leaders, has been one of the few places in Caracas where I, as a light brown-haired, white US citizen of Irish ancestry, would not receive curious looks from individuals on the street. In fact, in this part of the city, it was not uncommon to hear individuals speaking English. In contrast, in the western parts of Caracas where working-class individuals live, one is hard-pressed to hear English spoken or to find many light-skinned Venezuelans living and working. In these western parts of Caracas, citizens have historically supported Chavista politicians. The point of all this is to demonstrate that racial and class dynamics indeed characterize Venezuelan political life, and that many of the individuals who had pushed for Chávez's return to power in 2002 resided in many of the barrios that populate the western, and poorer, half of Caracas (Cannon 2008; Ciccariello-Maher 2013; Fernandes 2010; Kingsbury 2018).

In its program for CESAP, the NED continues to claim that a need existed for dialogue and reconciliation in the aftermath of the coup d'état. In addition, the NED claims that the opposition and government needed to dialogue concerning social conditions in the country. Unfortunately, though, the NED alleges that quality information concerning the country and its social conditions are lacking. NED funding for CESAP would attempt to generate accurate information and "monitor social expenditures, the impact of poverty-alleviation programs and social development and change in Venezuela. The project will monitor government budgets and programs, gather data through surveys, and monitor social development indicators to develop a national picture of the state of poverty and social programs in Venezuela" (NED 2002c, 5).

CESAP's project consisted of several specific goals. First, the group collected information on social development, including expenditure and impact, by obtaining figures from two offices focused on social development issues such as nutrition, housing, and health. Second, CESAP surveyed households in five cities throughout Venezuela to assess the impact of social programs. Third, with information garnered from the surveys and from the government, the group released a report on their findings with recommendations on how to strengthen social programs. While the group acknowledged and commended the Venezuelan government for bringing some social development issues to the forefront of national discussion and addressing a number of social development issues in the 1999 constitution, the group also offered recommendations for the government to attend to issues of crime, unemployment, and education. Finally, CESAP conducted a campaign to disseminate its findings, by contracting with local newspapers, holding forums in several cities, and holding a national forum with government and opposition members to discuss the group's findings.

The NED provided another $65,000 to CESAP for a program called

Monitoring Social Programs, which would run from August 2003 until August 2004. Similar to its previous grant, CESAP planned to collect information on social development in seven states throughout Venezuela, including on issues involving nutrition, housing, and health. Similar to its previous grant, CESAP also planned to generate and disseminate a report on social development in Venezuela with recommendations to the National Assembly on how they might improve their social policies.

The NED also assisted NGOs with their networking within and beyond Venezuela. The Asociación Civil Consorcio Justicia (ACCJ) was founded in 1992 for "the promotion and strengthening of democracy and the democratization of the Venezuelan justice system" through citizen initiatives (ACCJ n.d.). The NED funded ACCJ with its first grant for projects between February 2001 and February 2002. As its general objective, ACCJ was "to build up the capacity of civil society organizations in Venezuela to become active partners in the struggle against authoritarianism" (NED 2001c, 1). In this passage, we clearly find that by 2001 the NED had no qualms about referring to the Venezuelan government as an authoritarian institution. While the Venezuelan government was indeed far from perfect in all of its policymaking approaches, its most serious political moves during this period involved putting many of its policies, including the development of a new National Assembly and a new Venezuelan constitution, to a nationwide, democratic vote. The description of the Venezuelan government and its leaders as authoritarian indeed involves an external interpretation, rather than an objective reading of the facts, and it glosses over an entirely complex political situation in order to justify its funding for, primarily, opposition actors within the country or groups that aimed to combat Chávez government policies.

With NED funding, ACCJ organized and hosted a conference with prominent NGOs in Venezuela, including Amnesty International-Venezuela, Red de Apoyo, and Una Ventana a la Libertad, and a conference with representatives from prominent NGOs throughout the world, including representatives from the Inter-American Dialogue, the National Council of Mexican NGOs, and the Organization of American States (NED 2001c). ACCJ sought to bring NGOs together so that they could establish strategies that would allow them to survive under the Chávez administration. In addition, ACCJ sought to establish dialogue between Venezuelan NGO leaders and international leaders in order to share experiences and exchange recommendations concerning their interactions with governments abroad. ACCJ reported that one of the main successes of these conferences was that several NGOs established funding relationships with an assortment of private companies, including CANTV and Statoil (NED 2001c).

From January 2002 to February 2003, the NED provided $84,000 to ACCJ for additional projects. In its program description, the NED (2003b) laments the tighter restrictions placed on citizen groups as well as attacks and alleged surveillance on government critics. During this period, the NED funded ACCJ to host a two-day conference involving all NED funding recipients as well as academics, politicians, and business leaders in order to discuss how to defend political rights and build alliances. Since ACCJ organized the meeting for April 2002, the meeting was postponed due to the coup d'état. Instead, ACCJ organized a public meeting on the role of truth commissions, and several meetings on conflict resolution and peaceful dialogue between the government and opposition. Under these projects, ACCJ organized a workshop with the National Prosecutors' Office to investigate the killings that ensued during the coup d'état, trained two hundred members from the National Prosecutors' Office on Alternative Dispute Resolution Methods, and co-sponsored workshops on democracy and conflict resolution in the 23 de Enero neighborhood, with the Ministry of the Interior. While many NED recipients worked with groups that primarily criticized the Venezuelan government and worked to undermine its policies, some NED recipients, at some points in time, worked with national government offices, such as ACCJ's work with members from the National Prosecutors' Office and with the Ministry of the Interior in a notoriously left-leaning part of Caracas that had continually supported the Chávez government, the 23 de Enero neighborhood (Ciccariello-Maher 2013; Velasco 2015).

Following this tumultuous period, the NED provided a $54,000 grant to ACCJ for a project called Strengthening the Judicial System to run for a year beginning in April 2003. In its program description, the NED (2003b) claims that Chávez had "deepened and inflamed the polarization in Venezuela" and that he has politicized the judicial system in Venezuela by stacking the courts with provisional judges that could be terminated by the government at any point. This situation served as the justification for providing ACCJ with funding to "monitor the status of the judicial system and its operation and work with the Congress to improve legislation and laws" (NED 2003b). Indeed, although President Chávez claimed to have appointed several additional judges to the court in order to allow the court system to deal with its insurmountable amount of cases, several international rights groups and opposition politicians claimed that Chávez appointed these members in order to tilt the court system in his favor. The claim, however, that Chávez alone deepened and inflamed political polarization throughout the country is far from accurate. While Chávez referred to opposition politicians with names such as *la oligarquía rancia* (the rancid oligarchy) and *los escuálidos* (the squalid opposition), opposition politicians often developed their own obscene names for Chávez and other Chavista politicians; routinely and violently battled with Chavistas in the street; refused, at times, to participate in particular elections; and, of course, supported a coup d'état that deposed President Chávez. The contention that only Chávez and his supporters fanned the flames of political polarization is thus false. Opposition politicians and supporters continually engaged in polarizing tactics alongside the Chavistas, and, in doing so, both sides undoubtedly contributed to a polarized political environment.

ACCJ implemented two programs with NED funding for this project. First, they established an observatory to monitor a number of judicial issues including the nomination and approval of judges, the judicial budget, citizen perceptions and complaints, and judicial decisions. The group also produced quarterly reports concerning legislation involving the justice system and recommendations on how to improve it, and it held several forums throughout Venezuela with human rights activists and congressional members to discuss their findings. Second, ACCJ worked with community leaders to establish conflict mediation programs in several neighborhoods in the Libertador section of Caracas, instead of encouraging citizens to work through Venezuela's inefficient court systems. And so, following President Chávez's new appointments, ACCJ both monitored judicial proceedings and sought alternative methods of conflict resolution that would bypass the Venezuelan court system all together.

In addition to working with Venezuelan NGOs primarily focused on domestic happenings, the NED also helped Venezuelan human rights groups link up with multilateral human rights institutions. For example, the NED awarded the Center for Justice and International Law (CEJIL), which is headquartered in the United States but contains a contingent in Venezuela, with $84,000 for a project called Human Rights Defense, which would run from September 2003 until October 2004. In its program description, the NED (2003b) regretted the human rights situation in Venezuela, citing a lack of rule of law, lack of political will to keep the Revolutionary Armed Forces of Colombia members out of the country, and, once again, extreme political polarization. Due to this situation, the NED reports that human rights groups need to play an important role in Venezuelan society, and that funding for CEJIL will allow them to work with local human rights groups and help them prepare and bring cases before the Inter-American Human Rights System, a system that the Venezuelan government had historically criticized due to the alleged direction it received from the US government (Gill 2014).

CEJIL's program in Venezuela consisted of three objectives. First, CEJIL employed a staff attorney to bring human rights cases before the Inter-American Commission on Human Rights and the Inter-American Court of Human Rights, including requests for provisional measures to safeguard several human rights activists and journalists. The staff attorney also collaborated with local human rights organizations in order to collect information concerning the human rights situation in Venezuela. Second, CEJIL conducted three seminars for students, journalists, and human rights defenders on the

Inter-American Human Rights System and the rights of journalists and human rights workers under this system. Lastly, CEJIL sought to include Venezuelan human rights organizations in their meetings in the United States and keep them informed concerning Inter-American proceedings and activities.

Finally, the NED funded several, additional programs that promoted civil liberties, including freedom of the press issues, decentralization issues, and voting rights. First, from May 2002 until October 2003, the NED provided the Instituto de Prensa y Sociedad de Venezuela (IPYS) with $25,000 for a project called Professionalization of the Media. At the time, IPYS, which remained headquartered in Peru, did not yet possess a fully consolidated IPYS branch in Venezuela. In its program report, the NED (2002d) reports that the Venezuelan government had threatened freedom of expression in the country. Its report notes that journalists are often concerned with their safety and that the National Assembly had begun discussions on a media content law that would allow the government to oversee the quality of all news outlets, potentially allowing it more intensive abilities to censor content.

IPYS used funding for an international forum and to launch an IPYS Venezuela network. In May 2002 IPYS convoked an international forum that focused on issues related to the press in Venezuela, with topics including "the professionalization of the media, the role of the press in political crisis, self-censorship, and protection of journalists" (NED 2002d, 5). The forum involved individuals from countries throughout Latin America, including Argentina, Chile, Colombia and Peru, as well as journalist-activists from a range of international groups, including Reporters Without Borders and the Inter American Press Association. Following the meeting, IPYS distributed reports concerning recommendations and summaries of discussions from the forum. IPYS also used funding for a follow-up meeting in Caracas with a network of journalist-activists in Venezuela so they could launch the newly developed IPYS contingent.

From April 2003 until April 2004, the NED provided $45,000 to IPYS for a project called Supporting Press Freedoms. In its program report, the NED (2003c, 4) claims that Venezuelan press groups were at the time ill-equipped to monitor press conditions throughout the entirety of the country, as they deteriorated under the Chávez administration. With the funding, IPYS trained and funded five regional monitors of press freedoms that would receive and investigate complaints on a daily basis. Funding also allowed regional monitors to meet on several occasions concerning freedom of the press issues throughout Venezuela.

Second, from September 2000 until October 2001, the NED provided $50,000 to Programa para el Desarrollo Legislativo (PRODEL), a group founded in 2000 to promote and defend Venezuelan decentralization efforts, for a project called Regional Forum for Decentralization. In its program report, the NED (2000c, 4) questions whether President Chávez will "attempt to consolidate his plebiscitarian, direct democracy," and suggests that NED funding will serve to stall these attempts at consolidating a direct democracy. We thus see that the NED clearly evidences an inclination toward representative democracy and a willingness to attempt to steer Venezuelan political society in this direction and away from direct democratic efforts. In doing so, the NED demonstrates that it believes that it knows what Venezuelan citizens most need from their political institutions, despite the fact that Venezuelan citizens had routinely supported President Chávez at the polls, and had voted to pass the new Venezuelan constitution, which championed the development of a participatory and direct, rather than solely a representative, democracy.

The NED's report celebrates the decentralization of power in Venezuela and claims that local governments are charged with delivering state services and ultimately provide a check on executive power. The report also criticized the national government's use of the military to provide social services under its Plan Bolívar 2000. In addition, PRODEL organized a forum for state legislators from all parties to discuss decentralization efforts in Venezuela, the rise of executive power, and budgetary issues. PRODEL also established a horizontal network of legislators throughout Venezuela that would monitor national legislation on issues of decentralization as they surrounded issues involving ports, taxes, and the environment.

Lastly, from September 2003 until October 2004, the NED provided Súmate with $53,400 for a project called Elections Education. In its program report, the NED, once again, laments increased political polarization and acknowledges that a referendum was the way out of the then-current political crisis surrounding the country in the post–coup d'état period. In doing so, the NED suggests that it knows what the Venezuelan political system best requires in order to move forward in a democratic manner. With its funding, the NED (2003d, 4) claims that Súmate "will train voters throughout Venezuela on the voting process and encourage participation in the referendum voting process" with its funding.

This general program involved several objectives. First, Súmate planned to contact regional organizations throughout Latin America and review their elections-related material. Thereafter, it would design its own voter education related materials concerning the referendum process and procedures including voter registration requirements. Their media campaign would also include the production of television and radio spots encouraging Venezuelans to register to vote and ensure that they are included on voter registration lists. Second, Súmate established a presence in all states throughout the country and from there planned to train around twenty-five thousand people in "how to disseminate information on the referendum, the legal and constitutional basis for the referendum, how to conduct a get-out-the-vote campaign for the entire community, [and] how to monitor the electoral process" (NED 2003d, 6).

Although the US government funded Súmate for seemingly nonpartisan endeavors such as providing Venezuelan citizens with information concerning the referendum process and assisting Venezuelans in their efforts to sign up to vote, the organization indeed stood at the center of opposition efforts to displace President Chávez from power. On top of providing Venezuelan citizens with information on the referendum process, Súmate openly encouraged Venezuelan citizens to vote to end Chávez's presidential term within the 2004 presidential referendum (Golinger 2006). In addition, the group became the training ground for several, high-profile anti-Chávez politicians, including Maria Corina Machado, who has become one of the most prominent, national politicians throughout the country and sought the opposition nomination for the 2012 presidential race, which she would eventually lose to Miranda governor Henrique Capriles.

Indeed, in personal interviews with the researcher, many NGO representatives lamented the fact that Súmate had sought international funding and even described itself as an NGO with an absence of ties to any opposition group. For many NGO representatives, Súmate's suggestion that it remained independent and nonpartisan tarnished not only its own image but also the reputation of a multiplicity of Venezuelan NGOs that make a much stronger case for nonpartisanship and independence, and have not directly worked with the opposition or openly supported opposition campaigns. On several occasions, the Venezuelan government indeed directly targeted Súmate, including bringing court cases against several of its members, for, among other crimes, treason (Golinger 2006). Although the Venezuelan government never formally prosecuted its members for treason, many NGO representatives believe that the Venezuelan government pursued legislation that damages a variety of NGOs, due to the activities of Súmate and few other groups that pose as NGOs, but, in reality, completely align with the opposition. Nonetheless, Súmate continues to freely operate in Venezuela.

NED Funding

In contrast with civil liberties issues, the NED has also prioritized issues involving with conflict mediation, the military, and law enforcement. One particular NED focus under the Chávez administration included the politicization of the Venezuelan military, and military involvement in government and public affairs. In February 2001 the NED provided the Asociación Civil Compresión de Venezuela (ACCV), an NGO focused on issues of civil-military relations and the defense of civil liberties, with $57,820 for activities that would run for the next two years. In its program description, the

NED (2001d, 1) alleged that the Venezuelan government "worked to blur the boundaries between military and civilian lines of authority" by appointing military leaders to government posts, including some of Chávez's conspirators in his 1992 coup d'état, as well as using the military in the provision of public services and assistance with public works. The NED also notes that the 1999 constitution has allowed the executive branch greater control over the military and the promotion of its officers. As a result of these changes, the NED claims that "the military and civil society need to stop and examine the repercussions of this trend, before the role of the military is irreversibly altered" (2).

The NED allocated funding for ACCV to accomplish several objectives during this period. First, ACCV used funding to organize six public forums on the issue of civil-military relations, with themes including "The Importance of Civil Leadership to Achieve a Military Balance" and "Trends of the Military Budget in Venezuela." In these meetings, ACCV invited military members, academics, and congressional members to participate and lead discussions. In order to provide balance, ACCV reports that members from several political positions spoke at their events. These members included a former minister of defense and Chávez critic, as well as a former Supreme Court magistrate that supported Chávez, in addition to other speakers.

Second, ACCV used funding to organize five panel discussions involving civil-military themes, including "Democracy, Politics, and the Armed Forces" and "Visions Regarding the Role of the Armed Forces in Venezuela," as well as four roundtable discussions on topics including "The Armed Forces and the Media" and "Venezuela Military Doctrine in the Constitution." In one roundtable, for example, in July 2002 ACCV hosted a former Venezuelan vice admiral as well as a historian of the Venezuelan military to discuss the history and future of the Venezuelan military, which the group also arranged for the media to cover. Following the meeting, *El Nacional*, a prominent national newspaper, conducted and published an interview with the historian concerning civil-military relations, where he criticized Chávez for heavily involving military members in the political life of the country.

In addition to its focus on the military, the NED also remained concerned over general issues of conflict throughout Venezuela. In its program description for its funding for the Asociación Civil Acción para el Desarrollo (ACCEDES), the NED claims that rumors swirled concerning the Venezuelan government arming private militia groups. As a result, the NED (2003e, 1) reports that "middle and upper classes feel extremely insecure and fear for their lives and property." Interestingly, the NED seems to lay the blame for crime in the country at the feet of the Chávez government. It seemingly suggests that the Venezuelan government has encouraged violence against middle and upper classes, including threats against not only their property but also their lives. These suggestions, however, greatly diverge from the realities of a lengthy history of criminal issues facing contemporary Venezuela, which begin long before President Chávez took power. Due to this situation, the NED provided ACCEDES, a group they describe as an organization that promotes community justice and legal aid, with a $10,000 grant for a project called Local Civic Education, which would run from April 2003 to April 2004.

With this funding, ACCEDES planned to conduct workshops with local leaders from neighborhood associations in seven different poor neighborhoods in Caracas. The NED (2003e, 1) reports that these workshops would focus on "democratic values, the role of civil society and community organizations in democracy, how to negotiate and mediate local conflicts, the Bolivarian Constitution and the rights of Venezuelans, how to address the violation of political and human rights, and ways to replicate the workshop in the neighborhood associations." The group also planned to train 220 individuals in conflict mediation and distribute several bulletins concerning their training to other neighborhood associations throughout Caracas.

The NED initiated a similar program with the Asociación Civil Justicia Alternativa (ACJA). In its program description, the NED deployed the same language from its program description for ACCEDES—that is, blaming the Venezuelan government for encouraging violence against the middle and upper classes. Although ACCEDES focused on conflict mediation in Caracas, ACJA focused on conflict throughout the country. The NED (2002e) reports that it funded ACJA to assist with conflict mediation in a program that would run from September 2002 until October 2003 and cost $10,000. ACJA planned to conduct two workshops in Maracay, the capital of Aragua State, and two workshops in each of three communities elsewhere in Aragua state. In its workshops, ACJA trained fifteen new justices of the peace, citizens, and government members in justice of the peace law and how to mediate conflicts. The overall aim of the two workshops was to establish a local network of individuals committed to mediating local conflicts, which would allow citizens to bypass the official court system.

The NED again provided a nearly $15,000 grant for ACJA for a project called Conflict Resolution at the Local Level, which would run for a year beginning in October 2003. While its initial grant was for the creation of a local network focused on mediating conflicts, its new project focused on human rights and policing. Under this project, the ACJA sought to hold five, two-day workshops in Aragua state that would train five hundred individuals—including police officers, local officials, and justices of the peace—on human rights issues, conflict mediation, and the role of the police in the justice system and community. The ACJA also planned to use funding to develop proposals that would improve police-community relations and to bring such proposals to local government leaders.

In a final example involving conflict mediation, from October 2002 until October 2003, the NED provided $11,000 to Fundación Justicia de Paz (FJP) for a project called Conflict Resolution at the Local Level. With NED funding, the FJP worked in thirty-two communities in Monagas State to promote dialogue between disparate political actors by convoking roundtable discussions moderated by local justices of the peace. During these roundtable discussions, the FJP sought to bring together different actors and generate accords between them in order to reduce conflict on basic policy issues, including illicit consumption of alcohol and insecurity (NED 2002f). For projects ranging between October 2003 and October 2004, the NED funded the FJP for a project of the same name for nearly $12,000. The FJP once again planned to work in thirty-two communities throughout Monagas State to reach accords between different political actors on general policy issues, such as issues of human rights and polarization. The group also planned to train ninety individuals in conflict resolution and mediation techniques (NED 2003f).

Last, the NED focused efforts on groups that specifically worked with law enforcement members in Venezuela. In 2003, for example, the NED provided over $40,000 to the Asociación Civil Liderazgo y Visión (ACLV) for a project called Civic Education for Police, which would run from September 2003 until October 2004. Similar to ACAE, ACLV possesses a relationship to the 2002 coup d'état. During that period, ACLV director Oscar Garcia Mendoza published a letter in a local Venezuelan newspaper expressing his support for the coup d'état and its leaders (Weisbrot 2004). With its US government funding, the ACLV project focused on training Metropolitan Police officers in Caracas, who were also widely viewed as anti-Chávez, in democracy and human rights training. In its program description, the NED (2003g) claims that police officers in Venezuela had indeed become politicized and remained ill-equipped to manage escalating crime rates.

ACLV planned a project involving three stages, including the training of educators in the police academy, teaching twenty-five courses in the police academy, and a final follow-up with program participants and the training of individuals that would continue their democracy and human rights training efforts in the police academy in the future. ACLV planned to train four individuals to serve as facilitators of courses that would help approximately 750 members of the police force "develop concepts such as, constructing a shared vision of the country and its future; the importance of dialogue and the peaceful resolution of conflict; the theory of citizenship as both a right and an obligation; and the role of the police in securing and promoting citizenship" (NED 2003g, 5). Thereafter, the four initial facilitators planned to train several members of the police force to conduct future meetings on democracy and human rights in the police force.

The NED continues to play a key role within the US democracy assistance community. It remains clear that some of the NED's recipients played prominent roles within the opposition, and, in some instance, the NED openly recognizes this within their program descriptions. In doing so, the NED demonstrates that it is not entirely committed to nonpartisanship, but, in many instances, has openly funded civil society groups with clear political leanings. In addition, many of the groups that the NED has provided with funding and assistance openly planned to contest Chávez government policies. However, in some few instances, some groups have worked with the government and commended some of its efforts, such as, at times, CESAP, ACCJ, and the FMG. These groups commended some government institutions and some government policies, and, in the instance of ACCJ, the group worked with some national government offices on issues of conflict mediation.

In general, the NED depicted the Venezuelan government under Chávez as a flagrant violator of constitutional and human rights, as promoting violence against middle- and upper-class citizens, as instigating polarization, as unable to properly govern Venezuelan society, and as promoting policies with no place in a democratic system. These alleged issues indeed served the official justification for the NED's involvement in the country. In their documents, the NED does not reflect on the fact that citizens continually elected Chavistas, supported and voted for a new Venezuelan constitution that championed participatory and direct democracy, and that opposition politicians and supporters also contributed to a polarized environment. Instead, NED documents largely venerated the political opposition and illustrated agreement with the opposition's concerns with Chávez's form of governance. In several instances, the NED even worked with NGOs that clearly aligned with the opposition and, in some instances, supported the transitional government, including ACLV, Súmate, and ACAC, whose director accepted a temporary position in the transitional government as the new minister of education. And so, the NED clearly evidences a disposition toward supporting groups that have criticized and worked to undermine the Venezuelan government under Chávez.

The NED also demonstrates a clear pattern of paternalism that remains consistent with the history of US foreign policymaking throughout Latin American since the early nineteenth century. While the Venezuelan government promoted a participatory and direct democracy, and Venezuelan citizens as a majority clearly supported these moves, the NED found these policies unbefitting for a contemporary democracy, and, in order to combat these policies, the organization funded several groups that sought to reverse such government policies. In addition, the NED continually reduced Venezuelan government policies to a series of objectives that Chávez alone sought to pursue. That is, the NED belittled the government's democratic pursuits and generally failed to understand that Venezuelan citizens might possibly support endeavors pushed by the Chávez government. Lastly, the NED inaccurately portrayed the nature of the Venezuelan political situation by blaming President Chávez for the politically polarized climate in the country and allegedly encouraging violence against his fellow citizens; that is, the NED failed to recognize that the opposition also played a role in the development of political polarization in the country. While Chávez and his political allies were hardly innocent of inflammatory behavior, they were not unilaterally responsible for all the political problems facing the country. In the end, we see the NED constantly siding with the political opposition and working to push back against Chávez government policies, though it could never fully shape how several NGOs depicted the Chávez government in their own reporting.

Chapter 8

TRANSFORMING CHAVISTAS, ENCOURAGING PROTEST

The US Agency for International Development in Venezuela

In dozens of countries throughout the world, the US government has worked through the US Agency for International Development (USAID) to provide democracy assistance abroad. Though the Kennedy administration initially established the agency in 1961 in order to specifically promote economic development, the group entered into the area of political development in the late twentieth century, continuing into the present (Carothers 2011; Robinson 1996). In Venezuela under President Hugo Chávez, USAID directed a particular unit to carry out democracy assistance efforts in the country: the Office of Transition Initiatives (OTI), an agency focused on assisting with and helping to carry out political transitions in countries abroad. US government elites have described the OTI as a partially clandestine unit that operates programs with less oversight than traditional USAID programs, and, to make matters even murkier, USAID/OTI has even subcontracted with private organizations to carry out their daily efforts abroad. In Venezuela, this involved Development Alternatives, Inc. (DAI).

Given that a transition in Venezuela was not actually transpiring in the country when the OTI initiated operations in 2002–2003, these efforts unsurprisingly generated much controversy, and, following an investigation in 2009, abruptly ended. Still, for seven years, the US government sought to undermine the Chávez government through its USAID/OTI/DAI nexus. Following the April 2002 coup d'état in Venezuela, USAID charged the OTI with handling its newfound programs within the country. Though US government elites sought to dismiss any criticism of its initial foray into the country, the criticism that the OTI had set out to displace the Chávez government was not misplaced. In particular, USAID/OTI/DAI maintained programs wherein they deliberately sought to pull supporters away from President Chávez by surreptitiously putting them into contact with opposition activists as well as by initiating a program designed to train and support blossoming student movements protesting against Chávez government policies in places all throughout Venezuela. Indeed, these latter movements include the location where many contemporary opposition leaders began their involvement in public politics, including opposition leader Juan Guaidó of the political party Voluntad Popular.[1]

In 2009 the Chávez government initiated an investigation into USAID/OTI/DAI activities in Venezuela and issued several of their employees citations surrounding their use of funding for activities in the country. USAID/OTI/DAI subsequently shipped their documents abroad, closed their office, and their US employees left the country. In 2010 USAID formally closed its OTI program in Venezuela. In this chapter, I detail USAID/OTI/DAI programs in Venezuela and how their objectives included attempts to change the minds of Chávez's supporters, to embolden those already protesting President Chávez, and to block Chávez government moves. All the while, US government functionaries demonstrated their belief that it was their duty to show Venezuelans how to do politics, how to engage in democracy, and what political leaders they should support. Though this is not the same sort of imperial tutelage from the colonial period, it is a form of neocolonialism wherein the US government uses its economic largesse and cultural leverage in an attempt to steer global political-economic dynamics in a direction that is most agreeable with US foreign policy interests. In doing so, US government functionaries aim to cultivate support for political parties and social movements that do not threaten or challenge US global power, and, in the instance of Venezuela, embrace US global leadership.

The US Agency for International Development and Its Goals

As the US government attained global hegemonic status following World War II, many of its leaders believed it had a newfound role to play throughout the world, including President Harry S. Truman (Lorenzini 2019).[2] In the aftermath of the war, the Truman administration offered foreign aid to countries in Western Europe in order to cultivate global support for the US-led liberal international order and to dissuade countries from turning toward and developing any sympathies for the Soviet Union. In Western Europe, the US government provided funds for societal reconstruction and economic growth through the Marshall Plan. In addition, the US government secretly distributed anti-communist propaganda and funded centrist political parties in, for example, Italy and Greece during the 1940s so that they might defeat socialist and communist parties that had garnered considerable support among their respective populations (Defty 2004; Kinzer 2013; Miller 1983). In both endeavors, the US government largely succeeded: it won the ideological support of most leaders in Western Europe, and, when socialist movements and political parties developed in southeastern Europe that might potentially work with the Soviet Union in a substantial manner, it neutralized them at the ballot box.

Though the United States maintained influence over Western Europe, the Soviet Union controlled much of Eastern Europe and curried support in many locations throughout what was then termed the Third World, with its own foreign aid programs and support for like-minded political parties (Levin 2016; Lorenzini 2019; Walters 1970). Coupled with the example of its socialist industrialization policies and poverty reduction programs, the US government recognized that the Soviet Union provided inspiration to many anti-colonial and liberation movements throughout what was then called the Third World. As a result, the Kennedy administration believed that they might neutralize these initiatives by establishing US government programs specifically designed to promote economic development beyond Western Europe and into many low-income, formerly colonized countries (Carothers 2011; Field 2014). In 1961 President John F. Kennedy signed the Foreign Assistance Act into law, and, among other features, the new legislation established USAID as the US government's primary agency charged with handling and distributing foreign aid.

Although the Kennedy administration initially established USAID in an effort to promote economic development abroad, the agency has since expanded its activities into the realm of political development and democracy assistance beginning at the end of the twentieth century (Carothers 2011; Robinson 1996). USAID now features several programs that explicitly focus on political rather exclusively economic initiatives. In particular, the agency includes a thematic focus on democracy, human rights, and governance, and in 2012 established the Center of Excellence on Democracy, Human Rights, and Governance. In its programmatic description, USAID (n.d.) explains that "we are integrating democracy programming throughout our core development work, focusing on strengthening and promoting human rights, accountable and transparent governance, and an independent and politically active civil society across all our work. At the same time, we remain committed to fundamental democratic empowerment activities, including supporting free and fair elections, up-to-date technology for new and traditional media, as well as the rule of law." In addition, the agency details that its adjacent center "provides technical advice and support to USAID missions implementing programs in democracy, human rights and governance; generates and disseminates knowledge to build the evidence base for global advancement in the area; and elevates the role of DRG in key USAID, US Government, and multilateral strategies" (USAID n.d.). There is thus no question that USAID has transformed into an agency with an obvious political component alongside its traditional economic focus.

Following its formation, USAID initiatives primarily focused on economic development programs. Indeed, some of the thinking surrounding economic development at the time insisted that economic development would eventually spur political development. In the late twentieth century, however, thinking within the development community began to insist that both economic and political development could occur simultaneously, as discussed in an earlier chapter (Carothers 2011). Together with the end of the Cold War and its apparent requirement for the US government to support anti-communist regimes, USAID made its way into the realm of democracy promotion and remains the US government's primary agency formally charged with promoting democracy abroad, leading into the present-day.

USAID/OTI in Chavista Venezuela

Post–Coup d'état Period (2002–2004)

Alongside the National Endowment for Democracy (NED) and its associated groups, USAID has provided periodic funding to groups such as the National Democratic Institute (NDI) and the International Republican Institute (IRI), two groups discussed in earlier chapters, particularly in years following USAID's closure of its office in Venezuela. In addition, USAID operated its own program in the country through the Office of Transition Initiatives (OTI) for several years following the 2002 coup d'état that displaced President Hugo Chávez. The OTI (n.d.) describes its purpose as "support[ing] US foreign policy objectives by helping local partners advance peace and democracy. The OTI provides fast, flexible, short-term assistance targeted at key political transition and stabilization needs." In public reports and statements, USAID/OTI offered only vague descriptions concerning their programming in Venezuela, generally referencing topics such as democracy, dialogue, and civil society. Interviews with former US government functionaries and analysis of US diplomatic cables, however, reveal an explicit effort to undermine the Chávez government, and to assist and hopefully bring opposition politicians to office.

Following the April 2002 coup d'état, USAID charged the OTI with carrying out its efforts in Venezuela, and in August 2002 the OTI began to develop its programming. The US government decision to use the OTI in the first place was itself curious and led to much controversy. Indeed, Chávez was deposed for a brief period, but he had returned to office to finish his term. The OTI, however, normally operates in war-torn countries facing deep conflict, such as Iraq, Sudan, Syria, and Ukraine. As a result, the news that USAID would use the OTI to operate programs in Venezuela was met coldly by the Chávez government (Golinger 2006).

In an interview with a former member of the US Department of State and USAID who helped to devise broad US foreign policy efforts toward Venezuela, the individual described the thinking behind the decision to use the OTI in the country. First, this functionary viewed the Chávez government as a serious threat to US global interests. He described President Chávez as "very hostile to the US. His pitch was anti-US, and he had a desire to become a leader throughout Latin America." Even further, he said, "When I was in the Bush administration, Chávez was far down the list of concerns. There wasn't much concern about Chávez. 9/11 was the most important [concern]. I was literally to make the Freedom Agenda work, along with Elliot Abrams. We devised the Freedom Agenda." What this functionary, among others, wanted to achieve before going into Venezuela was to ensure that the Bush administration prioritized the country: "We would say 'It's not the Middle East, but it's not good to have that problem in our backyard.' We would try and lobby Latin America countries against the [United Nations] not to support him. If he didn't have any money, fine. But he was sitting on the oil, and this was a problem for us. If it was [Daniel] Ortega in some tiny country [Nicaragua], then fine."

This functionary clearly embraced an imperialist mind-set regarding the role of the US government in the Americas and the broader world. According to him, Latin America remains "the backyard" of the United States. This depiction dates back to the Monroe Doctrine in 1823, wherein US leaders understood it as their responsibility maintain security throughout the Americas and to police the entirety of the region (Fitz 2017; Grandin 2006; Schoultz 2018. The imagery of the backyard of Latin America evokes the idea that the United States remains the proprietor of the hemispheric territory and must manage the affairs of the region. Given that Chávez rejected US global leadership, the US government somehow needed to neutralize the threat he posed. In doing so, this functionary makes reference to how he sought to influence other countries not to support Chávez, while also working on projects to undermine his presidency within Venezuela.

The road was not easy, though, to get individuals on board with working to displace Chávez. This functionary recalled that many individuals within USAID proper were still resistant to the activities of the OTI and the Bush administration's Freedom Agenda. "The Bush administration wanted to do more with democracy instead of planting trees. I was brought in to be an enforcer," he told me. "USAID wasn't on board with the Freedom Agenda ... USAID people didn't like the OTI, they saw it as an encroachment." He explained that many USAID employees remained protective of their identity as an agency involved in economic development projects, such as building roads and constructing dams, and they did not prefer to get into activities that looked like Central Intelligence Agency (CIA) or military activities. As a result, this functionary insisted that he had "to enforce" some practices within the agency, telling employees that USAID "is not a charity, not an NGO. The world is hostile and dangerous and we need to try to move it. We are using taxpayers' money." According to him, "Venezuela fell into the category of 'hostiles,'" and, as a result, USAID/OTI needed to combat his government and its policies, regardless of whether or not other USAID employees wanted to engage in less politicized work involving development elsewhere in the world.

Indeed, the reason that the OTI specifically got involved in Venezuela in the first place as an agency remained rooted in the view that Venezuela was a "hostile country." This functionary explained that the "White House wanted to come after Chavez... OTI was a better way, it's easier to get the money to people. It's not clandestine like the Cold War, but it's just easier. What can we offer that can't go through traditional channels... With OTI, you're not sitting down with the government at that point. And that's the idea." Individuals working for USAID/OTI/DAI on the ground in Venezuela, implementing their programs, had a sharper view of precisely why the OTI became the agency to operate in the country. One employee recounted that "when the office was opened, the US government came with a wrong logic. They thought Chávez would lose the recall referendum, and that Venezuela would need a strong democracy. But Chávez won, and they were wrong." Following the 2002 coup d'état, the opposition organized to recall President Chávez from office, but they failed in their attempt to unseat him. Employees on the ground believed that this was why the OTI was initially there: to assist in the apparent ensuing transition that would follow the recall election. Another employee on the ground told me a similar idea: "The US, at the beginning, saluted the coup d'état, and they had to pull back, because the coup failed. That was really sloppy by the opposition. So then came the *revocatorio* [recall effort], so we wanted to get people to go to the *revocatorio* and remove Chávez democratically. Jimmy Carter we had brought to make the referendum. Referendum came and Chávez won, and opposition were mad... mad at the US."

Indeed, in these early years involving USAID/OTI/DAI efforts, USAID provided some sporadic funding for IRI and NDI initiatives, but the group also directly funded the Carter Center, an organization established by President Jimmy Carter to monitor elections, in order to mediate the conflict between President Chávez and the opposition, and to pave way for a recall election on Chávez. Ambassador Charles Shapiro, for instance, confirmed this in a diplomatic cable in February 2004 outlining the OTI's work throughout the previous year, writing that the "OTI funded the Carter Center's continuing mediation and electoral process observation efforts" (Cablegate 2004b). Thereafter, the group funded the Carter Center to monitor elections in an effort to verify Chávez's defeat up to and through the 2004 recall election, which Chávez would, instead, eventually win with their verification, angering the political opposition in the country, many of whose members rejected the results. One employee described how, in addition to the Carter Center, the OTI also trained poll watchers, telling me that they "did an electoral witnesses program, training people to be electoral witnesses with electoral authorities. We tried to cut off arguments about fraud from the opposition so they would stop that. We proved there was no fraud. We made sure it was a fair campaign."

Not only was the opposition upset with the US government, but people in Washington were also upset that with their employees in Venezuela and how Chávez remained in office following the recall election in 2004. One former employee recounted that "sometimes I came to Washington. They didn't like what I would say. They wanted me to just get rid of Chávez. Informally, individuals said this. I was presenting stats on turnout during the campaign. 'Yes, but,' he said, 'you lost the elections.'" All of this programming and its outcomes indicates how US government funding can have the opposite effect that it might sometimes seemingly intend to have. In the end, despite US government efforts to monitor and evaluate the recall election, Chávez defied US government expectations and won. As a result, the US foreign policy community decided to change its strategy in the country and to begin a more long-term project on building the capacity of the opposition, including through continued USAID/OTI/DAI efforts, so that they might defeat Chávez as well as his allies in future elections.

Post-Referendum Period (2004–2006)

In the post–recall election period, USAID/OTI programming more explicitly challenged President Chávez. In a diplomatic in November 2006, Ambassador William Brownfield described USAID/OTI programming during the post-referendum period up until the 2006 regularly scheduled presidential election, plainly describing how their "strategy's focus is: 1) Strengthening Democratic Institutions, 2) Penetrating Chavez' Political Base, 3) Dividing Chavismo, 4) Protecting Vital US business, and 5) Isolating Chavez internationally" (Cablegate 2006l). Lest there be any confusion, Brownfield clearly articulates how the US government remained intent on deposing the Chávez government, albeit with a focus on elections rather than a direct intervention of sorts.

In order to "penetrate and divide" Chávez's base of support, USAID/OTI worked with DAI to fund small groups and programs within the country in order to pull supporters away from Chávez. In conversations with employees, they highlighted these particular programs that the group prioritized in the country during these years. One particular program included their work in barrios, or poor neighborhoods, throughout the Caracas area. Deputy Chief of Mission Kevin Whitaker described this program in vague terms in a cable from 2006, writing that "Chavez continues to loudly define and distort what democracy is all about. To provide some balance—primarily in low-income neighborhoods—OTI has developed five highly inter-active training modules that focus on: rule of law, separation of powers, political tolerance, the rights and responsibilities of citizens, and the role of civil society. In the two months since this project launched, over 40 NGOs around the country are using the materials to push back on the Bolivarian brain-washing effort" (Cablegate 2006k). According to Whitaker, since the Chávez government sought to "brain-wash" Venezuelan citizens, "Venezuelan civil society need[ed] partners like OTI to help build and strengthen the democratic institutions necessary to move the country beyond its deeply flawed past" (Cablegate 2006k). While asserting that Venezuela required US tutelage to move beyond its "deep flaws," Whitaker sought to appeal to the apparently essential nature of Venezuelans, in contrast with President Chávez, writing that "working against Chavez's militaristic vision and hate-filled discourse is the Venezuelans' essentially pacific nature and appreciation of societal harmony" (Cablegate 2006k). In doing so, Whitaker claims that Chávez's behavior is at odds with an apparently, naturally peaceful nature of Venezuelan citizens. Indeed, this is what Whitaker claims that US government programs were attempting to cultivate in Venezuela, and, through the process, only engaging Venezuelans' true nature as understood by US government elites. Whitaker never considers the distinct possibility that perhaps Venezuelans were not "brain-washed" but truly supported Chávez for reasons of their own choosing. Instead, given that Venezuelans selected an individual who the US government opposed, they could not possibly have engaged in proper, rational behavior. As a result, in Whitaker's opinion, these conditions necessitated the use of the OTI—and hence the US government—to show Venezuelans how to properly engage in democratic processes and what individuals they should appropriately select to run their country.

Ambassador Brownfield also discussed and further delineated these efforts in a 2006 cable, writing that the "OTI supports local NGOs who work in Chavista strongholds and with Chavista leaders, using those spaces to counter this rhetoric and promote alliances through working together on issues of importance to the entire community. OTI has directly reached approximately 238,000 adults through over 3000 forums, workshops and training sessions delivering alternative values and providing opportunities for opposition activists to interact with hard-core Chavistas, with the desired effect of pulling them slowly away from Chavismo" (Cablegate 2006l). Some in the US democracy assistance community sometimes downplayed the impact and extent of their programs in interviews with me. However, if indeed these programs reached some 238,000 individuals, that is no small program in a country of approximately 25 million citizens at the time. Once again, too, we see that US government programs were designed to counter Chávez's government and to offer "alternative values" in an effort to turn folks away from supporting him and toward the opposition. Once again, we also find high-ranking US government elites who believed it was the duty and responsibility of the US government to show Venezuelans' their true interests and "to slowly pull" Chávez's supporters away from him.

USAID/OTI/DAI employees specifically working on these programs recounted that they knew and were advised that these programs were specifically designed to pull supporters away from Chávez. One employee described to me in detail how USAID/OTI sought to accomplish this particular objective in the *barrios*. This particular employee told me that the group secretly worked with individuals from opposition political parties in order to develop "new NGOs that were looking very neutral in the eyes of the [Chávez] government, by them we can help people in the poor neighborhoods. They looked neutral because they had no affiliation with no political party. They were people from the neighborhood, even though they were opposition. They create the organizations with no past relation to political parties. So when they work in the barrios, they looked very neutral. So we gave them money . . . They were pulling people away from Chávez in a subtle manner." In doing so, this employee revealed that USAID/OTI designed all the thinking and materials that were used by these seemingly neutral NGOs throughout poor neighborhoods. "We were telling them what democracy is and showing them what democracy means. We developed very nice materials and took care of every word to give them, so it didn't look like we were sympathizing with the opposition: how to be a good citizen, how to work in the community. The people wanted it. Our goal was participation to talk about democracy values. We figure out that this was the way that we could convince the people that what was happening [under Chávez] was not democracy." The employee seemed convinced in some moments that "the people" wanted these programs, but, at other moments, the same employee surmised that "many people went [to USAID/OTI events] because we had breakfast and orange juice" and perhaps such individuals were not truly interested in turning toward the opposition, particularly in light of the fact that Chávez ended up winning the 2006 presidential election.

In the end, the same functionary admitted that USAID/OTI/DAI programs failed in their ultimate objective to bring Chávez's supporters over to the opposition. "The idea would have been to work with Chavistas to tell them that it's not the right thing to do. But Chavistas didn't want to work with us. We wanted to make bridges between Chavistas and opposition, but it was not possible to accomplish. We wanted to bring the Chavistas over to the opposition, but it didn't work." Besides conducting workshops and seminars on the state of democracy in the country, this functionary also laid out they tried to initiate other programs in the barrios, such as concerts and events. In one instance, one of their projects was disrupted. This former employee said that "in one project, they start a concert in a poor barrio, a hip-hop group. One group of Chavistas came with arms and guns, and tried to disturb it.

They knew it was a young project, not Chavista. Just because of that, they didn't want that to show. We wanted to build bridges to bring people together so they could see Chávez was wrong and we could help the opposition." As a result of the failure of these programs and Chávez's continued success, USAID/OTI/DAI decided to switch its approach to confronting his government and emboldening the opposition.

Post-Electoral Period (2007–2009)

Following Hugo Chávez's victory at the ballot box in 2006, USAID/OTI began to work with student movements that were protesting against and providing an overt challenge to the Chávez government and its policies. Indeed, it was during this period that President Chávez more intensively pursued a socialist agenda and a new constitutional referendum that would abolish presidential term limits and expand his socialist agenda, among other objectives. This is also the time period that some USAID/OTI employees said included their most successful efforts to combat the Chávez government and its policies. As the US government teamed up with student and youth movements protesting the government particularly in the streets of Caracas, Chávez suffered his first real defeat as Venezuelans rejected the constitutional referendum in December 2007. Unsurprisingly, the US government sought to claim much credit for this, a familiar practice within the US foreign policymaking and democracy promotion community (Mitchell 2009).[3]

Student protesting erupted in Venezuela in May 2007 over the Chávez government's ruling not to renew the broadcasting license of longtime television station RCTV as a result of its alleged involvement in the 2002 coup d'état. This ruling still allowed RCTV to broadcast over cable networking, but it could no longer freely broadcast over public Venezuelan airwaves. Though Chávez had announced the coming decision in the previous year, its actual passage generated large protests, primarily from college students, particularly on the Andres Bello University and Central University of Venezuela campuses, but also on several other campuses throughout Venezuela. Though the RCTV decision precipitated the protests, much of the protesting targeted the Chávez government and its policies, broadly speaking. This is the time period that led to the development and public political profile of several opposition leaders affiliated with the protests, including opposition leader Juan Guaidó but also Yon Goicoechea, Stalín Gonzalez, and Freddy Guevara, all of whom persist as opposition leaders into the present (Gill and Hanson 2019; Daniels 2019).

As their efforts in the barrios largely failed, USAID/OTI sought to link up with these student groups and to provide them with support. One USAID/OTI/DAI employee told me that "the movement started with the protest against that TV channel closed. When we saw that potential, we start to talk to them." In doing so, they wanted to help them organize a long-term movement that could continue to challenge Chávez after protesting RCTV's closure in particular had ceased. One high-ranking USAID member stated that the "objective was that you had thousands of youth, high school and college kids that were horrified of this Indian-looking guy in power. They were idealistic. We wanted to help them to build a civic organization, so that they could mobilize and organize. How do you organize yourselves to vote? This is different than protesting." In chapter 3, I discussed the racist dimensions of US government support for the opposition. Indeed, US foreign policymakers plainly recognized the racist and elitist nature of many middle- and upper-class Venezuelans in the country, too, and how they looked down on their lower-class and darker-skinned citizen counterparts. Some individuals, nonetheless, said they somewhat pushed back against this sort of thinking among high-ranking US government elites and the Venezuelan opposition. For example, one USAID/OTI/DAI employee said quite plainly that "USAID/DAI funds all these white people . . . that were not democratic at all . . . They were led by elitist conduction. I'd say, 'I'm not saying you're racist, but you need to do something about it.' They didn't want to talk about it. The reaction was so brutal that they accused me of supporting Chávez." Reflecting on the 2006 election, the same employee said that "I remember in a meeting with [Julio] Borges [from opposition party Primero Justicia], and he wouldn't shake hands with people and so forth. Chávez would allow people to hug him, and he would listen to them. They were so detached and didn't get close to the poor. When they choose [Manuel] Rosales [from the opposition to run for president in 2006], I thought forget it! His baby looked like a Gerber baby."

Despite the fact that US government officials clearly understood that the Venezuelan opposition members included many young students possessing racist, classist, and elitist views, they still continually supported them in their efforts to undermine and unseat President Chávez. In the end, geopolitics trumped these issues. Another USAID/OTI/DAI employee claimed that the

> most successful time [for USAID/OTI/DAI] was during 2007 when the student movement developed . . . The US had a very daring movement and brought a lot of money to the students through OTI, and it grew a lot as a result. There was a referendum at that time, and Chávez lost and was pissed off about that. It was really a lot of money that the US gave to the student groups through [USAID/OTI/DAI] . . . I can say with pride that a lot of people in the [Venezuelan] Congress, I know them from our projects. A lot of them now in the Congress. They work in the cities in the governments in the cities. I'm proud. It's like you see your son and daughter grow up. I knew them when they grew up. It's amazing. So the potential leaders when, if there is a change of government . . . and we were the ones who showed them the first steps.

Similar to their seminars and workshops in the barrios, USAID/OTI/DAI also conducted similar events for the students who were organizing protests against Chávez. In their events, one employee told me that they discussed "What is democracy? What is the vote? All the pillars with the democracy system, to reinforce them. What language they have to use... We were not the only institutions working with them." In addition to hosting such training events, this employee also recalled that "[we also gave them] all the things they needed: microphones, things for presentations, paper, we gave them this." In addition, this employee revealed that they were not the only US agency working with the students. In addition, the employee said that another US agency, which could have possibly been the CIA, had provided students with "things, like, they can be used in the street and protect themselves, [like] masks, but it was not part of open grants." Indeed, while USAID/OTI at least acknowledged they were working in Venezuela, agencies such as the CIA often do not publicly acknowledge their work in countries abroad.

In a diplomatic cable from this period, Ambassador Patrick Duddy lays out how USAID additionally assisted student leaders throughout the country (Cablegate 2008). Duddy reveals how at the behest of USAID contacts in the country, a USAID officer flew out to Mérida to meet with student leaders from several universities, including student leaders from the University of the Andes in Mérida and the University of Zulia, who had, additionally, thanked USAID for earlier support. The gathering met at the "vacation home" of Carlos Tinoco, a USAID contact within the country, to discuss funding for a national conference for students in Maracaibo, the most populous city in western Venezuela and the second most populous city in the country. Duddy cabled that they "have invited 10 Venezuelan legal experts, professors, and former government ministers to participate, including Milos Alcalay, Venezuela's former Ambassador to the United Nations. They requested assistance to organize the conference, including airfare for some participants. USAID and the Embassy have approved this request" (Cablegate 2008). It is clear from this cable that USAID maintained a particularly strong relationship with such student groups throughout the country. Indeed, the cable describes the ease with which student leaders informally asked for USAID assistance, and how it was summarily provided with seemingly little debate.

In December 2007 President Chávez experienced his first electoral loss, amid increased protesting and organizing among student groups in the country. One USAID/OTI/DAI employee remembered how, following his defeat, the "White House had called to thank DAI when Chávez lost the recall referendum. They couldn't believe it." As workers on the ground included Spanish-speaking, Latin American individuals and some from Venezuela itself, this same employee expressed resentment toward the attitude of some folks the Bush administration. This same employee relayed to me that "they said, 'How's this fucking Latino gonna get this done and we can't?' One guy said this . . . To the White House, I was just a guy mowing the grass. They didn't care about me." Indeed, the same individual disclosed how they believed they had post-traumatic stress disorder from the stress of their political experiences in Venezuela, but that the US government did not seem to care at all about the well-being of their employees in the country. To this individual, they wanted Chávez gone, and that was it. Still, some seemed to find it confusing that the White House needed Latin American employees to accomplish these efforts, and that they apparently could not achieve these results with direct actions from Washington alone.

The End of USAID/OTI Programming

In 2010 USAID/OTI formally closed its programming in Venezuela. In the previous year, the Chávez government had launched an official investigation into the agency and its efforts. In some ways, this is surprising given that nearly a decade had elapsed since the US government initiated such programming in August 2002. President Chávez often took rhetorical aim at US democracy promotion efforts, but, in many ways, never fully pursued efforts against their activities until this period. In other ways, perhaps the timing is not all that curious. In earlier years, Chávez won elections and seemingly faced no serious electoral threats. Only after Chávez lost the December 2007 constitutional referendum did his government begin to take serious aim at US government funding and programming within the country. Despite the closure of the program, many of these employees believed in their efficacy, even if they did not ultimately displace Chávez from power.

In August 2009 Ambassador Patrick Duddy cabled Washington that USAID/OTI programs were now coming under closer surveillance by agencies within the Venezuelan state. Duddy reported that "on August 26, police officers from the Scientific, Penal and Criminal Investigations Corps (CICPC) arrived at the Development Alternatives, Incorporated (DAI) office in Caracas and presented citations . . . for the Investigation of Crimes Against the National Wealth" to some of its employees (Cablegate 2009d). Duddy further revealed that "the investigation was initiated by the Superintendent of Banks (SUDEBANS) following the detection of unusually large cash transfers in 2007 and 2008. This coincides with the December 2007 Constitutional Referendum and national state and local elections in 2008" (Cablegate 2009d). Indeed, it appears that given Chávez's defeat, his government began to look into the funding behind groups opposed to his proposed referendum.

One employee revealed that the Venezuelan government started "photographing me and calling me at night. And then one day they stormed into my office. In they came, and I left through the door. So we came back later and removed *everything*. Even the stickers on the wall. We wanted to protect the grantees. We sent it all to the US." Another employee recalled the same story, saying that "I found out we were under investigation, so we closed it. I was in charge of closing it. It was a very exciting job." When one DAI representative met with embassy officials in August 2009, he explained precisely why the Venezuelan government was targeting them, saying that "'the streets are hot,' referring to growing protests against Chavez's efforts to consolidate power, and 'all these people (organizing the protests) are our grantees.'" (Cablegate 2009d).

In the aftermath of the program's closure, many of the USAID/OTI employees who retained US citizenship either returned to the United States or moved on to work in other countries on additional USAID/OTI programs. Still, despite the program's abrupt end, many believed that they had shaped the country for the better. One employee believed they provided the foundations for leaders who might come to lead a new Venezuela, as recounted earlier. For this employee, although the opposition did not defeat Chávez in a presidential contest, there was a sense that they had laid the groundwork for a future Venezuela that the opposition might lead. The same employee claimed that "looking back, we at least put the seed in some of the groups that they have to fight for democracy, and they have the right to do it. We gave them some tools. That's what kept them alive."

Other employees believed that their success solely laid with the anxiety it might have caused Venezuelan government leaders. A high-ranking USAID member articulated this view, stating that USAID "wanted to keep alive democracy movements, in the students and the youth, and hope they could galvanize enough support. We know our work has been effective, look at [current president Nicolás] Maduro. If we don't help keep people alive, there will be nothing to take over when the state collapses. We are vexing dictators. As long as Chávez wakes up and is angry with what we're doing, that's good, that's good for freedom." Even further, this same individual asserted that "if everyday a dictator wakes up and knows that they have people pushing for democracy, then it's important to support democracy. That's a victory."

In the post–coup d'état period, USAID/OTI actively sought to combat the Chávez government and to depose him from office. The agency contracted with DAI and worked on a range of fronts to counteract President Chávez's influence in the country. This activity primarily included the creation of new nongovernmental organizations (NGOs) that sought to pull Chávez's supporters away from him and into the opposition camp. Even according to former USAID/OTI/DAI employees, these efforts, however, failed. Chávez's supporters continued to vote for him in the 2006 presidential election and generally displayed support for the government, even in the face of US government attempts to ideologically convince them otherwise.

USAID/OTI/DAI experienced more success throughout their efforts with student movements. Indeed, it is during this period that Chávez experienced one of few electoral setbacks, when citizens rejected his constitutional referendum package in December 2007. At the time, many students throughout the country had taken to the streets to express their rejection of the Chávez government, initially including the closure of RCTV, but eventually turning into more widespread protest of the government itself. US government funding flowed to assist the student groups in their meetings and in order to help them host conferences throughout the country. In the end, while many in the US government seemed to believe their funding resulted in Chávez's electoral defeat, the truth is probably more complicated. However, there is no doubt that US government funding for opposition student groups assisted them in the development of their infrastructure and increased the capacity for them to disseminate their messages.

Throughout all of this funding, though, what is much more consistent is the US government's attempt to steer Venezuelan politics in particular directions. What is more, US government functionaries believed it was their duty to reveal to Venezuelans what politicians they should support and what politicians they should not support. This involved an attempt to cultivate rejection among Chávez's supporters. These attempts did not succeed. Likewise, US government-funded electoral monitors had continually found that Chávez won at the ballot box and that no electoral fraud existed. All of this indicates that the US government is not omnipotent. In a new era of imperialism, the US government must work through global networks much more so than through gunboat diplomacy or military intervention. Military interventions are never off the table, but both the US populace and the global community only have so much appetite for such measures. In addition, the US government remains somewhat curtailed by international law and must at least present itself as a good-faith actor that does not engage in hypocrisy (Poznansky 2020). Nonetheless, US global power persists, and, given US economic largesse and military unipolarity, successful interventions have succeeded elsewhere. In Venezuela, however, Chávez resisted US intervention and, with the exception of a few days in April 2002, remained president until his death in 2013.

Chapter 9

CHÁVEZ RESPONDS

Terminating Foreign Funding for Political Parties and NGOs

Since the April 2002 coup d'état that temporarily ousted President Hugo Chávez, Chávez hardly let any public appearance pass wherein he did not lambaste the US government and its alleged attempts to end his presidency—either, he asserted, by supporting the opposition at the ballot box or through violence. In keeping with such rhetoric, Chávez denounced opposition political parties, opposition-oriented nongovernmental organizations (NGOS), and opposition supporters as *pitiyanquis* (subordinates and puppets of the US government), which Chávez, in turn, referred to as *el imperio* (the empire). There is no doubt that Chávez was fully convinced that the US government through the Central Intelligence Agency (CIA) wished to assassinate him, or, in the least, that the United States wished to help the opposition defeat him during elections. In previous chapters, I have shown that the latter objective was clearly the case when it came to US democracy assistance programs, which were all designed to help the opposition usher in a new, liberal democratic form of government.

Yet, despite the 2002 coup d'état, the Venezuelan government did not seriously target US government funding for political parties and NGOs in the country for nearly a decade. It was not until December 2010 that the government passed legislation that cracked down on such practices. In the meantime, President Chávez and his supporters dominated the legislature as well as the judiciary. From the perspective of sociological theories of the state, the eventual passage of such legislation that targeted NGOs is not puzzling. What is puzzling, though, is that nearly a decade elapsed after the coup d'état before Chávez passed legislation that took aim at this practice. Historically, political sociological theories, including pluralist and neo-Marxist theories of the state, have focused on domestic factors and looked to the composition of government—namely, the legislature—to understand the passage of laws. However, Chávez supporters, or Chavistas, had dominated the National Assembly since 2000, and legislation was not passed until 2010. This indicates that forces outside of the legislature played a serious role in the government's decision.

Rather than domestic factors, the Venezuelan government's redirection in international and domestic government relations are what eventually generated the opportunity for President Chávez to pass this controversial law. As we will see, in the immediate years following the coup d'état, the government maintained acrimonious but somewhat working relations with the US and Western European governments, and, to a lesser extent, domestic NGOs. When anti-NGO legislation came upon the agenda in these earlier years, all of these actors worked together to urge the government to reconsider its passage. By 2010, the year in which anti-NGO legislation was finally passed, the Venezuelan government had redirected its relations away from these groups to now primarily include several authoritarian governments and anti-imperial governments that had already passed similar legislation or were considering its passage. China and Russia, in particular, replaced the United States and Western Europe as Venezuela's major military and political-economic partners. Venezuela increasingly traded with and received political-economic and military aid from these countries as well as met with and established cooperative agreements with them. More than any other countries, China and Russia came to buoy Venezuela in the wake of deteriorating relations with the United States and Western Europe. Indeed, this is a situation that continues into the present. Amid this new set of relations, anti-NGO legislation was thus not considered transgressive, but normative, as these same governments were also drafting and passing similar pieces of legislation.

Anti-NGO Legislation in Venezuela

In the wake of the 2002 coup d'état, President Chávez directed much blame on the CIA and the US government writ large. As months went on, Chávez began to direct his attention at some lesser-known US government agencies, particularly USAID and the NED. While the CIA has long been condemned by leftist leaders throughout Latin America, USAID and the NED were nowhere near such common names. Following the release of several documents from these groups, USAID and the NED's involvement with the opposition garnered much attention throughout the country and within the halls of Miraflores Palace. Even more, the US government, through an inspector-general report, had admitted that some US funding from these groups had, in fact, flowed to some opposition groups that planned and participated in the coup d'état that nearly eliminated the Chávez government (OIG 2002).

Yet, although some sporadic court cases were opened up against some NGOs shortly following the coup d'état and 2004 recall referendum, the

Venezuelan government never sought to legally prohibit foreign funding for parties and NGOs until nearly a half decade later. In June 2006 the National Assembly proposed the Law on International Cooperation (LIC) in order to target US government funding for civil society organizations throughout the country. If passed, this law would have created a national fund where all outside groups—including cooperating states, multilateral organizations, foreign NGOs, and other private organizations—would need to direct their funding for Venezuelan development projects broadly conceived. The Venezuelan executive branch would then distribute these foreign funds to NGOs willing to cooperate on national goals and projects established by the national executive. In doing so, neither donors nor NGOs would possess discretion over how funds would be allocated. The law would have thus prohibited NGOs from directly receiving funding from foreign sources. Yet, the National Assembly failed to consider the legislation for full passage into law, all despite Chavistas dominating the National Assembly.

Fast forward to 2010. Despite Chávez continually railing against US imperialism, the Venezuelan legislature had yet to consider the passage of legislation that targets foreign funding for NGOs. In December 2010, however, the National Assembly successfully, and quickly, passed the Law for the Defense of Political Sovereignty and National Self-Determination (LDPS). Unlike the LIC, the LDPS focuses on citizens who aspire for political office, political organizations and political parties, and political NGOs, which includes "groups that promote, defend, spread or inform citizens . . . about the full exercise of their political rights." The LDPS restricts these organizations and persons from receiving funds and support from foreign organizations and persons, and it establishes a fine of twice the amount of funding received as a penalty. The law also allows the government to disqualify the heads of political organizations from political participation for a period between five and eight years for receiving foreign funding.

After nearly a decade after the coup d'état, which the Chávez government alleged had been buttressed by US government funding, the Venezuelan legislature finally targeted civil society and its reception of foreign funds. The timing and the passage of this funding is curious and quite puzzling, and it speaks to the complicated relationship between Venezuela and the international community. So, why did Chávez finally target foreign funding for domestic groups and pass this legislation when it did?

Classical Political Sociology and International Relations

Classical political sociological theories have looked to the composition of government as well as the populace to explain the passage of legislation. Pluralist theorists, for instance, posited that no one group continually dominates political life (Dahl 1961; Polsby 1963). In their view, power remains fragmented and diffused throughout government branches and state institutions. At different periods, interest groups and social movements can lobby these branches and institutions, and, depending on the political climate and composition of these units, potentially achieve their will. Neo-Marxists have generally disagreed with pluralist-oriented theorists in their analyses of the legislation process. Although some neo-Marxists have disagreed on the mechanisms through which capitalists influence the behavior of national governments, they reach the same conclusion: capitalist-class interests direct legislation. Ralph Miliband (1969), for one, argued that most legislators come from an upper-class background and are socialized into a capitalist-oriented worldview that prioritizes business interests over working-class concerns. In the end, he argued that legislators consider business interests above all else when voting. In more recent years, analyses centralizing the power of the capitalist class have looked at campaign contributions and the influence of interest groups, such as the American Legislative Exchange Council (ALEC), in drafting legislation (Clawson et al. 1998; Hertel-Fernandez 2014, 2019; Gilens and Page 2014; Page and Gilens 2020).

These two general research traditions, however, do not move an analysis of the legislation formation process in contemporary Venezuela very far. Chavistas have dominated state institutions and all branches of government since 2000. Since this time, neither organized interest groups that possess the capacity to influence legislation nor a business community that wields determinative influence over government policy has much existed. Instead, Chavistas have dominated political life and seldom faced any obstacles to passing legislation. Their decision to shelve the LIC illustrates a rare instance that we actually see such obstacles. Since Chavistas have dominated political life, we must consider what impediments exist beyond the domestic environment.

Instead of domestic factors, a shifting set of international relations allowed for political opportunities for the Venezuelan government and, at times, closed off other possibilities. Hugo Chávez—and now Nicolás Maduro—was incredibly sensitive to how the global community perceived Venezuela and political dynamics therein. President Chávez sought a leadership role for Venezuela's government throughout the world and certainly a leadership position within the hemisphere. At varying points in time, though, his international concerns transformed. While at some points Chávez and other government leaders seemingly desired better working relations the United States and Western Europe, they have not appeared concerned with their criticism at other points. All of this depended on the historical trajectory of political processes within Venezuela, and, more importantly, Venezuela's relationship with a shifting set of government actors across the world.

Javier Corrales and Carlos Romero (2013, 170) have shown that Venezuela incrementally cultivated relations with countries such as China and Russia to promote an identity built upon "radical anti-Americanism, or at least, an image of courageously standing up to US objectives." David Smilde and Timothy Gill (2013, 3) have also shown that Venezuela has embraced an "ideology that encourages the development of a multi-polar world and an 'anti-imperial' axis of countries." In doing so, the Venezuelan government has prioritized relations with countries that challenge US global hegemony and has sought to reduce its dependence on the United States and Western Europe by garnering support from a newfound network of authoritarian and anti-imperial governments; namely, China and Russia.

Over the last two decades, China and Russia have increasingly engaged in trade with Venezuela, loaned the government money, provided military support and training, and diplomatically met with their leaders. Such a situation continues into the present day. Representatives from the US and Western European governments that previously provided funding to Venezuelan NGOs eventually developed a sense that their relations with the government were no longer welcome, and domestic NGO representatives articulate that dialogue with the government would end following the 2006 presidential election. Altogether, this illustrates the Venezuelan government's commitment to redirecting its foreign and domestic relations outside US and Western European influence, and toward a newfound subfield of allies, particularly at the global level. In addition, these shifts in international relations also provided the context in which the Venezuelan government pursued harsher sanctions against opposition groups within the country.

Redirecting Venezuelan Foreign Relations

Although upon President Chávez's death in 2013 the media highlighted the hostile relationship between the United States and Venezuela, relations were not always conflicted. Upon taking office, Chávez pledged to respect foreign investments, allow continued foreign investment, and reduce the size of an expansive state. In June 1999 he visited the United States to attract investment, meeting with executives from JP Morgan, Citigroup, and the New York Stock Exchange, as well as President Clinton (Vogel Jr. 1999). He developed friendly relations with other, US-allied nations as well. In October 1999 Chávez traveled throughout Asia to encourage investment and visited leaders and businesspersons in South Korea, Malaysia, and Japan, and, in July 2000 he traveled to Germany's Hanover Exposition to secure Western European investment from investors throughout the continent.

In earlier years, President Chávez also strengthened relations with Organization of the Petroleum Exporting Countries (OPEC) nations, some of which clashed with US government expectations. In August 2000 he visited Nigeria, Indonesia, and Saudi Arabia, among others, and also became the first head of state to meet with Saddam Hussein. The US government condemned the visit and attempted to dissuade Chávez from taking the trip; however, Venezuela emphasized its sovereignty, and Foreign Minister Jose Vicente Rangel responded that "nobody can influence our decision . . . [Chávez is] going to arrive [in Iraq], whether it be on a skateboard or a camel" (BBC News 2000). Rangel noted that the trip "is not an ideological or political visit . . . [but] a visit that corresponds to our country's petroleum policy and OPEC's petroleum policy" (Olson 2000). Despite working relations with the US government, this demonstrated that Chávez would not shy from breaking with the United States.

President Chávez continued to travel throughout Western Europe in 2001, including visits to Italy and England, to continue promoting investment. During this time, he also traveled throughout Central and South America and promoted regional integration. However, by the end of 2001, Chávez began to place some limits on foreign investment and private enterprise with the Hydrocarbons Law and the Land Law. The former reversed efforts to open the oil industry up to foreign investment and allowed the executive branch greater control over it. The law continued to allow joint ventures, but mandated that PDVSA, the government-owned oil industry, would possess, at minimum, a 51 percent share. The Land Law permitted the government to expropriate idle lands from large landholders in order to breakup land concentration and put unused territories to use (Ellner 2008, 113–14; Wilpert 2007, 254). Both laws irritated large rural landholders and private urban business persons as well as stoking suspicion among investors that the government might not ultimately respect their investments, illustrating the growing legitimacy of government intervention into the economy to the detriment of free market capitalism. Such dismay with government policies formed the basis of the April coup d'état led by dissident military officers, angered PDVSA employees, and anti-Chávez politicians and citizens.

In its wake, President Chávez asserted that the US government instigated the coup d'état. More than anything else, this became the government's justification for incrementally drifting further away from a subfield of government actors involving the United States and Western Europe, and toward a new subfield of actors explicitly governed by ideas of multipolarity and counteracting the former countries' global domination. Yet, even despite these accusations, the Venezuelan government still continued to conduct high-level meetings with its US counterparts. Most importantly, though, the US government remained Venezuela's largest oil consumer and trading partner. Although the Venezuelan government would have seemingly preferred to diversify its trading clientele, no country could purchase petroleum quantities or provide any of the support required to offset dependence on the United States at this time. Preferably or not, the Venezuelan government realized that it could not afford to entirely sacrifice relations with the United States.

During these early years of Chávez's presidency, the government also prioritized economic and social relations with the European Commission (EC), the agency of the European Union (EU) that coordinates international development assistance, as well as the EU and its member states. The EC developed two programs with Venezuela for the 2001–2006 period: one aimed at preventing natural disasters and one promoting economic diversification by providing support for Venezuelan fisheries. The EC also developed relations with several political NGOs. This included funding several groups to monitor the 2004 recall referendum, the 2005 parliamentary elections, and the 2006 presidential elections. Chávez continued to seek relations with not only the EU but also several EU countries. In November 2004 he sought to repair relations with the Spanish government after it recognized the Carmona government in April 2002 and allegedly assisted some of the plotters (Radio Nacional de Espana 2004). In October 2005 Chávez also traveled to France to meet with Prime Minister Jacques Chirac and several investors to discuss foreign investment into Venezuelan oil (BBC News).

Although President Chávez continued to court foreign investment, he evidenced a desire to chart a new course and publicly endorsed socialism for the first time at the World Social Forum in January 2005. Not long after, he began to cultivate intensive relations with countries that opposed the US government, as well as the EU, demonstrating the diminishing legitimacy these governments possessed within Venezuela. Although Chávez briefly visited President Vladimir Putin in earlier years, these visits were cast as strategic relations between governments with energy sources, similar to his visit to Iraq. That is, they were not cast as an ideological alliance developed in opposition to the United States and Western Europe. By 2006, though, Chávez embraced Putin as a harbinger of a new multipolar global order struggling to combat US and Western European influence and to solidify a new global subfield of relations. In Russia, Chávez met with Putin and visited several arms factories from where he would purchase weapons to update the military. These initial purchases included over $1 billion in helicopters, fighter jets, and AK-103 rifles, a move that US government leaders asked Russia to reconsider (Smilde and Gill 2013). Chávez also initiated intense relations with Belarus and Iran. While in Belarus, Chávez proclaimed that it embodied a "model of a social state, which [Venezuela is] also starting to build" (ITAR-TASS 2006). In Iran, Chávez and Ahmadinejad emphasized enhanced economic relations and urged the world to support Iran's nuclear program (Islamic Republic News Agency 2006).

In August 2006 President Chávez made a special six-day visit to China to initiate several cooperative arrangements. While there, Chávez asserted that relations between China and Venezuela would produce a "great wall" against US hegemony and help to create a new multipolar global order that would counteract its influence (Watts 2006). Among the deals made during this trip, China pledged to construct twenty thousand houses in Venezuela, increase oil imports to five hundred thousand barrels per day in 2009 and one million by 2016, establish joint oil ventures with the Venezuelan government, and develop Venezuela's railway and farm irrigation systems. These agreements were the beginning of China's now-intensive involvement in buoying the Venezuelan government and its economy, extending over $60 billion in loans since this time.

With these newly redirected relations developing that were being built upon the ideas of multipolarity and counter balancing the influence of the United States and Western Europe, it was during this time that the National Assembly made a move to ban NGOs' direct access to foreign funding. In June 2006, the month before Chávez initiated visits and embraced leaders in Russia, China, Iran, and Belarus, the National Assembly proposed and successfully passed the LIC in a first discussion. All Venezuelan legislation, however, must successfully pass through two rounds of discussion before becoming available to convert into actual law. What is more, during this period, these countries were also considering similar pieces of legislation, evidencing how these political maneuvers were becoming normative within this newly solidifying subfield aiming to diminish US global power (Carothers 2006; Gershman and Allen 2006).

Rumors that Venezuela was preparing this legislation, however, allowed the international community to quickly respond to it. One month before the LIC's first discussion, US Deputy Chief of Mission Kevin Whitaker cabled nineteen US embassies throughout Western Europe and Latin America, stating that "the Embassy has been working with civil society, other diplomatic missions and interested groups to bring domestic and international pressure on [Venezuela] to postpone or modify the legislation" (Cablegate 2006b). In order to engage with the Venezuelan government on this issue, the "Canadian Embassy organized a meeting . . . attended by representatives of the World Bank, UNDP, and UNHCR, Sinergia, Foro Por la Vida and Paz Activia [sic], as well as the diplomatic missions of Canada, United Kingdom, United States, Belgium, the Netherlands, Germany and the European Union" to decide on a strategy to combat the LIC (Cablegate 2006b).

In the days before and after the LIC was proposed and passed in a first discussion, a number of governments—including Canada, Finland, Italy, the Netherlands, Sweden, Switzerland, and the United Kingdom—supplied demarchés to the National Assembly voicing opposition to the law and attempting to utilize what leverage remained (Cablegate 2006b; Cablegate 2006d). Whitaker suggested that it "would be a good time to push the issue with sympathetic governments, taking care ... not make it appear as a [US government]-led effort" due to its diminishing influence, and indeed the Canadian, Finnish, and UK embassies led the effort to persuade Venezuela from passing the LIC in a second discussion (Cablegate 2006e; Cablegate 2006h). The EU and the United Nations Development Programme additionally registered their opposition to the law, conveying that it would threaten their own assistance to Venezuela, which a Dutch diplomat suggested had alarmed Saul Ortega, the Chavista National Assembly member heading the LIC efforts (Cablegate 2006g). During interviews, two EC international cooperation officers stated that the international community made it clear to government members that the communal donation pot that the LIC would establish was not something that embassies and donors would provide funding for, and all funding—to both the Venezuelan government and NGOs—could be terminated as a result.

In the end, Ortega told the Finnish ambassador that they did not pass the legislation due to appeals from the international community, illustrating the government's "keen desire to preserve the appearance of democracy, and their sensitivity when it comes to criticism, particularly from abroad" (Cablegate 2006e). Yet, despite the Venezuelan government's interest in maintaining a democratic reputation, Ortega told the Finnish ambassador that the law would be reconceptualized and reconsidered in a congressional session in 2007 (Cablegate 2006e). Nonetheless, the legislative setback demonstrated that Venezuela had not yet been fully integrated into a new subfield and its relations with the United States, and, even more so, Western Europe remained moderately strong and that these governments still wielded some level of influence over the Venezuelan government and its decisions.

In September 2006 Chávez visited the United Nations and provided his most internationally memorable speech. Upon taking the podium, Chávez crossed himself and stated that the area smelled of sulfur from its recent visit from President George W. Bush. Standing before the global community, Chávez denounced US aggression in the Middle East and its promotion of capitalist policies. Three months later, he won reelection in Venezuela with nearly 63 percent of the vote, and, in the post-2006 electoral period, Chávez intensified his aims to push the socialist revolution forward. All the while, Chavistas continued to dominate all branches of government.

In the post-electoral period, Chávez consolidated relations with anti-US, anti–Western European governments and became fully integrated into a newfound subfield of countries built upon multipolarity and a rejection of free market capitalism. While Venezuela had yet to pass any anti-NGO legislation, Venezuela's authoritarian allies had enacted and were now enforcing legislation that regulated NGO activity. In Russia, for instance, the government enacted legislation in April 2006 mandating that NGOs register with the government and disclose all their funding and public activity in advance, and, in

Belarus, the government mandated that NGOs register all activities with the national government (Gershman and Allen 2006). Although Venezuela did not yet pass legislation and remained keyed into relations with Western European and North American governments, the passage of restrictive legislation in other countries illustrated the possibility of doing so and that a burgeoning norm of restricting NGO activity was diffusing among some countries throughout the world.

In the post-electoral period, Chávez made plans to continue to update the military by having some Venezuelan military personnel train with the Russian military and by purchasing more equipment from them (Romero and Romero 2008). On a second visit to Russia in under three weeks, the Russian government loaned Chávez $1 billion to purchase weapons, bringing Venezuelan total purchases over the previous years to over $5 billion (Schwirtz 2008). The most recent purchases included army tanks, assault rifles, and submarines. From 2000 to 2007, general trade with Russia increased from $55 million to $1.1 billion, as Putin and Chávez continued to embrace one another as fellow allies in the struggle against US global hegemony.

While Russia became Venezuela's primary military partner, China became Venezuela's most important economic partner. By 2010, trade between Venezuela and China rose forty-five-fold to $9.6 billion up from $218 million in 2000. On top of this trade, China has provided Venezuela with over $60 billion in loans since 2005, and in 2007 provided $4 billion for the Venezuelan National Development Fund. In light of deteriorating relations with the United States and Western Europe, the Chinese government has kept, and continues to keep, alongside Russia, Venezuela economically afloat.

Beyond China and Russia, Venezuelan relations with Belarus intensified in this post-electoral period. President Alexander Lukashenko visited Chávez for the first time in 2007 and again in 2010 and 2012, establishing several agreements. Although Venezuelan-Belarusian relations have largely centered on energy and trade, Chávez and Lukashenko also emphasized a shared struggle. In December 2007 in Venezuela, Lukashenko illustrated his own concern with creating a multipolar world and, in barely coded language, reducing US influence, stating that Venezuela and Belarus "pursue an independent foreign political course and a socially oriented domestic political course, seek building a multipolar world, [and we] need joint efforts to counteract pressure from the outside" (ITAR-TASS 2007).

While in earlier periods Venezuela existed as the sole Far Left government in the region, with the exception of Cuba. Several leftist political leaders, however, began to come to power within Latin America that also provided the country with regional support for its political-economic policies and its struggle with the United States and Western Europe. In January 2006 Evo Morales took office in Bolivia, and in January 2007 Rafael Correa took office in Ecuador. Both leaders came to the presidency riding an anti-neoliberal platform that admonished past policies and challenged the US government. The Bolivian government, for example, expelled its US ambassador in 2008 for alleged plots to destabilize the government, and, in later years, expelled US-AID for the same allegations. The Ecuadorean government also expelled a US ambassador in 2011 over events revealed by WikiLeaks and provided Julian Assange with diplomatic asylum within the Ecuadorean embassy in London until 2019. In Nicaragua, Daniel Ortega, the Sandinista revolutionary, won the presidential election, assuming office in January 2007, and loudly supported Chávez and the promotion of twenty-first-century socialism. When the US government decided to suspend $64 million in economic aid to Nicaragua over electoral concerns in 2009, for instance, Chávez provided Nicaragua with $50 million to nearly replace it.

While the Venezuelan government intensified relations with Russia, China, and other allies, relations with the United States continued to deteriorate. Most notably, US-Venezuela relations became so strained that the two countries no longer possess ambassadors. These relations have further strained even further into the present with the Obama administration initially publishing an executive order in March 2015 calling Venezuela "a national security threat," and President Donald Trump blocking oil sales and threatening to invade the country. These policies have continued under the Biden administration, albeit without explicit threats of invasion.

Although in Venezuela the National Assembly had not yet reignited the LIC in the immediate post-electoral period, as Saul Ortega said it would, the possibility remained. The Finnish, Belgian, and Canadian ambassadors sought to continually leverage what clout remained and requested that Venezuela halt attempts to pass restrictive legislation. However, similar to US influence, Western European influence had begun to wane. In interviews, two representatives from the EC stated that by 2010 the influence of the EU had perceivably dissipated. Not only were EC projects within Venezuela subject to end in 2013, but government officials had begun to appear less interested in cooperation with Western Europe. Although one official sensed interest from the Venezuelan government until 2007 "to bring more prestige and technological advance to [the government's] line of work," interest began to diminish thereafter and "over time it must have become clear, even to the last technocrat, that putting yourself into discussions on cooperation with the EU is maybe not as suspicious as asking for cooperation from the US but only just a little bit less so . . . if you were politically minded then obviously it was clear you would not propose cooperation with an entity that was at least doubtful in terms of its loyalty to Chávez . . . You would be much better off proposing a new cooperation with China or Belarus." That is, within its new subfield, relations with the EU were no longer perceived as legitimate.

Throughout 2009, the government continued to keep restrictive legislation off the National Assembly agenda. In 2010, however, following a considerable showing from the opposition during the September legislative elections, the Venezuelan government ramped up its efforts to pass several pieces of legislation before the new Congress would convene in the following year. During this election, the opposition nearly received the same percentage of the popular vote (47 percent) as the Partido Socialista Unido de Venezuela (48 percent). As a result, the opposition would come to possess around 40 percent of legislative seats. This would mean that the Partido Socialista Unido de Venezuela would no longer command a supermajority within the legislature.

In the wake of these elections, Venezuelan government leaders initiated a new push for anti-NGO legislation, among a push for other legislative measures that sought to consolidate the communal state, including with the passage of the Organic Law of Popular and Public Planning, and the Organic Law of Communes. In December 2010, in two quick discussions in just over a week, the National Assembly successfully passed the LDPS. Under this new legislation, Chavista congresspersons circumscribed the focus to prohibit political NGOs and political parties from receiving foreign funding as well as prohibiting these groups from inviting foreign individuals into the country that offend Venezuelan institutions and threaten Venezuelan national sovereignty, however vaguely conceived. During this time, US and EU government functionaries told me that Venezuelan government members possessed no regard for the alarm evidenced by Western European and North American diplomats as they did during earlier periods, and they displayed no interest in speaking with members from the North American and Western European international community concerning the passage of this legislation. During this time, many NGO leaders also point out that by this point, the Venezuelan government had severed most of its dialogic relations with them, and, similar to the United States and Western Europe, possessed no interest in discussing the legislation and its effects with them.

The Breakdown of Dialogic Relations with the NGO Community, 1998–2010

While in 1998 President Chávez campaigned on the idea of constructing a new constitution that would promote a protagonistic and participatory democracy, his government's relationship with most NGOs increasingly deteriorated throughout his time in office. In the end, his earlier relations with the NGO community would become replaced by relations with community councils and other popular power bases, a move running parallel with its integration into its new subfield of allies.

In 1998 Chávez corralled the support of various segments of society as he entered the realm of formal politics. What Chávez most clearly emphasized in his 1998 campaign was the need to rewrite the constitution to allow for participatory democracy, and, upon winning, he set out to rewrite the Venezuelan constitution with the assistance of several NGOs. An individual representing an NGO that focuses on public health and environmental conservation, and participates in Sinergia, an organization that represents the interests of a multiplicity of NGOs, recounts that "in 1999 Sinergia did a large consultation process with organizations around Venezuela to bring in proposals to the new Constitution . . . so there was a lot of participation in the process of writing the new Constitution. For example, the article that deals with the right of free association has an added phrase which says not only that every person has the right to associate freely but also that the state has the obligation to facilitate the exercise of social rights. That was added by Sinergia." At this time, relations between NGOs and the government were rather constructive, and dialogic relations existed wherein representatives could meet with high-ranking government members and express their demands (Garcia-Guadilla 2003; Salamanca 2004, 101). The head of an NGO that focuses on police brutality and human rights recounted in an interview that in 1999 her organization worked with the government on issues of impunity and pushed the government to address these issues within the constitution. She believes that during this time the government truly wanted to work with NGOs that also endorsed the move toward participatory democracy.

In fact, the new constitution identified civil society as an essential component of Venezuelan society writ large. Luis Salamanca (2004, 101–2) points out how "the constitution . . . confers the following attributes to civil society: Article 206 says that civil society should be consulted by the state-level Legislative Councils on matters of interest to the states . . . and Article 296 states that civil society nominates three members to the . . . National Electoral Council." However, who exactly would represent "civil society" and become considered as "the bearers of rights to intervene in public affairs" became contested terrain, as civil society encompasses any organization that sits between the market and the state (102).

If at the beginning of Chávez's presidency there was some ambiguity concerning who the government would recognize as the voice of civil society, the government clarified what groups possessed legitimacy in the post–coup d'état period. David Smilde (2009, 4) describes this period between 2003 and 2006 as a period in which the government began to actively sponsor the participation of only some select groups. Rather than consulting with various segments of civil society—including human rights groups, neighborhood associations, and the multiplicity of existing religious groups—it began sponsoring citizen groups that generally supported the Chávez government. As an example, "at the end of July 2004, several neo-Pentecostal groups received $400,000 from the government for a project to foment peace and dialogue. They used the money for several small workshops but also two large rallies... At the rallies, the organizers claimed to speak for the entire evangelical movement in throwing their support behind the Chávez government" (4–5). After the 2002 coup d'état, the Chávez government had also become increasingly suspicious of NGOs that received funding from the United States. In 2003 the government enlisted the support of several groups to assist with the transformation that would take place in the transition from the old to the new constitution. However, "criteria for participation excluded from official recognition those social organizations 'that receive foreign financing,' thus denying them the right to participate in the decision-making process" (Garcia-Guadilla 2003, 188).

During the period of sponsorship, the government also assisted in the development of communal councils throughout the country with the passage of the Law on Communal Councils in 2006. Smilde (2009, 4) describes the communal councils as "local initiatives in which 200–400 households within a self-defined geographical area, consisting of 20 percent of the population, hold elections and write a charter. They then write a history of the community, make a list of problems the community suffers, and translate these problems into projects. They request financial support from public institutions and then are charged with exercising supervision over these projects." Some individuals have asserted that while the communal councils might empower some communities to make changes and improve their neighborhoods, the councils are not truly autonomous groups as they rely on the national government for their funding. One former representative from Sinergia, the umbrella organization representing a number of Venezuelan NGOs, asserted:

> If you concentrate in your very local community, [and on their] practices, policies, or needs, you are listened to. Otherwise, forget it. If there is a major decision taken even though it affects you, you have no word, and you will not be listened to. So we are seeing a lot of people upset, people who strongly believed in this idea of participation... even if they get organized as an organization of the popular power, they are not listened to or have a major influence... so I think that more and more what we are seeing is the authoritarian face of the government ruling by decree laws... above the people and not really listening.

Others, however, view the communal councils as a countervailing check on unbridled state power and the true motor behind the creation of a new radically democratic, socialist society (Ciccariello-Maher 2013; Kingsbury 2018; Wilpert 2007).

By 2006, although the government had clearly demonstrated what groups it deemed to truly represent the interests of civil society, NGOs were not entirely cut off from discussions. In June 2006, when the government first considered the LIC, a representative from an NGO focused on the rule of law recalled that government members working on the law "invited [his organization and other organizations] to a kind of formal meeting. We spent perhaps a couple of hours . . . discussing what we thought, giving them our opinion, they gave us their opinion. We kind of shared both opinions, but that was it." Although he did not evidence much enthusiasm for the meeting that took place between the government and these groups, the event illustrates that the government still reached out to some NGOs concerning the law and were at least willing to hear their concerns. When these NGOs could no longer directly consult with the government, this representative stated that they worked through foreign embassies and international groups in order to convey their demands.

Smilde (2009, 4) describes the current period—that is, beginning in 2007—as characterized by government-centralized participation. Through constitutional reform, the Law on Communal Councils, and thereafter the Law of Communes, the Chávez government promoted the development of a communal state, wherein communal councils might group together to form an extensive commune. Within the communes, communities can possess jurisdiction over banks, communal projects, and state-allocated resources. While government supporters portray these changes as providing citizens with directly democratic mechanisms, critics have argued that these legislative changes create parallel governments that aim to undermine opposition mayoralties and states and are thus illiberal and undemocratic. Regardless of opinion, however, what is evident is a clear shift in perceptions of legitimacy. Throughout this current period, many NGOs have expressed feeling marginalized from the government and its discussions on various issues, and some have even reported harassment from the government. The same representative from the NGO focused on the rule of law that had a brief meeting with the government over the LIC, for example, recounted how the Chávez government denounced his and other organizations for their work: "They publicly insult you, they threaten in general: '[NGOs] are doing this,' 'they are not patriotic,' 'they are selling away the motherland,' and . . . accusations of being also even terrorist . . . or working for [the United States] in order to overthrow Chávez, for example."

When the LDPS came up for discussion in December 2010, NGO representatives were not consulted as they were in 2006. As one head of an NGO focused on promoting general human rights recalled: "When [the LDPS] was first discussed, I was on vacation . . . I think this is why they did it at this time [December], around the holidays. Most people were away and were not thinking about it . . . We really had no time to prepare a response and the government was not interested in speaking with us." As a result, space has largely closed for many civil society actors within the country to develop working relations with the socialist government in the country, even more so now under President Maduro, who has grown increasingly authoritarian and, in doing so, has had state forces raid the offices of several NGOs.

For much of the twentieth century, pluralists and neo-Marxists led the debate over the legislative process. While pluralists contended that interest groups ultimately condition the passage of legislation, neo-Marxists asserted that business interests ultimately prevail. In many places, we indeed see the importance of business interests, particularly within the United States. In the case of the LDPS in Venezuela, though, neither pluralist nor neo-Marxist theory helps us make sense of the passage and timing of the LDPS. In contemporary Venezuela, Chavistas dominated political institutions and socialism has garnered much societal legitimacy. This presses us to make sense of the obstacles to its passage and examine how international factors have played a role in shaping the government's initial decision to stall the passage of anti-NGO legislation and wait nearly a decade until passing such legislation in any capacity.

As we have seen, the Venezuelan government under President Chávez initially sought working relations with the United States and Western Europe, and, even when it became apparent that the US government funded some of the 2002 coup d'état supporters and even participants, it remained keyed into relations and programs involving these countries. Dialogic relations between Venezuela and multilateral groups also persisted. Even more, the United States and the European Union remained Venezuela's primary trading partners, effectively financing many of Chávez's social projects. Over time, however, the government came to embrace other anti-imperial and even some authoritarian governments that composed a newly developing subfield of actors championing multipolarity and looking to counteract US and Western European global influence, including through the passage of anti-NGO legislation. By 2010, when the Venezuelan government enacted the LDPS, its most prominent and celebrated political-economic relations existed with the authoritarian governments of China, Russia, Belarus, and Iran, and anti-neoliberal, Latin American governments, such as Cuba, Bolivia, Ecuador, and Nicaragua. This changing subfield was domestically paralleled by increasing emphasis on communal councils and communes within the country. While the Venezuelan government's formerly dialogic relations with the United States and Western Europe, and, to a lesser extent, domestic NGOs, stymied Venezuela's original efforts to pass restrictive legislation, these avenues were all but sidelined by 2010, as Venezuela became fully integrated into a new set of global relations.

By 2010, the subfield in which Venezuela had become embedded was a field in which authoritarian and anti-imperial governments, on the one hand, and popular power bases, on the other hand, commanded the Chávez government's concern. These newly prioritized relations between Venezuela and these entities—and deprioritized relations with formerly important governments and organizations—allowed the government the political opportunity to pass this legislation. By this point, no legitimate opposition stood in the way of the government's goals, and those groups and governments that had developed close relations with Venezuela were not governments or organizations that opposed restricting NGO operations. Instead, Venezuela's restrictive policies conformed to behavior that had begun to develop among its closest allies throughout the world.

Conclusion

MAKING THEORETICAL SENSE OF US DEMOCRACY ASSISTANCE EFFORTS IN VENEZUELA

Throughout this book, I have sought to detail US foreign policymaking efforts in Venezuela during the years of the Hugo Chávez administration, and, in particular, I have examined US democracy assistance efforts carried by the US Agency for International Development (USAID) and the National Endowment for Democracy (NED) and its associated groups. In this final chapter, I revisit the theoretical issues involving these efforts, and discuss how we might make the most sense of them in contemporary Venezuela. In basic summation, I find that the neo-Tocquevillian perspective on US democracy promotion thoroughly inaccurate. Instead, I have sought to build upon the insights generated by those working within the neo-Marxist tradition, and, in doing so, to incorporate the work of critical historical and postcolonial work into a deeper understanding of such US foreign policymaking efforts.

The neo-Tocquevillian perspective, for its part, paints a far more unbiased, nonpartisan picture of US government activities than what we find on the ground in Venezuela. Instead of funding a diversity of groups, the US government has principally worked with opposition political parties and highly critical, if not opposition-aligned, nongovernmental organizations (NGOs). In fact, during the early years of the Chávez administration, the US government even worked with Venezuelan actors who took part in the 2002 coup d'état that violently, but temporarily, displaced the Venezuelan government. While it is somewhat possible that US government members might not have understood that a coup d'état was necessarily in formation, several US government agencies continued to fund some of these actors even following such coup d'état efforts. And so, while US government elites might claim that they have funded opposition actors due to their democratic credentials, we find that in several instances such democratic credentials are actually quite dubious, as several of these groups had previously pursued anti-democratic and unconstitutional efforts to unseat the Chávez government.

In addition, the neo-Tocquevillian perspective does not precisely clarify what conceptual sorts of democratic features the US government promotes abroad. By neglecting to do so, neo-Tocquevillian scholars demonstrate that they are unreflective in their conceptual understanding of democracy. In Venezuela the US democracy assistance community has primarily encouraged liberal democratic features of governance, including decentralization, rule of law, civil liberties, and conflict mediation. Yet, there exists multiple understandings of how democracies should operate, and the programs and policies that the US government has promoted in Venezuela do not exhaust the full spectrum of all such variants of democratic governance. Indeed, the Venezuelan government has not entirely sidelined many liberal democratic features of governance. In contrast with the United States and its emphasis on liberal democracy, Venezuelan government leaders have most importantly sought to develop a strong centralized state that might assist with the redistribution of wealth and resources.

Unlike the neo-Tocquevillian perspective, the neo-Marxist perspective recognizes that clear differences might exist between the United States and other countries' understandings of democracy. What is more, this perspective underscores the importance of neoliberal economic policies within US foreign policymaking. Although there are some clear economic elements involved with some of the programs that the US government has promoted, the totality of US democracy assistance efforts is not reducible to the promotion of neoliberal economic policies. Instead, many US government efforts have involved promoting strictly political projects, which have encouraged rule of law, conflict mediation, civil liberties, and decentralization efforts. This is not to suggest that many scholars who have examined US foreign policy would necessarily disagree. However, the purpose of this text has been to highlight further dynamics at play involving contemporary US foreign policymaking, in addition to these economic dimensions.

As a result, I have sought to centralize the work of critical historians focused on US intervention in Latin America and postcolonial scholars who have long shown how government elites in the metropole aim to culturally justify their global efforts. Such a perspective helps to illuminate how liberal democratic concepts underpin the programs that US government agencies have established in Venezuela. Although private property rights feature into US government programs, they in no way command all their focus and all their funding. In fact, only one US democracy promoting agency, the Center for International Private Enterprise (CIPE), remains focused on promoting free market capitalist policies. Such a perspective also helps us to understand why the US government has continually worked with opposition-oriented NGOs and political parties during the Chávez administration. We can connect these sorts of opposition-focused democracy assistance programs to a history of US imperialism within the region.

Since the inception of the Monroe Doctrine in 1823, the US government has sought "to protect" Latin America. This has often involved the prevention of leftist leaders from coming to power. Indeed, during the Cold War, the US government assisted in the violent destabilization of a number of socialist/communist-oriented countries. What is more, the US government and its functionaries possess a lengthy history of depicting Latin American leaders and their citizens as political subjects that require tutelage in order to learn how to properly select leaders and effectively govern their population. Throughout interviews and within policy documents, we find continual racist and neocolonial understandings of the Chávez government and the policies it pursued, in addition to supporters of the government and Venezuelans more generally.

US Democracy Assistance and the Neo-Tocquevillian Perspective

Neo-Tocquevillian scholars have generally depicted US democracy assistance programs as operating in the general interest of democracy writ large. They in no way seriously interrogate, and/or potentially criticize, US democracy assistance programs and the conceptual politics that underlie them. In other words, such scholars uncritically accept the beneficence of US foreign policymaking, and they do not perceive such programs as containing any political-economic biases. In addition, they do not recognize the multiple meanings that the concept of democracy itself possesses and how the general concept of democracy remains contested.

In Venezuela the Chávez government prioritized the rights of economic and social majorities, and it sought to use state power to empower these groups. At times, although the Venezuelan government did not entirely eschew all liberal democratic features, the Chávez government pursued policies that contravened a liberal democratic emphasis on limiting state power. For instance, the Venezuelan government expropriated unused rural landholdings from large rural landholders, pushed for more executive control over the military and its usage, and sought to alter national curriculum and introduce Bolivarian-oriented schools for young children. The Venezuelan government also established a number of social missions that aimed to combat illiteracy, provide medical access, offer educational opportunities, provide adequate housing, and subsidize food and other basic products.

Instead of working with the national government, though, as USAID and the NED do in some contexts, US democracy assistance programs did not involve much participation from the Venezuelan government. Rather, most programs involved opponents of the Chávez government, including opposition political parties, opposition-oriented NGOs, and opposition activists. For example, the International Republican Institute (IRI) and the National Democratic Institute for International Affairs (NDI) established strong relations with several opposition parties, such as Primero Justicia, Proyecto Venezuela, and Acción Democratica. These parties continually opposed the Chávez government and sought ways to replace Chavistas in power. At times, some NDI and IRI programs involved members from pro-government parties, but such individuals' participation in these programs was quite minimal and considerably dwarfed by the participation of opposition politicians and their supporters.

Through their programs, the IRI and, to a lesser extent, the NDI, worked to enhance the capabilities of mostly opposition political parties. In order to do so, they primarily focused their energy on two sorts of efforts. These efforts included leading their own seminars on developing various political capabilities and sponsoring foreign politicians and strategists to lead seminars and to offer guidance to opposition political party leaders. This included providing guidance on how opposition political parties could enhance their political platforms, attract more party members, and develop more effective communication strategies. Although IRI reports contend that their representatives were at pains not to place continual blame on the Chávez government for the political polarization that characterized Venezuela, their representatives furnished opposition political party leaders with continual advice on how they could most effectively operate under a political system dominated President Hugo Chávez and his supporters.

Beyond political parties, the NED worked with a variety of NGOs that often aligned themselves against the Venezuelan government. In fact, some of these groups openly defined themselves as part of the opposition, including Súmate, a group from which several opposition leaders, including Maria Corina Machado, a former opposition presidential candidate, would emerge. In addition, the group also promoted a recall referendum against President Chávez, an obvious partisan position. Elsewhere, the NED promoted NGOs that contested legislation pushed or enacted by the Chávez government. For example, the NED promoted groups that contested legislation concerning the Land Law, changes to educational curriculum, and the involvement from the military in political life. USAID even more explicitly worked with opposition activists to create newfound NGOs in poor neighborhoods and to turn Chavistas toward the opposition. In addition, they worked closely with students protesting the Chávez government in the streets of major cities. It is thus clear that US democracy-promoting agencies active in Venezuela consistently and primarily worked with the Venezuelan opposition. In other words, there is a very strong bias in their funding for groups that opposed the Venezuelan government, and we cannot understand US democracy assistance efforts as in any way nonpartisan.

The NED and its associated groups' funding in Venezuela also demonstrate a proclivity for only particular democracy-related programs. This has included funding for groups that champion liberal democratic features of governance, such as decentralization, limiting state influence, and freedom of the press. Neo-Tocquevillians do not specifically identify what sort of democratic features of governance the US government promotes through its democracy assistance programs. In this way, the US government, as well as neo-Tocquevillian scholars, uncritically accept liberal democracy as synonymous with democracy writ large. Clearly, however, differences exist between the US and Venezuelan governments concerning what elements matter most for a truly democratic system. For the US government, this involves civil and political rights, such as the ability to vote and freely articulate one's political-economic perspective through the media. Within Venezuela, however, the government has become much more inclined to focus on economic and social rights, including its social missions and the redistribution of income and wealth.

In the end, neo-Tocquevillian scholars might object that the US government has supported opposition political parties and opposition-aligned NGOs because these parties and these NGOs were, and remain, the country's true champions of democratic policies, and, by contrast, Chávez and his supporters pursued anti-democratic and unconstitutional policies. Yet, there are several dimensions to contemporary US democracy assistance efforts that complicate these claims. It remains that the Chávez government routinely received electoral support from the Venezuelan populace, and that many of the parties and NGOs that received US government funding actually engaged in anti-democratic and unconstitutional behaviors themselves. While US government agencies might not have specifically supported these groups to engage in such anti-democratic behavior, they still continued to support many of these groups even after they had engaged in such anti-democratic and unconstitutional behaviors, such as providing support for the 2002 coup d'état that temporarily deposed President Chávez and the transitional government that displaced him.

Such claims sideline and discount the democratic aspirations of the majority of Venezuelan citizens. Venezuelan citizens continually exhibited their support for President Chávez and many of the changes that his government instituted at many intervals. Most notably, Venezuelan citizens elected and then recurrently reelected Chávez until his death in 2013. During the early years of his administration, Chávez won each election that he had participated in. This includes both elections wherein his presidency was on the line—including a recall referendum in 2004; elections that involved the passage of particular policies, such as a new Venezuelan constitution; and elections for legislative and other regional government members. In fact, with the exception of one constitutional referendum election in 2007 and one underwhelming showing in a parliamentary election in 2010, Chávez did not actually lose market capitalism and private property rights. However, while the US government promotes these issues through CIPE, and while these issues have a place in liberal democratic theory, the promotion of private property rights does not encompass the entirety of US democracy assistance efforts in Venezuela. Instead, we need to broaden the analysis of US foreign policymaking and highlight additional dimensions involving the practice.

A Deeper Perspective

To rectify existing limitations within the two aforementioned theoretical perspectives, I have developed a perspective on US democracy assistance efforts that brings in the work of postcolonial scholars and critical historians. I have explicitly laid out several dimensions involved with this perspective in chapter 2, and in that chapter I pointed out that US government elites often maintain their own specific set of interests in promoting liberal democratic features of governance abroad. This has primarily included the development of a state that minimally intervenes into the affairs of its citizens, and the enshrinement of the rights of the individual. For those that espouse a liberal democratic form of governance, the state should provide order and enforce contracts, but offer only minimal public services. Liberal democrats generally believe that the state should allow citizens to take control of their lives without much interference.

In chapter 2, I also linked US democracy assistance efforts with a racist and neocolonial history of US foreign policy efforts, which have involved land annexation, military invasion, and the destabilization of leftist governments throughout Latin America. I have sought to tie these efforts to a racist and neocolonial history involving treatment of Latin American leaders and citizens as political subjects who require tutelage and a political education in order to properly learn how to govern their subjects and select their leaders. President Chávez assuredly rejected much of what that the US government promoted within and beyond the hemisphere, including free trade and free market economic policies; counter-narcotics operations that, according to Chávez, violated countries' national sovereignty; and the global war on terror. Historically, when Latin American leaders have rejected the US government and its political-economic vision for the world, they have incurred imperial wrath, which, at times, and especially during the Cold War, has included violent regime change efforts. While a 2002 coup d'état transpired in Venezuela that was led by dissident military members and business leaders, among other individuals, US government members claimed that they played no role in such events. Although US government agencies had supported some individuals and groups who were involved with the coup d'état and the transitional government, US government members claimed that they possessed no knowledge that such individuals had planned to violently undermine the Chávez government (Cablegate 2004d). Some individuals have argued otherwise. That is, they have claimed that the US government indeed recognized that a coup d'état was in formation, and they strategically supplied groups with additional funding in the months and weeks leading up to April 2002 in order to strengthen the coup d'état's prospects (Golinger 2006; Robinson 2006).

Regardless of whether or not US government leaders had prior knowledge that the Venezuelan conspirators had planned to overthrow President Chávez, or if they provided them with assistance in their attempt to destabilize the Venezuelan government, we clearly see that the programs that the US government established and supported within the country show an obvious propensity toward liberal democratic forms of governance and for political parties and many NGOs that criticized the Chávez government and aligned with the opposition. For example, although the IRI and NDI at times worked with and involved Chavista government members in their programs, the bulk of their activities went toward assisting political parties that challenged the Venezuelan government, including Primero Justicia, Proyecto Venezuela, the Comité de Organización Política Electoral Independiente, and Acción Democrática. In fact, these political parties, among several additional opposition parties that the IRI and NDI established relations and regularly worked with, continue to mount challenges against the Venezuelan government and seek to displace the Chavistas from power. All evidence taken together thus demonstrates that US government agencies have continued to work with these parties in order to build up their political capacities long after the years that I have examined in this particular research project. Under the Trump administration, US diplomats regularly hosted, worked with, and publicly praised opposition leaders from many of these parties. Such a pattern has persisted under the Biden administration as well, albeit with less bellicose rhetoric.

During the period that I have examined, US government agencies primarily focused on increasing political pluralism and providing opposition political parties with technical skills to most effectively compete in electoral contests. These sorts of programs included showing party leaders how to boost their popularity throughout the country, how to amplify their public image, how to build up their youth bases, and how to effectively interact with journalists and citizens. In addition, these efforts included linking opposition party leaders up with ideological counterparts from the United States and beyond, including US Republican Party leaders from states such as California, Colorado, Oregon, and Mississippi. These activities also included linking leaders up with conservative politicians from other Latin American countries such as Chile, Colombia, and Mexico. Although some critics have alleged that the US government simply throws money at opposition groups as the Central Intelligence Agency (CIA) often did during the mid-twentieth century, the nature of such support remains much more technical than simply funneling money into the pockets of opposition politicians and parties.

In the civil sphere, the NED has worked with a number of organizations that have generally focused their efforts around two particular areas: (1) civil liberties and (2) conflict mediation and law enforcement. These two areas illustrate how US government agencies have specifically elected to push for civil and political rights throughout their programs, and how they have not exclusively pursued policies that would allegedly enfranchise a transnational, or any other particular, capitalist class. Indeed, while neoliberal capitalism requires law enforcement and order, socialist/communist-oriented societies also feature law enforcement and order. Nonetheless, while the Venezuelan government has not entirely eschewed civil and political rights, its main aim has surrounded social and economic rights. Under President Chávez, the Venezuelan government sought to prioritize the rights of the historically oppressed majority of the Venezuelan population. By contrast, US democracy assistance programs centered much less on such rights, and, instead, championed individual liberties, conflict mediation, rule of law, and freedom from state intervention.

Throughout the years of the Chávez administration, the NED focused its efforts on supporting groups that criticized the Venezuelan government for assuming more state power throughout society. The NED, for instance, supported a rural peasant group that criticized the Venezuelan government's expropriation of rural landholdings as well as a group focused on education that sought to temper the government's moves to alter national curriculum. In addition, the NED assisted groups that claimed that the Venezuelan government had generally targeted the abilities of NGOs. In doing so, the NED funded forums, such as one operated by the Asociación Civil Consorcio Justicia (ACCJ), that allowed domestic NGOs to initiate funding relationships with national and international businesses in order to persist. Yet, although US government agencies have generally claimed to support democratically oriented groups, the US government continually financed groups that took part in the anti-democratic and unconstitutional 2002 coup d'état and offered support for the transitional government. Therefore, in many respects, the US government has supported groups and parties within Venezuela, regardless of their democratic credentials. In addition, the US government has in only select few instances worked with the Chávez government and its members.

The NED has also focused many of its efforts on law enforcement and conflict mediation. At times, some of these programs involved national government agencies, such as when the NED funded the ACCJ to help to investigate deaths that transpired during the 2002 coup d'état. The NED also funded groups that criticized the Venezuelan government's use of the military, including the Asociación Civil Compresión de Venezuela, which funded several forums and workshops concerning this issue. In addition, the NED financed several groups that worked in neighborhoods in Caracas and beyond in order reduce violence and mediate conflict. Lastly, the NED funded the Asociación Civil Liderazgo y Visión to provide law enforcement officers with human rights training and initiate a legacy of human rights training within the Metropolitan Police unit.

In addition to underscoring how the US government often promotes liberal democratic features of governance, we must link US democracy assistance efforts to an imperial history of racism, paternalism, and neocolonialism in the region. Many US government elites often clearly articulated how their vision of democracy remains superior to all other visions of democracy. In interviews, such individuals were often quite clear in their zealous mission to "bring democracy" to Venezuela. Even though many individuals recognized existing racism among opposition members, they still believed they were worthy of US government support. In addition, US government elites often depicted Chávez as manipulating the minds of Venezuelan citizens, who, as a result, could not properly think for themselves. US government elites thus saw it as their objective to reveal the truth about Chávez to them and to, thereafter, move them toward the opposition. In doing so, USAID helped to establish and create materials for newfound NGOs expressly designed to subtly criticize Chávez and his policies, and to push his supporters to embrace the opposition.

We have also encountered several instances where the NED and its associated groups denigrated the Venezuelan government and its supporters within its program descriptions. For example, the NED often referred to the Venezuelan constitution that Venezuelan citizens had voted on in a referendum election as President Chávez's "pet Bolivarian constitution," without any consideration of citizen support for it. In addition, the NED claimed that the new constitution hardly affected Chávez's ability to govern and thus insinuated that its passage was generally useless for the Venezuelan populace. In other documents, the NED drew analogies between Cuban and Soviet policies and Venezuelan government policies. In other words, the NED sought to portray the Venezuelan government as a dictatorship under Chávez, and, by contrast, portrayed the organizations that it supported, and, by extension itself, as organizations that genuinely aimed to cultivate a true democracy within the country. In another example, the NDI took Chávez's electoral success to suggest that Venezuelan citizens had lost "faith in the democratic process." Of course, an alternative interpretation might be that many Venezuelan citizens were finally urged to politically participate as they felt connected with an outsider candidate.

Overall, this pattern of portraying Latin American leaders and their supporters as unintelligent, unaware of their true interests, and, in the instance of Chávez, unable to properly govern the Venezuelan populace, coheres with a pattern of US racism, neocolonialism, and regional paternalism. US government elites might object that President Chávez truly ruled in an undemocratic and unconstitutional manner. However, as illustrated several times throughout this book, Chávez regularly garnered electoral support from the Venezuelan populace. It is certainly possible to criticize Chávez for other sorts of objectionable methods of governance, such as illiberalism; however, it would be disingenuous at best for US government members to characterize the former president as obtaining support in an undemocratic manner. In addition, as also illustrated several times throughout this book, the US government supported groups that they themselves engaged in anti-democratic and unconstitutional policies. Although the US government might not have realized that some of the groups it had supported, such as the CTV and CEDICE, would go on to support the 2002 coup d'état and the transitional government that took Chávez's place, US agencies continued to support these and other groups following these anti-democratic and unconstitutional events, seemingly undeterred by support for such events within the country.

The totality of USAID and the NED and its associated groups' efforts illustrates a strong bend toward liberal democratic features of governance as well as a link with a historical pattern of racism, neocolonialism, and regional paternalism that understands Venezuelan citizens and leaders in a highly pejorative light. We must take US ideological interests in liberal democratic features of governance seriously and see how they remain connected with a history of racism, neocolonialism, and paternalism. These are the advances of such a perspective that illustrates the weaknesses of a neo-Tocquevillian perspective and aims to build upon the insights developed by scholars working within the neo-Marxist tradition.

As this book goes to press in April 2022, I would have predicted a continued plummeting in relations between the United States and Venezuela. Yet, amid the Russian invasion of Ukraine, the Biden administration has begun to meet and speak with members of the Venezuelan government. Their hope is to move Venezuela away from Russia, and the Venezuelan government hopes to sell its oil in the United States once again. Indeed, there remains a possibility that the United States might relax widespread sanctions on the Maduro government, allowing some of their oil to flow.

Nonetheless, several US Congress members and citizens are opposed to any opening in such a relationship. They continue to lambaste the Venezuelan government with regards to democracy and human rights. There is no doubt that Maduro has taken far more undemocratic steps than President Chávez ever did. Yet, it remains true that such US sanctions are only intensifying an existing economic crisis that is primarily affecting poor and working-class Venezuelans.

Trust between the two governments will surely complicate decision-making involving these issues. The United States, for its part, must come to terms with the fact that for decades it has engaged in a neocolonial and racist pattern of foreign policymaking. From government members' depictions of Chávez and his supporters, to the various schemes devised by several US government agencies to unseat Chávez and his allies, acknowledgment of these practices might go a long in paving way for better relations with the Venezuelan government in the future. This does not mean abandoning considerations of human rights abuses in foreign policymaking and public statements, but rather an acknowledgement that the United States has deliberately sought to unseat leaders in Venezuela and played a key role in such diminishing relations.

In the end, we must all come to terms with the fact that the United States continues to exercise a paternalistic approach to the rest of the world. In particular, US taxpayers have the right to know how it is that our money is spent and for what purposes. We must interrogate the continuing legacy of US interventionism and decide whether this is something that we should support. US foreign policymaking is notoriously undemocratic. With enough awareness and mobilization, my hope is that is one day citizens will become able to exercise more control over these policies, whether in Venezuela, Ukraine, or anywhere else.

NOTES

Introduction: The Venezuelan Government and US Empire in the Twenty-First Century

1. As of writing (April 2022), opposition leader Juan Guaidó of the Voluntad Popular party has also laid claim to the Venezuelan presidency, and, in fact, several dozen countries recognize him as the rightful Venezuelan leader. The world remains split over this issue.

2. Over the last several years, however, Venezuela has faced a grave economic crisis largely as a result of corruption and depreciating oil prices. The US government has indeed compounded the crisis by enacting economic sanctions against the Maduro government.

Chapter 1: The Rise of Hugo Chávez and the Evolution of US-Venezuelan Relations

1. Both parties remain part of the Venezuelan opposition to the socialists into the present.

2. In previous decades, Venezuela had featured military dictatorships, albeit with a three-year period of democratic rule from 1945 to 1948. After the fall of democracy in 1948, Venezuela once again featured a military dictatorship, which received support from the Eisenhower government in the United States. Under the Pact of Punto Fijo in 1958, though, major Venezuelan parties and key societal actors established an agreement between them to undertake a transition toward democracy and to ensure its stability (Hellinger 2004).

Chapter 2: Theoretical Perspectives on US Democracy Assistance

1. Somewhat relatedly, an embrace of postmodernism or postmodernity has ensued within some disciplines, particularly the humanities. Within the social sciences, however, such an open embrace of postmodern theory has also seemingly fallen out of favor, too, if it ever truly had any influence.

2. It developed in societies with little industrialization rather than within highly industrialized countries.

3. There are several social scientists who reject this idea and claim that the US government continues to dominate the world in its own interest. Some even point to continued inter-imperialist rivalry, albeit between the United States and China (Hung 2020). Leo Panitch and Sam Gindin (2005), for one, continue to view the US government as engaged in economic coercion through international financial institutions in order to maintain global domination. They ultimately view US foreign policy as undertaken to promote US capitalist interests. William Robinson (2001) does not disagree that the United States remains the world's dominant force and the headquarters of global capitalism, but he understands the US government as primarily acting in the interests of a transnational capitalist class. Similarly, David Harvey (2005) understands the US government as continuing to act in the interests of US capitalists and engaging in overseas military endeavors in order to pry open new areas for US investment and trade.

4. Such views also come through within writings praising the practice of democracy assistance itself, which I discuss earlier in this chapter. Though such authors might not explicitly discuss the United States as an empire, they generally praise the overseas endeavors of the country and much of its foreign policymaking. Such language concerning US global leadership also persists among most US politicians, though individual politicians might have some differing views on how exactly the US government should lead.

5. Instead of making such connections, at the time, most mainstream sociologists such as Talcott Parsons (1966) and his followers remained rather celebratory of the United States and its alleged value system.

6. US policymakers, however, have certainly attempted to present governments as threatening to US citizens such as in Panama and Grenada in order to justify military intervention (Poznansky 2020).

Chapter 3: Understanding Venezuelans, Understanding Chávez

1. The Trump administration, in contrast with the Bush and Obama administrations, more explicitly embraced policies such as the Monroe Doctrine and US global power more broadly. Secretary of State Rex Tillerson

and National Security Advisor John Bolton both openly praised the Monroe Doctrine.

2. Many early philosophers, political scientists, and sociologists, however, supported colonial and imperial relations throughout the world, including Franklin Giddings, John Stuart Mill, Paul Reinsch, and Edward Ross (Go 2011; Magubane 2016; Steinmetz 2013; Vitalis 2010). Into the present, some social scientists have supported US sanctions, regime change efforts, and military intervention in places all throughout the world. For instance, there were no shortage of political scientists and historians who supported the US- and British-led invasion of Iraq in 2003. There is also no shortage of social scientists who have called for US intervention in contemporary Venezuela to ultimately depose the Chávez and now Maduro government.

3. Bolívar became consecrated within the United States, with statues erected in his honor and several towns named after him (e.g., Bolivar, Ohio; Bolivar, Tennessee; Bolivar, Texas). Caitlin Fitz (2017) has also found that throughout the 1830s hundreds of families named their sons Simon Bolívar in a show of honor and respect for him.

4. Elsewhere, of course, the United States has used more violent forms of intervention, such as military warfare and drone strikes. However, such intervention is far less prevalent than the more mundane efforts of "promoting democracy" through funding and training by various US agencies for such internal groups. In some places like Iraq, too, this work has existed side by side with military intervention.

5. In later years and amid conflict with Mexico in the 1840s, John L. O'Sullivan famously termed this vision "Manifest Destiny."

6. More specifically, as Chávez's supporters referred to him with reference to his military service as *Mi Comandante* (My Commander), the opposition distorted the phonetics of the phrasing and referred to him as *Mico Mandante* (Monkey in Charge) (Herrera Salas 2005, 84).

7. Chávez routinely spoke of his Indigenous and African heritage, and extolled Indigenous and Afro-Caribbean communities within the country. By contrast, the opposition often portrayed Chávez as more dark-skinned than he actually was and even publicly likened him to a gorilla (Gottberg 2011).

Chapter 4: Coaching Opposition Political Parties I

1. López also remains the political mentor and advisor to opposition leader Juan Guaidó, the individual who, as of this writing, is recognized by the United States and several other countries as the rightful leader of Venezuela.

2. IRI documents confirm the existence of the vote monitoring program and their attempt to "increase transparency" in Venezuelan elections. The

FOIA-released documents, however, redact the names of the groups involved. Nonetheless, the diplomatic cables reveal the primary actors: Hagamos Democracia and opposition parties.

Chapter 7: Funding Anti-Chávez Voices in Civil Society

1. Unfortunately, in more recently released documents, the NED has shielded the precise NGOs they have funded abroad. Nonetheless, many of their efforts seem rather consistent with its earlier efforts pushing back against Chávez government policies, if not more intensively (see, e.g., Gill 2020 on NED support for rock bands to write anti-Chávez protest songs for distribution).

Chapter 8: Transforming Chavistas, Encouraging Protest

1. Voluntad Popular is a centrist political party in Venezuela founded in 2009 by Leopoldo López. It remains one of the most prominent political parties in the Venezuelan opposition. As of October 2021, its leader, Juan Guaidó, continues to claim that he is the legitimate president of the country, as a result of Venezuela's allegedly fraudulent 2018 presidential election.

2. Many scholars of development trace the rise of US foreign aid programs to President Truman's Point Four Program speech and his administration's subsequent efforts.

3. Lincoln Mitchell (2009), for instance, finds that while the Bush administration took credit for the Rose Revolution in Georgia, the truth, he says, was far more complicated, and that US foreign policy efforts were far less critical than the Bush administration claimed.

BIBLIOGRAPHY

Asociacíon Civil Acción Campesina (ACAC). n.d. https://www.accioncampesina.com/.
Asociación Civil Consorcio Justicia (ACCJ). n.d. https://accessinitiative.org/users/asociaci%C3%B3n-civil-consorcio-desarrollo-y-justicia.
Alexander, Jeffrey C. 2008. *The Civil Sphere*. Oxford: Oxford University Press.
Alexander, Jeffrey C. 2012. *The Performance of Politics: Obama's Victory and the Democratic Struggle for Power*. Oxford: Oxford University Press.
Almaguer, Tomas. 2008. *Racial Fault Lines: The Historical Origins of White Supremacy in California*. Berkeley: University of California Press.
Almond, Gabriel, and Sidney Verba. 1963. *The Civic Culture: Political Attitudes and Democracy in Five Nations*. Princeton, NJ: Princeton University Press.
Amin, Samir. 2001. "Imperialism and Globalization." *Monthly Review*, June 2001. https://monthlyreview.org/2001/06/01/imperialism-and-globalization/.
Anderson, Elisabeth. 2013. "Ideas in Action: The Politics of Prussian Child Labor Reform, 1817–1839." *Theory and Society* 42 (1): 81–119.
Anievas, Alexander, Nivi Manchanda, and Robbie Shilliam. 2014. *Race and Racism in International Relations: Confronting the Global Colour Line*. London: Routledge.
Appleman Williams, William. 1959. *The Tragedy of American Diplomacy*. Cleveland: World Publishing Company.
BBC News. 2000. "'Chávez' Iraq Visit 'to Go Ahead.'" BBC News, August 8, 2000. http://news.bbc.co.uk/2/hi/americas/871874.stm.
Babb, Sarah. 2009. *Behind the Development Banks: Washington Politics, World Poverty, and the Wealth of Nations*. Chicago: University of Chicago Press.
Baldoz, Rick. 2008. "The Racial Vectors of Empire." *Du Bois Review* 5 (1): 69–94.
BBC News. 2005. "US Planning Invasion, Says Chavez." BBC News, October 20, 2005. http://news.bbc.co.uk/2/hi/americas/4359386.stm.
Beck, Ulrich. 2005. *Power in the Global Age: A New Global Political Economy*. Cambridge: Polity.

Beckfield, Jason. 2010a. "The Social Structure of the World Polity." *American Journal of Sociology* 115 (4): 1018–68.

Beckfield, Jason. 2010b. "Transboundary Politics." In *The Handbook of Politics: State and Society in Global Perspective*, edited by Kevin T. Lecht and J. Craig Jenkins, 145–60. New York: Springer.

Becker, Howard. 1992. "Cases, Causes, Conjuncture, Stories, and Imagery." In *What Is a Case?: Exploring the Foundations of Social Inquiry*, edited by Charles C. Ragin and Howard Becker, 205–16. Cambridge: Cambridge University Press.

Behrens, Angela, Christopher Uggen, and Jeff Manza. 2003. "Ballot Manipulation and the 'Menace of Negro Domination': Racial Threat and Felon Disenfranchisement in the United States, 1850–20021." *American Journal of Sociology* 109 (3): 559–605.

Berg, Charles Ramírez. 2002. *Latino Images in Film: Stereotypes, Subversion, and Resistance*. Austin: University of Texas Press.

Bergesen, Albert. 1980. *Studies of the Modern World-System*. New York: Academic Press.

Bergesen, Albert. 1993. "The Rise of Semiotic Marxism." *Sociological Perspectives* 36 (1): 1–22.

Bevins, Vincent. 2020. *The Jakarta Method: Washington's Anticommunist Crusade and the Mass Murder Program that Shaped Our World*. New York: Hachette.

Bhagwati, Jagdish. 1966. *The Economies of Underdeveloped Countries*. New York: McGraw-Hill.

Block, Fred. 1977. "The Ruling Class Does Not Rule: Notes on the Marxist Theory of the State." *Socialist Register* 33:6–28.

Boli, John, and George M. Thomas. 1997. "World Culture in the World Polity: A Century of International Non-Governmental Organization." *American Sociological Review* 62 (2): 171–90.

Boot, Max. 2001. "The Case for American Empire." *Weekly Standard*, October 15, 2001.

Boot, Max. 2003. "Neither New nor Nefarious: The Liberal Empire Strikes Back." *Current History* 667:361–66.

Booth, William. 2021. "Rethinking Latin America's Cold War." *Historical Journal* 64 (4): 1128–50.

Boswell, Terry, and Christopher K. Chase-Dunn. 2000. *The Spiral of Capitalism and Socialism: Toward Global Democracy*. Boulder, CO: Lynne Rienner.

Bourdieu, Pierre. 1984. *Distinction: A Social Critique of the Judgment of Taste*. Cambridge, MA: Harvard University Press.

Bourdieu, Pierre. 1993. *The Field of Cultural Production: Essays on Art and Literature*. New York: Columbia University Press.

Bridoux, Jeff, and Milja Kurki. 2014. *Democracy Promotion: A Critical Introduction*. New York: Routledge.

Bulmer-Thomas, Victor. 2018. *Empire in Retreat: The Past, Present, and Future of the United States.* New Haven, CT: Yale University Press.

Burden-Stelly, Charisse. 2018. "W. E. B. Du Bois in the Tradition of Radical Blackness: Radicalism, Repression, and Mutual Comradeship, 1930–1960." *Socialism and Democracy* 32, no. 3: 181–206.

Buitrago, Daisy. 2010. "Venezuela Slams 'Meddling' by Nominee U.S. Envoy." Reuters, August 5, 2010.

Bureau of Democracy, Human Rights, and Labor (DRL). n.d. https://www.state.gov/bureaus-offices/under-secretary-for-civilian-security-democracy-and-human-rights/bureau-of-democracy-human-rights-and-labor/.

Burnell, Peter. 2000. *Democracy Assistance: International Co-operation for Democratization.* New York: Routledge.

Burron, Neil. 2012. *The New Democracy Wars: The Politics of North American Democracy Promotion in the Americas.* Burlington, VT: Ashgate.

Burstein, Paul, and C. Elizabeth Hirsh. "Interest Organizations, Information, and Policy Innovation in the US Congress." *Sociological Forum* 22 (2): 174–99.

Buxton. Julia. 2011. "Foreword." In *Venezuela's Bolivarian Democracy: Participation, Politics, and Culture under Chávez*, edited by David Smilde and Daniel Hellinger, ix-xxii. Durham, NC: Duke University Press.

Cablegate. 2004a. "DAS Deshazo's Meeting with Chief Justice Rincon." US embassy, Caracas, Venezuela, January 29, 2004.

Cablegate. 2004b. "Human Rights Strategy for Venezuela." US embassy, Caracas, Venezuela, February 9, 2004.

Cablegate. 2004c. "Update on the USAID/OTI Program." US embassy, Caracas, Venezuela, February 11, 2004.

Cablegate. 2004d. "Venezuela's VP Discusses Referendum and HR Cases, Proposes Improvements in Bilateral Relations." US embassy, Caracas, Venezuela, August 5, 2004.

Cablegate. 2005a. "Bolivarian Hubris: Chavez Warns of US Assassination Plot." US embassy, Caracas, Venezuela, February 24, 2005.

Cablegate. 2005ab "Chavez: China My Old Friend." US embassy, Caracas, Venezuela, January 5, 2005.

Cablegate. 2005c. "NDI and IRI Work to Strengthen Political Parties in Venezuela." US embassy, Caracas, Venezuela, April 11, 2005.

Cablegate. 2005d. "Update On the USAID-Funded Venezuelan Electoral Observation Organization 'OJO Electoral.'" US embassy, Caracas, Venezuela, January 19, 2005.

Cablegate. 2005e. "Why the Opposition Withdrawal Surprised Observers." US embassy, Caracas, Venezuela, December 9, 2005.

Cablegate. 2006a. "BRV Reacts to Country Report on Terrorism." US embassy, Caracas, Venezuela, May 4, 2006.

Cablegate. 2006b. "BRV Takes Aim at Independent Civil Society." US embassy, Caracas, Venezuela, June 5, 2006.

Cablegate. 2006c. "Chavez and the Rhetoric of Hate." US embassy, Caracas, Venezuela, June 19, 2006.

Cablegate. 2006d. "Demarche Delivered on Venezuela's Anti-NGO Law." US embassy, Oslo, Norway, June 16, 2006.

Cablegate. 2006e. "International Cooperation Law Stalled—For Now." US embassy, Caracas, Venezuela, August 23, 2006.

Cablegate. 2006f. "Is Chavez Losing It?" US embassy, Caracas, Venezuela, May 3, 2006.

Cablegate. 2006g. "Netherlands / Venezuela: Demarche on Anti-NGO Law." US embassy, The Hague, Netherlands, June 16, 2006.

Cablegate. 2006h. "NGO Law One Step Close to Passage." US embassy, Caracas, Venezuela, June 16, 2006.

Cablegate. 2006i. "Spain Opposes Venezuelan Anti-NGO Law." US embassy, Madrid, Spain, June 21, 2006.

Cablegate. 2006j. "Time to Re-Double Our Pro-Democracy Efforts in Venezuela," December 5, 2006.

Cablegate. 2006k. "What Our Foreign Assistance Is Really Doing in Venezuela." US embassy, Caracas, Venezuela, August 10, 2006.

Cablegate. 2006l. "USAID/OTI Programmatic Support for Country Team 5 Point Strategy." US embassy, Caracas, Venezuela, November 9, 2006.

Cablegate. 2006m. "USAID/OTI Venezuela Election Related Activities." US embassy, Caracas, Venezuela, December 4, 2006.

Cablegate. 2007a. "Chavez Names a "YES" Cabinet/Previews His "Socialist" Agenda." US embassy, Caracas, Venezuela, January 9, 2007.

Cablegate. 2007b. "Chavez's Self-Coronation; Goes after Electricity, Oil, and President Bush." US embassy, Caracas, Venezuela, February 2, 2007.

Cablegate. 2007c. "Chavez's Way Ahead: Words to Deeds." US embassy, Caracas, Venezuela, January 12, 2007.

Cablegate. 2007d. "Chavez to U.S.: 'Go to Hell.'" US embassy, Caracas, Venezuela, January 22, 2007.

Cablegate. 2007e. "Opposition Looks toward 2008." US embassy, Caracas, Venezuela, December 18, 2007.

Cablegate. 2007f. "To the Mat: Chavez Takes on Insulza and Church over RCTV." US embassy, Caracas, Venezuela, January 9, 2007.

Cablegate. 2007g. "Venezuela: A New Time Building Slowly." US embassy, Caracas, Venezuela, March 22, 2007.

Cablegate. 2007h. "We Aren't Making This Up: The BRV'S Bizarre Policy Highlights." US embassy, Caracas, Venezuela, September 17, 2007.

Cablegate. 2008. "Emerging Student Leaders Outline Future Strategies." US embassy, Caracas, Venezuela, February 21, 2008.

Cablegate. 2009a. "As Chavez Expands Control, Opposition Implodes." US embassy, Caracas, Venezuela, March 18, 2009.

Cablegate. 2009b. "Chavez As He Sees Himself—The Revolutionary Battling the Empire." US embassy, Caracas, Venezuela, April 1, 2009.

Cablegate. 2009c. "GRBV Police Target USAID/OTI-Funded Democracy Programs." US embassy, Caracas, Venezuela, August 27, 2009.

Cablegate. 2009d. "International Community Working Quietly To Stop NGO Law." US embassy, Caracas, Venezuela, May 11, 2009.

Cablegate. 2009e. "Ten Tenets of Chavismo." US embassy, Caracas, Venezuela, June 16, 2009.

Cablegate. 2009f. "What's Wrong with the Opposition?" US embassy, Caracas, Venezuela, November 3, 2009.

Campbell, John. 1998. "Institutional Analysis and the Role of Ideas in Political Economy." *Theory and Society* 27, no. 3: 377–409.

Canache, Damarys. 2002. "From Bullets to Ballots: The Emergence of Popular Support for Hugo Chavez." *Latin American Politics and Society* 44:69–90.

Cannon, Barry. 2008. "Class/Race Polarisation in Venezuela and the Electoral Success of Hugo Chavez: A Break with the Past or the Song Remains the Same?" *Third World Quarterly* 2 (4): 731–48.

Cardoso, Fernando Henrique, and Enzo Faletto. 1979. *Dependency and Development in Latin America*. Berkeley: University of California Press.

Carothers, Thomas. 1999. *Aiding Democracy Abroad: The Learning Curve*. Washington, DC: Brookings Press.

Carothers, Thomas. 2006. "The Backlash against Democracy Promotion." *Foreign Affairs* 85 (2): 55–68.

Carothers, Thomas. 2011. *Aiding Democracy Abroad: The Learning Curve*. Washington, DC: Carnegie Endowment.

Castells, Manuel. 2000. *The Rise of the Network Society*. Malden, MA: Wiley-Blackwell.

Castells, Manuel. 2009. *The Rise of the Network Society*. Malden, MA: Wiley-Blackwell.

Centeno, Miguel. 2012. "The Arc of Neoliberalism," *Annual Review of Sociology* 38:317–40.

Center for the Dissemination of Economic Knowledge for Liberty (CEDICE). n.d. https://cedice.org.ve/.

Center for International Private Enterprise (CIPE). n.d. https://www.cipe.org/.

Center for International Private Enterprise. 2001. *Quarterly Report*. Washington, DC: CIPE.

Center for International Private Enterprise. 2002a. *Program Report*. Washington, DC: CIPE.

Center for International Private Enterprise. 2002b. *Program Report*. Washington, DC: CIPE.

Center for International Private Enterprise. 2002c. *Program Report*. Washington, DC: CIPE.

Center for International Private Enterprise. 2006. *Program Report*. Washington, DC: CIPE.
Center for International Private Enterprise. 2009. *Program Report*. Washington, DC: CIPE.
Center for International Private Enterprise. 2011. *Program Report*. Washington, DC: CIPE.
Center for International Private Enterprise. 2012. *Program Report*. Washington, DC: CIPE.
Center for International Private Enterprise. 2013. *Program Report*. Washington, DC: CIPE.
Center for International Private Enterprise. 2017. *Program Report*. Washington, DC: CIPE.
Chandler, Nahum D. 2007. "The Possible Form of an Interlocution: WEB Du Bois and Max Weber in Correspondence, 1904–1905." *CR: The New Centennial Review* 7 (1): 213–72.
Chase-Dunn, Christopher, Yukio Kawano, and Benjamin D. Brewer. 2000. "Trade Globalization since 1795: Waves of Integration in the World-System." *American Sociological Review* 65:77–95.
Chorev, Nitsan. 2005. "Making and Remaking State Institutional Arrangements: The Case of U.S. Trade Policy in the 1970s." *Journal of Historical Sociology* 18:3–36.
Chorev, Nitsan. 2007. *Remaking U.S. Trade Policy: From Protectionism to Globalization*. Ithaca, NY: Cornell University Press.
Chorev, Nitsan. 2012. "A Civil Religion for World Society: The Direct and Diffuse Effects of Human Rights Treaties, 1981–2007." *Sociological Forum* 27:937–60.
Christian, Michelle. 2019. "A Global Critical Race and Racism Framework: Racial Entanglements and Deep and Malleable Whiteness." *Sociology of Race and Ethnicity* 5 (2): 169–85.
Christensen, Darin, and Jeremy M. Weinstein. 2013. "Defunding Dissent: Restrictions on Aid to NGOs." *Journal of Democracy* 24 (2): 77–91.
Ciccariello-Maher, George. 2013. *We Created Chávez: A People's History of the Venezuelan Revolution*. Durham, NC: Duke University Press.
Ciccariello-Maher, George. 2016. *Building the Commune: Radical Democracy in Venezuela*. New York: Verso.
Clawson, Dan, Alan Neustadtl, and Mark Weller. 1998. *Dollars and Votes: How Business Campaign Contributions Subvert Democracy*. Philadelphia: Temple University Press.
Clement, Christopher. I. 2005. "Confronting Hugo Chávez: United States 'Democracy Promotion' in Latin America." *Latin American Perspectives* 32 (3): 60–78.
Cole, N. Scott. 2007. "Hugo Chavez and President Bush's Credibility Gap: The Struggle against US Democracy Promotion." *International Political Science Review* 28:493–507.

Cole, Wade M. 2012. "A Civil Religion for World Society: The Direct and Diffuse Effects of Human Rights Treaties, 1981–2007." *Sociological Forum* 27 (4): 937–60.

Concheso, Aurelio. 2013. "The Private Sector and the Future of Venezuela." *CIPE blog*, December 17, 2013. https://en.paperblog.com/the-private-sector-and-the-future-of-venezuela-748346/.

Conti, Joseph A., and Moira O'Neil. 2007. "Studying Power: Qualitative Methods and the Global Elite." *Qualitative Research* 7 (1): 63–82.

Corrales, Javier, and Carlos A. Romero. 2013. *U.S.-Venezuela Relations since the 1990s: Coping with Mid-Level Security Threats*. New York: Routledge.

Corrales, Javier, and Michael Penfold-Becerra. 2011. *Dragon in the Tropics: Hugo Chavez and the Political Economy of Revolution in Venezuela*. Washington, DC: Brookings Institution Press.

Cottam, Martha L. 1994. *Images and Intervention: US Policies in Latin America*. Pittsburgh: University of Pittsburgh Press.

Cox, Oliver Crowell. 1959. *The Foundations of Capitalism*. New York: Monthly Review Press.

Craner, Lorne, and Kenneth Wollack. 2008. *New Directions for Democracy Promotion*. Washington, DC: Better World Campaign.

Crisp, Brian F. 2000. *Democratic Institutional Design: The Powers and Incentives of Venezuelan Politicians and Interest Groups*. Stanford, CA: Stanford University Press.

Crisp, Brian F., and Daniel H. Levine. 1998. "Democratizing the Democracy? Crisis and Reform in Venezuela." *Journal of Interamerican Studies and World Affairs* 40 (2): 27–61.

Dahl, Robert A. 1961. *Who Governs? Democracy and Power in an American City*. New Haven, CT: Yale University Press.

Dahl, Robert. 1971. *Polyarchy: Participation and Opposition*. New Haven, CT: Yale University Press.

Daniels, Joe Parkin. 2019. "Venezuela: Who is Juan Guaidó, the Man Who Declared Himself President?" *Guardian*, January 23, 2019.

Davidson, Alastair. 1974. "Gramsci and Lenin, 1917–1922." *Socialist Register* 11:125–50.

Defty, Andrew. 2004. *Britain, America and Anti-Communist Propaganda 1945–53: The Information Research Department*. London: Routledge.

De Tocqueville, Alexis. (1835) 2003. *Democracy in America*. New York: Penguin.

Diamond, Larry. 2009. *The Spirit of Democracy: The Struggle to Build Free Societies throughout the World*. New York: St. Martin's Griffin.

Domhoff, G. William. 1996. *State Autonomy or Class Dominance?: Case Studies on Policy Making in America*. Herndon, VA: Aldine Transaction.

Doty, Roxanne Lynn. 1996. *Imperial Encounters: The Politics of Representation in North-South Relations*. Minneapolis: University of Minnesota Press.

Du Bois, W. E. B. 1900. "The Present Outlook for the Dark Races of Mankind." In

The Problem of the Color Line at the Turn of the Twentieth Century: The Essential Early Essays. New York: Fordham University Press.

Du Bois, W. E. B. 1903. *The Souls of Black Folk*. Oxford: Oxford University Press.

Du Bois, W. E. B. 1915. "The African Roots of War." *Atlantic Monthly* 115 (5): 707–14.

Du Bois, W. E. B. 1920. *Darkwater: Voices from Within the Veil*. New York: Harcourt.

Du Bois, W. E. B. 1945. *Color and Democracy: Colonies and Peace*. New York: Harcourt.

Du Bois, W. E. B. 1947. *The World and Africa: An Inquiry into the Part Which Africa Has Played in World History*. New York: Masses & Mainstream.

Du Bois, W. E. B. 1951. "Peace is Dangerous." W. E. B. Du Bois Papers, 1803–1999. https://credo.library.umass.edu/view/collection/mums312.

Dupuy, Kendra, James Ron, and Aseem Prakash. 2016. "Hands Off My Regime! Governments' Restrictions on Foreign Aid to Non-Governmental Organizations in Poor and Middle-Income Countries." *World Development* 84:299–311.

Ellner, Steve. 2008. *Rethinking Venezuelan Politics: Class, Conflict, and the Chávez Phenomenon*. Boulder, CO: Lynne Rienner.

Enríquez, Laura J., and Simeon J. Newman. 2016. "The Conflicted State and Agrarian Transformation in Pink Tide Venezuela." *Journal of Agrarian Change* 16 (4): 594–626.

Evans, Peter B. 2012. *Embedded Autonomy: States and Industrial Transformation*. Princeton, NJ: Princeton University Press.

Eyal, Gil, Iván Szelényi, and Eleanor R. Townsley. 1998. *Making Capitalism without Capitalists: Class Formation and Elite Struggles in Post-Communist Central Europe*. London: Verso.

Fan, Yun. 2004. "Taiwan: No Civil Society, No Democracy." In *Civil Society and Political Change in Asia: Expanding and Contracting Democratic Space*, edited by M. Alagappa, 164–90. Stanford, CA: Stanford University Press.

Feagin, Joe R. 2009. *The White Racial Frame: Centuries of Racial Framing and Counter-Framing*. London: Routledge.

Ferguson, Niall. 2005. *Colossus: The Rise and Fall of American Empire*. New York: Penguin.

Fernandes, Sujatha. 2010. *Who Can Stop the Drums?: Urban Social Movements in Chávez's Venezuela*. Durham, NC: Duke University Press.

Field, Thomas. 2014. *From Development to Dictatorship: Bolivia and the Alliance for Progress in the Kennedy Era*. Ithaca, NY: Cornell University Press.

Finkel, Steven E., A. Perez-Linan, and M. A. Seligson. 2007. "The Effects of Us Foreign Assistance on Democracy Building, 1990–2003." *World Politics* 59: 404–30.

Fioramonti, Lorenzo, and Antonio Fiori. 2010. "Civil Society after Democracy: The Evolution of Civic Activism in South Africa and Korea." *Journal of Civil Society* 6 (1): 23–38.

Fischer, Claude. 2010. *Made in America: A Social History of American Culture and Character*. Chicago: University of Chicago Press.

Fitz, Caitlin. 2017. *Our Sister Republics: The United States in an Age of American Revolutions*. New York: W. W. Norton.

Flyvbjerg, Bent. 2006. "Five Misunderstandings about Case Study Research," *Qualitative Inquiry* 12 (2): 219–45.

Fourcade-Gourinchas, Marion and Sarah Babb. 2002. "The Rebirth of the Liberal Creed: Paths to Neoliberalism in Four Countries." *American Journal of Sociology* 108 (3): 533–79.

Frank, Andre Gunder. 1966. *The Development of Underdevelopment*. Boston: New England Free Press.

Fukuyama, Francis. 1993. *The End of History and the Last Man*. New York: Avon.

Fung, Archon. 2003. "Associations and Democracy: Between Theories, Hopes, and Realities." *Annual Review of Sociology* (2003): 515–39.

Gaddis, John Lewis. 2005. *Strategies of Containment: A Critical Appraisal of American National Security Policy during the Cold War*. Oxford: Oxford University Press.

Galeano, Eduardo. 1971. *Open Veins of Latin America: Five Centuries of the Pillage of a Continent*. New York: New York University Press.

Gallie, Walter B. 1956. "Essentially Contested Concepts." *Proceedings of the Aristotelian Society* 56 (1): 167–98.

Garcia-Guadilla, Marcia Pilar. 2003. "Civil Society: Institutionalization, Fragmentation, Autonomy." In *Venezuelan Politics in the Chávez Era: Class, Polarization, and Conflict*, edited by Steve Ellner and Daniel Hellinger, 179–98. Boulder, CO: Lynne Rienner.

Gates, Leslie C. 2010. *Electing Chavez: The Business of Anti-Neoliberal Politics in Venezuela*. Pittsburgh: University of Pittsburgh Press.

Geogehan, Kate. 2018. "A Policy in Tension: The National Endowment for Democracy and the U.S. Response to the Collapse of the Soviet Union," *Diplomatic History* 42 (5): 772–801.

German Press Agency. 1999. "Venezuela's Chávez Meets Chinese Premier." October 12, 1999.

Gershman, Carl, and Michael Allen. 2006. "The Assault on Democracy Assistance." *Journal of Democracy* 17 (2): 36–51.

Gilens, Martin, and Benjamin I. Page. 2014. "Testing Theories of American Politics: Elites, Interest Groups, and Average Citizens." *Perspectives on Politics* 12 (3): 564–81.

Gill, Timothy M. 2016. "The Venezuelan Government and the Global Field: The Legislative Battle over Foreign Funding for Nongovernmental Organizations." *Sociological Forum* 31 (1): 29–52.

Gill, Timothy M. 2019. "Shifting Imperial Strategies in Contemporary Latin America: The U.S. Empire and Venezuela under Hugo Chávez." *Journal of Historical Sociology* 32 (3): 294–310.

Gill, Timothy M. 2020. "Why Did the US Fund Anti–Hugo Chávez Rock Bands in Venezuela?" *Jacobin*, June 5, 2020. https://www.jacobinmag.com/2020/06/us-intervention-venezuela-hugo-chavez-ned.

Gill, Timothy M., and Rebecca Hanson. 2019. "How Washington Funded the Counterrevolution in Venezuela." *Nation*, February 8, 2019. https://www.thenation.com/article/archive/venezuela-washington-funded-counterrevolution/.

Go, Julian. 2007. "The Provinciality of American Empire: 'Liberal Exceptionalism' and US Colonial Rule, 1898–1912." *Comparative Studies in Society and History* 49 (1): 74–108.

Go, Julian. 2008a. *American Empire and the Politics of Meaning: Elite Political Cultures in the Philippines and Puerto Rico during US Colonialism*. Durham, NC: Duke University Press.

Go, Julian. 2008b. "Global Fields and Imperial Forms: Field Theory and the British and American Empires." *Sociological Theory* 26 (3): 201–29.

Go, Julian. 2011. *Patterns of Empire: The British and American Empires, 1688 to the Present*. Cambridge: Cambridge University Press.

Golinger, Eva. 2006. *The Chávez Code: Cracking US Intervention in Venezuela*. Northampton, MA: Olive Branch Press.

Golinger, Eva. 2008. *Bush versus Chávez: Washington's War on Venezuela*. New York: Monthly Review Press.

Gómez, Laura E. 2020. *Inventing Latinos: A New Story of American Racism*. New York: New Press.

Gottberg, Luis Duno. 2011. "The Color of Mobs: Racial Politics, Ethnopopulism, and Representation in the Chávez Era." In *Venezuela's Bolivarian Democracy: Participation, Politics and Culture under Chávez*, edited by David Smilde and Daniel Hellinger, 271–97. Durham, NC: Duke University Press.

Gramsci, Antonio. 1971. "State and Civil Society." In *Selections from the Prison Notebooks*, 206–76. New York: International Publishers.

Grandin, Greg. 2006. *Empire's Workshop: Latin America, the United States, and the Rise of the New Imperialism*. New York: Metropolitan Books.

Gratius, Susanne. 2010. *Assessing Democracy Assistance: Venezuela*. FRIDE report.

Hammersley, Martyn, and Roger Gomm. 2000. "Introduction." In *Case Study Method*, edited by Roger Gomm, Martyn Hammersley, and Peter Foster, 1–16. London: SAGE Publications.

Harvey, David. 1990. *The Condition of Postmodernity*. Malden, MA: Blackwell.

Harvey, David. 2005. *The New Imperialism*. Oxford: Oxford University Press.

Hellinger, Daniel. 2003. "Political Overview: The Breakdown of Puntofijismo and the Rise of Chavismo." In *Venezuelan Politics in the Chávez Era: Class, Polarization, and Conflict*, edited by Steve Ellner and Daniel Hellinger, 27–53. Boulder, CO: Lynne Rienner.

Held, David. 1997. *Models of Democracy*. Stanford, CA: Stanford University Press.

Hetland, Gabriel. 2017. "From System Collapse to Chavista Hegemony: The Party Question in Bolivarian Venezuela." *Latin American Perspectives* 44 (1): 17–36.

Herrera Salas, Jesús María. 2005. "Ethnicity and Evolution: The Political Economy of Racism in Venezuela." *Latin American Perspectives* 32 (2): 72–91.

Hertel-Fernandez, Alexander. 2014. "Who Passes Business's 'Model Bills'? Policy Capacity and Corporate Influence in US State Politics." *Perspectives on Politics* 12 (3): 582–602.

Hertel-Fernandez, Alexander. 2019. *State Capture: How Conservative Activists, Big Businesses, and Wealthy Donors Reshaped the American States—and the Nation.* New York: Oxford University Press.

Hertz, Rosanna, and Jonathan B. Imber. 1995. *Studying Elites using Qualitative Methods.* Thousand Oaks, CA: SAGE Publications.

Hidalgo, Manuel. 2009. "Hugo Chávez' 'Petro-Socialism.'" *Journal of Democracy* 20:78–92.

hooks, bell. 1982. *Ain't I a Woman: Black Women and Feminism.* London: Pluto Press.

Horne, Gerald. 2016. *The Counter-Revolution of 1776: Slave Resistance and the Origins of the United States of America.* New York: New York University Press.

Horne, Gerald. 2020. *The Dawning of the Apocalypse: The Roots of Slavery, White Supremacy, Settler Colonialism, and Capitalism in the Long Sixteenth Century.* New York: Monthly Review Press.

Horsman, Reginald. 1981. *Race and Manifest Destiny: Origins of American Racial Anglo-Saxonism.* Cambridge, MA: Harvard University Press.

Hung, Ho-Fung. 2020. "Disintegrating US-China Economic Symbiosis and the New Inter-Imperial Rivalry." *Marxist Sociology* (blog), July 2, 2020.

Hunt, Michael H. 2009. *Ideology and US Foreign Policy.* New Haven, CT: Yale University Press.

Ignatieff, Michael. 2003. "America's Empire Is an Empire Lite." *New York Times*, January 10, 2003.

Immerman, Richard. 2010. *Empire for Liberty: A History of American Imperialism from Benjamin Franklin to Paul Wolfowitz.* Princeton, NJ: Princeton University Press.

Immerwahr, Daniel. 2019. *How to Hide an Empire: A History of the Greater United States.* New York: Farrar, Straus and Giroux.

Information Telegraph Agency of Russia (ITAR-TASS). 2006. "Venezuelan President Praises Belarus as 'Social State.'" July 23, 2006.

Information Telegraph Agency of Russia (ITAR-TASS). 2007. "Belarus, Venezuela Set up Oil Production Joint Venture." December 9, 2007.

Islamic Republic News Agency. 2006. "No Limit in Cooperation between Iran, Venezuela—President." July 30, 2006.

International Republican Institute (IRI). n.d. https://www.iri.org/.

International Republican Institute. 1998. *Venezuela's 1998 Presidential, Legislative, and Gubernatorial Elections: Election Observation Report*. Washington, DC: IRI.
International Republican Institute. 2001a. *Quarterly Report*. Washington, DC: IRI.
International Republican Institute. 2001b. *Quarterly Report*. Washington, DC: IRI.
International Republican Institute. 2002a. *Quarterly Report*. Washington, DC: IRI.
International Republican Institute. 2002b. *Quarterly Report*. Washington, DC: IRI.
International Republican Institute. 2002c. *Quarterly Report*. Washington, DC: IRI.
International Republican Institute. 2002d. *Quarterly Report*. Washington, DC: IRI.
International Republican Institute. 2003a. *Quarterly Report*. Washington, DC: IRI.
International Republican Institute. 2003b. *Quarterly Report*. Washington, DC: IRI.
International Republican Institute. 2005a. *Quarterly Report*. Washington, DC: IRI.
International Republican Institute. 2005b. *Quarterly Report*. Washington, DC: IRI.
International Republican Institute. 2005c. *Quarterly Report*. Washington, DC: IRI.
International Republican Institute. 2007a. *Quarterly Report*. Washington, DC: IRI.
International Republican Institute. 2007b. *Quarterly Report*. Washington, DC: IRI.
Itzigsohn, Jose, and Karida Brown. 2020. *The Sociology of W. E. B. Du Bois*. New York: New York University Press.
Jackson, Jeffrey T. 2005. *The Globalizers: Development Workers in Action*. Baltimore: Johns Hopkins University Press.
Jung, Moon-Kie. 2011. "Constituting the US Empire-State and White Supremacy: The Early Years." In *State of White Supremacy: Racism, Governance, and the United States*, edited by Moon-Kie Jung, João H. Costa Vargas, and Eduardo Bonilla-Silva, 1–23. Stanford, CA: Stanford University Press.
Kaplan, Robert. 2014. "In Defense of Empire." *Atlantic*, April 2014. https://www.theatlantic.com/magazine/archive/2014/04/in-defense-of-empire/358645/.
Kaplan, Robert. 2020. "The Afterlife of Empire." *National Interest*, October 16, 2020. https://nationalinterest.org/feature/afterlife-empire-170803.
Karl, Terry Lynn. 1997. *The Paradox of Plenty: Oil Booms and Petro-States*. Berkeley: University of California Press.
Keck, Margaret, and Kathryn Sikkink. 1998. *Activists beyond Borders: Advocacy Networks in International Politics*. Ithaca, NY: Cornell University Press.
Keen, Mike Forrest. 1992. "The Freedom of Information Act and Sociological Research." *American Sociologist* 23 (2): 43–51.
Kelly, Janet, and Carlos A. Romero. 2002. *The United States and Venezuela: Rethinking a Relationship*. New York: Routledge.
Khan, Shamus. 2012. *Privilege: The Making of an Adolescent Elite at St. Paul's School*. Princeton, NJ: Princeton University Press.
Kingsbury, Donald. 2018. *Only the People Can Save the People: Constituent Power, Revolution, and Counterrevolution in Venezuela*. Albany: State University of New York Press.
Kinzer, Stephen. 2006. *Overthrow*. New York: Times Books.

Kinzer, Stephen. 2013. *The Brothers: John Foster Dulles, Allen Dulles, and Their Secret World War*. New York: Macmillan.

Kitschelt, Herbert P. 1986. "Political Opportunity Structures and Political Protest: Anti-Nuclear Movements in Four Democracies." *British Journal of Political Science* 16 (1): 57–85.

Klein, Naomi. 2007. *The Shock Doctrine: The Rise of Disaster Capitalism*. New York: Metropolitan Books/Henry Holt.

Kluegel, J. R., D. S. Mason, and B. Wegener. 1999. "The Legitimation of Capitalism in the Postcommunist Transition—Public Opinion about Market Justice, 1991–1996." *European Sociological Review* 15:251–83.

Kolko, Gabriel. 1969. *The Roots of American Foreign Policy*. Boston: Beacon Press.

Krasner, Stephen D. 1978 *Sovereignty: Organized Hypocrisy*. Princeton, NJ: Princeton University Press.

Krasner, Stephen D. 1999. *Sovereignty: Organized Hypocrisy*. Princeton, NJ: Princeton University Press.

Krenn, Michael. 2006. *The Color of Empire: Race and American Foreign Relations*. Lincoln: University of Nebraska Press.

Kurki, Milja. 2013. *Democratic Futures: Re-visioning Democracy Promotion*. London: Routledge.

Lacayo, Celia Olivia. 2017. "Perpetual Inferiority: Whites' Racial Ideology toward Latinos." *Sociology of Race and Ethnicity* 3 (4): 566–79.

Lander, Luis E., and López Maya, Margarita. 1999. "Venezuela. La victoria de Chávez." *Nueva Sociedad* 160:4–19.

Latham, Michael E. 2000. *Modernization as Ideology: American Social Science and 'Nation Building' in the Kennedy Era*. Chapel Hill: University of North Carolina Press.

Lean, Sharon F. 2012. *Civil Society and Electoral Accountability in Latin America*. New York: Palgrave.

Lenin, V. I. 1902. "What Is to Be Done?" Marxist Internet Archive. https://www.marxists.org/archive/lenin/works/1901/witbd/.

Lenin, V. I. 1917. *Imperialism: The Highest Stage of Capitalism*. New York: Penguin Classics.

Levin, Dov. 2016. "When the Great Power Gets a Vote: The Effects of Great Power Electoral Interventions on Election Results." *International Studies Quarterly* 60 (2): 189–202.

Lipset, Seymour Martin. 1959. "Some Social Requisites of Democracy: Economic Development and Political Legitimacy." *American Sociological Review* 53 (1): 69–105.

Lipset, Seymour Martin. 1997. *American Exceptionalism: A Double-Edged Sword*. New York: W. W. Norton.

López Maya, Margarita, and Luis E. Lander. 2000. "Ajustes, costos sociales y la agenda de los pobres en Venezuela: 1984–1998." *Revista Venezolana de Economía y Ciencias Sociales* 6 (3): 185–206.

López Maya, Margarita. 2003. "The Venezuelan Caracazo of 1989: Popular Protest and Institutional Weakness." *Journal of Latin American Studies* 35 (1): 117–37.

Lorenzini, Sara. 2019. *Global Development: A Cold War History*. Princeton, NJ: Princeton University Press.

Lowe, David. 2013. *Idea to Reality: NED at 30*. Washington, DC: National Endowment for Democracy.

Mac an Ghaill, Maírtín. 2000. "The Irish in Britain: The Invisibility of Ethnicity and Anti-Irish Racism." *Journal of Ethnic and Migration Studies* 26 (1): 137–47.

Magubane, Zine. 2016. "American Sociology's Racial Ontology: Remembering Slavery, Deconstructing Modernity, and Charting the Future of Global Historical Sociology." *Cultural Sociology* 10 (3): 369–84.

Mann, Michael. 1987. "The Autonomous Power of the State: Its Origins, Mechanisms, and Results." In *States in History*, edited by John A. Hall, 109–36. New York: Basil Blackwell.

Mann, Michael. 2013. *The Sources of Social Power: Volume 4, Globalizations, 1945–2011*. Cambridge: Cambridge University Press.

Martin, John Levi. 2003. "What Is Field Theory?" *American Journal of Sociology* 109 (1): 1–49.

Marx, Karl. 1978. *The Marx-Engels Reader*. Edited by Robert Tucker. New York: W. W. Norton.

Mathias, Matthew D. 2013. "The Sacralization of the Individual: Human Rights and the Abolition of the Death Penalty." *American Journal of Sociology* 118 (5): 1246–83.

McAdam, Doug. 1982. *Political Process and the Development of Black Insurgency, 1930–1970*. Chicago: University of Chicago Press.

McCarthy, Thomas. 2009. *Race, Empire, and the Idea of Human Development*. Cambridge: Cambridge University Press.

McCoy, Alfred W. 2017. *In the shadows of the American Century: The Rise and Decline of US Global Power*. Chicago: Haymarket Books.

McCoy, Jennifer, and David J. Myers. 2004. *The Unraveling of Representative Democracy in Venezuela*. Baltimore: Johns Hopkins University Press.

McFaul, Michael. 2004. "Democracy Promotion as a World Value." *Washington Quarterly* 28 (1): 147–63.

McFaul, Michael. 2009. *Advancing Democracy Abroad: Why We Should and How We Can*. Lanham, MD: Rowman and Littlefield.

McPherson, Alan. 2016. *A Short History of US Interventions in Latin America and the Caribbean*. Hoboken, NJ: John Wiley & Sons.

Mearsheimer, John J., and Stephen Walt. 2008. *The Israel Lobby and U.S. Foreign Policy*. New York: Farrar, Straus and Giroux.

Melia, Thomas O. 2006. *The Democracy Bureaucracy: The Infrastructure of the Ameri-*

can Democracy Promotion. Princeton, NJ: Princeton Project on National Security Working Group on Global Institutions and Foreign Policy Infrastructure.

Meyer, John W., John Boli, George M. Thomas, and Francisco O. Ramirez. 1997. "World Society and the Nation-State." *American Journal of Sociology* 103 (1): 144–81.

Mill, Charles. 1997. *The Racial Contract*. Ithaca, NY: Cornell University Press.

Miller, James E. 1983. "Taking off the Gloves: The United States and the Italian Elections of 1948." *Diplomatic History* 7 (1): 35–56.

Miller, Aragorn Storm. 2016. *Precarious Paths to Freedom: The United States, Venezuela, and the Latin American Cold War*. Albuquerque: University of New Mexico Press.

Mills, C. Wright. 1956. *The Power Elite*. New York: Oxford University Press.

Miliband, Ralph. 1969. *The State in Capitalist Society*. London: Weidenfeld & Nicolson.

Mitchell, Lincoln. 2009. *Uncertain Democracy: U.S. Foreign Policy and Georgia's Rose Revolution*. Philadelphia: University of Pennsylvania Press.

Mitchell, Lincoln. 2016. *The Democracy Promotion Paradox*. Washington, DC: Brookings Institution Press.

Morris, Aldon. 2016. *The Scholar Denied: W. E. B. Du Bois and the Birth of Modern Sociology*. Berkeley: University of California Press.

Morgenthau, Hans J. 1951. *In Defense of the National Interest: A Critical Examination of American Foreign Policy*. New York: Knopf.

National Endowment for Democracy (NED). n.d. https://www.ned.org/.

National Endowment for Democracy. 2000a. *Program Report*. Washington, DC: NED.

National Endowment for Democracy. 2000b. *Program Report*. Washington, DC: NED.

National Endowment for Democracy. 2001a. *Program Report*. Washington, DC: NED.

National Endowment for Democracy. 2001b. *Program Report*. Washington, DC: NED.

National Endowment for Democracy. 2001c. *Program Report*. Washington, DC: NED.

National Endowment for Democracy. 2001d. *Program Report*. Washington, DC: NED.

National Endowment for Democracy. 2002a. *Program Report*. Washington, DC: NED.

National Endowment for Democracy. 2002b. *Program Report*. Washington, DC: NED.

National Endowment for Democracy. 2002c. *Program Report*. Washington, DC: NED.

National Endowment for Democracy. 2002d. *Program Report*. Washington, DC: NED.

National Endowment for Democracy. 2002e. *Program Report*. Washington, DC: NED.

National Endowment for Democracy. 2002f. *Program Report*. Washington, DC: NED.

National Endowment for Democracy. 2002g. *Program Report*. Washington, DC: NED.

National Endowment for Democracy. 2003a. *Program Report*. Washington, DC: NED.

National Endowment for Democracy. 2003b. *Program Report*. Washington, DC: NED.

National Endowment for Democracy. 2003c. *Program Report*. Washington, DC: NED.

National Endowment for Democracy. 2003d. *Program Report*. Washington, DC: NED.

National Endowment for Democracy. 2003e. *Program Report*. Washington, DC: NED.

National Endowment for Democracy. 2003f. *Program Report*. Washington, DC: NED.

National Endowment for Democracy. 2003g. *Program Report.* Washington, DC: NED.
National Democratic Institute for International Affairs (NDI). n.d. https://www.ndi.org/.
National Democratic Institute for International Affairs. 2002a. *Program Report.* Washington, DC: NDI.
National Democratic Institute for International Affairs. 2002b. *Program Report.* Washington, DC: NDI.
National Democratic Institute for International Affairs. 2003. *Program Report.* Washington, DC: NDI.
National Democratic Institute for International Affairs. 2004a. *Program Report.* Washington, DC: NDI.
National Democratic Institute for International Affairs. 2004b. *Program Report.* Washington, DC: NDI.
National Democratic Institute for International Affairs. 2005a. *Program Report.* Washington, DC: NDI.
National Democratic Institute for International Affairs. 2005b. *Program Report.* Washington, DC: NDI.
National Democratic Institute for International Affairs. 2006. *Program Report.* Washington, DC: NDI.
National Democratic Institute for International Affairs. 2007. *Program Report.* Washington, DC: NDI.
National Democratic Institute for International Affairs. 2008a. *Program Report.* Washington, DC: NDI.
National Democratic Institute for International Affairs. 2008b. *Program Report.* Washington, DC: NDI.
National Democratic Institute for International Affairs. 2008c. *Program Report.* Washington, DC: NDI.
National Democratic Institute for International Affairs. 2009. *Program Report.* Washington, DC: NDI.
National Democratic Institute for International Affairs. 2010. *Program Report.* Washington, DC: NDI.
National Democratic Institute for International Affairs. 2013. *Program Report.* Washington, DC: NDI.
Neuman, William. 2013. "Venezuela Stops Efforts to Improve U.S. Relations." *New York Times,* July 20, 2013.
Nkrumah, Kwame. 1966. *Neo-Colonialism, the Last Stage of Imperialism.* New York: International Publishers.
Nye, Joseph. 2015. *Is the American Century Over?* Hoboken, NJ: John Wiley & Sons.
O'Callaghan, Sean. 2013. *To Hell or Barbados: The Ethnic Cleansing of Ireland.* Austin: University of Texas Press.
Office of the Inspector General (OIG). 2002. *A Review of U.S. Policy toward Venezuela November 2001—April 2002.* Washington, DC: OIG.

Office of Transition Initiatives (OTI). n.d. https://www.usaid.gov/who-we-are/organization/bureaus/bureau-conflict-prevention-and-stabilization/office-transition-initiatives.

Olson, Alexandra. 2000. "Venezuela Defends Chávez Iraq Trip." Associated Press, August 8, 2000.

Page, Benjamin I., and Martin Gilens. 2020. *Democracy in America?: What Has Gone Wrong and What We Can Do about It*. Chicago: University of Chicago Press.

Panitch, Leo, and Sam Gindin. 2005. *The Making of Global Capitalism*. New York: Verso.

Parmar, Inderjeet. 2013. "The 'Knowledge Politics' of Democratic Peace Theory." *International Politics* 50 (2): 231–56.

Parsons, Talcott. 1966. *Societies: Evolutionary and Comparative Perspectives*. New York: Prentice Hall.

Penfold-Becerra, Michael. 2007. "Clientelism and Social Funds: Evidence from Chavez's Misiones." *Latin American Politics and Society* 49:63–84.

Petras, James. 1997. "Imperialism and NGOs in Latin America." *Monthly Review* 49 (7): 10–27.

Petras, James. 1999. "NGOs: In the Service of Imperialism." *Journal of Contemporary Asia* 29 (4): 429–40.

Platt, Jennifer. 1992. "Cases of Cases . . . of Cases." In *What Is a Case?: Exploring the Foundations of Social Inquiry*, edited by Charles C. Ragin and Howard Becker, 21–52. Cambridge: Cambridge University Press.

Polsby, Nelson. 1963. *Community Power and Social Theory*. New Haven, CT: Yale University Press.

Poulantzas, Nicos. 1969. "The Problem of the Capitalist State." *New Left Review* 58 (1): 67–78.

Poznansky, Michael. 2020. *In the Shadow of International Law: Secrecy and Regime Change in the Postwar World*. Oxford: Oxford University Press.

Putnam, Robert D. 1993. *Making Democracy Work: Civic Traditions in Modern Italy*. Princeton, NJ: Princeton University Press.

Putnam, Robert. 1995. "Bowling Alone: America's Declining Social Capital." *Journal of Democracy* 6:65–78.

Quijano, Aníbal. 2000. "Coloniality of Power, Eurocentrism, and Latin America." *Nepantla: Views from South* 1 (3): 533–80.

Quisumbing King, Katrina. 2019. "Recentering U.S. Empire: A Structural Perspective on the Color Line." *Sociology of Race & Ethnicity* 5 (1): 11–25.

Radio Nacional de Espana. 2004. "Venezuelan President urges Spaniards to 'Unmask Neoliberalism." November 22, 2004.

Ragin, Charles. 1989. *The Comparative Method: Moving Beyond Qualitative and Quantitative Strategies*. Berkeley: University of California Press.

Ramirez, Mark D., and David A. M. Peterson. 2020. *Ignored Racism: White Animus toward Latinos*. Cambridge: Cambridge University Press.

Rid, Thomas. 2020. *Active Measures: The Secret History of Disinformation and Political Warfare*. New York: Farrar, Straus and Giroux.
Ritzer, George. 2003. "Rethinking Globalization: Glocalization/Grobalization and Something/Nothing." *Sociological Theory* 21:193–209.
Robertson, Roland. 1992. *Globalization: Social Theory and Global Culture*. London: SAGE Publications.
Robinson, Cedric. 1983. *Black Marxism: The Making of the Black Radical Tradition*. London: Zed Books.
Robinson, William I. 1996. "Globalization, the World System, and 'Democracy Promotion' in US Foreign Policy." *Theory and Society* 25 (5): 615–65.
Robinson, William I. 2001. "Social Theory and Globalization: The Rise of a Transnational State." *Theory and Society* 30:157–200.
Robinson, William I. 2003. *Transnational Conflicts: Central America, Social Change, and Globalization*. New York: Verso.
Robinson, William I. 2006. "Promoting Polyarchy in Latin America: The Oxymoron of 'Market Democracy.'" In *Latin America after Neoliberalism: Turning the Tide in the 21st Century?*, edited by Eric Hershberg and Fred Rosen, 96–119. New York: New Press.
Robinson, William I. 2007. "Beyond the Theory of Imperialism: Global Capitalism and the Transnational State." *Societies without Borders* 2:5–26.
Rodney, Walter. 1972. *How Europe Underdeveloped Africa*. London: Bogle-L'Ouverture Publications.
Romero, Simon, and Clifford J. Romero. 2008. "Venezuela Announces Early Plans for Military Exercises With Russia in Caribbean." *New York Times*, September 8, 2008.
Rostow, W. W. 1960. *The Stages on Economic Growth: A Non-Communist Manifesto*. Cambridge: Cambridge University Press.
Ryan, Alan. 2012. *The Making of Modern Liberalism*. Princeton, NJ: Princeton University Press.
Said, Edward. 1978. *Orientalism*. New York: Vintage.
Salamanca, Luis. 2004. "Civil Society: Late Bloomers." In *The Unraveling of Representative Democracy in Venezuela*, edited by Jennifer L. McCoy and David J. Meyers, 93–114. Baltimore: Johns Hopkins University Press.
Sassen, Saskia. 2006. *Territory, Authority, Rights: From Medieval to Global Assemblages*. Princeton, NJ: Princeton University Press.
Solidarity Center (SC). n.d. https://www.solidaritycenter.org/.
Solidarity Center. 2000. *Quarterly Report*. Washington, DC: SC.
Solidarity Center. 2002. *Quarterly Report*. Washington, DC: SC.
Solidarity Center. 2006. *Program Report*. Washington, DC: SC.
Solidarity Center. 2010. *Program Report*. Washington, DC: SC.
Solidarity Center. 2012. *Program Report*. Washington, DC: SC.
Solidarity Center. 2013. *Program Report*. Washington, DC: SC.

Schoultz, Lars. 2018. *In Their Own Best Interest: A History of the U.S. Effort to Improve Latin Americans*. Cambridge, MA: Harvard University Press.

Schwirtz, Michael. 2008. "Russia Loans Venezuela $1 Billion for Military." *New York Times*, September 27, 2008.

Scipes, Kim. 2005. "Labor Imperialism Redux?: The AFL-CIO's Foreign Policy since 1995." *Monthly Review* 57 (1): 23–37.

Scipes, Kim. 2010. "Why Labor Imperialism? AFL–CIO'S Foreign Policy Leaders and the Developing World." *Working USA* 13 (4): 465–79.

Scott, James M., and Carie A. Steele. 2011. "Sponsoring Democracy: The United States and Democracy Aid to the Developing World, 1988–20011." *International Studies Quarterly* 55 (1): 47–69.

Sikkink, Kathryn. 2007. *Mixed Signals: US Human Rights Policy and Latin America*. Washington, DC: Century Foundation.

Sklair, Leslie. 1995. *Sociology of the Global System*. London: Prentice Hall.

Sklair, Leslie. 2001. *The Transnational Capitalist Class*. Malden, MA: Wiley-Blackwell.

Skocpol, Theda. 1985. "Bringing the State Back In: Strategies of Analysis in Current Research." In *Bringing the State Back In*, edited by Peter B. Evans, Dietrich Rueschemeyer, and Theda Skocpol, 3–43. Cambridge: Cambridge University Press.

Smilde, David. 2009. "Three Stages in the Chávez Government's Approach to Participation." In *Woodrow Wilson Center Update on the America*, edited by Adam T. Stubits, 2–7. Washington, DC: Woodrow Wilson Center.

Smilde, David. 2011. "Participation, Politics and Culture: Emerging Fragments of Venezuela's Bolivarian Democracy." In *Venezuela's Bolivarian Democracy: Participation, Politics and Culture under Chávez*, edited by David Smilde and Daniel Hellinger, 1–27. Durham, NC: Duke University Press.

Smilde, David, and Timothy M. Gill. 2013. "Strategic Posture Review: Venezuela." *World Politics Review*, September 17, 2013.

Smith, Phillip. 2005. *Why War?: The Cultural Logic of Iraq, the Gulf War, and Suez*. Chicago: University of Chicago Press.

Smith, Tony. 2013. "Democracy Promotion from Wilson to Obama." In *US Foreign Policy and Democracy Promotion: From Theodore Roosevelt to Barack Obama*, edited by Michael Cox, 13–36. New York: Routledge.

Somers, Margaret R., and Fred Block. 2005. "From Poverty to Perversity: Ideas, Markets, and Institutions over 200 Years of Welfare Debate." *American Sociological Review* 70 (2): 260–87.

Steinmetz, George. 2005. "Return to Empire: The New US Imperialism in Comparative Historical Perspective." *Sociological Theory* 23 (4): 339–67.

Steinmetz, George. 2013. *Sociology and Empire: The Imperial Entanglements of a Discipline*. Durham, NC: Duke University Press.

Sussman, Gerald. 2006. "The Myth US 'Democracy Assistance': US Political Intervention in Post-Soviet Eastern Europe." *Monthly Review* 58 (7): 15–29.

Tuman, John P., and Craig F. Emmert. 2004. "The Political Economy of U.S. Foreign Direct Investment in Latin America: A Reappraisal." *Latin American Research Review* 39:9–28

Uggen, Christopher, and Jeff Manza. 2002. "Democratic Contraction? Political Consequences of Felon Disenfranchisement in the United States." *American Sociological Review* 67 (6): 777–803.

US Agency for International Development (USAID). n.d. https://www.usaid.gov/.

US Chamber of Commerce. n.d. https://www.uschamber.com/.

US Congress. 2010. "Hearing on Human Rights and Democracy Assistance: Increasing the Effectiveness of U.S. Foreign Aid. Committee on Foreign Affairs." Statement of Howard Berman, June 10.

US Subcommittee on the Western Hemisphere. 2009. *U.S. Policy toward Latin America in 2009 and Beyond*. Washington, DC: US Government Printing Office.

Velasco, Alejandro. 2011. "'We are Still Rebels': The Challenge of Popular History in Bolivarian Venezuela." In *Venezuela's Bolivarian Democracy: Participation, Politics and Culture under Chavez*, edited by David Smilde and Daniel Hellinger, 157–85. Durham, NC: Duke University Press.

Velasco, Alejandro. 2015. *Barrio Rising: Urban Popular Politics and the Making of Modern Venezuela*. Berkeley: University of California Press.

Vitalis, Robert. 2010. "The Noble American science of imperial relations and its laws of race development." *Comparative Studies in Society and History* 52 (4): 909–38.

Vogel Jr., Thomas T. 1999. "Venezuela's Chávez Must Woo Skeptical Investors on U.S. Trip." *Wall Street Journal, Eastern Edition*, June 8, 1999.

Vucetic, Srdjan. 2011. *The Anglosphere: A Genealogy of a Racialized Identity in International Relations*. Stanford, CA: Stanford University Press.

Wallerstein, Immanuel. 1974. "The Rise and Future Demise of the World Capitalist System: Concepts for Comparative Analysis." *Comparative Studies in Society and History* 16:387–415.

Walters, Robert S. 1970. *American and Soviet Aid: A Comparative Analysis*. Pittsburgh: University of Pittsburgh Press.

Waltz, Kenneth Neal. 1979. *Theory of International Politics*. Reading, UK: Addison-Wesley.

Watts, Jonathan. 2006. "Chávez Says China Deal 'Great Wall' against US." *Guardian*, August 25, 2006. https://www.theguardian.com/world/2006/aug/25/venezuela.china.

Weber, Max. (1914) 1978. "Basic Sociological Terms." In *Economy and Society: An Outline of Interpretive Sociology*, edited by Guenther Roth and Claus Wittich, 3–61. Berkeley: University of California Press.

Weber, Max. (1919) 1958. "Politics as Vocation." In *From Max Weber: Essays in Sociology*, 77–128. New York: Oxford University Press.

Weber, Max. (1922) 1978. "The Types of Legitimate Domination." In *Economy and*

Society: An Outline of Interpretive Sociology, 212–301. Berkeley: University of California Press.

Weber, Max. 1978. *Economy and Society: An Outline of Interpretive Sociology*. Berkeley: UC Press.

Weber, Max. (1917) 1994. "Socialism." In *Weber: Political Writings*, edited by Peter Lassman and Ronald Speirs, 272–303. Cambridge: Cambridge University Press.

Wedel, Janine. 2000. *Collision and Collusion: The Strange Case of Western Aid to Eastern Europe*. New York: Palgrave Macmillan.

Weiner, Melissa F. 2018. "Decolonial Sociology: WEB Du Bois's Foundational Theoretical and Methodological Contributions." *Sociology Compass* 12 (8): 1–16.

Weisbrot, Mark. 2004. "On the State of Democracy in Venezuela." Center for Economic and Policy Research, June 24, 2004. https://cepr.net/democracy-venezuela/.

Whitehead, Laurence. 1996. "Concerning International Support for Democracy in the South." In *Democratisation in the South: The Jagged Wave*, edited by Robin Luckham and Gordon White, 234–72. Manchester: Manchester University Press.

White House. 2015. "FACT SHEET: Venezuela Executive Order." March 9, 2015.

Wiarda, Howard J. 2003. *Civil Society: The American Model and Third World Development*. Boulder, CO: Westview Press.

Williams, Eric. 1944. *Capitalism and Slavery*. Chapel Hill: University of North Carolina Press.

Wilpert, Gregory. 2007. *Changing Venezuela by Taking Power: The History and Policies of the Chávez Government*. London: Verso.

Wright, Winthrop R. 2013. *Café Con Leche: Race, Class, and National Image in Venezuela*. Austin: University of Texas Press.

Yin, Robert. 2017. *Case Study Research: Design and Methods*. Thousand Oaks, CA: SAGE Publications.

Zemko, John. 2012. "Venezuelan Elections: Role of the Private Sector." *CIPE blog*, October 12, 2012. https://www.cipe.org/blog/2012/10/22/venezuelan-elections-role-of-the-private-sector/.

INDEX

ACAC (Asociacón Civil Acción Campesina), 158–59, 173
ACAE (Asociación Civil Asamblea de Educación), 159–62, 172, 212
ACCEDES (Asociación Civil Acción para el Desarrollo), 170–71
Acción Democratica (AD): and Carbajal, 98; and CTV, 147; and democracy bureaucracy, 95, 117, 122, 210, 215; and Maduro, 36; in the mid-twentieth century, 19; and youth members, 160
ACCJ (Asociación Civil Consorcio Justicia), 102, 164–66, 173, 216
ACCV (Asociación Civil Compresión de Venezuela), 169–70, 216
ACJA (Asociación Civil Justicia Alternativa), 171
ACLV (Asociación Civil Liderazgo y Visión), 172–73, 217
activists: and ACAC, 158; human rights, 166; and IRI, 31, 98; journalist, 167; opposition, 32, 91, 175, 209–10; and OTI, 92; and Rosales, 114; trained in social media and information technologies, 125–27
Adams, John Quincy, 76, 93
ads/advertisements, 32, 96, 145
advocate/s, 47, 61, 133, 146
Afghanistan, 18, 23, 30, 72
Africa, 8–9, 52, 67, 78

African Americans, 6, 75, 94
African/s: Chávez's heritage, 223n7; and racist-imperialism, 67, 75, 77; slavery, 6, 71, 74, 91
agenda: anti-NGO, 16, 191; Carter administration's, 43; Chavez's, 22, 125, 135, 184; and CIPE, 136, 138; National Assembly, 201; socialist 26; US foreign policy, 44
agriculture, 28, 46, 158–59
aid, 112; and Chávez, 28; from China, 191; from CIA, 19; criticized and prohibited by world leaders and governments, 11–12; for "economic modernization," 41, 43, 45; legal, 171; to middle-income countries, 10; neo-Tocquevillian view of, 38; Nkrumah on, 65, 80; Plan Bolívar 2000, 22; and Russia, 191; from Soviet Union, 177; as a tool of foreign control, 9; from Truman administration, 176; USAID, 46; US diplomat on Chávez's use of, 88; US suspension of Nicaraguan, 200
Allende, Salvador, 4, 30, 42
allies, 3, 194; Chavez's 13, 16, 33, 72, 90, 94, 97, 123, 129, 132, 174, 181, 198–201, 206, 219; Guaidó's, 115; Maduro's, 36; Reagan's, 43; Rosales', 114; Solidarity Center's, 150; US-Venezuela as, 37

247

ambassador/s: Brownfield, 83–85, 109–11, 121, 181–82; Chilean, former, 119; Duddy, 34, 84, 113, 186, 187; expulsion of, 12, 18, 34–35, 124, 200; Finnish, 198, 200; US, 35, 50, 90, 93, 97, 120, 131–33, 200; Shapiro, 109, 121, 180; Venezuelan UN, 98, 186
amendment/s, constitutional, 26, 123
Americas, the: Central, 7, 106, 119; and democratic political systems, 55; and Monroe Doctrine, 6, 179; North, 65, 69, 71, 76; and racist-imperial mentalities, 72, 76; South, 28, 78, 195
annexation, land, 71, 78, 94, 214
Anzoátegui, 106–7, 109
Aragua, 140, 171
Argentina, 43, 167
aristocracy, 48, 64
Asia, 9, 45, 67, 78, 194
Assange, Julian, 82, 108, 200
authoritarian: allies, 198; anti, 52; depictions of Chávez, 86, 121–22, 148–49, 164; governance, 10; governments, 9, 29, 42, 58, 191, 194, 205; leaders, 49; regimes, 40, 44
authoritarianism, 72, 120, 164
Azerbaijan, 9, 29

"backyard," 70, 131–32, 179
ballot box, 177; alternative to revolution, 28, 44; Chávez's success, 89, 184, 189; to undermine Chávez, 115, 123, 129, 190
banks, 26, 80, 204
Baruta, 99, 118, 156
Belarus: regulation of NGOs, 11, 199; US democracy assistance to, 10; and Venezuela, 4, 16, 30, 33, 72, 196–97, 200, 205
Biden, Joe, 36, 115, 200, 215, 218
Blum, Pedro Diaz, 99, 107
Bolivia, 4, 11, 16, 33, 124, 199–200
Bolivarian Revolution, 5, 159
Bolívar, Simón, 6, 73, 223n3

Borges, Julio, 99, 112, 115, 185
bourgeoisie, 54–55, 63
brigades, 159–60
Brownfield, William, 83–85, 109–11, 121–22, 181–82
Building Consensus on a National Agenda, 138–39
Bukharin, Nikolai, 56, 79
bulletins, 137, 143, 171
Bureau of Democracy, Human Rights, and Labor (DRL), 46–47
Bush, George W., 98; administration, 24, 33, 34, 82, 179, 186; Chávez's critiques of, 33, 83, 85, 88, 97, 198
business/es, 59, 60, 79, 84, 138, 140, 160; and ACCJ, 165, 216; and Chávez, 17; and CIPE, 141–46, 152; coalition with labor, 147; domestic, 10, 136; groups, 15, 31–32, 134, 138; Miliband on, 193; people/persons, 137, 194–95; US, 4, 181, 205; US Chamber of Commerce, 133; Venezuelan, 23, 102–3, 130, 214

cabinet, 153, 162
cables: Ambassador Brownfield's, 122; diplomatic, 15, 72, 82, 85–86, 88, 111, 178; embassy, x, 83, 89, 108; indicative of racist-imperial mentalities, 84
Caldera, Rafael, 19, 96
California, 65, 78, 108
Canada, 22, 74, 129, 197
capitalism, 60, 216, 222n3; anti-colonial rejection of, 73; Chávez's rejections of, 22, 25–26, 198; and Du Bois, 79; and Gramsci, 57–58; and Land Law, 195; liberal democratic, 39; liberal internationalist view of, 40; and Marx, 54–56; and neo-Marxists, 11; NGO promotion of, 15, 130, 133–34, 141–42, 214; racial, 71, 74; and Reagan, 44; Smith, Adam, 62; stability for, 10, 59; US government promotion of, 152

Capriles, Henrique, 144, 156, 169; election defeats, 27–28, 36, 127; and Primero Justicia, 31, 99, 113; US support for, 115, 118
Carabobo, 21, 103, 107, 140
Caracas: ACAC in, 158; ACCEDES in, 171; ACCJ in, 165, 166; ACLV in, 172; Carbajal in, 99; CEDICE in, 135; and Chávez, 17, 23, 34; CIPE in, 144; eastern, 163; IPYS in, 167; IRI in, 97, 101, 106–7, 109–10; NDI in, 117, 128; NED in, 217; neighborhood of, upper-middle class, 114; neighborhoods of, working-class, 15; protests in, 20, 184; SC in, 150; USAID/OTI, 181; US embassy in, 72, 83, 88; US filmmaker arrested in, 35; western, 162
Carbajal, Rogelio, 98–99
Cardenas, Francisco Arias, 98, 101–2
Cardozo, Dr. Elsa, 105
Caribbean, 7, 28, 38, 71, 132, 137, 223n7
Carmona, Pedro: Decree, 32, 162; in hiding, 24; as interim president, 23, 24, 31, 96, 104, 138, 152, 162, 196
Carter Center, 180
Carter, Jimmy, 43, 180
Carvajal, Leonardo, 160–62, 212
Castillo, Julio, 118
Castro, Fidel, 4, 17
Catholic Church, 18–19, 85, 138, 147
Caulfield, John, 84, 86–88, 114
CD (Coordinadora Democrática), 32, 121, 139
CEDICE (Center for the Dissemination of Economic Knowledge for Liberty): and CIPE, 134–40, 142–45, 151–52; 212–13, 218; and coup d'état, 218; and IRI, 102, 104; and NED, 32
CEJIL (Center for Justice and International Law), 166–67
Central Intelligence Agency (CIA): and Chávez, 37, 190–91; and democracy bureaucracy, 30, 41, 179, 186, 215–16; and Guatemala, in, 4, 33; Venezuelan military, assistance for, 19
Central University of Venezuela, 105, 139, 184
CESAP (Centro al Servicio de la Acción Popular), 162–64, 173
Chacao, 21, 99, 114
Chávez, Hugo: CIPE and SC efforts to undermine, 130–52; IRI efforts to undermine, 95–108, 110–13, 115; NDI efforts to undermine, 116–25, 127–29; NED's efforts to undermine, 153–74, 224n1; racist-neocolonial depictions of, 72, 81–94; USAID/OTI efforts to undermine, 175–76, 178–89; theoretical implications of, 53–54, 60, 63, 70; 207–12, 214–19; and US government, 4, 11–37, 190–205
Chavistas, 150, 166; efforts to coopt/defeat, 14, 30–31, 115, 118–19, 182–83, 210, 215; in the National Assembly, 190, 192; political domination, 193, 198, 205; and poor barrios, 162; and protests, 23, 165; racist-neocolonial depictions of, 89
children, 46, 65, 74, 159, 209
Chile, 133, 137, 167, 215; US-backed coup in, 4, 9, 30, 33, 42, 43, 44
China, 3, 79, 199; and empire 3, 4, 9, 222n3; and Chávez, 16, 30, 33, 81, 191, 194, 196–97, 199–200, 205
CIPE (Center for International Private Enterprise): function, 11; and NED, 43, 47, 153; Venezuela, in, 14–15, 32, 130–31, 133–52, 208, 212, 213–14
civil liberties, 208; and Gorbachev, 10; and liberal democracy, 14, 55, 69; and NED funding, 154, 156, 167, 169, 213
civil society: and ACAE, 161; and ACCJ, 164; and Chávez, 27, 202; and CIPE and CEDICE, 138–39, 144; concept of, 45; Egypt, in, 11; and Gramsci,

57; and IRI, 97, 99, 102–3; and LIC (Law on International Cooperation), 192, 197, 203–4; and NED, 157–58, 170–71, 173; and neo-Marxist scholars, 58; and neo-Tocquevillian scholars, 50; and SC, 150; and Smith, Adam, 62; South Korea, in, 52; and Tocqueville, 13, 48–49, 55; and USAID/OTI 15, 32, 92, 177, 182; US support for, 12, 29–31, 35, 51, 70, 156
class/es, 21, 52, 86, 134; capitalist, 38, 55, 193, 212–13, 216; lower, 185; and Marxism, 55–57, 59, 63; multi, 162; upper and middle, 20, 114, 156, 170–71, 173, 185, 193; working, 15, 20, 29, 55, 82, 108, 163, 193, 219, 222
Clinton, Bill, 28, 33, 82, 194
"clown," 83, 85, 89
CNE (National Electoral Council), 97, 128, 20
Cold War, 53, 180; end of, 58, 178; and Hollywood, 7; US support for dictators and suppression of leftists, 9, 33, 44, 209, 214
Collins, Mike, 31, 102
Colombia, 10, 23, 28, 106, 128, 166–67, 215
colonialism: and abolition, 73; and capitalism, 74; European, 8, 78; Locke, 62; settler, 71–72. *See also* neocolonialism
US, 66, 77, 79, 93, 94
colonies, 7–8, 64–66, 68, 73, 75, 91
colonization, 8, 76
color line, 14, 66–67, 78
communism, 5, 10, 44, 58, 79; anti, 42
Concheso, Aurelio, 104, 137–38, 144
conflict mediation, 154, 166, 169, 171–73, 208, 219
Conflict Resolution at the Local Level, 171–72
Constituent National Assembly, 22, 25
constitution/s: Marx's critique of, 55;

"pet Bolivarian," 156–57, 171, 217; Venezuelan, 21–23, 163–64, 168, 170, 173, 201–3, 211
contractor/s, 46–47, 91, 97–98, 111, 115
cooperatives, 15, 130, 149–50, 152
COPEI (Comité de Organización Política Electoral Independiente): and CTV, 147; and democracy assistance, 95, 99–102, 104–7, 112–13, 115, 119, 122, 147, 215; and Pact of Punto Fijo, 22; Sáez, endorsement of 21; Venezuelan politics, domination of, 19; youth development, 160
corporations, 3, 10, 11, 14, 60, 79, 80–81
Correa, Rafael, 11, 199
corruption, 19, 36, 51, 87, 126, 221n2; anti, 45
councils: community/communal, 26–27, 123, 136, 149–50, 201, 203–5; worker, 15, 130, 149–50, 152
counterrevolutionary, 4, 42, 68
coup d'état, 80; of Chávez, 15, 23–25, 31–33, 83–84, 96, 102–5, 117, 146–48, 161, 195; MBR-200 failed, 20; post, 178, 180 184, 188, 190–92, 202–3; US and NGO support for, 54, 70, 108, 119–20, 138, 140, 151–53, 155, 161–63, 165, 168, 170, 172, 175, 205, 207, 211–12, 214, 215–16, 218
court/s, 3, 62, 114, 165–66, 169, 171, 191
crime/s, 136, 154, 163, 169–70, 172, 187
crisis: economic, 130, 138, 219, 221n2; political, 37, 106, 167–68, 119
Cromwell Cox, Oliver, 56, 74
CTV (Confederación de Trabajadores de Venezuela), 15, 23, 138–39, 146–49, 151–52, 212, 218
Cuba, 199; Chávez, 17, 30, 33, 72, 84, 205; and guerillas, 18–19, 60; influence in Venezuela, 160, 217; and US, 4–7, 44, 60, 69, 77
culture/s, 57, 67, 81, 88, 94

decentralization: and Law on Municipal Governance, 156; NGO/liberal democratic promotion of, 13–14, 69, 97, 103, 139, 141, 157, 167–68, 208, 211, 213
demagoguery, 88–89
democracy assistance: and civil society, 45; definition, 43; and Department of State, 47; origins of, 10–12, 41, 44, 154; and theory, 38–39, 48–49, 52–54, 58–61, 63, 69–70, 207–14, 216–17, 222n4 ; and USAID, 46, 53, 175, 177, 207; US leaders on, 51; Venezuela, in, 5, 13–14, 16, 18, 24–25, 29–30, 32–33, 37, 74, 90, 93, 94, 96, 115, 135, 156, 173, 175, 190, 207–14, 216–17
democracy bureaucracy, 11, 45, 47
democracy, liberal: and development, 41; internationalist, 40; and NED, 153–54, 218; politics of, 13–15; and racist-imperialism, 79; and theory, 41, 54–57, 61–65, 68–70, 210–11, 214; Venezuela, in, 5, 18, 28, 39, 91, 104, 139, 190, 208–11, 214–15, 218
democracy, participatory: and Chávez, 17, 21, 22, 25, 30, 39, 91, 93, 119, 168, 173, 202; conflicting definitions of, 91, 93, 136
democracy promotion: definition, 43; liberal, 40; origins, 10, 41; racist-imperialist, 79; theories of, 42, 47, 49, 53, 59–60, 63, 207; and USAID, 178; US leaders on, 51; Venezuela, in, 12, 134–35, 153, 164, 184, 187
democracy, representative, 29, 62–63, 168
Democratic Party, US, 3, 116
democratization, 49, 53, 122, 164
deregulation, 11, 59, 131–33, 136
destabilization, 30, 209, 214
Development Alternatives, Inc. (DAI), 32, 111, 113, 175–76, 180–81, 183–89
dictator/s, 9, 10, 59–60, 113, 137, 188

dictatorship, 6, 18, 40, 42, 60–61, 63, 217
diplomacy, 7, 46, 98, 189
diplomat/s: on Chávez, 83–90, 92–94; US, 65, 92–94,109, 111, 114, 120, 123, 128, 131–32, 215; Dutch, 198; removal of, 34; Venezuelan, 124; Western European and North American, 215
discourse, 42, 48, 66, 120–21, 182
Dominican Republic, 4, 7, 94, 100, 112
donors, 192, 198
Drug Enforcement Agency (DEA), 4, 23, 30
Du Bois, W.E.B., 12, 14, 56, 66–68, 78–79
Duddy, Patrick, 34, 84–85, 113, 186–87

EC (European Commission), 196, 198, 200
"economic modernization," 41, 44
economics: free market, 79, 130, 134, 142, 145; and neocolonialism, 58; neoliberal, 38, 59; "neo-stupid," 85, 132–33; professor, 139; of US Empire, 80
economy: free market, 63, 143; market-, 135–36; and network society, 60; Northern Italian, 50; and state intervention, 132, 152, 195; and US government, 3, 133; Venezuela, in, 137–40, 43, 152, 195, 197, 213
Ecuador, 11, 16, 34, 200, 205
education, 85; and Chávez, 26, 31, 154–56; cultural, 57; and NED in Venezuela, 159–63, 173, 212, 216; tutelary, 65, 141, 214; and US aid, 28, 41, 45, 51, 159
educators, 103, 158, 160, 172
Eisenhower, Dwight D., 4, 221n2
Election Day, 108, 110, 144
election, recall: of Chávez, 25, 32–33, 53, 60, 120–21, 128, 139, 155, 180–81, 186, 191, 196, 210–11
electoral monitoring/observation: and

democracy assistance, 15, 33, 45, 53, 60, 96, 117, 127–28, 130, 147, 156, 223n2
electorate, 15, 110
elites: British, 73; European, 67; private sector, 136; transnational, 59; US, 6, 13, 39, 65, 72, 74–77, 81–83, 86, 94, 108, 110, 131, 133, 154, 175, 182–83, 185, 207–8, 213–14, 217–18; Venezuelan, 113, 136, 155
emancipation, 6, 55
embassy, 16, 204, 186, 188, 198, 204; cables, 83, 88–89, 108; Ecuadorean, 200; UK, 198; US 35, 72, 88, 89, 108, 111, 128, 131–32, 197
empire, 3, 6–9, 190; British, 42, 65, 72–75; European, 64, 78; informal, 42, 66; liberal, 64–65; and McKinley, William, 13. *See also* US Empire
employees, 176, 179, 180–81, 183–84, 187–88, 195
energy, 26, 29, 132, 136, 196, 199
England, 6, 48, 74, 75, 195
enslavement, 74–75
environment, the, 45, 106, 128, 168
EU (European Union), 129, 196–97, 205
Europe: and Du Bois, 79; Eastern, 9, 16, 45, 177; and Guaidó, 36; and liberal democracy, 55; and racialist thinking, origins of, 74; Western, 16, 58, 67–68, 176–77, 191, 193–201, 205
European/s, 112; and colonialism, 7–8, 42, 62, 64, 72, 73, 90; and Marshall Plan, 41; and national movements, 40; and neocolonialism, 80; and racism, 67–68, 71, 74, 76–78, 93; and Venezuela, 91, 121; Western, 16, 191, 194, 196, 198, 200–201, 205. *See also* EC (European Commission); EU (European Union)
exceptionalism, 8, 13, 48, 54, 64
exploitation, 68, 78, 80; super, 79

FARC (Revolutionary Armed Forces of Colombia), 23, 34, 166

farmers, 158–59
Fedecámaras (Venezuelan Federation of Chambers of Commerce): and Carmona, 23, 96, 162; and Chávez, 23, 96, 138–39, 144, 152, 162; and Entrepreneurship Clubs, 145; and SC, 147, 151–52, 162
Fernandez, Eduardo, 99, 104, 113
"fiscal discipline," 142
FMG (Fundación Momento de la Gente), 31, 156–58, 173
Folsom, George, 96, 103, 212
Fondren, George, 99–100
food, 22, 26, 148, 154, 156, 159, 209; stuffs, 79
fool, 83, 85, 89
Foreign Assistance Act of 1961, 41, 46, 177
forums: and ACCJ, 166, 216; and ACCV, 170; candidate, 96; and CEDICE, 136, 152, 213; and CESAP, 163; and the NED, 96, 161, 163, 166, 170, 216–17; and OTI, 182
foundations, 11, 18, 46
France, 41, 48, 55–56, 196
Franklin, Benjamin, 6, 75, 93
fraud, 110, 181, 189
freedom, 7, 10, 46, 68, 75, 79, 95, 113, 133–35, 137, 142, 188, 216; of expression, 148–49, 167; "fundamental human," 51; of the press, 12, 167, 211; of speech, 51, 119; and theory, 55, 61–64
Freedom Agenda, 179
Freedom of Information Act (FOIA), 47, 108, 119, 134, 148
free market: and democracy assistance, 44, 54, 59, 208, 213; and Du Bois, 79; and liberal democracy, 62–63; and Venezuela, 4, 15, 130–36, 138–39, 141–46, 152, 195, 198, 213–14
free trade, 23, 29, 141, 214
Fundación Pensamiento y Acción, 99–100

Galeano, Eduardo, 56, 58
GDP, 7, 42, 132
genocide, 68, 71
Germany, 56, 194, 197
Gershman, Carl, 103, 107, 138
globalization, 56, 59
Globovisión, 27, 104, 138
God, 71, 75, 93
Golinger, Eva, 24, 30–33, 120
goods, 46, 79, 134
Gramsci, Antonio, 57
grantees, 30–32, 95, 146, 153, 188
grants, 135, 158, 186
grassroots, 20, 101, 103, 110, 121
Great Britain, 41–42, 56, 71
Grenada, 5, 68, 69, 222
Guaidó, Juan, 36–37, 114–15, 176, 184
Guam, 6, 7, 77
Guatemala, 4, 5, 44, 106, 128
guerillas, 18–19, 28
gunboat diplomacy, 7, 189

health care, 21–22
hegemon, 42, 65
hegemonic, 3, 7, 57, 58, 65, 68, 176
hegemony, 9; Chavista, 26; US, 29, 34, 59, 94, 115, 132, 194, 197, 199
historians, 12, 48, 69, 208, 214, 223n2
Hobbes, Thomas, 61–62
housing, 22, 26, 28, 163–64, 209
Howard, Darryl, 101–2
Hussein, Saddam, 17, 29, 68, 195
Hydrocarbons Law, Organic, 22, 30, 134, 152, 195

ideals, 79, 86, 91, 112
ideology, 39, 101, 123, 136; and communism/socialism, 44, 89; and democracy, 43; Gramsci on, 57; neoliberal, 59; and Venezuela, 94; WASP, 81
identity, 21, 142, 194
image/s, 215; anti-US, 194; of Chávez, 83; and IRI, 102, 105, 108; and NDI, 120; and Súmate, 169
imagery, 132, 179

imperial, 74; anti, 16, 73, 191, 194, 205; and democracy assistance, 217; modalities, 9, 42, 65, 66; racist, 66–67, 69, 70–71, 81, 84, 94, 154; US, 6, 7, 9, 39, 64, 68, 70–71, 73, 78–80, 94, 176, 214; Venezuela, efforts in, 5
imperialism: capitalist, 71, 74; and Du Bois, 67; and Lenin, 56; and neocolonialism, 80; new era of, 189; US, 5, 7, 9, 64, 69, 70, 78, 79, 80, 92, 160, 189, 208
imperialist: British, 56; inter, 56; Lenin, 58; mind-set, 179; racist, 72, 75–79, 81
independence, 9, 73–74, 77, 80, 189
Indigenous, 5, 45, 53, 67, 76–77, 91, 94
individualism, 159–60
industry: national, 46; nationalization of, 136; nationalized, 11, 134; oil 18, 22–23, 134, 155, 195; petroleum, 150; private, 213; privatization of 11, 131; public relations, 68
industrialization, 56–57, 177; de-, 79
inequality, 12, 17, 55, 86–87, 139
Instituto Zuliano de Estudios Políticos, Económicos y Sociales (IZEPES), 106, 108
instruction, 43, 69, 101
Inter-American Human Rights System, 166–67
interdependence, 40, 62
International Monetary Fund (IMF), 3, 20
International Republican Institute (IRI): funding efforts, 14; and interviews, 82; and NED, 11, 43, 47, 90; president of, 51; and the Venezuelan opposition, 30–32, 95–115, 116–20, 122–23, 129–30, 140, 146, 153, 178, 180, 209–10, 212–13, 215, 223n2
interviews, 182; ACAE, 145; Chavistas and non-Chavista, 118; and CIPE, 145; EC, 198, 200; journalists and academic, 119; mock, 123; NDI, 120; personal, 169; USAID and

OTI, 15, 111, 115, 178; US elite 72, 82, 108, 131; white US Americans, 81
investment, 20, 28, 132, 137, 157, 194–96, 222n3
investors, 17, 194–96
Iran: and the US, 9, 10, 44, 60; and Venezuela, 4, 16, 33, 72, 196–97, 205
Iraq, 63; and Chávez, 17, 23, 29, 72, 195–96; invasion of, 9, 18, 223n2; and OTI, 178; and US, 68; and Venezuela, 30
Ireland, 56, 73–74
Italy, 50, 57, 176, 195, 197

Japan, 63, 194
Jefferson, Thomas, 6, 75, 85, 93
journalists: and Chávez, 26; and democracy promotion, 108, 143–44, 150; and NGOs, 53; and US Empire, 3, 73; Venezuela, in, 31, 102, 119–20, 166–67, 215
judges, 25, 62, 165–66
judiciary, 23, 62, 120, 162, 190
justice, 51, 141, 154, 165, 173; community, 171; social, 59, 86, 119; system, 164, 166, 171
justification: and Chávez, 90, 93; communism as, 5; imperial, 71, 74; neocolonial, 81; racist, 94; state, for the, 61; US democracy assistance, for, 81; for US intervention, 13

Kautsky, Karl, 56, 79
Kennedy, John F., 4, 41, 46, 175, 177

labor, 15; cheap, 59, 212; and coup d'état, 31; and dependency theory, 79; and Lenin, 56; and Nkrumah, 80; unions, 103; Venezuela, in, 130–31, 136, 138, 146–49, 151–52, 213
landholders, 14, 137, 157–58, 195, 209, 213
landholdings, 156, 158, 216
landowners, 23, 156, 158, 213

Land Law, 22, 134, 137, 152, 154, 158, 195, 210, 213
Latino/s, 81, 187
law enforcement, 11, 35; and NED, 14, 153–54, 169, 172, 213, 216–17
Law of Communes, 201, 204
Law of Popular Participation, 149–50
Law on Communal Councils, 203–4
LDPS (Law for the Defense of Political Sovereignty and National Self-Determination), 12, 192, 201, 204–5
leftist: and Chávez, 25; and NED, 159–60, 191; and US intervention in Latin America, 4–5, 19, 33, 66, 68, 199, 209, 214
legitimacy, 36, 52, 129, 162, 195–96, 202, 204–5
Lenin, V.I., 56–59, 79
libertarian, 15, 31, 45, 102, 135, 213
liberty, 87, 135, 141; and Locke, 62; and Marx, 55; and Tocqueville, 48–49, 55, 64; and US Empire, 7
LIC (Law on International Cooperation), 192–93, 197–98, 200, 204
loans, 80, 197, 199
Locke, John, 55, 61–62, 68
López, Leopoldo, 99, 112–14
Louisiana, 8, 65
Lukashenko, Alexander, 199

Machado, Maria Corina, 169, 210
Machismo, 86, 89, 94
Maduro, Nicolás; and authoritarianism, 205; Chávez's successor, 28, 125, 130; democracy bureaucracy 15, 130, 137, 144, 151–52, 188; and Leopoldo López, 99, 114; and socialism, 63; and the US, 4, 16, 35–36, 218, 221n2, 223n2
Manning, Chelsea, 82, 108
Maracaibo, 106, 114, 145, 156, 186
market economies, 79, 134
Marshall Plan, 41, 176
Marx, Karl, 54, 56, 63

mayor/s: opposition, 14, 21, 99, 101–2, 104, 110, 114, 118, 122, 156, 204
MBR-200 (Movimiento Bolivariano Republicano-200), 20–21
McFarland, Stephen, 88, 109, 128–29
McKinley, William, 6, 7, 13, 77
media, 211; and Chávez, 120, 194; opposition, 26–27, 99–105, 96, 117, 123, 137–38, 143, 145, 149, 159, 161, 167–68, 170, 177; social, 3, 114, 125–27; US, 81, 88, 106
"megalomaniac," 83–84
Mérida, 145, 186
Metropolitan Police, 172, 217
Mexican-American War, 13, 39, 78
Mexicans, 6, 77, 78
Mexico: and Maduro, 36; and US colonialism, 6, 36, 65, 71, 77–78; and Venezuelan opposition, 98, 112, 128, 215,
Middle East, 10, 69, 131, 179, 198
military: and Chávez, 17, 18, 20, 22–24, 31, 87, 102–3, 154, 156, 159, 161, 170, 199, 209, 223n6; and China, 191, 194; and democracy assistance, 43, 49, 137, 168–70, 179, 189, 191, 195, 196, 210, 214; and informal empire, 42, 65; and Marxism, 57–58; and Nkrumah, 80; and Russia, 191, 194, 196, 199; South Korea, in, 52; and Truman, 41; and Trump, 36–37; and US intervention, 3–4, 6–7, 9, 23, 28, 68, 77, 189, 221n2, 222n6, 223n4; Venezuela, in, 18–20, 34, 221n2
minister, 119, 128, 162, 170, 173, 186, 212
minority, 46, 53–54, 60, 87
Miraflores Palace, 23–24, 191
Miranda, 27, 31, 99, 147, 169
Mises, Ludwig von, 62, 135
modalities, of empire: and democracy assistance, 44, 49, 58, 69; and economic coercion, 3; imperial, 9, 16, 42, 65, 66, 74, 80; and military intervention, 3

modernity, 67, 135
modernization, 41, 43–45, 118
money: and Chávez, 203; and China, 194; and corruption, 27; and democracy assistance, 131, 179–80, 183, 185, 215–16; and neocolonialism, 65; and opposition NGOs, 33, 91; and Russia, 194
mongrel, 67, 77–78
Monitoring Social Programs, 60, 162, 164
Monroe Doctrine: and democracy assistance, 154, 179; and racist-imperialism, 6, 13, 39, 69, 71, 77, 81, 209, 222n1
Morales, Evo, 11, 199
movements: anti-colonial, 177; communist, 41; democratic, 40, 59; and democracy promotion, 79, 99, 112–13, 118, 143, 146, 176, 184, 188–89; mass, 60; national, 40; nationalist, 8; and pluralism, 193; revolutionary 8; social, 10, 18, 52, 99, 176; and South Africa, 52; and Soviet Union, 42, 45
Movimiento al Socialismo, 31–32
MUD (Mesa de la Unidad Democrática), 114, 126–27
multipolar/arity, 4, 132, 155, 195, 196–99, 205
MVR (Movimiento Quinta Republica), 99–100, 106–8, 117

Nacional, El, 104, 128, 137–38, 170
nationalism, 42, 66, 86
nationalist, 8, 22, 125, 154–55
nationalization, 26, 44
national security, 10, 35, 51, 68–69, 98
National Security Council, 51, 82–83, 88, 111
Native American, 6, 67, 69, 71, 75
NDI (National Democratic Institute for International Affairs): and anti-Chávez opposition, 31, 90, 95–96, 99, 107, 109–11, 115–30, 140, 146, 209–10, 212–13, 215, 217; and

NED, 11, 14, 43, 47, 90, 153; and "regime change," 51; and USAID, 178, 180
NED (National Endowment for Democracy): and Chamber of Commerce, US, 133; and democracy bureaucracy, 46–48; documents, 47, 82, 108, 140, 173, 191, 224n1; grantees, 95, 130, 146, 153; and liberalism, 63; and Reagan, 43, 146; Romania, in, 52; and the US government, 5, 10–11; Venezuela, in, 14–15, 24, 30–32, 90, 95–97, 102–3, 107–8, 115–16, 138, 140, 153–74, 178, 191, 207, 209–10, 212–13, 216–18, 224n1
neocolonialism, 13, 58, 61, 65, 80, 176, 217–18
neoliberal: anti, 22, 81, 200, 205; capitalism, 22, 60; economics, 38, 59; policies, 10, 11, 15, 18–19, 23, 34, 38, 54, 83, 208, 212–13
neo-Marxist/s: and democracy, 11–12, 38–39, 47–48, 54, 60–61, 70, 207–8, 212–13, 218; and dependency theory, 58; and globalization, 56; and Latin America, 34; and the state, 190, 193, 205
neo-Tocquevillian/s: criticisms of, 53–54, 61, 69–70, 115, 152, 207–9, 211, 218; and democracy, 12–13, 38, 48–50
newsletters, 137, 162
newspaper/s, 127–28, 144–45, 163, 170, 172
New York Stock Exchange, 17, 194
Nicaragua: and Chávez, 16, 33–34, 205; and the Contras, 68; and NGOs, 11; and Ortega, 112, 179, 200; and Sandinistas, 25, 30, 42, 68; and Somoza, 43, 60; and US imperialism, 4, 10, 44, 60, 69, 94
Nkrumah, Kwame, 58, 65, 80
nomination, 34–35, 166, 169
non-profit, 32, 95, 116, 146
nutrition, 163–64

Obama, 33–36, 82, 87–88, 200
oil, Venezuelan: and AD, 19; and Chávez, 23, 25, 29, 155, 179, 196; and China, 197; and CIPE, 142; and Organic Hydrocarbons Law, 22, 134, 195; and PDVSA, 151, 195; strike, 25; and Trump, 200; and the US, 30, 36, 131, 195, 200, 218; value of, 5, 18, 130, 136; vulnerability, 19–20, 36, 118, 130, 221n2
Ojo Electoral, 117, 127–29
omnipotent, 155, 189
Organization of American States, 85, 164
Organization of the Petroleum Exporting Countries (OPEC), 194–95
Orientalism, 14, 93
Ortega, Calixto, 106–7, 124
Ortega, Carlos, 147
Ortega, Daniel, 11, 112, 179, 200
Ortega, Saul, 99, 198, 200

Pacific Ocean, 6, 75, 94
Pact of Punto Fijo, 18, 22, 221n2
paternalism: and Chávez, 132, 218; in Latin America, in, 14, 81, 93, 173, 217–18; and the NED, 173; and neo-Marxism, 61; and neo-Tocquevillians, 38; Venezuela, in, 13, 132, 218
patriarchal, 6, 61
PCV (Communist Party of Venezuela), 106
PDVSA, 151, 195
Peña, Alfred, 101–2, 115
Peru, 167
petroleum, 150, 195
Philippines, 6–7, 39, 65, 77
Pinochet, Augusto, 4, 9, 30, 137
Plan Bolívar 2000, 22, 168
pluralism, 38, 54, 119, 215
pluralist, 13, 39, 51–52, 190, 192–93, 205
Poland, 45, 52
polarization, 105–7, 119–21, 165–66, 168, 172–74, 210

police: and Gramsci, 57; Venezuela, in, 21, 148, 154, 171–72, 179, 187, 202
poll/s, 159; and Chávez, 117, 144, 168; training, 33, 97, 109, 180
poverty, 30, 51, 132–33, 139, 163, 177
presidency: Bush's, George W., 98; and Chávez, 18, 22, 24, 26, 34, 72, 87, 93, 135, 137, 139, 144, 147, 179, 190, 196, 202, 211; in Ecuador, 200; and Guaidó, 37, 221n1; Maduro's, 36–37; of Woodrow Wilson, 40
Primero Justicia (PJ), 185; and IRI, 32, 95, 99–107, 109, 112–15; and the NDI, 117–19, 122–24, 126, 129, 210, 215; and youth, 160
prison, 20, 114
private enterprise, 10, 133–34, 135–36, 139
private property: and democracy promotion, 110, 134, 137, 141, 156–58, 208, 213–14; and liberal democracy, 13; and Locke, John, 62; and the Venezuelan government,14, 39
privatization, 20, 59, 131–32, 134
PRODEL (Programa para el Desarrollo Legislativo), 167–68
production, 22, 54, 56–57, 59, 80, 168
products, 7, 67, 79, 209
professor/s, 105, 138–39, 186
profit, 36, 55
progress, 48, 55–56, 81, 133, 145, 161
propaganda, 141, 176
protest/s: in Caracas, 20; and Chávez, 112, 138, 162, 184, 188–89, 224n1; and communist governments, 10; against Maduro, 99; opposition, 23
Providence, 71, 75–76
Proyecto Venezuela: and COPEI, 21; and IRI, 30, 32, 95, 98, 215; and NDI, 118, 210, 215
PSUV (Partido Socialista Unido de Venezuela), 26–27, 99, 126–27, 149–50, 201
public transport, 20, 22
Puerto Rico, 6, 7, 39, 65, 77, 94

puppet/s, 68, 129, 190
Putin, Vladimir, 11, 196, 199

Quijano, Aníbal, 14, 66, 67–68, 93

race/s, 67–68, 75–77, 78–79, 86–87
racial: capitalism, 71; and Chávez, 87, 162–63; dictatorship, 6, 40, 61; ideology, 81; imperialism, 71, 74–78; inequality, 86; mentalities, 82
racism: and Chávez, 81; cultural, 81; and Du Bois, 78; and neo-Marxist insight, 61; and US, 13, 38, 16, 78, 81, 217–18; Venezuela, in, 76
racist-imperialist mentalities: 72, 81, 76–77, 79, 81–82, 84; and WASPs, 75,
radio, 88, 96, 127, 130, 143–44, 152, 168
rallies, 160, 203
rapprochement, 33, 36
RCTV, 26, 84–85, 112, 184–85, 189
Reagan, Ronald, 4, 10, 43, 44, 68, 116, 146
Recall referendum. *See* election, recall
recruitment, 105, 107
redactions, 111, 120
Red Innovación, 126–27
redistribution, 44, 63, 136, 142, 158–59, 208, 211
reelection, 122, 198
referendum, constitutional, 26, 113, 12, 129, 184, 187, 189, 211
regulations, 11, 140–41, 158
religion, 51, 67, 76, 160
renewal, 118, 121–23
rents, 19, 136,
Republican National Committee, 97, 99, 100, 108
Republican Party: Mississippi, 99, 215; Oregon, 101, 215; US, 3, 31, 95, 98–103, 105, 115, 215
revolution, 28, 44, 56, 57, 92, 198
revolutionaries, 6, 40, 56, 60, 72, 73
rhetoric: and Biden, 215; and Chávez, 85–86, 89, 97, 121, 182, 190; of

liberal democracy, 61; of modernity, 67; populist, 135; religious, 112
rifles, 196, 199
Robinson, William, 10, 56, 58–60, 212, 222n3
Römer, Henrique Salas, 21, 98–99
Rosales, Manuel, 90, 110–15, 122, 156, 165
Russia: democracy assistance in, 10; and empire, 3, 9; and Lenin, 56–57; and NGOs, 198; and Putin, 11; and Venezuela, 4, 16, 30, 33, 72, 81, 191, 194, 196–97, 199, 200, 205, 218

Said, Edward, 14, 66, 67–68
sanctions, 36, 43, 158, 194, 218, 221n2, 223n2
Sandinistas, 4, 25, 30, 42, 68, 200
Saudi Arabia, 9, 29, 195
schools, 109, 159, 160, 209
seminars: CEJIL, 166; CIPE, 143; FMG, 158; IRI, 14, 95, 103, 108, 210; NDI, 121, 210; SC, 148; USAID/OTI/DAI, 183, 186
services: access to, 134; decentralization of, 13; and informal sector workers, 148; municipal, 21; public, 170, 214; social, 19, 22, 26, 168
Shapiro, Charles, 109, 121, 180
Sinergia, 197, 202–3
slavery, 56, 68, 71, 74, 76, 91
socialism: and Chávez, 25–26, 72, 89, 91, 133, 140–42, 146, 149, 155, 196, 200; and democracy assistance, 44, 140–43, 150; and Marx, 55; twenty-first century, 25–26, 72, 133, 10–42, 146, 200; and the US, 58; Venezuelan, 5, 152
sociologist/s, 7, 47, 58, 67, 77, 148, 223n2
solidarity, 48, 124
Solidarity Center (SC): and democracy bureaucracy, 11, 14, 43, 47, 153; and Venezuelan labor, 15, 130–31, 138, 146–52, 213
Somoza, 43, 60

South Korea, 52, 194
sovereignty: and Chávez, 214; and Latin America, 4, 77; and liberal democracy, 62; and Nkrumah, 80; and norms, 50; and US, 73; Venezuelan, 27–29, 195
Soviet Union: and Chávez, 26; and Gramsci, 57; and Latin America, 4; and US, 7–8, 10, 42–44, 58, 66, 134, 176–77; and Venezuela, 19, 160
Spain, 7, 71, 112, 114
Spanish-American War, 8, 77–78
speech/es: and Chávez, 85–86, 88–89, 198; freedom of, 51, 119
stability: and democracy assistance, 47, 118; domestic, 68; for global capitalism, 10; and imperialism, 64; and polyarchy, 59; Venezuela, in, 19, 139
statehood, 8, 65
Strengthening Political Parties: IRI's, 97–98, 102, 107, 109, 111; and NDI's, 118, 120–21
strike/s, 15, 25, 32, 146–48, 152, 223n4
student/s: Romania, in, 52; Venezuela, in, 15, 19, 35, 9 99–100, 108, 112, 117, 122–23, 143, 160–61, 166, 176, 184–86, 188–89
subfield, 194–98, 200–201, 205
subsidies, 20, 43
sulfur, 33, 198
Súmate, 25, 32, 155, 168–69, 173, 210
Summit of the Americas, 22, 34, 87
superpower, 4, 7
supremacy: US, 13–14, 66, 68–70, 75, 93–94; WASP, 71
surveillance, 165, 187
surveys, 159, 163
Syria, 34, 178

tactics, 58, 66, 98, 166
taxation, 136, 213
tax/es, 20, 136, 168
taxpayer/s, 131, 150, 179–80, 219
teachers, 143, 159–61
technology, 96, 101, 116, 125–27, 177

television: and Chávez, 20, 33, 84, 88; and DAI, 32; and Globovisión, 104, 138; and IRI, 96; and RCTV, 26, 112; Súmate, 168
term limits, 28, 184
theorists: dependency 56, 58, 79; globalization, 59; liberal, 61; modernization, 41, 45; neo-Marxist, 212; pluralist, 192–93; world systems, 59
theory: of citizenship, 172; dependency, 34, 79; and empire, 16; and liberal democracy, 61, 214; Marxist, 57; and neocolonialism, 80; neo-Marxist, 34, 205; postmodernist, 221n1; sociological, classic, 16
think tank, 15, 99, 130, 145
Third World, 79, 177
Tocqueville, Alexis de, 13, 48–49, 55, 63
totalitarian/ism, 48, 61, 86
trade: and China, 194, 199; free, 23, 29, 141, 214; and Latin America, 79; liberalization, 11, 22, 59, 131–34; and Russia, 194, 199; and Soviet Union, 44; unions, 143, 148; US-Venezuela, 34, 37
tradition, 14, 64, 193, 207, 218
transparency: and democracy assistance, 15, 53, 60, 118, 123, 126, 157, 223
treaties, 6, 50
Trinidad, 34, 73
Truman, Harry S., 41, 76, 224n2
Trump, Donald, 3, 36–37, 115, 200, 215, 222n1
tutelage: CIPE, 135; US, 39, 66, 69, 72, 77, 92–94, 132, 176, 182, 209, 14; Western, 67

Ukraine, 4, 16, 178, 218, 219
Union para El Progreso, 30, 98, 101–2
union/s, 19, 23, 103, 138, 146–50
United Nations: ambassador, 98, 186; and Bush administration, 179; and Chávez, 198; Declaration on Human Rights Defenders, 50; General Assembly, 33, 35, 85

Universal, El, 137–38
university: and ACAE, 160–61; and Marx, 63; professors, 138; recruitment, 102, 108, 145; students, 99–100, 108; and USAID, 186
UNT (Un Nuevo Tiempo), 110, 112–14, 117, 122–23
US Agency for International Development (USAID): and democracy assistance, 46–48, 53, 177, 207; and "democracy bureaucracy," 4–5; documents, 82, 128; and economic development, 130, 177–78; and interviews, 82, 120; and IRI, 95, 109, 111–13, 115; and LDPS, 12; and liberalism, 63; and NDI, 116, 127–28; and NED, 10–11; origins of, 41, 46, 175, 177; and Putin, 11; Romania, in, 52; Venezuela, in, 12, 14–15, 28, 30, 32, 47, 87, 89, 90–93, 108–9, 111–13, 115, 127–28, 175–76, 178–81, 183–89, 191, 207, 209–10, 217–18
USAID Office of Transition Initiatives (OTI), Venezuela, in, 15, 32, 82, 92, 109, 111–13, 115, 175–76, 178–89
US Congress: and CIA, 4; and "democracy bureaucracy," 11, 43, 47; and Foreign Assistance Act of 1961, 41; and Venezuela, 218
US Department of State: democracy assistance and promotion, 10–11, 30, 46–47, 63; interviews, 51, 82, 131–32, 178; investigation into Chávez coup d'état, 24; and IRI, 95, 97; and NDI, 116
US Empire: and authoritarianism, 72; and British Empire, 73; and Chávez, 190; definition of, 3; and democracy assistance, 70; and Du Bois, 78; and ideology, 13; and informality, 42, 66, 73; and Latin America, 70; origins of, 7–9; and scholarship, 64–66, 222n4; twenty-first century, 9, 13; and Venezuela, 4–5, 13

US military, 4, 6, 23, 28, 68, 77
US populace, 6, 189

values: Christian, 45; and democracy assistance, 91, 100, 122, 137, 141, 146, 160, 171, 182–83; liberal democratic, 91; libertarian, 45; US, 19, 51, 64; world cultural, 50
Venezuelan National Assembly: and ACAE, 161; and CEDICE, 137, 140; and CESAP, 164; and Chavistas, 190–91, 198; and CIPE, 143; and IRI, 97, 99, 103–4; and LDPS, 192, 201; and LIC, 197–98, 200–201; and NED, 156–57, 167; and presidential term limits, 26; and PSUV, 27; and SC, 149–50
Venezuelan Supreme Court, 103, 170
victory, 17, 25–28, 97, 125, 184, 188
Vietnam, 7, 9, 68
violence: and Caracas, 20; and Chávez, 23–24, 103, 190; and democracy assistance, 118, 159, 170–71, 174, 217
Voluntad Popular, 36, 95, 99, 114, 160, 176
voter/s: anti-Chavez, 91; database, 126–27; and IRI, 100, 105, 108–10, 114; and motorcyclists, 144; poor, 120; registration, 33, 168; youth, 98, 120

warfare, 49, 80
war on terror, 4, 23, 29–30, 33, 214
Washington Consensus, 131–32, 139
Washington, DC: and democracy, 51, 59; and neo-Toquevillianism, 50; and racist-imperialism, 69; and totems, 51; and Venezuela, 87, 99, 101, 103, 106–7; 111–12, 119, 138, 181, 187
wealth, 28, 63, 130, 136, 208, 211
weapons, 20, 40, 196, 199
website: and ACAE, 161; CEDICE, 135; and CIPE, 133, 143; IRI, 97, 114; NDI, 116; Red Innovación, 125–26; WikiLeaks, 108

Whitaker, Kevin, 84–86, 89, 92, 110, 122–23, 181–82, 197
White Anglo-Saxon Protestant (WASP): and racist-imperialism, 6, 66, 68 ,71, 74–78, 81, 93, 94
White House, 83, 180, 186–87
whiteness, 67, 76
WikiLeaks, 108, 200
women, 19, 45–46, 53, 95, 108, 116–17, 124
workers: and CEJIL, 167; and CTV, 23, 148; Egypt, in, 11; and Gramsci, 57; informal, 140, 148, 213; poor countries, in, 79; and SC, 146, 148, 150, 213; USAID, 15, 186
workshops: ACAE, 161; ACCEDES, 171; ACCJ, 165; ACJA, 171; CEDICE, 138, 140; and Chávez, 203; CIPE, 144; IRI, 95, 101–3, 106, 112; and NDI, 117, 120–21, 123–24; SC, 150; and NED, 217; USAID/OTI, 182–83, 186
World Bank, 3, 197
World Social Forum, 25, 196
World War II, 7–9, 41–42, 49, 63, 66, 73, 176

youth: activism, 31; bases, 215; and Carbajal, 98–99; and Gramsci, 57; groups, 19; leaders, 105, 107; members, 110; and NDI, 117, 122–24, 126; and NED, 159–60; participation, 95–96, 99, 108; from PJ, 102, 112, 117; recruitment of 14; Romania, in, 52; and UNT, 112; and USAID, 113, 184–85, 188; Washington, in, 101

Zemko, John, 137, 144
Zulia: and CEDICE, 140; and Chávez, 27; and CIPE, 145; and IRI, 106–7, 109, 114; and NED, 156; University of, 186